THE
SPECTATOR
BOOK OF
WIT, HUMOUR
AND MISCHIEF

By Marcus Berkmann

Rain Men: The Madness of Cricket

Zimmer Men: The Trials and Tribulations
of the Ageing Cricketer

A Matter of Facts: The Insider's Guide to Quizzing

A Shed of One's Own: Midlife Without the Crisis

Ashes to Ashes: 35 Years of Humiliation
(and About 20 Minutes of Ecstasy)
Watching England v Australia

THE
SPECTATOR
BOOK OF
WIT, HUMOUR
AND MISCHIEF

edited by
Marcus Berkmann

Little, Brown

LITTLE, BROWN

First published in Great Britain in 2016 by Little, Brown

3 5 7 9 10 8 6 4 2

A CIP catalogue record for this book
is available from the British Library.

ISBN 978-1-4087-0743-2

Typeset in Bembo by M Rules
Printed and bound in Great Britain by
Clays Ltd, St Ives plc

Papers used by Little, Brown are from well-managed forests
and other responsible sources.

MIX
Paper from
responsible sources
FSC® C104740

Little, Brown
An imprint of
Little, Brown Book Group
Carmelite House
50 Victoria Embankment
London EC4Y 0DZ

An Hachette UK Company
www.hachette.co.uk

www.littlebrown.co.uk

To Jenny Naipaul

INTRODUCTION

I started reading *The Spectator* in the early 1980s, as a recently unemployed graduate with too much time on my hands. Although I never truly shared its politics, I identified from the beginning with its maverick spirit, its wilful non-conformism. Under Alexander Chancellor's editorship, the magazine had become a place where good writers could say what they liked, as long as it was legal, decent, honest and truthful. Newspapers were duller than they later became, and *The Spectator* provided a vital counterpoint of flair, drollery and inside knowledge. Having decided that I too wanted to be a writer and dedicated most of my early twenties to learning how, I saw an opening in 1986, when over the course of a year the magazine published three pieces about pop music. Each was by a different writer, and each was less than distinguished. The magazine clearly wanted someone to perform this challenging task. Why shouldn't it be me? I wrote three sample columns and sent them in. Astoundingly I thought someone might read them, recognise my talent and give me a regular column.

In most magazines the unsolicited manuscripts sit in a huge cardboard box in a corner, before finding their way into a black bin-liner. If you are lucky, they send you a rejection slip. I was luckier. The editor's secretary, Jenny Naipaul, had injured her back and was in hospital in traction, bored to distraction. She offered to read the unsolicited manuscripts, found mine and liked it. When she left hospital and returned to work, she rang me up and invited me in to see her new boss, Charles Moore.

In those days *The Spectator* occupied an elegant Georgian town house in Doughty Street, Bloomsbury, which I believe it owned outright. Its legendary summer parties were held within its rooms and in its modest back garden, where the great and good of London political, literary and journalistic life drank free gin until there was none left anywhere in the world. My friend David Taylor, who writes under the name D. J. Taylor, had attended a couple of these parties and narrowly escaped with his life. Now I was sitting on the sofa in Charles Moore's office on the first floor at the front of the building, a room full of books, paintings, old furniture and teetering piles of paper: the study of all our dreams. Behind his desk sat Charles himself, barely three years older than me, and wearing the brightest red corduroys I had ever seen. If a pair of trousers can ever be said to be intimidating, these could. I had to concentrate not to stare. Charles being Charles, he was effortlessly courteous and encouraging, and by the end of the meeting I had been commissioned to write something on the tenth anniversary of punk, on which Charles was possibly not an expert. But then nor was I. Like any young scribbler on the make, I was winging it.

I wrote a couple of pieces about pop, both of which were published, and then everything went quiet. New to this game, I hadn't worked out that it was up to me to pitch ideas if I wanted to write for the magazine. But I now had a second stroke of luck. The arts editor left and was replaced by Jenny Naipaul, my first champion. She rang me up and offered me a monthly column. This was in May 1987, and it kick-started a freelance career that has lasted nearly 30 years. Where would I be now without Jenny? For purely selfish reasons, I have dedicated this volume to her.

The pop column continued until late 2015, when I did something no sensible freelance ever does: I gave it up. 'Why did you resign?' people kept asking, echoing the 1960s TV series *The Prisoner.* Indeed, I was half expecting to wake up the following morning in Portmeirion, wearing a natty blazer and being chased everywhere by giant barrage balloons. I told everyone that I had run out of ideas. Fellow hacks looked at me askance. As one said, 'If we all gave up columns because we had run out of ideas, there would be no columns anywhere.' I had let the side down.

As it turned out, I realised the column had to end while I was working on this book. *The Spectator Book of Wit, Humour and Mischief* had been conceived, possibly over lunch, as a belated follow-up to Christopher Howse's 1990 volume *The Wit of 'The Spectator'*, and as the first of a putative series of themed books using the vast and rarely tapped resource of the *Spectator* archive. My publisher and friend Richard Beswick and I pitched the idea to the magazine's seniors, and they embraced it with enthusiasm. They gave me the run of the website and the digitised archive, but being the sort of person who writes for *The Spectator*, I favoured a more old-fashioned approach. I asked if I might come into the office once a week and leaf through binders of old magazines, prospecting for gold. I thought it might take three months of Fridays. It took nearly a year.

The magazine has new and elegant offices in Old Queen Street in St James's, a short stagger from the Houses of Parliament. The building has five storeys and an ancient lift, which I have been in once. (It manages to be both slow and terrifying. I didn't breathe during its long, creaky ascent. It felt like a nineteenth-century equivalent of a dangerous sport.) On the top floor is the office of Andrew Neil, former editor of the *Sunday Times* and now chairman of the Press Holdings group, which owns *The Spectator*. It's a glorious space, but a little out of the swim of things, so he prefers to use the mahogany-panelled conference room in the basement. This left the office free for me to use on Fridays, and the occasional Thursday, throughout 2015. I sat at his meeting table, reading old articles and taking care not to spill crumbs from my sandwiches on his floor. A more unscrupulous individual, or a better journalist, would have rifled through his desk drawers or the pockets of the spare suit (pinstripe) hanging in the corner. But I am far too well brought up to do any of that. I just read and read and read, did some photocopying, and read some more.

After ten months and many sandwiches, I had three box files full of photocopied articles. I had already decided on a chronological structure for the book because I felt it best reflected the changing tone of the magazine over the years. Six men have edited the magazine since I started there: very different men who shaped the magazine in different ways. Charles Moore (1984–90) presided at the peak of the Young Fogey terror, but he is a good and kindly man, and a wittier writer than many give him credit for. Dominic Lawson (1990–95) was, and probably still is, deeply eccentric. He had a fearlessness that occasionally verged on recklessness, and got into more scrapes than most editors. He was also obsessive about the Diary, which he constantly sent back for rewriting, no matter how eminent the writer. Twenty years later, the Diaries under his tenure still glisten and gleam. Frank Johnson (1995–9) was the only editor I never met. He was so utterly indifferent to my subject that I thought it best to keep my head down and hope not to be fired. But I loved his writing, his utterly distinctive voice, the half-smile, the perennially raised eyebrow. Boris Johnson (1999–2005) is, of course, a phenomenon. There is disappointingly little of his humorous writing in this book, as he saves most of it for the *Telegraph*. The magazine loosened and lightened during his years in charge, although how much of that was down to him and how much to the tireless editorial team who were pretty much left to get on with it remains a subject of debate.

Matthew d'Ancona (2006–9) I met only once, at a lunch for arts contributors. As a Smiths fan he took a dim view of my relentless mockery of Morrissey, and spent the rest of lunch talking to his more glamorous neighbour on the other side. I suspected that he found the public role of *Spectator* editor more irksome than the deeper, more introverted pleasures of editing the magazine. Fraser Nelson (2009 to date) seems to balance the roles more happily, although every time I bumped into him in the magazine's offices, a look of terror came into his eyes. I mentioned this to one of his colleagues, who said he probably had no idea who I was. But I am a great admirer, as I'm not sure the magazine has ever been livelier and funnier than it is now.

It is also younger and (to use a slightly *Guardian*-ish word) more inclusive than it used to be. In 1990 the magazine was still very male and bufferish. Craig Brown's 'Wallace Arnold' column, which adorned the inside back cover, was such an unerring parody of certain *Spectator* contributors it's astonishing he was allowed to get away with it. The parodies demonstrated two habits of *Spectator* writers that would need careful handling. One was all the moaning about modern life. You cannot believe how many diarists used to complain about TV remote controls, or wonder what had happened to proper steak and kidney pies. I cut all this stuff out. If you had read it 20 years later, you would have screamed. The moans that survive into this book have done so because they are still funny. The iceberg of grumpiness beneath these few would have holed a bigger ship than the *Titanic*.

The other early casualty of the blue pencil was all the feuding. I had forgotten how energetically *Spectator* columnists used to enter into long-running feuds with friends, enemies and frenemies within the magazine and without. The letters column alone could keep an argument going for months. Not many feuds remained amusing for long, though, and in almost every case the participants were palpably enjoying them more than their readers. Did anyone still care? In most cases, I decided not.

This book starts in 1990 because that's where *The Wit of 'The Spectator'* ended. Though relatively brief, Christopher's book was rich in Auberon Waughs and Jeffrey Bernards, and included Kingsley Amis's justifiably famous 'Sod the Public' essays from 1985 and 1988. All three writers are represented here as well, although not as comprehensively. Waugh ended his long association with the magazine in 1995, and as Bernard's health started to fail (he died in 1997), he was compelled to dictate his columns, and their quality became more variable. But as one generation departs, possibly in a drunken haze, the next one steps forward. Indeed, in my first edit, certain writers cropped up so often I had to pare back their contributions with a scythe. Mary Killen's etiquette column, 'Dear Mary', was like Japanese knotweed, while Jeremy Clarke's 'Low Life' pieces proliferated like leylandii. Later on came Deborah Ross's wonderful stream-of-consciousness restaurant reviews and the wild, frothing (but elegantly sculpted) rage of Rod Liddle.* But there are also countless Diary entries, many letters, a handful of book reviews and even one or two pieces by me. The book is strictly chronological, partly, as I said, to distinguish different eras of the magazine from each other, but also because I liked the idea that the book should be a lucky dip, that you

---

* Who, for some reason, and I cannot even begin to justify this, I always think of as 'Rid Loddle'.

would never know what was coming next. For the same reason there is neither an index nor a contents page that is any use at all. This isn't a work of reference, it's an entertainment. For similar reasons, I have kept explanatory footnotes to a minimum. I have also have kept the type of pieces that need explanatory footnotes to a minimum. Detailed knowledge of the Maastricht Treaty is not required in these pages, although it might help to remember that Robert Maxwell died by falling off a yacht.

A swift word on general editorial policy. Many of these entries are excerpts from longer pieces, but very few 'internal' cuts have been made within those excerpts. These few are marked by the shorthand [. . .]. The easily offended should be aware that there is a fair amount of swearing in the book, but I have retained the form in which the swear-word was originally printed, so some writers say 'fuck' and others say 'f***'. As *The Spectator* has traditionally been *laissez-faire* about this sort of thing, I have assumed that these formulations were chosen by their writers, and thus are to be respected. One or two misspellings and grammatical infelicities have been corrected. *Spectator* subs were always reluctant to change copy, so if you had written something particularly stupid or clumping, there it would be in the magazine the following Thursday. If nothing else, this kept us on our toes.*

So why end the column? Because as well as reading everyone else's contributions, I reread my own. I saw that as the years had passed, I had become technically more adept and was writing better and funnier columns, while having less and less to say. It was also chastening to realise that having written a column in, say, 1993, I had written it again in 2001, and then again in 2008 and was thinking of doing it again in 2015, having forgotten that I had written any of the previous ones. The towel was asking very politely to be thrown in.

But it has been wonderful to be associated with the magazine for so long. I believe that the best magazines are like clubs. Writers are members

---

* The process wasn't infallible. When Mark Mason filed a review of Sebastian Coe's autobiography, he included quotes that contained both dominant Anglo-Saxon four-letter swearwords. He wasn't sure of the magazine's policy, so he transcribed these as 'fuck' and 'c***'. When he opened the magazine on Thursday, they had been changed to 'f***' and 'cunt'.

as much as the readers: in fact, if you feel you are a member, then you are, automatically. (The best selection policy of all: self-selection.) So I have tried to make this book the Christmas present that members of that club would like. I don't think we need worry too much about non-members. They can have something else. A nice tie, perhaps.

1990

Jeffrey Bernard; Wallace Arnold; Taki;
Auberon Waugh; Hilary Mantel; John Wells;
Martyn Harris; Alan Watkins

LOW LIFE

Jeffrey Bernard

6 January

If I hadn't wanted to take my daughter to lunch on Christmas Day I would have stayed in bed. It was pretty awful for me but seemingly OK for a 19-year-old who only four years ago was sustained by fish fingers. We should have walked around the corner to Chinatown and had the crab and ginger and a row with one of the waiters. I usually feel like a member of that crazy institution, the Dangerous Sports Club, when I go into most Chinese restaurants apart from The Ming in Romilly Street. There is something oddly reassuring about being addressed as Jeff as opposed to the usual snapped, barked or screamed, 'What you want?' They are benign in the Ming, but in most other Chinese restaurants I am reminded of the fact that they invented gunpowder. How lucky they didn't have any nitric acid and glycerine.

Anyway, the Churchill Hotel in Portman Square could have done us a bit better. Only the starter was good. Gravadlax, and they ruined that by not turning up with the sauce until we had half finished it. The turkey was so dry it took an entire sauce-boat of gravy to swallow it. Where was the black meat? The paper-hatted party at the next table kept staring at Isabel and me. That may have been because she is so pretty, but I suspect that they thought they were gazing at a dirty old man with his bit of fluff.

After a mediocre Christmas pudding – it is so easy to buy a really good one – the waitress asked me if I wanted coffee. When I told her no she said, 'It is inclusive, sir.' My God. Do I look as though I couldn't buy a cup of coffee if I wanted one? I didn't say anything because she was a Chinese waitress and I do not want to get stabbed or blown up in front of my own daughter. That will be a private happening when it comes to pass. After I had paid the bill (£80) I put Isabel in a taxi to send her home, and then Christmas simply petered out into limbo.

After that it was home to television, tea, forbidden biscuits and then vodka in the evenings in an attempt to seduce that elusive sandman. It is not a good thing to attempt to use booze as an anaesthetic at night but it can work wonders during the day when Norman is waffling about the success of the play. After about four large ones I can barely hear a word he waffles; I just sit there watching him raising his fists to the ceiling like some idiot who has just scored a goal. In his case it is usually an own goal. He only opens his mouth to change step as they say.

But since Christmas there has been a lot of yawning in this attic. If I hear, read or see any more summings up of the Eighties or predictions for the Nineties I shall cancel the papers and send the television set back to the people I rent it from. Do you really want to know what some idiot actress or stand-up comedian thinks may happen on the political front over the next ten years? It is asinine and angry making.

Nevertheless, as a man who lives in the past, if not from day to day, I must say something about the Eighties. They were good for me apart from 1987 when I had nowhere to live. That was hell, carting carrier bags around to any bed I could find. Thank God for the Chelsea Arts Club which bailed me out from time to time. Then in 1988 Keith Waterhouse said he wanted to make a play of this column and I thought he was mad. Since it appeared, life has changed a little and thanks to him, Peter O'Toole and Ned Sherrin I sometimes find myself walking about with a fixed smile on my face, like babies have when they are busy farting. Peter says you can't live from peak to peak and have to learn to walk in the valleys. Thanks to those three gentlemen I can now walk in the valley without even looking over my shoulder.

AFORE YE GO

Leaves from the commonplace book of Wallace Arnold

6 January

It was with no little regret that, while casting my eye o'er the list of members who had expressed their intention of resigning from the Garrick Club, I came across the name of Noriega, Gen. Manuel just one down from Noakes, John. Of course, in recent years he has been able to muster precious little time to pop his head around the portals of the club – though I am told that he put our reciprocal arrangement with the Cavalry and Pump-Action Shotgun Club, Panama, to good use – but in his present situation his hopes of swapping Tales from the Green Room with some of our most illustrious thespians in a small but light-hearted gathering around the Garrick hall fire seem, frankly, a mite wee.

I remember well the time – it must have been late '67, early '68 – when the young Manuel Noriega, then cutting something of a dash as a stringer for the estimable Peterborough column on the *Telegraph*, approached me, even then a distinguished Man of Letters, with a view to securing membership. Though already afflicted with a by-no-means inconsiderable skin problem – my espousal of a goodly dash of Clearasil went unheeded, I fear – Noriega exuded a sort of rugged charm and devil-may-care enthusiasm which I for one found positively infectious. 'You make me Garrick member, I no kill your mama,' he quipped, over a perfectly acceptable glass o' port in the RAC, of which he was already making quite a name for himself as Joint Chairman – with the young David Astor, as then was – of the Adult Movies Committee. 'No need,' I countered. 'Dead already!'

We both had a good chuckle over that one, I remember, and by the very next week I was introducing him to all the leading Garrick big-wigs, among them the leading theatrical impresario Mr Paul Raymond, the distinguished comedy actor Mr Reg Varney and the young George

Weidenfeld, then earning an immensely pocketable sum as a part-time tap-dancer at Quaglino's.

Duly elected, Manuel took to the club like the proverbial feathered biped to H_2O, and it was after listening to the after-dinner banter of Mr Terry Worsthorne that he set his heart upon becoming a Supreme Head of State. Posted back to Panama for a few weeks by the top guns on Peterborough with a view to spying out humorous road-signs and ticklish menu translations, he grasped the opportunity to parade about the sun-soaked streets in his Garrick Club tie, thus gaining the respect of the military junta of the time. It then took only one or two appropriately placed retellings of backstage anecdotes concerning Johnny Gielgud and his sieve-like memory (!) for Manuel to be accepted as one of their own by the Panamanian High Command. The rest, as they say, is history.

LOW LIFE

Jeffrey Bernard

3 February

Life has been lower than low over the past few days. It reached rock bottom last Saturday with an incident of such squalor that I thought I must seek sanctuary in a monastery for a while. A woman came into the pub and ordered herself a pint of cider. I took no notice, but I did fleetingly think that it was a fairly unusual order for a lone lady to make. After a while she had a refill. Ten minutes after downing that she approached the bar again and said to the barman, 'Have you got a plunger?' He said, 'What do you want a plunger for?' and she said, 'Because I've just been sick in the ladies and it's blocked up.' Well, I thought, this is really delightful. All a man needs while he is quietly meditating on his bar stool.

The barman went into the ladies to inspect the damage and then, beyond the call of duty and the terms of his contract, cleared the mess up. When he had done that and returned to his post behind the bar, the vomitee asked, 'Could I have a large rum and blackcurrant juice please?'

You don't have to dress up as Napoleon to tell the world that you are mad. She was refused and asked to leave. What an awful episode. Well, I'm still thinking about it, aren't I? Now why did she own up in the first place? Bravado? And why choose the sink to put the breakfast in and not the lavatory? Such imponderables make my insomnia almost unbearable. And she was as coherent as a television newsreader.

AFORE YE GO

Leaves from the commonplace book of Wallace Arnold

24 March

Harry Smethwick, the distinguished journalist who died last week, was commonly known by his friends simply as 'Niffy' Smethwick. He didn't wash much, if at all, and his breath was of such ferocity as to clear the public bar, but we loved him all the more dearly for it.

In writing this warm-hearted tribute to a dear and trusted friend, I must begin by tracing the source of our acquaintance. Upon first meeting in the downstairs bar at the National Gallery, we immediately recognised each other as soul mates. I was the more intelligent, attractive and popular, but he knew more about greyhounds, or so he claimed. Even then – and I am now talking about the late Fifties, that remarkable era – he possessed the purple face and idiosyncratic gait (saving on shoe-leather, he chose to hop everywhere) that endeared him to all that tolerated him.

His taste in women was patchy. Often, when we were arguing long and noisily over our cream stouts in the upstairs bar of the Sir John Soane Museum, a discarded woman would arrive at our table, placing a naked breast somewhat disconcertingly into his pint-pot so as to interpose a barrier between him and his beloved beverage. On other occasions, while we were putting the world to rights in the saloon bar of the Imperial War Museum, a fiancée or other would appear, decked out in full wedding garb, pages and bridesmaids trailing, demanding to know why he was not at the altar.

He would treat his women appallingly, often forcing them to give him piggyback rides to work rather than succumbing to the more expensive option of catching the tube. But they loved him for it, and, in turn, were invited to join him on the office floor, where he would entertain them with his passionately held views on Archbishop Makarios or the rise of skiffle.

But it would be wrong to give the impression that Niffy was a plaster saint. If he had any faults, they were many and varied. He had a mulish streak, delivering a swift kick to anyone who stood immediately behind him, and going 'Eeyore! Eeyore!' whenever the subject of food cropped up in the conversation. By the late Sixties, his purplish hue had become tinged with green, so he would oft find himself perused in the Lounge Bar of the British Museum by passers-by who had inadvertently mistaken him for a wall-map of the Western Isles.

He delighted, of course, in my friendship, as I in turn grew to tolerate his. I offered him social standing, a keen intellect, political savoir-faire and the easy charm of the well-bred, while he would from time to time offer me a slim panatella. Many were his qualities. He was always courteous, except when rude. He was quite good at cooking broccoli. He could tell a joke, though not well. He was rarely slow to join us in laughing at himself, and, if the need arose, could be laid out with a swift jab to the chin. Through it all, he was sustained by his friends, or friend. He was a difficult man, but he loved me dearly.

HIGH LIFE

Taki

7 April

ATHENS

This is a painful confession to make, but as this is the last column I write for Charles Moore, I might as well come clean.* I have been writing

---

* Taki wasn't leaving the magazine. Charles Moore was, to go and edit the *Daily Telegraph*.

horrendous fibs these last 13 years, ironically ever since I joined *The Spectator*. Needless to say, not to you, dear readers, but to the fair sex in general, and girls under the age of 28 in particular. It all started in 1977, when I was living in SW10, in the house I eventually dropped to my buddy John Aspinall when No. 11 refused to come up. I had just begun this column for the then-sainted one, Alexander Chancellor, and being rather nervous about writing in a foreign language, I'd sit and practise when not in Tramp or Annabel's.

How does one practise? Why, by writing love letters, of course. Back then I was in love with an English girl who wouldn't give me the proverbial time of day, so one night I decided to go for broke. Here is what I wrote:

Dear X. There is a marvellous line in Romeo and Juliet, *when Romeo – having avenged Mercutio's death – is advised to flee Verona. 'But heaven's here, where Juliet lives,' he cries. However corny this may sound, this is exactly how I have felt towards you ever since the first moment I met you. Love, Taki.*

The reason, I'm ashamed to admit, that I know the letter by heart is not because I have kept a copy, but – horror of horrors – because the epistle served its purpose so spectacularly, I decided right there and then to try it again. Three weeks later I met an American lady in the Big Bagel and dropped off my R and J letter to her the next day. I changed only her name and added the word Shakespeare because she was a Yank. Incredible as it may seem, it worked again. I was hooked for life.

As it is with most drugs, things were hunky dory for a while. Mind you, it didn't always work, but I was doing better when I used the letter than when I didn't. Then I made a terrible mistake. I began writing it in lavatories and passing it around night-clubs, and even restaurants. One evening in 1985, fresh out of jail and raring to go, I dined with Sophie Stapleton-Cotton, her room-mate Sasha Nott, daughter of the lugubrious-looking Falklands man, and my friend Oliver Gilmour.

Sophie wasn't paying the slightest attention to me, so when I got home that night I yet again wrote The Letter. And that is when the proverbial you-know-what hit the fan. Sophie read the form epistle, laughed, and told Sasha that she thought me ridiculous, but that I did write nice letters. That is when la Nott got suspicious. 'Let me see,' she said, and then she began to roar like the MGM lion. As it turned out, four other friends of hers had received it also. With Sophie that made five. Word got out, and in no time I was the laughing-stock of London, Oxfordshire, Wiltshire, Somerset, Gloucestershire, and even some other shires not chic enough to mention. Being found out did for my sex life what Bomber Command did for Dresden. I tried it on some Greeks but my heart wasn't in it. By 1986 I stopped it altogether.

Until last week in London, that is. During a birthday party for Emily Todhunter, I was seated between Cassy Neville and Susannah Constantine. I fell madly in love with both, got drunk, and went home to try it once again. But I think I got the names and addresses mixed up, so as I'm bound to be found out, and in order to commemorate Charles Moore's editorship, I now do penance. And swear I will never write the R and J letter again. At least not in England.

AFORE YE GO

Leaves from the commonplace book of Wallace Arnold

21 April

I wonder if anyone other than I managed to get all the way through the farewell article written by our dear departed editor in the *Sunday Telegraph* the other week? He entertained his reader(s) with an agreeable saunter through some of the highlights of his brief stint at the steering wheel, including by no means uninteresting anecdotes concerning some of the more colourful characters who have supped at the celebrated *Spectator* high table o'er the years.

Might I add one or two of my own reminiscences from my somewhat longer association with the journal? Well do I remember sitting in a celebrated *Spectator* high chair in the March of 1968. My fellow guests were Mr Enoch Powell, the leading politician and academic; Miss Sandie Shaw, the *chanteuse*, whose magnificent efforts with 'Puppet on a String' had gained Britain first place in the Eurovision Song Contest of that year; Mr Bernard Jeffrey; the Ayatollah Khomeini, at that time an up-and-coming humorous essayist and co-presenter with Miss Muriel Young of BBC TV's *Six O'Clock Club*, whose waspish tongue and severity of judgement was even at that early stage earning him something of a name for himself; the Duke and Duchess of Windsor, fresh from a successful season at the De La Warr Pavilion, Bexhill-on-Sea; Mr Somerset Maugham; the Kray Brothers, taking a well-earned break from rehearsals for that week's *What's My Line?*, hosted by the irascible Gilbert Harding; and George Weidenfeld, or Gorge Widenfed as he then was, owing to a proof-reader's error.

Others who gathered to partake of the assorted sweetmeats at that memorable luncheon included Mr Reg Varney, later to achieve an international reputation for his leading role in *On the Buses*; Emperor and Mrs Hirohito, over here on a flying visit to catch Dame Anna Neagle in *Carousel*; Mr 'Teasy-Weasy' Raymond, then famous as the initiator of the celebrated 'Peregrine Worsthorne' humorous column in the *Sunday Telegraph*, later to become better known as a world-class hairdresser; four members of the now defunct 'Black and White Minstrels' team, including a fully blacked-up Mr Kenneth Rose, later to gain prominence as a diarist and biographer but then concentrating his energies on light-hearted renditions of the early hits of Al Jolson; Professor Hugh Trevor-Roper, who had arrived as a Tinned Peach in Heavy Syrup, having been misinformed that it was one of those Come-as-a-Fruit luncheon parties that were then enjoying something of a vogue; Mr and Mrs Bamber Gascoigne and the two competing teams from an early edition of *University Challenge*, plus jocular mascots; and last but by no means least, our then proprietor, the Scandinavian band leader Mr James Last, accompanied by leading members of his rhythm section. Oddly enough, with such an illustrious guest-list, it now seems extraordinary that I am unable to remember a thing that happened before, during or after that luncheon, though we might well have had a rather good brie, and perhaps a stick or two of celery.

LETTERS

5 May

Sir: Paul Johnson tells us (The press, 21 April) that 'a woman would prefer to be raped by a man of her own race'. Well I hadn't thought about the subject in quite those terms before, but I suppose my ideal rapist would be an Oxbridge man with at least a good Upper Second, a lover of early Baroque music, a keen gardener and a competent croquet player, but not an Anglican, a food and wine bore or a habitual *Spectator* reader.

D. A. Roberts
Canterbury, Kent

ANOTHER VOICE

Auberon Waugh

19 May

Whatever one may have against butterflies – and I agree that in the present plague affecting the entire West Country, they can be intensely irritating – at least they make no noise. Nor, unlike Rottweilers and ladybirds, do they often attack human beings. Many have forgotten the old age pensioner who was bitten to death by ladybirds outside Minehead in the last great plague of 1976. Up to then, people had thought that ladybirds were disappearing, and a few old dears had written to the newspapers saying what a shame it was. Then they came back, like something out of Hitchcock. Another such plague is promised for this year.

The rumour went round West Somerset that the corpse of the old age pensioner, when they eventually got to him, was a more horrible sight than anything seen in the Blitz. What made the man's death particularly poignant was that he was a visitor to the neighbourhood, who had come to enjoy the beauties of the countryside. We countryfolk are used to the hazards and know how to protect ourselves against them by various wily tricks, like never going out of doors unless we have to, or covering ourselves with sacks and binder-twine when we do.

As I say, I have never yet seen butterflies attack a human being, but then we had never heard of homicidal ladybirds before 1976, and I would not be at all surprised to learn of some appalling tragedy, almost certainly in Somerset, where the whitened bones of an amateur naturalist, or ecologist, or environmental enthusiast, or whatever these people now call themselves, are found with only a pair of damp, horn-rimmed spectacles glinting optimistically over the eye sockets to serve as a clue. I have no doubt that even butterflies can be goaded beyond endurance by the yelps and coos of these people. It will be a brave butterfly fancier who ventures down to West Somerset this summer. The fields are swarming with vipers, too – another protected species – and in the present state of government cuts, it is unlikely that any anti-snakebite serum will be available.

I must admit that I am on the side of the butterflies against the butterfly-fanciers, if only because butterflies make no noise. Where egg-collectors are concerned, my sympathies are different. A recent survey of noise pollution, identifying the noises which people found most troublesome, was conducted recently by Bupa. It had two significant omissions. The first was the noise of other people's television sets, which must surely be the biggest single source of annoyance for people living in towns. Dogs, pneumatic drills and burglar alarms were mentioned, even children (or 'kids', at any mention of which even the most toughened criminal is expected to burst into tears), but not television.

The other significant omission, affecting most particularly those who live in the suburbs and country places, was the racket set up every morning at this time of year by songbirds and other feathered friends, sometimes called the Dawn Chorus. Birds, too, you see, are sacred. At least half of all country and suburban dwellers must suffer from this persecution, and nobody dares complain because we have all been brainwashed into thinking birdsong pretty. So it is, sometimes, when you have two or three of them on the job of an evening; six or seven hundred of them, yelling and shrieking their silly heads off at five o'clock in the morning, are more than anyone can be expected to endure. I have often observed how soon majors and other people who retire to live in Somerset tend to go mad, but I always attributed it to the influence of loneliness, and listening to BBC radio. Now I tend to think it is the result of being woken up every morning by the hideous cacophony of these warbling cretins. But what finally drives so many country dwellers round the bend is the social inhibition on complaining about it. We are simply not allowed to say that songbirds are anything but delightful. Then the poor old things turn on their radios and, as often as not, have to listen to more birdsong . . .

I do not think it is because I am getting older, although my mother-in-law, who spent her married life in suburban Surrey, was complaining about it 30 years ago. I honestly think the problem is getting worse. When I was young, nearly every boy in the neighbourhood and several girls used to collect birds' eggs. The same was true of our parents' and grandparents' generations, as several mouldering collections of birds' eggs in the attics – and in most people's attics I imagine – testify. For my own part, I had no patience with birds' eggs as a boy but used to shoot small birds with an air-rifle, sometimes accounting for five or six a day. Between us, we kept the brutes in their place.

With the new sentimentality about birds, which is no more than a reflection, as I see it, of a sinister burgeoning misanthropy, this is no longer possible. The Royal Society for the Protection of Birds, which disposes an income of many millions of pounds a year, runs its own paramilitary police force, owns or controls vast tracts of land, claims the right to enter and search any citizen's home, let alone his land, has now set up an infra-red surveillance system and is trying to set up a nationwide system of informers, along the lines of Cuba's Citizens' Council for the Protection of the Revolution, or Stalin's secret police.

In my time I have complained about the activities of the American Drugs Enforcement Agency in certain benign and easy-going countries of the Far East; even about the excessive powers of our own Customs and Excise, with its small army of snoopers and informants. But the RSPB is a greater threat to the liberty and sanity of this country than an oppressive government agency, because it has for members single-issue fanatics who appear completely impervious in their self-righteousness and in their ignorance of the civil rights of others.

Spokesmen for the RSPB this week claimed that extra powers were necessary to protect our British birds against greedy German and Arab collectors: 'The Germans don't have many birds of their own, so there's a strong market for ours. Falconry is a big pastime in the Middle East so the birds are worth even more money if they are sold to Arabs.'

But among the new powers demanded by Mr Peter Robinson, described as 'Chief RSPB Investigator', was a curfew on all egg collectors, forcing them to report to the police every day during the breeding season. Am I alone in feeling that I would be perfectly happy to see every surviving osprey eaten by German war criminals if the RSPB would confine its activities to rescuing seagulls and encouraging suburban bird-baths?

LOW LIFE

Jeffrey Bernard

7 July

I only found out the other day that the tax inspector who is hounding me nigh unto death is a woman. When my accountant informed me of the fact I gave what I can only describe as a cynical shrug of my drooping shoulders. There has been some sort of acid in my mouth ever since. I thought I had got rid of women once and for all. It is quite extraordinary that when things have been going well and smoothly a 'Did I hear someone use the word ethical?' woman will appear and bring me to a halt with a short, sharp jolt.

I remember some years ago winning £100 on a horse at Newbury, a bundle at the time, and standing in the bar toasting my good fortune, and my then wife walked in and said, 'You'll be able to buy that Hoover now.' That anybody can seriously believe that money is for Hoovers or for a rainy day is beyond my comprehension. Every day is a rainy day. No, income tax inspector is a very suitable job for a woman and it is surprising that no Chancellor of the Exchequer has ever been a woman. In that event a large vodka would cost £100.

But there are other aspects of money which are troubling me at the moment. A month ago, I had to write to an old friend to ask him for £1,000 he has owed me for a while. I have erected a wall of silence. He can keep it, but I do not like having the piss taken out of me in that sort of way. Three years ago I gave an old friend £500 and he hasn't spoken to me since and, in fact, he doesn't even come into the Coach and Horses any more. Just think of how many people you could get rid of with £1 million. What this woman income tax inspector wants to go away and leave me alone is ridiculous and *Jeffrey Bernard is Unwell* is not *The Mousetrap*. Incidentally, Norman says that *The Mousetrap* is a better play than *King Lear*. I asked him how come and he said, 'It's had a longer run'. There is no answer to that.

Last week he was sitting this side of the bar looking particularly gloomy and I overpaid him with a penny for his thoughts. He said, 'I just wish I could see England beat the West Indies 5–0 in a Test series before I die.' He then asked me what I would like to see before I die and I told him a barman in his employ who knew what he was doing and who could speak English. In recent weeks he has taken to employing Serbo-Croats who have been bitten by long-range tsetse flies. It is the only pub I know of in which prudent customers carry a hip flask. But I suppose it is somewhere for an aimless man to go.

CINEMA

Hilary Mantel

18 August

Once in a while we all need to see a spectacularly bad film, and it is a bonus that Zalman King's *Wild Orchid* (18) features Mickey Rourke. These days the man's career has a gruesome fascination, like the site of an especially gory road accident.

Emily (Carre Otis) is a vacant-looking virgin from the boondocks. (I have looked this word up; it is derived most respectably from the Tagalog for 'mountain'.) In the first scene her tearful mother waves goodbye to her as she boards the bus for the big city. Mother would lie in the road and scream if she knew what was in store for her darling. But the first impression is that Emily will prosper, for she's being interviewed for a major post in a swish law firm. In addition to her dazzling legal qualifications she has six languages, 'including rudimentary Chinese'. (I am reminded of a sign in a shop window in Windsor – 'Scandinavian spoken here'.) Miss Otis, regrettably, does not manage English too well, but delivers her lines with the aplomb of someone sliding into a coma.

Suddenly, Emily is in Rio; cue the dancing girls, the carnival masks, the fevered rhythms, the heat of the night. She has been sent to negotiate a deal on a hotel complex, along with brisk businesswoman Claudia (Jacqueline Bisset). Now, there was an innocent time, before JB, when a wet T-shirt was just something you slopped out of a washing machine. These days, like other mature lovelies, JB asserts that beauty has been a burden – though you notice that these people never have plastic surgery in reverse. Her character speaks in a clipped English accent, as if interviewing the assorted sweaties and swarthies for a post at Cheltenham Ladies' College. Except that these are her lines: 'So what's happening, boys – talk to me – what's the word on the streets?'

Enter Mickey. He has been dyed a strange yellow colour, and he plays Wheeler, a man of fabulous wealth. He is a property developer, who may mess up the deal for the girls; but the plot is secondary to the sex. Claudia is obsessed with Wheeler, but he won't touch her; she casts Emily in his path to see what will happen. Wheeler is impotent, though it's not put quite so brutally: 'I'm just not very good at being touched, Emily.' This does not mean we are short on action: the shuddering Emily is forced to witness sundry couples getting down to it, while Mickey salivates in the shadows. A curious thing is that clothes in this film almost self-destruct. You'll remember those chairs in old westerns, that used to snap with such ease over brawlers' heads. Here it's the same with garments. One tiny pull and there's a shocking rending of seams and boondocks are falling out all over the place. For much of the film Mickey affects a dusty black suit, like an old Irish priest. But there is no shirt underneath; presumably it unravelled while he was trying to put in his cuff links. Ofttimes, too, he broods astride a throbbing Harley Davidson, while the cries of the libidinous issue from beach and bush. 'My investors are flying across the world', snaps Bisset, 'and planning a celebration ... dancing girls.' Oh, shucks. You'd been hoping for a whist drive.

When she acquires a lover, Claudia keeps Emily on hand to translate. 'Tell him to take off his pants.' Since he is not Chinese, this does not tax Emily's skills. 'Ask him if he understands the tremendous pleasure women get looking at naked men.' We never do get to understand it, really; once we are acquainted with Mickey's life story, the writhing bodies are visible only through a blur of tears. 'He was an orphan on the streets of Philadelphia ... stuttered so badly as a child he could hardly talk ... ' At times the whole enterprise seems to be slipping gently into aphasia.

It is unfair to categorise this film as soft porn. The sex is straight, dull, and noisy, but the whole is far funnier than most of the comedies on the circuit. No connoisseur of the preposterous should miss it.

DIARY

John Wells

13 October

I always enjoy the ritual standing ovation at the Tory Conference. My earliest experience of it was at Blackpool when it was performed for Ted Heath in his first year as leader of the party. Desperate-eyed activists stood at the back of the hall, slapping the wall when their hands got worn out with clapping, one eye grimly on the second hand of their wrist-watches, but Ted seemed really to believe it, and lifted his arms again and again, beaming from ear to ear as only he can. William Rushton and I were standing by the swing doors when he came reeling out of the hall 20 minutes later, eyes still unfocused, looking like an orgasmic pink baby. I am afraid Rushton and I were simultaneously moved to shout with laughter, and at very close range. So bemused was he with the adulation that he immediately split the same ecstatic grin and raised his arms again in triumph.

TELEVISION

Martyn Harris

24 November

Well before the leadership ballot on Tuesday I had grown weary of the sight of Mr Michael Heseltine stalking about his garden in beige pullie and green wellies. For reasons I don't understand, whenever a television programme profiles a politician it is felt necessary to show him wandering about in the background, doing something pointless. The most popular is to have him take a piece of red paper from a red box and study it closely in the light of a green-shaded lamp. The paper is often upside down.

Mr Macmillan used to be seen climbing out of a big car and then shooting something; Lord Whitelaw used to do the washing up; Mr Heseltine pulls on his very clean gumboots and harvests the suckers from the bole of one of his trees. This would be better left until the spring. At one point I think I lip-read Mr Heseltine saying, 'Bloody silly, talking to a tree,' but I cannot be positive as his mouth has almost vanished over the last five years – a possible result of remaining so tight-lipped.

DIARY
Alan Watkins

1 December

Llew Gardner, who has died at 60, was one of the pioneers of disrespect-ful by-election reporting when he was with the *Sunday Express* before 1964. He was an equally unaccommodating political interviewer with various television companies afterwards. His career, however, did not flourish as it should have done following his departure from Thames over a decade ago. Part of the reason lay in Llew's approach to people. As Winston Churchill remarked of F. E. Smith, he would as soon keep a live coal in his mouth as a witty saying. One Saturday night I was in a Fleet Street pub, the Falstaff, with Llew and a few colleagues. With one of them I was having what one might call a Cambridge conversation. 'No, no, Bloggs wasn't at Jesus. He was at Christ's.' That sort of thing. Mr Peter Paterson, who was of our group, became restive at the turn the talk was taking and volunteered: 'I was educated at the University of Life myself.' Gardner: 'Failed, I assume.' On another occasion a colleague who had served gallantly throughout the war was about to re-embark on a description of his experiences. Gardner: 'I'm sorry, Wilfred, I haven't got time to cross the Rhine tonight.' I was talking of cricket grounds: 'I'm not really an Oval man.' Gardner: 'I should have thought that described you pretty accurately.'

LOW LIFE

Jeffrey Bernard

1 December

Last Monday I went to the *Sunday Express* Book of the Year Award at the Café Royal and sat at Frank Muir's table. What a charming man he is. But I couldn't help wondering, every time I looked at him, what on earth must it be like to be Geoffrey Wheatcroft's father-in-law. It makes me wonder which unlikely journalist will lay siege to my daughter one day. My brother, Bruce, has suggested the wine correspondent of the *Cork Examiner* but it doesn't really matter as long as my son-in-law-to-be does not work for the *Sun*.

These lunches, like the *Evening Standard* Drama Awards one, are strange dos. You see the same faces at most of them. I think that maybe Ned Sherrin is sustained by 365 of them every year. Laurie Lee was at the Café Royal again but he sat too far away from me to keep an eye on him. Last year I sat next to him and he shovelled four lamb cutlets into his jacket pocket without even bothering to wrap them up in a napkin. I said to him, 'I didn't know you had a dog.' He said, 'I haven't. They're for me. I shall heat them up again tonight for my supper.' This year we had roast lamb served with a thick brown gravy, so God alone knows the state of his pockets the next day.

1991

Frederic Raphael; Craig Brown; Wallace Arnold;
Miles Kington; John Mortimer; Martyn Harris;
Auberon Waugh; Dear Mary

DIARY

Frederic Raphael

5 January

During the autumn, travelling in Australia, we began to suffer from biblio-penury; we ran out of paperbacks. Hotel kiosks offered a diet of Stephen King, whose monarchy I deny. In time-I-learned-how modesty, I bought a three-in-one volume of Ruth Rendell's short stories. She was, the cited puffs insisted, 'the Queen of Crime'. Although this office harks back to the Magna Mater, *la* Christie (whose works I only ever enjoyed when translated into Spanish), I hoped Ms Rendell might instruct me in the art of suspense, as well as eliding the time between one Ansett flight and another. After a prolonged tasting, I declined to read on. I have rarely read such bloody, awful stories so slackly assembled, so meagre in characterisation, so trite in vocabulary. Since our return, the eagerness of editors and television executives to promote Ms Rendell's enthronement has continued. My Christmas pleasure was supposed to be enhanced by her contribution to the *Weekend Guardian*. It began,

> Jenny's friend, who was not crying yet, who seemed on the verge of crying or even screaming, a desperate woman, said in the voice she could only just control, 'Then who am I to turn to? What can I do?'

If such a manuscript were to be sent me by some beginner seeking praise under the rubric of unsweetened advice, I should cross out everything which preceded the (very lame) dialogue and ask if the force of the narrative was not strengthened by the excision. Whether or not 'creative writing' can be 'mentored' (as an advertising sophist put it recently in the *Writers' Guild News*), it is certain that the blue pencil, not to mention the raspberry, deserves to be wielded mercilessly in the campaign against literary obesity. Can virtue be taught? Vice can at least be stigmatised.

LETTERS

19 January

Sir: I would have entered Jaspistos's competition (5 January) asking for parodies of *Private Eye* had you not prematurely published what I presume to be Frederic Raphael's winning entry – an excellent if somewhat extreme parody of *Private Eye*'s parody of the *Spectator* diary – in the same issue.
John Diamond
London SE1

DIARY

Craig Brown

2 March

I spent two hours over lunch with Charles Moore a fortnight ago and failed to notice that he was going bald, then last week I read his moving lament to his lost hair. Oddly enough, I have been going bald since the age of 20, yet for most of the day I am able to wander around under the happy illusion that I have an almost unmanageably extravagant head of hair, along the lines of an English Jimi Hendrix or even Carmen Miranda. Only when I catch sight of myself in shop windows am I brought face-to-face with the realisation that I more closely resemble Mr Robert Robinson. Though I am grateful to Mr Moore for pushing a new line in baldy propaganda to the effect that bald men are excitingly power-crazed, I'm afraid that it won't wash with the world at large. One of the many upsetting aspects of hair loss is having to read flagrantly baldist fiction in which walk-on characters are described as 'dull and balding' as if the two adjectives went together as naturally as 'happy and glorious'. Those who do not suffer from it suspect that baldness is as much a character defect as a physical defect. This is why Gerald Kaufman, who is really not so bad as politicians go, seems to inspire convulsions of irritation. Perhaps if he were to invest in a Lionel Blair-style bouffant hairpiece, his pronouncements would gain a new authority. Other politicians have gone in for hair replacement therapy, some of it bizarre. The late Mark Boxer had as sharp an eye for hair as he had a nose for gossip. As a cartoonist, he found that when he got the hair of a caricature right, the rest followed. A year or so before he died, he told me with great glee that he had been chatting to a dermatologist at a party. This dermatologist had told him of a new method of hair replacement which involved planting the patient's pubic hair on the bald patch. He assured Mark that a senior Tory politician was undergoing this treatment, but discretion forbade him to reveal which one. Coincidentally, the very next day, Mark visited the opera, and found that the head behind which he sat belonged to Mr (as he then was) Norman St John-Stevas. But even diarists must exercise discretion from time to time, so I think I will close Mark's story there . . .

AFORE YE GO

Leaves from the commonplace book of Wallace Arnold

23 March

I must confess myself a little surprised that Mr Edward Pearce has not seen fit to include me in his new biography of Mr John Major for I have, of course, been on intimate terms with our new Prime Minister for close on 20 years. Might I come to the aid of future historians and fill in those gaps that Pearce, perhaps from jealousy, perhaps out of misguided deference, chose to leave unfilled?

I first met John back in 1969, when he served me a bag of 6″ screws from behind the counter of a leading ironmongers in the Brentford area. If it was indeed him – and I have no reason to suppose that it was not, for this assistant, too, had a deferential air and very pronounced spectacles – then our conversation went like this:

W.A.: A bag of 6″ screws please.

J.M.: Certainly, sir. That'll be 35 new pence, please.

W.A. *(handing over correct change)*: Thank you.

J.M.: Who's next, please?

It was another ten years before I renewed our brief acquaintance. He had just been elected to the House of Commons, and on his third day as an MP he was delighted to be invited to a small cocktail party where 'new boys' could mix freely with what one might call the 'grandees' of the party such as W. Arnold Esq. I was expounding on, as I remember, the Common Market (dread words!) when, out of the corner of my eye, I saw him approach. I immediately thrust out an empty glass in his general direction.

'A touch more fizz for me, please, waiter,' I exclaimed, by way of greeting.

'B-b-but I am the new MP for Huntingdon,' he explained.

'*Excusez-moi* – they're spreading such a wide net these days that it's deuce hard to keep up!!!' I explained, seeking to put him at his ease. 'What's your name, laddie?'

'Major,' he replied, jigging from foot to foot.

'Major by name,' I muttered to my old quaffing partner Julian Critchley, 'but Corporal by nature!!!'

John couldn't help but overhear this good-natured quip, and he was, as I remember, the first to join in the merriment, looking down with a straight face at his somewhat over-shone shoes in, I believe, silent laughter.

For the next eight years, we did not, I seem to remember, exchange so much as a word, though mutual friends now tell me that he used to nod and smile enthusiastically in my direction if we ever passed in a Westminster corridor. It was on his elevation to Chief Secretary of the

Treasury in 1987 that I became aware that our friendship was of a more enduring type than I had previously suspected. 'My dear John,' I wrote, 'heartiest congrats on your appointment! Delighted that Margaret took my advice! Must have lunch soon! Yrs ever, Wallace. P.S. Love to the wife (if any).' And do you know, I still keep his reply to this day. 'The Chief Secretary read your recent communication with great interest,' it says. 'He appreciates all comment from members of the public and has asked me to convey his thanks.'

DIARY

Miles Kington

4 May

Any day now I am due to reach my fiftieth birthday, and I had hoped to arrive at that safe haven without ever having to go ski-ing, enjoy opera, become a poker player or wear a white tie. I was wrong about one of them. Last week I was invited to a grand dinner at Lincoln's Inn and accepted because the guest list also contained my boss, Mr Andreas Whittam-Smith of the *Independent*, a man whom I never get to meet otherwise. I did not notice until it was too late that it was white tie. So I rang Philip Howard at *The Times* for his advice. He does not run an advice column but until four years ago he was my neighbour in Notting Hill and I know that he knows about dressing grandly for strange affairs. After all, he went to Eton, which is five years of dressing grandly for strange affairs.

'When I go to Moss Bros to hire this stuff, Philip, what do I ask for exactly?'

'Dear boy, you don't go to Moss Bros. If you go there you will spend £35 or so, and go to Lincoln's Inn looking like a man who has just spent £35 or so at Moss Bros. Now, I have at home a whole selection of stuff inherited from uncles and fathers and if you go to my place and let my wife sort you out, you will go to Lincoln's Inn looking like a man whose white tie has been in the family for three generations.'

And so it was. The best-fitting jacket was somewhat frayed, but cosily so. It was also missing a button, but Myrtle Howard flourished a spare one and sewed it on.

'It's tartan, but very dark,' she said.

'From Philip's old days in the Black Watch?'

'From the sofa.'

I entered my white tie and evening dress like a man becoming his own effigy at Madame Tussaud's. Like a waiter going to a restaurant, Myrtle thought. Or a conductor, she thought more kindly, off to the Albert Hall.

'A conductor wouldn't go on a bike,' I said.

'You're going on a *bike?*' she said. 'This I must see.'

Bicycling is the quickest way round London. Everyone knows that. So when I moved to Bath four years ago, I found it made sense, every time I had to come back to the capital, to put the bike in the train at Bath, get it out at Paddington and tackle London at speed. Even cycling past the taxi queue at Paddington makes it feel worthwhile. But cycling all the way to Lincoln's Inn in white tie seemed a little ambitious, so I left the bike at Paddington en route, took a taxi and arrived at Lincoln's Inn in time to be introduced to the 100 other diners, most of whom were judges, and silks, and common law advocates, and benchers of the Inn. I was confused, partly because a knowledge of the legal hierarchy seems to me as unnecessary as a love of poker or knowledge of opera, partly because I realised I was the only man in the room whose waistcoat did not cover the top of his trousers, though this could be overcome if I bent over like an old tree. Every time I was introduced to someone, I bent over *and did not return to the vertical.* It was in this position that I met Kenneth Clarke, the education supremo, and fellow guest.

'Do you get out to hear much jazz these days?' I enquired.

'No,' he mourned. 'I only got to Ronnie Scott's once last year. And the trouble is that when I do go out to jazz, I am recognised and get heckled.'

But everyone gets heckled by Ronnie Scott, I would have told him, if dinner had not been announced. The meal was held in a hall that would have made a very fine Tudor railway terminus. At one end were

400 or so junior lawyers, occasionally dropping their cutlery or their portable phones as they ate; at the other, above us, was a huge mural painting which I was informed by a kindly judge, or silk, or something, was insured against theft. 'The insurance company, however, returns the premium to us every year as it is incapable of theft,' he smiled. This is the kind of donnish joke which I suspect keeps lawyers of all ranks reconciled to their strange way of life. Not always successfully: the man opposite me suddenly said, halfway through dinner, 'I have been in the law for 32 years, and it has been 32 years of total tedium.' No wonder they need these dinners.

DIARY

John Mortimer

15 June

Life is full of marvellous stories. The following account was given to me, during a local dinner party, of how a neighbour came to break her arm. Her husband came home drunk one night and fell asleep at the foot of the stairs. The two sons came home later, found their father sleeping, went to the refrigerator from which they extracted a turkey's giblets, unzipped their father's fly and inserted these pieces of offal. The unfortunate mother awoke and came out onto the landing to see the cat apparently eating her husband's private parts. She was so appalled that she fell down the stairs. Yes, life is full of marvellous stories, but if you put them in a book no one would believe them.

DIARY

John Mortimer

22 June

Can it be only 20 years since the *Oz* trial? It seems in another century. These were the distant days of beads and Nehru jackets and Afghan waistcoats, when we were arguing about 'Children's Lib' and the 'alternative press' and whether that lovable character Rupert Bear might be depicted in a high state of sexual arousal. Two moments stand out in my memory. One was when the comedian Marty Feldman, whom I had unwisely put forward as a witness for the defence, called the judge a 'boring old fart'. On his way back from the witness box after this display of tact Marty whispered to me, 'Great to be working with you at last.' The other was when a witness was asked where *Oz* magazine was printed and gave an address in Buckingham Palace Road. 'For Heaven's sake!' the judge was roused to a rare moment of passion. 'Can't we keep the Royal Family out of this?'

TELEVISION

Martyn Harris

29 June

The highlight of any Wimbledon, and true test of a commentator's mettle, is the complete day's washout, though this should ideally start in the middle of a tense singles battle between two top seeds rather than, as this year, on the first day of the tournament.

Harry Commentator was our carpenter for this event, as Frank Bough used to say, and Harry filled the void brilliantly with a fine drizzle of factoids laid over the usual mournful shots of uneaten strawberries and unclaimed silver trophies. It was only the 26th time in 100 years we had lost an entire day's play, Harry told us, and his heart went out to those who had travelled hundreds, even thousands of miles. We should console ourselves with the thought of poor Mats Wilander, pulled out with knee injury, just as in rainy days of yore we used to dissipate our grief in contemplation of Bjorn Borg and his grojn strajn.

Leaving 'this wet Wimbledon' for a moment we went over to 'last week at Eastbourne', where Pam Shriver and Martina Navratilova ('the old firm of Shrive and Nav', as Harry called them) were chatting away in the kind of guest-house bedroom which has peach nylon sheets that spark with static and a complimentary Kit-Kat in the puddle beside the electric kettle. Both Shrive and Nav have the stitched-on squint that goes with 25 years of serving into the sun and the unforced fluency of a thousand Harry Carpenter interviews. Shrive asked if Nav remembered that second-set battle with Christine Truman that was interrupted in '74. Nav said did she ever.

Harry plucked us away then to consider the really big question of the tournament, which was whether André Agassi would wear white socks. Agassi has taken time off from his Nike commercials to appear at Wimbledon this year, though it is not certain whether 'this baby-faced exponent of rock 'n' roll tennis' (Harry Commentator) will condescend to win it.

'What do you expect from Wimbledon?' Harry asked him searchingly.

'I expect to go there nervous and excited,' said André.

'And what will Wimbledon expect from you?'

'About the same,' said André, mystifyingly. 'But Wimbledon was there years before me and will be there for years afterwards.'

Which seemed to be a safe bet, and so André went off to work on his squint, and Harry Commentator to his carpentry box.

ANOTHER VOICE

Auberon Waugh

7 December

Twenty-four years ago, when I was enrolled as *The Spectator*'s political correspondent and started the regular columns which have continued, with only two breaks, ever since, I was so poor that when I covered party conferences for the magazine in Brighton I used to stay in some rooms over a Cypriot café. The café was called the Brighton Belle, and its welcome in those days was warm but distinctly homely, with nylon sheets on the beds and a shared bathroom for the whole corridor.

Among the Cypriot waiters there was an exceptionally lively – some might say impudent – youth with the short legs and low-slung bottom characteristic of northern Cyprus. His chief delight was to pretend that his clients were drunk as he served them in the bar. He was called Costas, I think, as in Costas Lotta, and we had many merry exchanges along these lines. Later I saw him again, as I thought, at a cocktail party in the Boltons, where he had presumably been hired as a waiter. He was addressing himself to a very attractive blonde whom I had never seen before and have never seen since, a mother of four as I later discovered, divorced from a rich Greek.

'Hello, Costas,' I said, or words to that effect. 'Things looking up, eh?' Costas gave me a blank stare and informed me that he was the Greek middleweight boxing champion, an Olympic yachtsman, and a noted sprinter. Later he was introduced to me by the host, Mr Alistair Horne, who said that he was called Taki Theodoracopoulos and was a mysterious millionaire from Greece with connections in the hotel trade.

That was over 20 years ago. I did not expose Taki then as a Cypriot waiter from Brighton on a razzle, nor have I done so since, even when old friends like Alexander Chancellor and Nigel Dempster came up to tell me about this exciting new Greek millionaire they had met. I certainly do not propose to do so now, particularly as it is always possible that I am wrong, that Costas and Taki are not the same person at all. The end of the cocktail party at the Boltons was that the attractive blonde lady said to me: 'Thank you so much for rescuing me from that dreadful man. But you must be careful. He will kill you.'

In those 20-odd years since the Brighton Belle – if my identification is correct – Taki has achieved universal acceptance as a Greek million-aire, with a large yacht moored somewhere over the horizon, as well as breaking through as a much-loved *Spectator* columnist, dope-smuggler and gaol-bird.

How can I explain why it was that, asked by *The Spectator* to give his own short-legged, hairy-bottomed, baboon-like opinion on the best or most overrated books of the year, he should plump for my autobiography, *Will This Do?* (Century £15.99) as the most overrated ('disappointing, rather, as few rated it at all')? I would be most surprised if he had read the book. My guess is that he spent a total of six minutes on it, probably in somebody else's house, to check his name in the index and flick through the pictures. 'For his sake, he should have kept out the pictures of his family. They're so ugly . . . ' he writes, as his only substantive criticism.

But why, given the opportunity to insult any of the tens of thousands of unread books published last year, should he pick on my own brilliantly funny, unusual and informative memoirs? I do not mind in the least being singled out in this way, and in Taki's case am rather grateful, seeing it all as part of the rough and tumble of show business, but what are we to suppose the punters make of it all? Is there really so much entertainment to be derived from the contemplation of a small, self-regarding group of acquaintances, not particularly well known outside their own circle, slagging each other off?

Last week, Rory Knight Bruce, a former *Spectator* boxwallah, now editor of the *Standard* Diary, wrote a weasellish piece against journalistic feuds, obviously scared out of his mind by the prospect of a vendetta from John Osborne. In the course of it, he pompously took me to task for an alleged feud against Lord Gowrie, the popular black auctioneer and expert on modern art. It was one of 11 references to myself by other contributors in last week's magazine (not counting the letters page). My point is that this has got to stop or else the magazine will collapse in on itself like one of Adrian Berry's Black Holes in space.

YOUR PROBLEMS SOLVED

Dear Mary . . .

7 December

Q. I have an elderly bachelor aesthete coming to stay for Christmas. He is extremely good value but can also be rather sharp and touchy. For this reason I feel I cannot risk being frank with him about his clothes, of which he has one set, and which smell appalling. (He lives in Norfolk so tends to sleep in them during the winter.) What should I do?
  – V.M., London W11

A. Invite your guest to sit in the kitchen while you make some large, custard-based confection for consumption over Christmas. This will enable you to 'accidentally' spill a good pint or so of milk over the clothes, which you can then insist on stripping off him. Have to hand a spare outfit of men's clothing in his size which he can wear until you have effected the cleaning process on the offensive set.

1992

Dear Mary; Michael Frayn; Keith Waterhouse;
Martyn Harris; Dominic Lawson;
Julie Burchill; Jeffrey Bernard

YOUR PROBLEMS SOLVED

Dear Mary . . .

1 January

Q. They say that the late Robert Maxwell used to turn heads when he entered a room. I have the same effect but the heads turn away. Is it possible to acquire charisma, to make oneself more interesting? What do you suggest?
  – T.H., Luton, Beds

A. I have noted, on the social circuit, that certain people can attain a spurious charisma by wearing a knowing smile on their lips and saying little. Their demeanour serves to unnerve others who presume that there must be more to such a person than meets the eye. Inevitably, this success is short-lived and the practitioner very soon unmasked, unless he is a younger person moving in drug-taking circles and the silences are taken to denote wisdom. Many of the most pointless people of the 1960s and '70s got away with being cyphers for years by using this method. You may, of course, not wish to build your social life around drug-taking. If you are a man, another way of gaining charisma is to make passes at virtually every woman you meet. Englishwomen are so surprised that roughly four out of ten will accept the overture. The confidence which accrues to you as a sequel to such submissions will help to develop any latent charisma you may have.

THE ROOT OF ALL DELAY

Michael Frayn

1 February

No more Wechsel. The last of the summer Cambio. The real sadness of the Single European Currency is that it would mean the end of European money-changing as we know it.

I recall many delightfully unhurried exchanges of currency and traveller's cheques all over Europe, many delicious stews of noughts and decimal points, many entertaining failures to have my passport with me or to remember that banks close for lunch. But if I had to select just one occasion to recall in the bleak years ahead it would be a certain Monday morning in late June at the Banque de France in Laon.

Laon, appropriately enough, is at the crossroads of Europe. It's in the Aisne, in northern France, situated just off the motorway that runs from Strasbourg and Germany to the French Channel ports, at the point where it crosses the N2 from Paris to Brussels. Whichever road you're on you can see it coming from miles off – two ancient Gothic cathedral towers perched on a fortified hilltop islanded in the great agricultural plain. Two stars in the Michelin – three for the nave of the cathedral – wonderful views.

This charming town was full of sunshine and the bustle of market day when we found ourselves in need of a little financial refreshment there. We were on our way back from south Germany, and we needed a little more French currency to see us through to Calais. We had it in mind to change some £40 worth of left-over German marks, together with a £20 sterling traveller's cheque. The Banque de France seemed like a good choice for our custom. Its appearance was discreetly imposing, its name suggested solidity and extensive reserves. We were right. The feast of fine banking that ensued was worth another three stars in the Michelin. I was so impressed that I made a complete note of it, course by course, from the moment we pressed the yellow button beside the heavily armoured front door.

1. A red light comes on to indicate that our application for entry is being considered. We are instructed to wait for a green light before attempting to push the door.

2. The green light comes on, and we enter, to be confronted by a second door, with a second yellow button. A second red light comes on, while our credentials are examined all over again.

3. We pass through the second door, and enter a great hall divided by a counter. On the other side of the counter are a dozen or so employees of the bank. On this side is a spacious emptiness occupied only by us. We are the only people in Laon to have passed both tests.

4. We advance towards the counter and the waiting staff. We choose the nearest clerk, on the right-hand side of the bank, and present our £20 traveller's cheque, our passport, and our 130 deutschmarks. The clerk examines the cheque. She examines the passport, then takes a printed form and writes down by hand the number of the passport, together with my name and address. She examines the DM50 note, then the three 20s, then the ten and the two fives. She goes away to consult the bank's files.

5. She comes back and performs various computations upon a small pocket calculator. The calculator is for some reason balanced half on and half off an open ledger, so that it gives to the touch like a pudding. She writes down by hand on the printed form the quantities of sterling and deutschmarks involved, the rates for each currency, and the two sub-totals in francs. She performs another wobbly computation, and writes down the total. So far, a dignified but not unusual display of traditional handcraft money-changing.

6. But this is merely the *amuse-gueule* before the meal proper. The clerk takes the form she has filled up, together with the

passport, the traveller's cheque, and the seven deutschmark
bills, to a more senior-looking woman, who has drawn-back
grey hair and steel-rimmed spectacles. She checks the two
multiplications and the addition. She re-examines the passport,
the traveller's cheque, and the German bank-notes, and returns
them to the clerk. Everything is in order. The clerk returns
to the counter and hands us back our passport. She retains
the traveller's cheque – but she hands back our deutschmarks.
What?

7. She indicates a male cashier in a small fortified enclosure a
    kilometre or two away on the left-hand side of the great hall.
    Of course. A division of functions familiar from many such
    occasions in the past.

8. We walk across to the cashier. The clerk, on the other side of
    the counter, also walks across to the cashier. *We* are holding
    the passport and the returned DM130; *she* is holding the £20
    traveller's cheque and the form she has filled up, as checked and
    authenticated by her senior. We wait for the cashier to take the
    deutschmarks through the front of the security grille; she waits
    for the cashier to open a special window in the back of it and
    take the traveller's cheque and the form.

9. The clerk returns to her post on the right-hand side of the
    bank.

10. The cashier examines the traveller's cheque once again, then
    consults another set of files. He reworks the computations on
    the completed form. He takes the seven deutschmark bills
    from us, and examines them again in their turn – first the 50,
    then the three 20s, then the ten and the two fives. They all
    apparently pass muster once again. Nothing has changed, in
    this rapidly changing world, since they were first examined and
    re-examined on the right-hand side of the bank.

11. Or has it? The cashier is evidently shaken by a sudden doubt. How about the exchange rates? Some fair amount of time has now gone by since they were checked and double-checked on the other side of the bank. There may have been dramatic developments in the markets since then. The Federal Government may have fallen. The pound may be soaring even as the deutschmark goes into free fall. He looks up both the rates again. Nothing has happened. Pound and mark alike are rock-steady.

12. This steadiness in the markets makes a pleasing contrast with the cashier's pocket calculator, which is balanced half on and half off a ledger, just like the clerk's, so that it gives like a second helping of pudding as he punches each button, and recomputes all the computations that he has just reworked manually.

13. There is evidently something a little unsettling about the result of this fourth trip through the sums. I suspect the trouble is that the new results are exactly the same as the earlier ones, which may of course tend to confirm them, but which may, on the other hand, suggest the possibility of systematic error in the bank's methodology for multiplication and addition. The cashier summons a second cashier, who goes through all the rates and calculations for a fifth time. I notice that he too keeps the calculator balanced half on and half off the ledger as he works. Sponge *calculatrice* is obviously a *spécialité de la maison*.

14. And yes – steps are being taken. Action is in hand. The first cashier has let himself out of his cage. He is walking all the way back across the bank towards the right-hand side. We cross back as well, separated from him by the counter, in parallel, anxious to stay in touch with events. I believe he is carrying the traveller's cheque and the German bank-notes, but he evidently doesn't have everything with him, because after he has spoken to the clerk on the right-hand side she leaves her position, and we all walk back again to the left-hand side.

15. I'm not sure that it's the correctness of the mathematics that are at issue now – the calculator has been left to one side. I have the impression that they have moved on to more general questions. After all, not two but three different currencies are involved in this transaction, and there may be problems of protocol and precedence. Should the Bundesbank or the Bank of England be informed first?

16. A long time goes by. It is very quiet and still inside the bank, and my attention wanders. I find myself covertly watching some of the other staff. I become fascinated by one particular man. He is recklessly handsome, with a moustache and a three-piece suit, and he has nothing at all to do. The desk in front of him is completely empty. He rubs his hands together and gazes into space, with a look of wistful tenderness. I don't believe he is thinking about high-interest savings accounts, or even ways of making the bank's foreign exchange procedures more secure. I believe he is thinking about some member of the opposite sex.

17. I notice that there is in fact a young woman sitting just in front of him, typing rapidly, until there is nothing more to type, when she, too, leans on her empty desk and gazes into the great spaces of the room. I believe her thoughts have also strayed to her private life. They do not talk to each other. They do not look at each other. I get the impression that it's not each other that they are thinking about. Their separate reveries seem strangely deep and poignant in the quiet, lofty room.

18. Just a moment. Something's happened . . . I don't know what it was, but the clerk is walking back to her place on the right-hand side of the bank. It's been settled. Everyone's anxieties over the transaction have been set to rest.

19. The clerk fills out a second form to replace the first one.

20. She walks back to the cashier with the new edition of the form. I have the impression that she is moving a little more slowly than before. Her footwear, I think, is not entirely suitable for active pursuits like currency exchange.

21. The cashier checks the new figures and the current state of the foreign exchange market. He pays over Fr636.27.

22. We exit through the double security system.

The sun is still shining. We are in no hurry, and Laon is a delightful place to be. I look at my watch; the whole entertainment has taken 25 minutes.

So what's going to happen to everyone in the Banque de France in Laon when the ecu comes? How are the rest of us going to fill our time? We're all going to end up staring into space, thinking about our loved ones.

DIARY

Keith Waterhouse

22 February

The race is on to make *Maxwell: the Movie*, with at least three contenders at the starting post. My money is on Mike Molloy, former editor-in-chief of the *Mirror* group, who has a wealth of first-hand Maxwelliana in his television film treatment – for example, the time Cap'n Bob was reduced to a cowering wreck by the arrival of Mother Teresa and a heavy mob of nuns, hell-bent (if heaven-sent) on relieving him of a million pounds before they left the office. (He didn't have his cheque-book.) Then there was the highly placed woman executive who accompanied the old rogue on a business trip to Tokyo, where he tried to send her out to buy him a pair of socks. The lady was most indignant. 'Bob, you are paying me many tens of thousands a year for my professional skills. They do not include sock-buying.' An apparently contrite Cap'n Bob dug into his pocket and produced a brick-thick wad of yen which he pressed upon his offended senior employee. 'My dear, I'm most truly sorry and you must forgive me. Now you've been working very hard and I want you to take the afternoon off and devote yourself to shopping. Buy yourself something very silly.' As the mollified executive made for the door he added, 'And bring me back a pair of socks.' If Molloy's version gets off the ground, I have offered to play a small cameo scene. When Robert Maxwell was trying to persuade me not to transfer my act from the *Daily Mirror* to the *Daily Mail*, he asked whether I belonged to the Mirror pension scheme. I told him that as a freelance I had my own arrangements. Sloshing more champagne into my glass, he invited me to outline my private pension plan, listening, as I did so, with the amused tolerance of a rich uncle hearing a favourite young nephew boast of having saved up four and sixpence. At the end of my account he patted me confidentially on the knee, and in a fog-siren purr promised, 'I could enhance that pension scheme, Keith.'

TELEVISION

Martyn Harris

14 March

Inspector Morse is a cult, which means it is impossible to argue for or against it, or ever to understand why anybody should watch it. 'But it's so smug and hammy and badly plotted and plodding,' I say to *Morse* morons, and they giggle and hug themselves and say, 'Yes, isn't it wonderful!'

At the start of last week's episode (ITV, 8 p.m., Wednesday) in a fit of indignation I wrote down a piece of dialogue between batty old Lady Emily, who is brushing her hair, and her nasty rich husband:

He: 'Brush, brush, brush. Ha! I don't know why you bother. You're getting old just like the rest of us.'

She: 'What a cruel, cruel man you are!'

He: 'Better a cruel than a foolish one!'

Can't they see this is bad writing, I ask the *Morse* morons in my house, and they say, 'Yes, isn't it wonderful?'

So the next thing I do is make a careful note of the plot. This involves the murder of the nasty husband, followed by the murder of his two nastier sons, followed by the murder of Lady Emily by a nutty girl she believes is her illegitimate daughter. Morse thinks the killer is first one son, then the other, then the brother of a murdered stonemason who once had an affair with Lady Emily.

When he lights, completely by chance, upon the real killer, it turns out to be a kindly psychiatrist lady living in a cottage on the estate, who has had little to do so far with the rambling storyline, but is now the only member of the cast left alive, apart from Sergeant Lewis. This nice, plump, middle-aged lady, we are asked to believe, has beaten the brains out of two strong men and shot a third, for no better motive than that she thinks this carnage will secure Lady Emily's inheritance for the nutty girl, who is actually no relation at all. 'It is all too idiotic for words,' I say, and the *Morse* morons say, 'Yes, isn't it wonderful!'

YOUR PROBLEMS SOLVED

Dear Mary . . .

14 March

Q. I don't wish to have to police my guests when they come to stay, so how can I stop them from putting glasses and mugs down on polished tables without being a bore? I find they do it even when you have put out plenty of coasters. One can partly get round it by always serving coffee and tea in cups with saucers, but then people tend to go and make themselves great steaming mugs of tea in the middle of the day.

– S.M., Sussex

A. The best way to deal with this problem is to hide the mugs where only you can find them so that guests are forced to use cups and saucers to consume the tea they have made. Alcoholic drinks should be served to persistent offenders in glasses with coasters superglued onto the bottom.

DIARY

Dominic Lawson

21 March

Some of our readers appear to think that the 'Dear Mary' etiquette column is a concoction. They are wrong. Mary is Mary Killen, and the letters are genuine cries for social help. Last weekend I found myself sitting at lunch next to an elegant woman who told me, eyes brimming with gratitude, that she had taken Mary's advice, and it had worked. She had had a call for jury service. So, following Mary's suggestion, she wrote to the Central Criminal Court roughly as follows: 'Dear Sir, Thank you very much for your letter. You can be sure I will do my duty to rid our streets of vermin. I shall certainly obey the judge's instructions when he asks us to send down vile criminals, so brilliantly apprehended by our wonderful police force. Yours sincerely . . .' By return of post she received a letter saying that the court would not after all be requiring her services as a juror.

YOUR PROBLEMS SOLVED

Dear Mary . . .

21 March

Q. My passport has almost expired (its validity) and I need to supply an up-to-date photograph of myself in order to renew it. I am 58 years old and my problem is that, though in real life I am remarkably well preserved by any standards, in posed photographs I look about 68. I believe this is because the face, when not animated, seems to sag downwards and forwards at my age. I cannot face carrying around a hideous picture of myself for ten years. What can I do? I just look like a loony if I try to 'animate' myself in the booth.

   – A.C., London W8

A. Why not give yourself a temporary face-lift before entering the photo booth? This is only slightly painful and involves dragging the extra folds of sagging skin back and securing them with elastoplast behind your ears and at the top of your forehead. The elastoplast itself can then be masked by fluffing locks of hair over it. You will find the results to be remarkably effective.

TELEVISION

Martyn Harris

28 March

The Old Devils (BBC 2) is the best thing on television this year: a wonderful adaptation of Kingsley Amis's novel by Andrew Davies, who cannot have had much natural sympathy with the pit-bull of Primrose Hill. Someone told me, in fact, that when Davies and Amis met, the screenwriter was rash enough to remark that he didn't think Amis's recent novels were as good as the earlier ones, whereupon he of the crimson wattles snarled: 'And what on earth makes you think I am interested in the opinion of a silly young shag like you?' It might be true as well, for the incident finds its way, word for word, into the first TV episode.

YOUR PROBLEMS SOLVED

Dear Mary . . .

4 April

Q. I have always found anything to do with noses disgusting.
I adore children but cannot understand why their noses have
to be running all the time. I usually bring tissues when I go to
visit friends with children and simply wipe their noses for them
so I can bear to look at them. However, I have one friend in
particular whose three children's noses seem to be permanently
caked with undislodgeable matter. What should I do as I am
shortly to pay a visit there?
  – L.G., Ludgershall

A. Most toy shops sell Sir Roy Strong-style false faces comprising
glasses, nose and moustache. Why not make a purchase of a set
of three false faces – costing only about £1.50 – and request that
your friends' children wear the false faces for the duration of your
visit? In this way the entire offending nose areas will be screened
from your view.

DIARY

Julie Burchill

11 July

On 18 July my old alma mater, the *Face* magazine, is throwing a fund-
raiser at the Atrium, Millbank, London SW1. The proceeds will help pay
the (chivalrously reduced) damages to Jason Donovan, who claims that
the *Face* called him a screaming mimi. When I heard that Mr Donovan
had won his libel case, I immediately wired the editor of the *Face*, my old

drinking pal Sheryl Garratt, with an offer of help. Rather dashingly, I asked, 'Will a grand do?' Over the next week, this fax was reproduced in around half a dozen reports on the case and its aftermath. To my astonishment, both Sheryl and the publisher, Nick Logan, wrote separately soon after, both apologising for this awful breach of etiquette, claiming that their hacks had seen my fax 'accidentally'. Let me use this opportunity to put their minds at rest once and for all – Sheryl, Nick: the only reason I gave you the lousy money was so that people would write about it.

LETTERS

18 July

Sir: Charles Moore (Politics, 4 June) admits having reached the age of 35 without knowing the meaning of the word 'twat'. He is not the only man to have been so sheltered from the real world. One day Robert Browning came across a seventeenth-century couplet:

> *They talk'd of his having a Cardinalls Hat,*
> *They'd send him as soon an Old Nuns Twat.*

From this he concluded that 'twat' meant 'a nun's head-dress'. So, towards the end of *Pippa Passes*, we find the (unconsciously) hilarious lines:

> *Then, owls and bats,*
> *Cowls and twats,*
> *Monks and nuns, in a cloister's moods,*
> *Adjourn to the oak-stump pantry!*

Christopher Howse
London W12

LETTERS

15 August

Sir: I, too, am surprised that Charles Moore didn't hear the word 'twat' until so late in his life (Another voice, 4 July). Surely he is not too young to have been told the legendary but I suspect not apocryphal story of my old friend Tallulah Bankhead being asked, on an aeroplane flight, by the stewardess, 'Miss Bankhead, would you like some of our TWA coffee?' Tallulah raised an eyebrow. 'No, but I'll have some of your TWA tea.'

Nicholas Haslam

London SW7

LOW LIFE

Jeffrey Bernard

5 September

Norman's daughter, Natasha, was married a few days ago and it was an honour for me to be invited to the wedding and the reception after. It was the first time I had ever been into a synagogue. At the entrance I was given a yarmulka and then Norman ushered me to the front row of the stalls, so to speak, where I had a good and clear view of the couple standing at the chupa. It looked delightful, and a trio comprising clarinet, fiddle and harmonium made it a truly joyous occasion. It bordered on show business and for the duration of the ceremony even Norman looked as though he had forgotten how much the day was costing him. Natasha looked lovely and it occurred to me that she is lucky that, as any bloodstock agent will tell you, breeding is not an exact science. [. . .]

There was a long line of wellwishers and friends waiting to congratulate the happy couple but Norman, being particularly solicitous, took me to the head of it and then put me at a table and chair with a drink and where I overlooked the river. I sat there sipping away and nibbling on potato pancakes while the room gradually filled up with guests. Norman's brother-in-law, a loquacious minicab driver, took a photograph of me wearing the yarmulka which will go into my scrapbook. That may well give my grandchildren something to wonder about one day.

The champagne flowed, Norman beamed and Michael, the boss barman and only other representative from the Coach and Horses, cut a dash in his dinner jacket. Never have I been surrounded, I thought, by so many Jews, not even at Brighton races. It was then that my train of thought led me to think about the Holocaust and that was depressing until Norman diverted my attention with one of his philosophical observations like, 'Drink up. It's free today.'

1993

Dominic Lawson; Keith Waterhouse;
Auberon Waugh; Dear Mary; Alan Rusbridger;
Ian Hislop; Stephen Fry

DIARY

Dominic Lawson

9 January

Mr Alan Clark, who is drawn to controversy as a housefly is to rotting fruit, has done it again by writing an article in *The Times* accusing Churchill of being 'obsessed' with fighting Hitler, and denouncing our great war leader for failing to sue for peace with the Nazis in 1941. Mr Clark somehow left out from his article the fact that Hitler broke every one of the six treaties he signed between 1933 and 1939. But I am surprised that anyone is surprised by the ravings of the former defence minister. It is widely known that Mr Clark is a man who keeps a Rottweiler called Eva, named after Eva Braun, and is a keen collector of Nazi memorabilia. There are times when I think that Mr Clark is the only good argument against inherited wealth, as it is that which gives this particular unemployed ex–MP the time to devote to his historical researches and his subsequent verbal venting of them through his least useful orifice. Without his inherited millions Mr Clark might have to spend his time more usefully, working as a chauffeur perhaps, or as a commissionaire. I must therefore take issue with our diarist of last week, Mr Nigel Dempster, who stated here that Mr Major's failure to ennoble Mr Clark was 'the most glaring omission' in the New Year's Honours List, since 'his innate honesty in the witness-box led to the collapse of the Matrix Churchill trial in November and the acquittal of three directors who otherwise would probably have been found guilty and jailed.' The fact is that Mr Clark had earlier made statements to the police which were instrumental in the decision to prosecute the three innocent men. It was only in court, when confronted by a defence counsel in possession of hitherto suppressed Government documents detailing Mr Clark's role in the affair, that the former defence minister blurted out the words which led to the acquittal of the Matrix directors. Mr Clark, as one minister regularly put it to him face to face, is 'a bad man'.

DIARY

Keith Waterhouse

23 January

I am very nervous of being approached in the street by strangers. Asked if I am who I am, my instinct is to hedge cautiously, 'Not necessarily.' Two recent encounters left me no less wary. A young man came up to me in Shaftesbury Avenue and said, 'You're that Keith Waterhouse, aren't you? You wrote *Billy Liar*, didn't you? My favourite book of all time.' As I pumped his hand warmly, he added, 'Mind you, you haven't done much since, have you?' A few days later a well-dressed lady stopped me in the King's Road. 'I don't make a practice of accosting people, Mr Waterhouse, but I just wanted to say how much I enjoyed your novel *Our Song*. It made me laugh and cry.' Thanking her kindly, I said, 'Now go and see the play – it will make you laugh and cry even more.' Her demeanour changed at once. 'See the play? See the play? Do you know the price of a theatre ticket these days? Look at my coat – I can't even afford to have it dry-cleaned!' And before I could burble, 'But madam, we are thinking of giving a Sketchley's £1-off voucher with every pair of tickets!' she was off. I did not fare much better at my club, where an elderly party I found myself standing next to at the bar barked, 'Goin' to see that thing with O'Toole. Know anythin' about it?' 'Yes, I wrote it.' The rheumy old eyes did not flicker. 'Any good?'

ANOTHER VOICE

Auberon Waugh

10 April

On Sunday we learned how Sir Peregrine Worsthorne, in order to celebrate the 50th birthday of Mrs John Birt a week earlier, allowed himself to be put into a charabanc at 8.30 in the morning for a mystery tour which took him, after various stops, to a hamburger bar where the roisterers were served in their seats with boxes of hamburgers accompanied by Coca-Cola for their luncheon.

The other guests, who were 'media executives, journalists etc.', were somewhat surprised to be given a non-alcoholic luncheon. 'But again,' says Peregrine, 'John Birt pulled it off.' It was only when he got home that he began to pay the price. 'Ever since returning home in the small hours last Sunday, I have been in bed with a viral infection,' he reveals. 'It is no exaggeration to say that I have not recovered yet.'

Few people will be more distressed than I if it should prove fatal. For years I have been writing about the effect of hamburgers on people in this country, which might be compared to the effect of Marmite on the French or salt on slugs. Where hamburgers are concerned, one does not need even to eat them to suffer from their deleterious effects. In Rome, where a hamburger bar was proposed in the *centro storico* near the Spanish Steps, it was discovered that the cooking process gives off a form of gas which attacks ancient buildings. The Pantheon itself was covered by a sort of stone-devouring slime, until the City Fathers stepped in.

In America, the home of the hamburger, there are no ancient buildings worth talking about, so this anxiety does not arise. But it should be evident to any European – by which I mean anyone belonging to the common culture of Europe, shaped by classical history, Catholicism, the Renaissance, reformation, counter-reformation, the Holocaust, the fascist and socialist illusions – that the hamburger, wherever it is found, is the emblem of American cultural colonialism. It is more than a food preference: it is an existential choice, a philosophical statement, a way of life.

The American culture, based on the dictatorship of the mass market, can be imposed by economic forces or it can be adopted almost by accident as a result of slipping into a number of easy choices. It is something which any half-educated Englishman (or French, Dutch or Belgian man) would wish to oppose with all his strength. If only I had the time, I would be happy to spend it picketing hamburger bars, as others picket abortion clinics.

YOUR PROBLEMS SOLVED

Dear Mary . . .

17 April

Q. I live in a tiny village in an area of outstanding natural beauty. There are obvious restrictions on building but there are none on buying hideous, amoeboid, white plastic furniture for your garden at £23.99 for four chairs and a table. My nearest neighbour has made such a purchase and, most offensively, has cut back the hedgerow between us to such an extent that I see these items of furniture each time I look out of the window on the south side of my house. What can I do about this? (Incidentally he also has purple and white festoon blinds in the windows at the front of his cottage.)
  – Name and address withheld

A. Pop into your local auction-house and buy up some acceptable garden furniture costing at least £23.99. Then enter your neighbour's garden under cover of darkness and remove the offensive furniture, replacing it with the inoffensive. There should be no need for you to leave a note to explain your actions.

DIARY

Alan Rusbridger

29 May

It has always surprised me how few Trotskyists read the *Tatler*. Pick up any magazine of the far Left and you will find page after page of impenetrable articles about the corruption of the ruling classes and the shape of the revolution to come. How much more effective it would be simply to reproduce pages from the Bystander, that hugely enjoyable photo album of rich young things pulling off each other's trousers at hunt balls. Hand that out at the factory gates at Dagenham of a Monday morning and you might really start the revolution. Similarly, if I were editing the *Socialist Bugle* this week I would run huge chunks of Alan Clark's diaries. Was there ever a Tory minister who so conformed to the wildest Trot stereotype of a Tory minister: a minister with a castle, a personal fortune of £40 million and a dog called Eva Braun? From the current serialisation in the *Mail on Sunday* I would reprint three passages which fall into the category of things no self-respecting revolutionary would dare make up. First, there would be the intimate dinner party of Tory bigwigs at which there was much talk of 'too many jewboys in the Cabinet'. Then there would be the episode in which a minister debates with himself whether to jump on a shop assistant he meets on the train, mesmerised as he is by the fact that 'she was not wearing a bra, and her delightful globes bounced prominently, but happily, under a rope-knitted jersey'. Finally, I would reprint the same minister's dictum on dirty tricks: 'As far as I'm concerned, "dirty tricks" are part and parcel of effective government.' Subversive and entertaining though the diaries are, they have so far failed to explain Clark's eleventh-hour decision not to stand for re-election last year. During the week of the election itself he put off an interview with the *Guardian*, pleading to me that he was imminently to be translated to the House of Lords. It would be interesting to know why that never came about. It may well be that the diaries will come to be seen as the

most spectacular act of revenge in the long and tortuous annals of the
Conservative Party.

The other passage that caught my eye in the Clark diaries was his
entry for 23 June 1983, while Minister of Employment. 'There is a
tiny *balcon* below knee height. Sometimes I get a wild urge to relieve
my bladder over it, splattingly on the ant-like crowds.' The only other
person I knew who was troubled by this urge was my former employer,
Robert Maxwell, except that he was altogether less inhibited. Someone
who travelled with him a fair amount told me that, after landing on the
helipad on top of the Mirror building, the fat old crook would often
walk over to the side of the building and urinate on to the heads of the
ant-like crowds going about their daily business in Holborn Circus. The
psychological origins of this syndrome are obscure. One wonders if it
already has a name: Alan Clark's syndrome by proxy?

DIARY

Ian Hislop

5 June

You can't keep a bad man down. There are now plans to stage a musical
about Robert Maxwell in the West End and the producers are looking for someone to play him. Names such as Mel Smith and Robbie
Coltrane are being suggested, but this is hardly very imaginative
casting. I would go for Arnold Schwarzenegger myself. The action-
hero-turned-hamburger-salesman has just been in this country, and
every time he gave an interview it struck me how good he would be
in the Maxwell role. Arnie's combination of ruthlessness and humour-
lessness is ideal, and his leaden attempts at buffoonery are exactly in
the style of the late Captain Bob. When you add in the constant sense
of threat lurking behind any conversation, you have an almost perfect match of subject and actor (all right then, star). Arnie's accent is
almost right as it is and he would have to do very little in the way of

psychological preparation. The immigrant background, the self-made struggle, the financial empire, the interest in politics (rightish for Arnie, leftish for Bob) are all there already. I hope the producers have got the sense to see this because it could be a huge success. The scene where Arnie/Bob strides into the Mirror building and shouts '*Hasta la vista, pension-scheme*' before bursting into song might be one of the great moments of musical theatre.

Maxwell was something of an actor himself. In the celebrated court case against *Private Eye* his performance in the witness box was sufficiently powerful to win him large libel damages from the jury. I always believed that the case hinged not on any of the financial evidence (or lack of it), but on the question of the 'Lookalikes'. This is a feature in *Private Eye* that points out famous people who look like each other. On one occasion, it was suggested that Maxwell looked like the more handsome Kray twin. Unsurprisingly, Maxwell's barrister brought this to the attention of the court, but he then continued with various other 'Lookalikes' including the Duke of Edinburgh and Adolf Eichmann. No jokes are ever very funny when they reappear in a courtroom (though everyone laughs at anything the judge says in the hope that it will make him more sympathetic to their side) and this was no exception. However, not only did no one laugh but Maxwell suddenly broke down in tears and, producing a large handkerchief, began to sob uncontrollably. He explained that the mention of Eichmann brought back memories of the loss of his family at the hands of the Nazis. A solemn hush descended on the court. *Private Eye*'s solicitor wrote, 'Maxwell takes out onion' on the pad in front of him, but his cynicism was not shared by anyone else. The scene had a great impact on the jury. I even felt mildly guilty myself. I was therefore greatly relieved this week to meet Lord Spens, the former Guinness defendant, who told me at a lunch that he had spent the evening with Maxwell on that very day seven years ago. When Spens had asked him about the tears in the court, Maxwell had roared with laughter, pointed to himself and shouted, 'Forget Rada.'

LETTERS

10 July

Sir: I do not think that Taki can claim to be 'the greatest Greek cricketer ever' (High Life, 26 June). That honour surely has to go to his compatriot Xenophon Balaskas, whose Test career for South Africa stretched to eight games in the 1930s and included one century against New Zealand in the season 1931–32.

Revd Jonathan Edwards
Honiton, Devon

ANOTHER VOICE

Auberon Waugh

11 September

In a single, 20-line paragraph of his brilliant 'Diary' in last week's *Spectator*, A. N. Wilson disposed of a matter which has troubled my waking hours for as long as I can remember. It was on the subject of titles, their place in British society, the way we feel about them etc. By 'we' of course I mean chaps like me, Andrew, Angus and the rest of us – chaps who might reasonably have given a certain amount of thought to the matter. Wilson's disposal of the whole subject in 20 lines at the beginning of his 'Diary' hinted that he had other, more important things to talk about, and I confess I was most grateful to learn that the bursar of Exeter College, Commander Simon Stone, a former signals officer on the royal yacht *Britannia*, will be known as Ms Susan Marshall from the first day of next term.

But an awareness of titles is almost universal among Britons, whereas the temptation to change sex is still restricted, even among former naval officers. An Englishman who generalises on such a subject in no more than 20 lines must be either hiding something or suppressing more emotions than are usually considered healthy to suppress. Let us examine Wilson's statement line by line:

> I rather admired a friend of mine who inherited a baronetcy this summer and decided not to use his title. He and his wife both lead middle-class lives in London and felt it would be vaguely ridiculous to dub themselves Sir This and Lady That.

On the face of these two sentences, it is hard to see how Wilson's friend has done anything to be admired. Many might have admired him for inheriting the baronetcy in the first place. Despite everything said and written on this subject in recent years, it is extraordinary how many of our less sophisticated fellow countrymen continue to admire anyone with a title, just as it is extraordinary what complicated emotions titled people stir in the breasts of the more sophisticated. Again, it is a perfectly normal thing for people to take action to avoid being made to look ridiculous, even 'vaguely ridiculous'. There need be nothing shameful in that. But one does not admire someone simply because he does not wish to look ridiculous.

Nor is it true that Wilson's friend and his wife would have had to dub themselves Sir This and Lady That. They would have been invested with their new dignity and acclaimed in their titles by the social custom of their country. It would be easy to condemn Wilson's friend and his wife as traitors to their class and to the system which once distinguished Britons from lesser breeds, gave our nation its character and pre-eminence, created the culture of the English country house, which is the highest point of western civilisation, to which French, Germans, Dutch, even distant Poles and Czechs once aspired.

But perhaps it is not reasonable to accuse people of betraying a cause which is already lost. In the foolish, muddled perceptions of our time, by no means everyone is agreed that the collapse of the class system is the chief mark of our national decline. There are those who feel they have done well out of the collapse, or that they would not have been able to do so well under the previous system. I do not really wish to accuse the mysterious Mr This and Mrs That of betraying their class when they refuse to call themselves Sir This and Lady That like everyone else.

'There is an inevitable embarrassment factor where titles are concerned,' writes A. N. Wilson. No doubt it is felt by all the peers of Britain – 24 dukes, at my last count, 29 marquesses, 157 earls, 105 viscounts, 441 hereditary barons ... what business, one asks oneself, have mere baronets, as they go about their middle-class lives in London, to feel embarrassed in this company? Last time I made an emergency call on a London dentist, I found rather to my surprise that my root canals or whatever were being attended to by a hereditary baron. The crime of which A. N. Wilson's friends might reasonably be accused is not so much that of betraying their class, but of treason to something much more sacred, an Englishman's sense of the absurd.

I wonder how many people have the faintest idea how many baronets there are. I held a sweepstake last weekend in Somerset. A local landowner (younger brother of a Shropshire earl) put it at 150. His daughter, married to an insurance executive, said 200. A daughter of mine, married to a businessman, said 100. My wife (sister of a Surrey earl) put it at 75. Her brother (the Surrey earl, himself a baronet) came through on a cellular telephone to announce confidently that the figure was 3,000. In fact, as I eventually discovered from the Home Office which keeps the Roll, there are between 1,230 and 1,330, the higher figure allowing for unclaimed baronetcies and those whose claims have not been properly established. Any group as large as that, scattered through the country, many no doubt working as vets, accountants, journalists, is part of the warp and weft or woof of society.

Perhaps one should say it is part of the woof. Undoubtedly, it is one of the more absurd ingredients in our national comic opera, and those born to it are required to play a slightly absurd role. There are some advantages to it, if not many. A Polish count to whom I put the question told me he wears his 'title' like a dinner-jacket, only on those occasions which seem to demand it. But it is this enjoyment of life's rich absurdity which distinguishes the English, at least, from apes, Americans, Germans and most of the rest of the human race. We must all play our parts. To decline to do so on the grounds that you find it embarrassing or socially constricting is to renounce any meaningful participation in British life.

Of course it might turn out that A. N. Wilson's friend works for Murdoch, in which case the humour even of his renunciation is lost. We cannot throw too many stones. Even if we accept the Murdoch presence as part of an enemy occupation of our country, how many of us can be certain that we would have acted heroically as Frenchmen in occupied France? No doubt most of us would have continued editing literary journals as before. A. N. Wilson ends his famous 20 lines with a trenchant observation:

> It is hard not to wince [he says] when the widows of knights insist on calling themselves 'Lady' This or That, or when the children of life peers deem it worthwhile to dub themselves 'Honourable'.

What on earth does he expect widows of knights to call themselves? As I say, it is extraordinary what complicated emotions titled people continue to stir in the breasts even of the most sophisticated. At least A. N. Wilson is happy to remain part of our national comic opera. As Mark Steyn observed recently, 'Britain has always been best at good middle-brow art. Gilbert and Sullivan rather than Beethoven; P. G. Wodehouse, not Goethe.' It does *The Spectator* no harm to be edited by the child of a life peer. Even *Literary Review* might carry more weight if it were edited by a baronet.

DIARY

Stephen Fry

6 November

The recent humiliation of the Canadian Conservative Party has given me a slight twinge of guilt over one of my favourite books. I was in the city of Oxford some years ago, in one of those streets that they call the Wide or the Long or the Tall, and I drifted into the Oxford University Press bookshop. I had been meaning for some time to treat myself to the brand-new edition of the *OED* – this was in the days when it was presented in many-volumed book form rather than as a CD or interactive game. I ordered the full set, which cost something in the region of £1,400 and would, I was promised, be dispatched to my home address from the OUP's warehouse in Corby. Before paying I browsed for a while and happened upon an item called *The Oxford Book of Canadian Political Anecdotes*. I think you will agree that titles like this do not pop up every day and cannot be passed over. It ranks with the American classic *Utilising Road Kills* and every bibliophile's favourite, *With Rod and Reel in Northern Bechuanaland*. I grabbed the only two copies on the shelf and went up to pay. As I did so, who should come into the shop but the thinking man's cinnamon muffin, Jeremy Paxman? We chatted awhile and I showed him my find. He was suitably impressed, but had to clutch the counter to save himself from falling when the shop assistant said to me, 'That'll be one thousand four hundred and fourteen pounds ninety-eight, please.' Paxman could see no purchases I had made other than those two copies of *The Oxford Book of Canadian Political Anecdotes*. 'What the . . . ?' he mouthed. 'Ah,' I said, 'rare and valuable item, *The Oxford Book of Canadian Political Anecdotes*. Worth every penny.' I left him gaping like a landed perch and wondering at what kind of an arse would pay fifteen hundred quid for a kitsch joke. I think he knows now, but for a while he was easily the most flabbergasted *Newsnight* presenter in the Thames Valley region.

DIARY

Stephen Fry

13 November

The experience of reading newspapers for a week [for an appearance on *The News Quiz*] has reminded me of our great national genius for headline writing. I spotted a screaming banner in a tabloid last week which ran 'Nude Etonian Murdered By A Hooker's Junkie Lover'. This I thought deserved some kind of palm for containing six words each of which is a sub-editor's dream. Only 'By' and 'A' are redundant. It managed to be free of word-play too. Some years ago I was invited to lunch by the late Mark Boxer, who was editing the *Tatler* at the time. He wanted to offer me a job, but was being rather coy about describing it. 'I need you to take a look at each month's edition and smell it,' he said. 'Find some way of linking everything together. Think about how various features and articles can be reflected on the cover.' At last, after much puzzlement, I suddenly grasped what he was driving at. 'You want me to write the puns!' 'Yes!' he cried, thumping the table with joy. For a few months I did as I was asked. If the front cover contained a girl in a scarlet frock, then the 'spine line' would say 'Red Dress The Balance'. Even date puns were obligatory: 'Feb. & Groovy', 'June Know Where You Are Going?' and 'Nov. Under You're Feeling Blue'. If there was a major feature about Catholic families inside, the cover would promise 'The Smart Sect: Roman Britain revealed' or some such tummy-rubbish. Fashionable film and book titles would dictate headlines too. An article decrying the influence of Britain's leading design guru would, as a matter of course, be headlined 'Conran the Barbarian', just as profiles of the Chancellor today are invariably subbed 'Beyond Our Ken' or 'Kenneth Clarke Ha Ha Ha'. I lasted no more than three months in this atmosphere. My friends just couldn't take it. 'Ah, the Articulate Laurie,' I would say, 'Hugh are you?' There is no sign of the epidemic being halted. Last week's *Spectator* could not resist headlining Simon Courtauld's article on fish 'Absolutely brill'. It may be time for legislation.

1994

Dear Mary; Keith Waterhouse;
Dominic Lawson; John Mortimer; Robert Harris;
Richard Littlejohn; Jeffrey Bernard

YOUR PROBLEMS SOLVED

Dear Mary . . .

1 January

Q. My 21-year-old sister, who has come to live with me in London, keeps losing the front-door key to our flat. It seems not to be an affectation but to stem from genuine absent-mindedness and to be incurable. It is too dangerous to leave a key hidden somewhere outside the flat, so what do you suggest? Your solution urgently, please, as she keeps coming back in the middle of the night without one and sometimes I am not in myself to admit her.

   – M.S., Beaufort Street, SW3

A. You must insist that your sister wears traditional school knickers with a pocket in which she can keep her key. This should preclude the syndrome of her laying down the key on some social surface to be certainly forgotten. These voluminous garments are so far out of fashion as to be on the cusp of surging back in again. Indeed one fashion leader has deliberately driven to a school outfitter's in Dorset in order to stock up with a quantity in navy which she wears on top of the traditional white 'liners' or lining pants. Not only has she enjoyed an unprecedented level of pelvic warmth this winter, she also claims to have excited copy-cat purchasing amongst virtually all the girlfriends in front of whom she has recently undressed.

DIARY

Keith Waterhouse

8 January

Dinner with a veteran foreign correspondent, now grounded. I asked him what, in all the wars and uprisings and other skirmishes he has covered over the years, was his hairiest moment. He thought for a bit and then said, 'It was in Beirut. There was some shelling going on and a colleague and I ran for cover in an abandoned hotel. The shelling got uncomfortably nearer and we thought we'd better make a run for it. Just as we were about to duck out through the back, my friend pointed through a hole in the wall where a doorway had been, leading to the front desk. "Look!" he exclaimed. "Shan't be a tick – I must get it!" Get what? The hotel cat? An abandoned child? He darted through the gap and, just in that second, a shell hit the building and the whole bloody wall came crashing down. I was sure he was a goner, but I had to find out. I started clambering through the rubble, calling his name, then through this curtain of dust staggered my friend, covered in blood and plaster and shards of glass but holding something aloft in triumph. "I've got it, I've got it!" he cried. It was the hotel's credit card embossing machine, together with enough blank American Express vouchers to keep two correspondents in expense account receipts for the rest of their stay.'

And that was his hairiest moment?

'No, my hairiest moment was when we clambered aboard the truck that stopped to give us a lift, and I thought he'd dropped the bloody thing.'

DIARY

Dominic Lawson

19 February

I am sorry if some readers were shocked by the abrupt nature of the message in place of the Low Life column last week. But its absent author wanted the explanation 'Jeffrey Bernard has had his leg off'. He had become irritated by the now legendary apology 'Jeffrey Bernard is unwell'. A couple of weeks earlier, Jeff had rung me up to complain, 'I'm not unwell. I'm fucking dying.' I am delighted to report that Jeff, while not a picture of health, has survived an operation for the removal of the lower half of his right leg. When I went with Michael Heath to the Middlesex Hospital to visit the slightly edited columnist last Wednesday, the day after the operation, Jeff's condition could best be described as uncritical. 'Look,' he said, as I was hanging up my coat. I turned round, and it took me a little while to realise that Jeff was pushing his stump as near to my face as it would reach. 'The doctor says it's beautiful.' Michael suddenly began to look rather unwell. 'The things I'll do to get a subject for the column,' the patient continued, pointing to the remains of his right leg. Jeff is brave. He had been rushed into the hospital to have the amputation in the morning, but because of some more pressing emergency was forced to wait a whole day for the gangrenous leg to be removed. As he was explaining this to us, a glamorous woman, who can have been no more than half Jeff's age, walked into the room. 'I suppose,' she addressed the Low Life columnist, 'you'll be wanting to show me the leg.' Michael and I looked at each other, made our excuses, and left.

DIARY

John Mortimer

12 March

It seems a long time since we got back from Morocco and said goodbye to the sunshine. Michael Codron, the impresario who's done so much to introduce new writers, turned up in the hotel where we stayed. We were remembering old times and the days when Michael put on *A Voyage Round My Father*. After Alec Guinness left, the part of my father was taken by Michael Redgrave, then coming to the end of a distinguished career. I knew he had had difficulty in remembering his lines and wore a sort of hearing aid into which they were repeated, together with stage directions, from the prompt corner. I didn't know what Michael told me in Morocco, that one night the hearing aid picked up messages from radio taxis. The great actor sat down on a sofa beside the actress who was playing my mother and said, loudly, impressively and to her complete astonishment, 'I must now proceed immediately to number four Flask Walk.'

YOUR PROBLEMS SOLVED

Dear Mary . . .

19 March

Q. I don't think anyone has asked what can be done about a slow eater at a dinner-party. Is it all right to clear away the plates and leave him lagging along? If not, how can he, or even she, be hurried?

– M.B., Longstowe, Cambs

A. Why not keep a starving cat on your premises and release it into the dining-room at the necessary moment? Such cats are brazen about snatching food from wherever they can find it, and can even be introduced earlier to hurry along the type of guest who keeps pieces of food dangling on his fork for minutes at a time as he finishes off what he was saying. These tardy eaters will soon learn their lessons as the cat flies into action.

DIARY

Robert Harris

16 April

Modern life holds few greater pleasures than flying first class at some-body else's expense. Personally, if I had to pay for the privilege myself, I wouldn't enjoy it. I'd spend the entire flight thinking how much more wisely I could be spending the money. But if somebody else is paying – in my case, the occasional foreign publisher – flying abruptly ceases to be a chore and becomes a luxury. My heart was therefore touched last week when I heard the story of Albert Goldman, the American biographer of Elvis Presley and John Lennon, notorious for dwelling on the more sordid aspects of his subjects' lives. It seems that at the end of last month Mr Goldman agreed to fly from Miami to London to give an interview to the BBC arts programme *The Late Show*, but only on condition his seat was first class. Imagine his distress on arriving at the check-in desk and discovering his reservation was only for club class. Mr Goldman promptly threw a tantrum of epic proportions – so epic that the BBC had to be telephoned in London and his seat upgraded. Alas, the author's victory was short-lived. Possibly as a result of his exertions at the ticket desk, Mr Goldman suffered a heart-attack and died mid-flight.

YOUR PROBLEMS SOLVED

Dear Mary . . .

11 June

Q. I am a former mistress of Alan Clark. As a Lloyd's loser, I would welcome some extra income at this most difficult of times, particularly as I am planning a holiday on the Côte d'Azur in midsummer and my car badly needs replacing. Please could you advise me as to how much my story would fetch on the open market?
   – Name and address withheld

A. I am afraid that your experience, though of obvious interest to your friends and close relations, has now become too commonplace to be able to sell to any real commercial advantage in an already overcrowded market. If, however, you can prove that three generations of the same family – say, you, your children and your mother – have all enjoyed physical intimacy with Mr Clark, then you may well be able to pick up approximately £625 including VAT from a tabloid newspaper. This will serve as a down payment on a Lada motorcar, which costs £5,200 new.

DIARY

Richard Littlejohn

9 July

Is Tony Blair in the wrong party? That is the question being asked increasingly in political circles. He strikes me as a model Christian Democrat, of the kind to which Conservative MEPs cheerfully align themselves. Apart from a burning desire for office, he seems to have little in common with an overwhelming number of his colleagues in the Labour Party, especially his rival for the leadership, Margaret Beckett. He is a charming, intelligent man, without a hint of malice or vindictiveness. He frightens nobody. Mrs Beckett and Mr Prescott give the impression of not only wanting to destroy all the reforms of the past 15 years, regardless of merit, but to take revenge on everyone they believe has prospered under the Conservatives. They belong to Labour's dark ages. It is not so long ago that Labour MPs were appearing on Trotskyist platforms and writing in the agitprop press for publications such as the *Morning Star* and *Socialist Worker*. I have discovered that Mr Blair was also a contributor to a political sheet considered extreme by many. In 1979 and 1980 he contributed articles to *The Spectator*. So while his comrades were rubbing shoulders in print with the likes of Tariq Ali, the young Blair was sitting comfortably alongside such well-known socialists as Auberon Waugh. In those days he called himself Anthony Blair. The Tony came later, in the cod-proletarian manner of Mr Wedgwood Benn. So perhaps he is in the right party after all.

YOUR PROBLEMS SOLVED

Dear Mary . . .

6 August

Q. As far as I am concerned, the whole point of a drinks party is to meet as many people as possible. I therefore like occasionally to glance over the shoulder of whoever I am talking to in order to ensure that I am not missing any key person. I know that an extraordinary number of people find this habit offensive and wonder how one can prevent their noticing. Please advise.

– C.H., London SW1

A. Why not use the method employed by one of the country's most competent socialisers? H.B. finds that, provided he keeps his eyes fixed in an intent stare on those of his interlocutor, it will stand him in good stead when he swivels his head suddenly backwards or sideways as though someone is nudging or pushing him. On the return sweep he can usually take in the room without suspicion. H.B. also points out that as long as one is staring intently at an interlocutor there is no need to listen to what he or she is saying. This leaves the ears free to eavesdrop on other nearby conversations.

LOW LIFE

Jeffrey Bernard

13 August

A certain amount of loneliness is beginning to creep into my life – very different from being alone, which I like – and it has prompted me to put an advertisement into the personal columns of this journal, stating quite simply, 'Alcoholic, diabetic amputee seeks sympathy fuck.' I'm not sure that our editor would wear this final 'cry for help' and I suppose that anyone who might answer it would be as daft as a brush.

YOUR PROBLEMS SOLVED

Dear Mary . . .

10 September

Q. 'Willy' seems to have become ubiquitous, acceptable from Radio 4 to the *Daily Telegraph* to the dinner table. What is the acceptable female equivalent?
– T.Q., Birmingham

A. This perplexing question was originally printed on the Letters page (27 August). 'Fanny' is on the boundaries of social acceptability. It achieved something of a breakthrough in the late Seventies when a Chelsea hostess threw a party for all the women she knew named Fanny and all the men she knew named Willy in the hope of forging some permanent relationships. In recent years, however, the expression 'front bottom' has gained most currency amongst the sophisticated. It was first used in a national broadcast by Dame Edna Everage in 1990 when talking to Douglas Fairbanks Jr about his relationship with Joan Crawford. On the subject of the pet names they used, Dame Edna asked Fairbanks, 'And did you have a special name for her . . . front bottom?'

LETTERS

24 September

Sir: I am a regular reader and subscriber and would like to say how much we enjoy *The Spectator* keeping us in touch with the unpleasant aspects of English life.
  A. M. King
  Harare, Zimbabwe

LOW LIFE

Jeffrey Bernard

24 September

Four or five years ago, I was sitting in the Groucho Club one afternoon whiling away the time with a vodka, when one of the few men I've ever seen paralytically drunk in that club lurched over to where I was sitting and punched me in the face. He was too drunk for it to be very effective and, anyway, I was very resilient in those days, so I just said to him, 'What was that for?' He said, 'You're Michael Foot, aren't you?'

I have always admired Michael Foot, duffel coat and all, and he is an excellent writer. So, in a way, I felt quite flattered but also quite irritated, considering that I am just over 20 years younger than he is. The mistaken identity cropped up again last week when another customer came over to my table with a large vodka saying, 'That's for you.' I said, 'That's very kind of you, but I don't even know who you are.' He said, 'Maybe, but I know who you are. You're Michael Foot, aren't you?' If Michael Foot happens to read this, I hope he isn't too upset. As for myself, I'm getting slightly fed up with mistaken identity, although thanks to it I have brought considerable happiness into a couple of lives. Quite a few years ago I was having a drink in the Queen's Elm in Fulham Road, standing near a bit of a lookalike when a woman suddenly screamed at him, 'You're that shit Jeff Bernard, aren't you?' and promptly threw a pint of beer at his face. He ducked and I got the lot which gave me something of a drenching. When the misunderstandings, all of them apart from whatever it could have been to make her think I was a shit, had been cleared up, the angry woman and my lookalike fell instantly in love and are, to this day, living happily in a fairyland castle that I can see in my mind's eye surrounded by sunshine and cherry blossom.

There was a time when I would tell bookmakers, bailiffs and the police that I was my twin brother but both of my brothers have two legs each so I can't get away with that any more. What I do puzzle about is what on earth I could have done to the beer-throwing woman in the Queen's Elm. It certainly must have been more complicated than going to bed with her and then not telephoning her the next day, otherwise I'm sure that I would have remembered her, but I must admit that my memory started failing me years ago and has done so frequently ever since. Perhaps I was born with premature Alzheimer's syndrome. There is usually some way of talking oneself out of such messes but I am still trying to think of an excuse to offer my wife of 22 years ago who, one

Sunday, came into our village pub wearing a black wig which someone had lent her for fun. She looked rather sensational and I'm afraid that I started talking to her – and I have never been in the habit of talking much to women without having had a formal introduction – when she pulled me up short by suddenly calling me one of the rudest words in the dictionary.

Lunch was difficult to swallow that day and another pint of beer in the face would have been more welcome or even some of the whisky I used to drink before I was mistaken for being Michael Foot. Probably the worst one, although happily they kept it to themselves at the time, was a man in the pub who thought I might be Herbert von Karajan. Now there was a shit of the first order. And I don't think that Taki would be pleased to have seen and heard a man looking at a picture I have on the wall of the two of us who said to me, 'I didn't realise you knew Bob Monkhouse.' I wonder where the next punch on the nose or large vodka is coming from. Perhaps I should try getting up in drag. That could spread the rumour that Dame Edith Sitwell was still alive.

YOUR PROBLEMS SOLVED

Dear Mary . . .

3 December

Q. What can one do when driving past Slough on the M4? I find the smell absolutely disgusting.
  – M.W., Marlborough

A. The only effective solution is to travel by train. Many rail routes to the West Country give Slough a wide berth, and in this way you need not expose yourself to the five to seven minutes of toxic gases which must be endured when travelling on the M4 by car.

1995

Theodore Dalrymple; Keith Waterhouse;
Craig Brown; Dear Mary; Dominic Lawson;
Charles Moore; Jeffrey Bernard; Alan Clark

IF SYMPTOMS PERSIST ...

Theodore Dalrymple

7 January

The entire nation has been plunged into deep, indeed inconsolable, mourning over the untimely demise of Frederick West. News of his death came as a shock, to me as to others, and naturally I began to ponder the big questions, as philosophers call them, such as whatever happened to Smith, to whom I was called out some time ago while I was on duty for the prison, who had eaten an entire fluorescent light tube in his cell, glass, metal, attachments and all?

It was lucky for Smith, I thought, that he was not in the ex-Soviet Union: there, in the good old days, he would have been charged with stealing socialist property.

I asked him why he had done it. He was trying to kill himself, he said, before the prison food, which he thought was poisoned, could do so.

I phoned the surgeon at the nearest hospital.

'I've heard the food in there isn't very good,' he said. There was much joking in the casualty department about light snacks.

It isn't only about prison suicide that the Government is concerned, of course. We doctors have been given the responsibility by the Department of Health of reducing the numbers of suicides in the nation as a whole by 15 per cent by the year 2000. The way to achieve our goal is through the coroners' courts, of course. Some time ago a wealthy and successful man I knew swallowed 200 tablets and a bottle of rum. The coroner asked me whether I thought he might have taken them by accident.

I was about to answer with a ringing and confident no, when the coroner made himself a little clearer: was there even a one in a million chance he had taken them by accident?

'Er, well, I suppose so,' I replied.

The coroner (and the man's family) relaxed, an open verdict was returned, the family was £750,000 the richer and an insurance company the poorer by an equivalent sum, at least until it put my premiums up.

DIARY

Keith Waterhouse

28 January

I thought for a while there that I should be kicking off my stint on this Diary with a riddle fit for the pages of the *Fortean Times*. Switching on the radio in my bedroom, I was rewarded with about ten seconds of music, and then the set went dead. I fiddled about with it aimlessly to no avail, and then noticed that the cleaning lady must have unplugged it to accommodate the vacuum cleaner. I reconnected the thing and it worked. But here was the mystery: how did an unplugged radio come to have ten seconds' worth of, at a guess, Mozart sloshing about inside it? And was it from the current programme (it was Beethoven by the time I had got it working again, so there was no clue there), or had this ten-second snatch been, so to speak, trapped inside the set when it was unplugged? I did not dare ask an electrician, since I knew he would laugh at me the way motor mechanics used to in my driving days – and as did all my friends, who said the phenomenon I had described was a technical impossibility and I must have imagined it. Since none of them is in the Faraday class I finally consulted an ex-wife who knows about fuse wire and how to change light bulbs and suchlike matters electrical. She reported briskly, 'What you clearly have there is a mains radio which can also work on batteries. Being the idle slob that you are, you have never changed the batteries, with the result that they have now run out of juice. What you heard was the last gasp of your radio running on its batteries before they expired altogether. If you do not change them at once, they will corrode and the set will be ruined.' The diagnosis was correct. How disappointing.

*

The late Gilbert Harding, one of the earliest television personalities, when crossing the Canadian border into the United States had to fill in a form containing a question on the lines of 'Is it your intention to overthrow the United States Government?' Harding replied, 'Sole purpose of visit' – and was refused entry. I thought they had long ago given up all that sort of nonsense, but apparently not. Travelling to San Francisco I was given the wrong immigration form – a thing called a visa waiver. Among a list of routine questions about the amount of currency I was carrying and whether I was importing cactus, there was this: 'Have you ever been or are you now involved with espionage or sabotage, or in terrorist activities, or genocide? Tick box. If yes, please contact the American Embassy since you may be refused admission to the United States.'

BOOKS

Craig Brown

4 February

Who's Who 1995
(A. & C. Black, £90, pp. 2131)

Was there ever such a happy book? It is so long, so detailed, with a greater range of characters than anything yet dreamed up by the South American magic realists, and yet every page sings of triumph and joy, of success and achievement and lives fulfilled.

Harvey Proctor, who will obviously be best remembered as the author of *Billericay In Old Picture Postcards* (1985), has been the director of Proctor's Shirts and Ties since 1992, John Ernest Douglas Delavalette Browne has been Managing Director of Falcon Finance Management Ltd since 1978, while Ernest Saunders MA has been President of Stambridge Management ever since 1992. Happily neither Sir David Frost nor President Nelson Mandela ever had to go through the trauma of a divorce, for they have only been married once, and it is reassuring to see that both Kurt Waldheim and President Mitterrand had such uneventful wars.

One or two of the characters do not play ball, but they are in a tiny minority. All we are told of the mysterious (Sir) Felix Roland Battan Summers, 2nd Bt, cr. 1952, for instance, is that 'he does not use the title and his name is not on the Official Roll of Baronets'. In contrast, the life of the 7th Earl of Lucan seems a lot fuller, furnished with a date of birth, a wife, children, parents, an education and a spell in the army, though alas no recreations and no address, just the delicately parenthesised italics beneath his entry – [*The Earl has been missing since Nov. 1974*].

Such glimmers of mystery and suspense, of secret lives lived between the lines, are what make *Who's Who* so compelling. In no other work are all the characters permitted to write their own stories, and retrospectively to plot their own destinies, jigging the facts and figures about from year to year, leaving this out, putting that in, rather like a painter returning again and again to improve his self-portrait. Back in 1986, Peter Bruinvels described himself as an MP. Come 1988, thrown out by the electors of Leicester East, he became: 'Management consultant; Director, Aalco Nottingham Ltd since 1983'. This year, he appears as: 'Principal, Peter Bruinvels Associates, media management and public affairs consultants, founded 1986; news broadcaster, political commentator and freelance journalist.'

It must be hard to know what to leave out. Dame Barbara Cartland bites the bullet, and puts it all in, from 'designed and organised many pageants in aid of charity, including Britain and her Industries at British Legion Ball, 1930' through 'carried the first aeroplane-towed-glider-mail in her glider, the Barbara Cartland, 1931' to a complete list of all her novels (22 last year alone), with separate sections devoted to Sociology (*Be Vivid, Be Vital, Men Are Wonderful*, etc.), Philosophy (*Touch the Stars*), Biography (*Polly, My Wonderful Mother*) and Autobiography, the most recent being *How to Write Like Barbara Cartland, Vols 1 and 2* (1994). Sir David Frost is similarly never backward in coming forward, least of all here, where his entry contains his own name repeated no less than 45 times – *David Frost Live by Satellite from London*, 1983, *David Frost Presents Ultra Quiz*, 1984, and so on. Looking through his long list of achievements, it is hard to know which of them one should feel most regret at missing. Personally, I swing between *Elvis – He Touched Their Lives* (1980), *Frost Over Canada* (1982) and *Abortion – Merciful or Murder?* (1975).

Less public figures find it harder to signal the living, breathing personalities waving beneath the avalanche of posts acquired. For them, the spot marked 'Recreations' must come as a mixed blessing – too dull (Reading, Walking, Music) and you sound like all the others, too off-beat and you sound either pious ('keeping friendships in constant repair') or arch ('thinking about writing the Great British Novel') or both ('Mother Earth'). Sir Ronald Millar lists 'All kinds of music, all kinds of people', which immediately makes one want to send The Beastie Boys round to his house for a sing-song. Meanwhile, Andrew Neil has increased his recreation over the years from the off-putting 'Dining out in London, New York and Aspen' to the proportionately more off-putting 'Dining out in London, New York, Aspen and the Côte d'Azur.'

Intimations of marital tension may be daintily plucked from the opposing recreations of married couples. Virginia Bottomley says 'family', which includes her husband, while Peter Bottomley says 'children', which excludes his wife. Why should Peter be a recreation for Virginia, but Virginia not be a recreation for Peter? Actually, I think the reasons are perfectly obvious, but it is interesting to see the evidence presented so forcefully. Similarly, though Lord Archer of Weston-Super-Mare numbers his recreations as 'theatre, watching Somerset play cricket (represented Somerset CCC in benefit match, 1981; Pres., Somerset Wyverne, 1983)', his wife Mary numbers hers as 'village choirmistress, cats, squash, picking up litter'. This raises a number of questions. Does the village choirmistress know that she is Mary Archer's recreation? Who creates the litter that Mary spends her leisure hours picking up? Or is it a metaphor?

Of the ho-ho recreations, the most overused must surely be sleeping, named by, among many others, Terry Jones, Jeremy Paxman, Roy Hudd, David Lipsey of *The Economist* and Lord St John of Fawsley (who combines it with 'appearing on television', which goes some way to explain his recent drawling, droopy-eyed performances at all hours of day and night in defence of the Royal Family). There are one or two recreations, however, which make one view their practitioners in a new light. I never knew that David Bowie was a keen skier, for instance, or that the mad-eyed astronomer Patrick Moore composes music on the xylophone. Indeed, anyone wishing to test the enthusiasm of Sir Ronald Millar might do worse than purchase him the 1979 waxing *The Ever Ready Band Plays Music by Patrick Moore*.

The prize for the most tortured recreation goes to the playwright Edward Bond. It used to be 'the study of physics, because in physics the problems of human motives do not have to be considered'. However, after I sneered in print at such galumphing, he has now extended it, adding '. . . for the benefit of newspaper reporters: this is a joke, as anyone who had attended a rehearsal with actors would know'. We can only hope that Mr Bond's long-awaited excursion into comedy is not too far off.

Bond can be counted among those avowedly anti-elitists who have boldly managed to hold their noses long enough to fill in the Entry Form, some for so long that by the end they must have been gasping for breath. Pat Arrowsmith, 'pacifist and socialist', awards herself 27 lines, Tony Benn 24, Dennis Skinner ('good working-class mining stock') 9, Professor Eric Hobsbawm 19 and 'Hero of Socialist Labour' Georgi Alexandrovich Zhukov, *Pravda* columnist since 1962, double-holder of the Order of Lenin, 31. But at least Pat Arrowsmith, alone among the 29,000 included, mentions her spells in prison – 'awarded Holloway Prison Green Band, 1964', no less. She is similarly uncagey when tackling her private life: '*m*, Mr Gardner, 11 Aug 1979, separated 11 Aug 1979; lesbian partnership with Wendy Butlin, 1962–76'. For me, such frankness knocks spots off the mealy-mouthed entry of Jeanette Winterson ('partner: Dr M. Reynolds').

The essential question to be asked of *Who's Who* is whether or not the editors have achieved their stated aim of recognising those whose 'prominence is inherited, or depending upon office, or the result of ability which singles them out from their fellows in occupations open to every educated man or woman'. I would say they have a success-rate of 80 or 90 per cent, which is pretty good going, though in some areas their choices appear far more random than in others. On foreign soil, and in particular among foreign politicians, they are nervy and hesitant, hitting the small fry, but missing the big fry. Many dictators and ex-dictators are excluded – no Castro, no Saddam, no Amin, no Bokassa, no Gaddhafi – whilst some of their underlings are in. Deng Xiaoping is out but Zhao Ziyang, the General Secretary of the Chinese Communist Party, is in. Perhaps Deng couldn't be bothered to fill in his form, whereas Zhao simply leapt at the opportunity. If so, wouldn't it be wiser for *Who's Who* to earmark foreign politicians for compulsory inclusion, however brief, just as they do our homegrown politicians?

Other exclusions suggest strangulated cries of 'Oh my god, *must* we?' at the final editorial meeting. No Cilla Black, no Paul Gascoigne, no Noel Edmonds, yet the minor lyricist Don Black is in, and so are the quizmaster Bamber Gascoigne and Mr John Edmond, the Professor of Marine Geochemistry at the Massachusetts Institute of Technology. Prominence linked with youth poses a particular problem. When sportsmen have been around long enough for inclusion, they have also been around long enough to retire. This produces peculiarities: this year, Torvill and Dean are finally in, just as they are on their way out.

If there is a bias, it is, perhaps unexpectedly, towards poets and professors. Any British poet who has sold over 1000 copies stands a good chance (Carol Ann Duffy makes it this year) and there are professors galore. Indeed, it is hard to find a page without a professor: pages 36–37 offer a choice of no less than six Professor John Andersons alone.

But these are quibbles. *Who's Who* is a book of unrivalled interest and amusement on all sorts of different levels. Page 1156, for instance, offers us brand new characters with the gorgeously Firbankian names of Harry George Lillicrap, Sir Edouard Lim Fat, Professor Lim Pin, Sir (John) Gordon (Seymour) Linacre, Rambahadur Limbu, Edward Horace Fiennes Clinton, the 18th Earl of Lincoln, and – perhaps the happiest name in the entire volume – The Rt. Rev. Edward Flewett Darling, Bishop of Limerick and Killaloe.

Reading such a page, or, indeed, any other, it is hard not to feel in some eerie way that these are the Beautiful, and the rest of us are the Damned, and that *Who's Who* is a slightly more jaunty Raft of the

Medusa, everyone on it frantically waving their CVs in the direction of the ship of immortality as it sails away over the horizon. When Dame Barbara eventually drops off, I suppose there will be room for a good ten more, or 20 if they each agree to be modest. But we must all await our turn, and I'm afraid to say that, for this particular raft, it is definitely not women and children first.

YOUR PROBLEMS SOLVED

Dear Mary . . .

11 February

Q. How should one respond to young women who march through a door I hold open for them and do not have the manners or breeding to acknowledge my courtesy?
 – B.G., Hale, Cheshire

A. Although it is a tremendous nuisance to carry a loaded water-pistol at all times, a short sharp spurt aimed at the necks of offenders as they swan by will send them spinning round in surprise. Water is a harmless substance and this method can be applied to other commonplace discourtesies. It is also invaluable for catching the eye of a recalcitrant waiter.

LETTERS

1 April

Sir: Any slight reservation one might have entertained regarding *The Spectator* being 'magazine of the year' (Leading article, 25 February) was instantly suppressed by the matchless Paul Johnson review in the same issue.

The elegance of the title, 'Get stuffed, Poussin', and the urbanity of the article itself, with its references to the painter being a Frog (a crucial point, often overlooked), dispel all doubt.

Here indeed is a journal worthy of today's Britain.

Michael Bertram

Eltham, Victoria, Australia

YOUR PROBLEMS SOLVED

Dear Mary . . .

6 May

Q. I should like to get my revenge on an odious little hack who has been attacking me in print and on television for many years. I would also like to take up the cudgels on behalf of some of the less able-bodied victims of his distorting lens. As we are certain to be attending at least one of the same literary parties this summer, I feel some sort of public gesture would be appropriate. What is your view on wine-throwing?

– C.H., London W11

A. There is no doubt that wine-throwing, though *passé*, would certainly excite media interest and might open up the debate *vis à vis* whether or not this person *is* an odious little hack. Yet you run the risk of being dissatisfied with the conclusions drawn and even of incurring further personal attacks by new persecutors. Meanwhile, the hack in question will hardly have been punished by merely having to pay a dry-cleaning bill. Far better to exact a more certain revenge. Your tiny tormentor, I gather, is known to be extremely vain. He is also a famous wearer of white suits. Why not, therefore, simply pop a small jar of Marmite into your bag when setting out for one of these parties? In the crush it should be no trouble for you to deposit the merest trace of Marmite onto an appropriate area of the seat of his white trousers. It only remains for you then to take up a position by the door of the party so that, when your victim is leaving, you can ensure satisfaction by being able to alert him to his condition with the words, 'Oh dear, you seem to have had some sort of accident. Bad luck.'

DIARY

Keith Waterhouse

13 May

There can be no one so smug as the writer who has just finished a book – particularly if he has friends who are only in the middle of theirs, or, better (meaning worse), just about to start. Such is the happy position I find myself in. The relief is physical rather than mental – like stepping down off the treadmill or coming in out of the garden after a hard day's digging. And suddenly, in a gush, there is a great avalanche of time – time to have lunch with friends, time to pick pencils up off the floor, time to answer letters, time to water the dead pot plants, time, now that it's spring, to buy a new winter overcoat, time to read and browse in bookshops, time to watch afternoon television, time to empty the wastepaper baskets, time to look at the damp patch in the lavatory and judge whether it's getting worse (it is), time to pay the final notices, time to change the dead light bulb on the landing which expired on New Year's Eve, time to restock the stapling machine, time to write that long-promised article for the *British Journalism Review* (it's coming, it's coming – as soon as I have cleaned my tennis shoes!), time to straighten out the kink in the bedside rug, time to get the month-in, month-out jacket and trousers dry-cleaned at last, time to tidy the slag-heap of a desk, time for a haircut, time, now, to have a bath on rising instead of bashing away at the typewriter in a muck sweat until five in the afternoon. And time to jangle one's change and look at the flowers. This euphoria, in my experience, lasts about four days, whereupon – having sworn to take the summer off – I find myself itching to get back to my desk, with the first sentence of the next damned thick book demanding to be set down on paper. No wonder there are too many books. All writers are recidivists.

YOUR PROBLEMS SOLVED

Dear Mary . . .

8 July

Q. I have only just caught up with your Christmas Celebrity Problems and felt I must offer you my solution to the Duchess of Devonshire's letter regarding calls of nature arriving when one is trapped on the motorway. Haven't you ever wondered why people keep a single green wellington boot in their car? I always have one in mine, and when I empty it out of the window people who see me just think, 'Oh, he must have been flighting ducks, what a sporty type!'
 – A.G., Bruton, Somerset

A. Thank you for your tip, which might well be useful for a man but would hardly be appropriate for a woman being driven by a chauffeur. In fact, after the publication of the Duchess's query, one of her friends has written to her making the admirable suggestion that she purchase a camper-van for future long-distance journeys.

DIARY

Dominic Lawson

28 October

It does seem to be the habit of great men to write their last published words in *The Spectator*. My stepfather, Freddie Ayer, did so while I was on the staff ('Reflections on the French Revolution', 9 July 1989). Now Sir Kingsley Amis seems to have followed in the tradition, albeit in the form of a letter to the editor which we published last month. In case you have forgotten, Sir Kingsley took it upon himself to criticise Auberon Waugh's occasional use of 'don't' when 'haven't' was grammatically correct. Waugh's usage, said Amis, was 'easier for monoglot immigrants, though'. Brutal stuff, and it is characteristic of Bron's forgiving nature – which he tries so hard to hide in his columns – to have eulogised his late critic so unstintingly over the past few days.

MEMORIES OF A GREAT NOVELIST

Charles Moore

28 October

When the Fairfax organisation bought *The Spectator* in 1985, it was decided that we should advertise the paper on television. I rang up Kingsley and asked him if he would shoot the ad. He agreed readily and cheerfully, and was surprisingly patient when he had to go and sit in a studio in west London and recite for an entire day until he found the right emphasis, 'Now that's what I call good writing.'

Unfortunately, there was a misunderstanding about payment. I had asked Kingsley to do the thing out of the kindness of his heart, but that was a quality which, though he did in fact possess, he liked to use sparingly. He wanted money. In the end we compromised by sending crates of malt whisky and by my giving him lunch at the Connaught.

We set off from Doughty Street after Kingsley had already consumed a quarter of a bottle of whisky. At the hotel he drank about the same again before we ordered the food. I had a stomach infection picked up in India and was not allowed to drink, so I gave him the wine list. 'Have anything you like,' I said, hoping he would remember that *The Spectator* was a very poor publication. His eyes lit up: 'Do you mean anything I like?' 'Well,' I said, laughing with an affected insouciance, 'I suppose I'd be a bit cross if you chose something that cost £260.' He surveyed the list. 'What about £160?' he said. I could only nod.

The wine waiter arrived with a bottle of Haut-Brion '61 and Kingsley drank it to its thick dregs. Then he had Calvados.

I bumped into Kingsley a few weeks later. 'I say,' he told me, 'that was a bloody good lunch. You know, when you have really good wine like that you are supposed to let the sommelier have a glass; but when I tasted it I suddenly thought, "No, why bother?"'

LOW LIFE

Jeffrey Bernard

28 October

I have had to weigh in again, this time at University College Hospital. I tipped the scales at a horrific 48 kilos which means that I could make a comeback as a fly-weight, especially since both Benny Lynch and Jackie Patterson are out for the count. Just for once the medical staff didn't hang about for too long or keep me waiting on a stretcher in a corridor, but quite quickly gave me some morphine. Yesterday, in the light of day, I turned around and, to my alarm, saw that the patient in the next bed to me was none other than Joe-Joe, the Maltese odd-job man who hangs around Soho. I once employed him myself to put up some bookshelves and now the poor chap has had a tracheotomy and can't speak at all. Do all the roads in Soho lead to hospital?

But if I still feel slightly sick, it is not because of my pancreas but because of a news item in last week's papers about a two-year-old girl who fell into a river but floated and was rescued by a German tourist. Her parents said she had been playing by the river bank and that she had fallen in because she was trying to reach the quack-quacks. There is something I found slightly awful and disgusting about teaching a child to call a duck a quack-quack, and moo-cows may be slightly worse. But it is not surprising nowadays. What is amazing, though, is that the child should have been rescued by a German tourist. An American or Japanese tourist would have simply taken a few snapshots of the incident and allowed the child to drift on out to the North Sea.

DIARY
Alan Clark

4 November

How lovely to be invited to write for *The Spectator* again. Now that the loathsome sneering features, pastily glistening, of its former editor[*] peer slit-eyedly out at the reader from the op ed page in the *Sunday Telegraph*, I may occasionally be granted this, the most eclectic of all privileges in journalism. 'The circulation will go down, of course,' I congratulated the new editor[†] in tones more of hope than prediction, 'and you are the person to bring this about.' Down, down and deliberately down, so that soon we are left with just the tiniest elite: those who pine for the quintessential elixir of high intellect and discernment. And then, at the very last moment – Whoosh! Dropping everything, there will arrive *ex machina* Ms Tina Brown, because to edit *The Spectator* must be the grandest and most desirable position on Fleet Street (the expression, of course, being adjectival now rather than geographic). Better even than owning it which, as is quite widely known, I once tried to do myself. But Algy Cluff, a friend, very splendidly wouldn't sell to me. For no better reason (as far as I could judge) than deference to the widely disseminated precept that What-Al-wants-Al-must-be-prevented-from-getting.

Still smarting from my rejection in the second round of the Kensington and Chelsea parliamentary selection. The auguries seemed favourable. After I had got through the first round, the local paper, the *K & C Mail*, wrote: 'His special qualities could endear him to members of the local

[*] Dominic Lawson
[†] Frank Johnson

Tory Association, and many are already talking about him as the ideal choice to represent the Royal Borough in Parliament. Stylish, charming, patriotic, raffish [I, *even* I, could not have written all this] ... experienced, fearlessly outspoken ... ' The Committee were delightful: intelligent and politically sophisticated. They laughed with me, sometimes stamped their feet with approval during my speech and answers. Maybe that was the trouble. Afterwards a friend in the Government said, 'They think you're a playboy. You've got to convince them you're serious.' But I'm deadly serious. Why else would I be swimming against the tide?

Gravitas. I am trying, but not, plainly, hard enough, I won't go into a television studio containing David Mellor. I won't write in any series or category where the name 'Roy Hattersley' did, or is likely to, appear. The moment I hear the word *light-hearted* – 'We're looking for a light-hearted piece on ... ', 'It's going to be quite a light-hearted programme ... ', 'If you could take a light-hearted look at ... ' – I head for the hills. I won't write about restaurants, or wine. I won't do Late Shows. 'Just a lot of men sitting around in shirt-sleeves,' said Jane, 'but you know underneath they're all wearing woolly vests.' I won't (the sums of money on offer are enormous) do 'extended' travel programmes, wandering about in a muck sweat in a pale suit with vicious tummy trouble and enduring the 'shall we just do that once more, Alan, only this time when you've finished trying to make yourself understood to her, half turn, and kind of wink at the camera'. It all raises one's recognition factor, of course, which is important for those in the public eye. But at what point do the graph lines of familiarity and exposure-fatigue intersect? I hate show business, but am addicted to its senior branch – politics. And one thing I have learned: you can pontificate, in print or on camera, all night long, but unless you have submitted yourself for endorsement or rejection to the electorate, you count for very little.

Unlike, it seems, practically everybody else, I never knew Kingsley Amis – nor his wealthy, denture-wearing son. This could well be related to the fact that, although many people have suggested that they propose me for the Garrick, when I say 'yes' they go coolish and nothing more happens. And I try and avoid the Groucho Club, whose very low ceilings, noise and accents put me in mind of the sergeants' mess at 3507 Fighter Control Unit at Budloe Manor just after the war. But *Lucky Jim* is the only book (besides, of course, *The Ordeal of Gilbert Pinfold*) which still makes me laugh on re-reading it for the umpteenth time. Nothing else he did was any good. *The Old Devils* got a prize, but it was really meant for *Lucky Jim*; just as Hemingway's Nobel, although nominally for *The Old Man and the Sea*, was in reality in recognition of *For Whom the Bell Tolls*.

LETTERS

11 November

Sir: How comely it is and how reviving to discover Alan Clark again in your columns. His limpid prose and unveiled insults soothe and threaten by turns.

David Steel
Hillesden, Buckingham

1996

John Wells; Simon Hoggart; Craig Brown;
Dear Mary; Keith Waterhouse; Matthew Parris;
Simon Courtauld; Barry Humphries

BOOKS

John Wells

20 April

Below the Parapet: The Biography of Denis Thatcher
by Carol Thatcher
(HarperCollins, £16.99, pp. 303)

The best anecdote in Carol Thatcher's appreciation of her father is about Denis boarding a train at Paddington in which the only empty compartment was reserved for Rosewood Psychiatric Hospital. Denis travelled alone and in comfort as far as Reading when 'all these chaps piled in', accompanied by a male nurse, who counted them before the train moved off. 'One, two, three, four ... who are you?' 'I'm the Prime Minister's husband.' 'Six, seven, eight, nine ...'

Whether or not the story is true it hits the nail on the head. Denis only appears to have had one serious nervous breakdown, but the strain of living with Queen Kong is evident in every line of the book, and *Below the Parapet* is the story of Den and Carol, two brave but badly damaged survivors. Carol's mum, referred to throughout as 'Margaret', never looks up at the nursery window on her way to work, has violent tantrums, addresses her daughter by the names of all her secretaries before she remembers she's called Carol, feeds them on the rare occasions she is there with frozen lasagne, and ignores them so fiercely that even the television turned up to a deafening level fails to rouse her.

Carol's tape recorder is not always reliable. When she asked me about the kind of language Richard Ingrams and I used as a basis for the 'Dear Bill' letters I quoted a remark I had overheard after a memorial service for one of 'the Few' in Alderney at which one old boozer had said he would probably be next and his friend said, 'Oh no, old boy, I'd be very sorry to see you trickle down the sink!'

This comes out as 'I'd be very sorry to see you crippled under.' Bill Deedes has admitted in print that he knocked the book into shape in exchange for a couple of cases of Beefeater, and his pencil is noticeable in phrases like 'a shade under six feet tall', but there are still passages where neither author nor subject seems to be entirely all there.

Historians may be grateful to Denis for reporting that Margaret's cry of 'What a terrible waste' about a battlefield in the Falklands was provoked by the sight out of the car window of an unused ammunition box. Baroness Thatcher may not. The same is true of Carol's description of 'charging after' Margaret at a photocall in a supermarket, cramming rolls of lavatory paper and 'really useful things' into the Prime Minister's cosmetically draped basket. As with some of the crueller glimpses of the boy Mark – Denis sitting with his head in his hands saying he never thought he'd see his family name on the front page of a Sunday paper in connection with a fraud – there are moments when a naive garrulousness does even more damage than understandable malice and the desire for revenge.

Denis's story begins in Wanganui, New Zealand, where the Thatcher fortune was founded on a substance Carol herself is too delicate to mention, called 'arsenite', which proved invaluable for dipping sheep and cleansing railway lines. It was invented by a Mr W. T. Owen and patented as Owen's Sheep Dip. The fact that his partner, Denis's grandfather Thomas, brought it to England as the mainstay of his own company, Atlas Preservatives, makes one wonder if the enterprising spirit jumped a couple of generations before alighting on the boy Mark.

There is, then, a good deal of Pooter life, with Tom Thatcher actually living in a house called 'The Laurels', keen involvement in freemasonry, a wife who ran a boarding house in Earl's Court and drank tea in a toque, and a son – Denis's father – who married a rackety girl from Camberwell who liked a flutter and whose father sold horses. Tom died insane.

From Mill Hill Denis went straight into the family business, flogging Atlas Ruskilla Triplecote. In the war he rose to the rank of major, exposed to danger only once when making gin in the bath in Marseilles, his best friend the song writer Jimmy Kennedy, who wrote *April in*

Portugal and *The Teddy Bear's Picnic*. He thought Montgomery was a first-class ****. On leave he had a long erotic entanglement at the Grosvenor House Hotel with a blonde called Margot Kempson, and was briefly married to her. Carol found her irresistible, and notes that her father became strangely wistful at the mention of her name.

Denis then caught the eye of the future Leader, who as a young politician, in Carol's words, 'needed a husband and children'. He described their honeymoon as 'quite pleasant'. There is nothing new or very surprising about his life as consort, and apart from a habit of saying 'sure as hell' he talks very much as we imagined him talking in the Letters. The Falklands were 'miles and miles of bugger all', the accommodation provided at a Commonwealth Heads of Government Meeting in Goa – CHOGM, the real Denis said, stood for Coons Holidaying On Government Money – was 'very high on the buggeration factor'. He hated the unions, worshipped South Africa, consoled himself in his solitude with Old Mill Hillians, once tried to stuff a banana up the trunk of a sacred elephant in India, and shared a table with Billy Graham at the Reagans' farewell dinner. He has never read his wife's memoirs, but then it is possible that she hasn't either.

Denis Thatcher is a rum bird. He was, Carol says, 'no mean catch' as a husband. He had a family firm, a flat off the King's Road in Chelsea, a car he referred to as his 'tart trap', and a winning simplicity of spirit. Whether, had he not been snapped up by the ambitious and impoverished Margaret Hilda Roberts, he would have merited our cruel satires or HarperCollins' generous outlay remains a topic for debate.

DIARY

Simon Hoggart

27 April

Many of the tributes paid to the Queen recently have described how quickly she puts commoners at their ease, or, alternatively, how someone who makes a *faux pas* can be frozen with a basilisk stare. I have never met her myself, but I have talked to Princess Di twice, and can confirm that meeting royalty does have a terrifying effect on the synapses. The first time, she had just flown out to Australia on her first big tour with Prince Charles. I found myself having one of those sympathetic, 'oh-I-know' type of conversations with her on the subject of how difficult it is to fly long distances with small children. (Prince William was not yet one year old.) What gave this banal conversation its surrealist tinge was the fact that she had flown in a private plane with a staff of (I think) 35, and – even weirder – I had completely forgotten that I did not then have any children. Later I met her at the British embassy in Washington where someone asked what she would be wearing at the White House dinner that night, and she replied, 'A little black number – it's the last new thing on the whole tour.' I piped up, 'So it's a sweater and jeans from now on then?' and was favoured for this tiny pleasantry with that wonderful, vast, heart-melting, knee-buckling smile which has enslaved so many men. They say that at this stage the great danger is over-confidence. She complained amiably about formal meals, and the embarrassment of finding something to say to distinguished people who were tongue-tied anyway. I said casually, 'Well, with any luck they'll put you next to Clint Eastwood, and you won't have to say a word all night,' which I thought was funny, but which she didn't get, and caused her to give me a blank, numbing stare.

YOUR PROBLEMS SOLVED

Dear Mary . . .

22 June

Q. Among our friends who regularly join us here in the summer are a delightful couple whom we always love to see. However, this year the man has taken to socialising around (and swimming in) the pool 'in the raw'. Although our daughters and their friends are broad-minded, they find this rather disconcerting, but we cannot agree on the best way to persuade our friend to wear a swimsuit! Can you suggest how we may achieve this – without impugning his virility?

   – A.J.W., France

A. The best method is to pour a sugary and colourless liquid such as 7-Up onto the patch of your friend's reclining chair which will be graced by his general buttock area. An army of ants will soon march towards the invisible strip with inevitable results, and will send him screaming into the house for suitable protective clothing.

DIARY

Keith Waterhouse

3 August

Does anyone know what I can do with the first act of an abandoned play, working title *Hitting the Fan*? It was to have been a dramatisation of the Alan Clark *Diaries* – a sort of political *Jeffrey Bernard is Unwell*. Or maybe a Westminster *Rosencrantz and Guildenstern*, since I had elected to regard the PM and her Secretaries of State as noises off, leaving the stage to Clark and his strutting Young Turk pals and their scheming civil servants. It was going rather well, no particular thanks to me – some of Clark's lines need only the lightest of dramaturgical touches to become an actor's dream: 'Nowhere in this fucking castle, with its 17 outhouses, garages, sheds and 18 vehicles, can I find pliers. I am surrounded by unreliables. My new, red, vintage tool-locker was empty. I ransacked the China Room, where I keep all my most precious things . . . ' My own main contribution was a Walking Footnote who reminds the audience, with the occasional aside, how all these people slotted into the parliamentary passing show. For instance, when Clark wonders who told Mrs T about his reference to

Nigeria as Bongo-Bongo Land, the Walking Footnote confides behind his hand, 'It was Douglas Hurd.' Ned Sherrin, who was to direct, had some interesting casting ideas, and it looked as if we were shaping up for a lively and unusual theatrical experience. Alas, as rehearsal dates loomed, our protagonist began to have second thoughts. For one thing, he wanted control. A politician in charge of a play is as ludicrous a prospect as a dramatist in charge of defence procurement. And then the Clarks were doorstepped for a week by the *Sunday Times*, culminating in a half-page piece raking up some of the choicer Clark nuggets and illustrated by a mock-up theatre poster: 'Alan Clark Is Unsure'. Whereupon, I gather, the long-suffering Mrs Clark asked, 'Do we really want to go through all this again?' And that was that. Shame. It would not have been 'all this again', it would have been great fun for everyone, and good for the ego. Where Ned and I perhaps made our mistake was in not inviting Alan Clark to help audition beautiful young actresses for the part of the shop assistant on the train with the 'delightful globes'.

ANOTHER VOICE

Matthew Parris

24 August

Fewer twentieth-century quips have become more famous than Groucho Marx's remark that he would not wish to join the kind of club which would accept people like him. May I add that I should not wish to be protected by any secret service which would offer employment as a spy to people like me? They did, you see.

The episode is brought to mind by reports that MI5 are finally bring-ing their recruitment programme out into the open. This year a glossy brochure is available to new university graduates: *Graduate Opportunities in the Security Services*. The document is decorated with a discreet coat of arms portraying a flying lion whose bottom half is a snake with a fish's tail, ringed by portcullises. '*Regnum Defende*', says the motto. This openness has to be good news, for it is vital that our intelligence services cast their net wide enough to recruit the best. And not a moment too soon. Previously they were frankly scraping the barrel. I know.

Have you ever read those spy novels in which mysterious men in rain-coats arrange rendezvous at Cambridge with undergraduates, to discuss the possibility of serving their country in an unusual way? Well, it really was like that.

I hope I do the present Bishop of Birmingham no injustice when I seem to recall (memory could be playing tricks, it sometimes does) that in 1972, as my tutor at Clare College, Cambridge, it fell to him to enquire whether I might be interested in rendering such service. I had just told him that a career in the diplomatic service interested me. Spying, it was suggested, might be a variation on that theme. To be fair to my tutor, I was not encouraged or advised to apply: the possibility was simply pointed out to me.

I expressed interest. Next came a telephone call from a man who gave me an address to visit in Cambridge, for a chat. This led to a journey to London where, at an elegant address to divulge which would break the Official Secrets Act, I rang a doorbell and was met by a young lady with a posh voice who held out my exact train fare, coins and all, on a silver tray. I met some more men. They warned me that spying was not a matter of steamy sex romps with beautiful blonde women: news which cheered me more than my interviewers could know. I remarked that, despite this, I was still interested.

The *Sunday Telegraph* said last week:

The names of undergraduates who might 'fit in' – who were predicted for firsts and who could slip unobtrusively into any social situation – were passed to the agencies by a select band of Oxbridge dons, discreetly talent-spotting among the young intellectuals of the day.

I have to report that I was not predicted for a first, I was hardly an intel-lectual and, whatever poor talents I may possess, slipping unobtrusively

into any social situation was never one of them. I could not slip unobtrusively into so much as a T-shirt, let alone a social situation.

The civil service examinations followed: you had to go through these
in the normal way, and I was anyway applying for a position in the regular
diplomatic service. My plan was to see whether either side or both offered
me a job, and only to choose if and when necessary. I was successful in
these examinations. The next test was the Civil Service Selection Board.
I did clear this hurdle, but received the distinct impression that, had I
failed, that was not necessarily the end of the road so far as Intelligence
was concerned. This may have been a misapprehension, but if I am right
then it was easier in 1972, not harder, to get into Intelligence than into
the above-board Foreign Office.

I had offered two character referees: my tutor and a friend, Elizabeth
Bingley. Elizabeth's name came up when I was asked to report to another
secret address in central London for a final interview. This took place at
an oak table before an array of distinguished and mostly elderly gentlemen chaired by a retired military officer with such an unusual name that
it could not possibly have been an alias. With much embarrassed clearing
of the throat I was assured by this gentleman that everyone present was a
man of the world. Some, he averred, had undoubtedly drunk too much
on occasions, while others knew about drugs. They realised I too might
have come into contact with drink or drugs. That was to be expected
these days. But (more clearing of throat) was I addicted to hard drugs, or
an alcoholic? I said no, neither.

With more clearing of throats I was asked, most apologetically, whether
Miss Bingley was ' . . . er – a *friend*'. Quick as a flash my laser-sharp brain
discerned their devilish purpose in asking me this. 'A good friend,' I
replied, with a manly, confiding glance. They looked encouraged. 'A
very good friend,' I said, warming to my tactic. They looked pleased.

'*A very good friend indeed*,' I breathed significantly. Relieved faces
beamed at me from around the table. Elizabeth was, indeed, a very good
friend, but never more. There were no further questions on this subject.
Shortly afterwards, I was offered the job.

I actually turned it down. On reflection it struck me that I was far too unreliable a chap to be a spy. I am not discreet, not self-effacing, not patient, not heterosexual and, besides, I am completely mad. I should have thought that was perfectly obvious. Mrs Thatcher certainly realised it, straight away.

I chose the regular diplomatic service.

And the more I thought about it, the more outraged I became that anyone should be trying to place responsibility for the security secrets of the nation into the hands of a fruitcake like me. A chilling thought, is it not? If inadequates such as I were turning down employment in Intelligence in 1972, who was accepting such jobs? These people will be in charge, by now. Can any of us sleep safely in our beds?

It has been remarked that the one person who must, beyond shadow of doubt, be an atheist is the Pope. This is because as Pope he will know that if there is a God, He will have contacted him; and as he knows He has not contacted him, he must know He does not exist. Likewise, life's confidence tricksters, all of us, live haunted by the knowledge that *nobody is in charge*. We know this because we know we are of limited talents and not particularly clever; yet we know that – just because we sound confident – people keep offering us jobs to which we are quite unsuited. We conclude that this must be how others got to the top. All over Britain, key positions are being occupied by total nincompoops.

The secret service has been trying to recruit – can you believe it! – the sort of bounder who would then write *Spectator* articles about his interviews. It is most unsettling.

WHEN SPIRO MET EDNA

Simon Courtauld

28 September

The editorial lunch at *The Spectator* has seen some interesting guests over the years. The best lunches have usually been those at which a clash of personalities has occurred, or embarrassment has been caused to one of those present.

Graham Greene was there one day, sitting next to a fairly humourless Tory politician. It was just before the publication of Andrew Boyle's book *The Climate of Treason*, revealing Anthony Blunt as the 'Fourth Man', and names of other likely candidates – Maurice Dobb, Fred Warner – were being tossed around the table. The politician did not think this a very dignified topic of conversation, but he was a lot less amused when Graham Greene said that while he was uncertain about the identity of the Fourth Man, he had just had a postcard from the Third Man, Kim Philby, in Moscow – which he then proceeded to remove from his breast pocket and hand round the table.

On another occasion I recall the then political correspondent, Peter Paterson, who had good socialist credentials, goading Jessica Mitford by talking about 'blackamoors'. (Paterson also caused some consternation by once bringing Alger Hiss to lunch.) When Lord Longford was telling the lunch table how well he had got on with the Kray twins when he visited them in jail, Jeffrey Bernard made a memorable interruption. 'Don't be bloody naive,' he said dismissively. 'They're f***ing social climbers.'

One day an attaché from the Soviet Embassy was a guest. He was talking of having spent some time in Mongolia, while Jennifer Paterson, *The Spectator*'s magnificent cook, now cookery writer and soon-to-be television star, was clearing the plates.

'Did you see much of my brother?' Jennifer asked him, in her endearingly loud and jolly way. One could see the attaché's brow furrow; he was irritated and uncomfortable, his expression seeming to say, 'Why this cook speak with me?' Brother of cook? Was this some coded message? The attaché could scarcely be blamed for not knowing that Jennifer's brother, at the relevant time, had been British Ambassador in Ulan Bator.

Unfortunately, Jennifer was not present at the most entertaining *Spectator* lunch of those times, which was attended by the former US vice-president Spiro Agnew, who died last week. It must have been almost 20 years ago: Agnew had been forced to resign in 1973 because of tax evasion charges, and he was in London to promote his book (a 'novel' about a vice-president). The editor, Alexander Chancellor, put together a lunch party consisting of Agnew, Barry Humphries, Kingsley Amis, Peter Ackroyd, then *The Spectator*'s literary editor, and myself. It was certainly a heterogeneous gathering.

No one can remember whether Kingsley Amis was on good, combative form, which probably means that he wasn't. Perhaps he was in one of his brooding moods, nodding his head at Agnew's more reactionary remarks, and enjoying his whisky. (As I recall, in Alexander's day only wine was offered before and during lunch, to which three exceptions were permitted: Kingsley Amis [whisky], Jeffrey Bernard [vodka] and Sam White [pink gin]. One day the gin bottle was not on the tray when Sam arrived, and he was heard to growl, 'No gin – no lunch.')

Barry Humphries, soberly dressed in a dark, pin-striped suit, conversed seriously with Agnew on such subjects as the future of Nato and Australia's involvement in the Vietnam war. Presumably the ex-vice-president had been briefed on the other guests – he would at least have known that Humphries was a comedian – but he cannot have been prepared for what happened next.

Alexander knew that a change of clothes for Barry Humphries had been delivered to the office, because he was due to go on somewhere straight after lunch, where he was to appear as Dame Edna Everage. Under pressure from Alexander, he agreed to leave the dining-room during lunch and, having changed, return as the housewife superstar.

Peter Ackroyd took him into his office, where, having just published one of his first books, on the history of transvestism, he was fascinated to observe the metamorphosis taking place. When Dame Edna appeared in the dining-room, we were on to the cheese, but from that moment Agnew lost his appetite. We could see that he was inwardly troubled: who is this woman? What's happened to the Australian guy sitting here just now? Yet this woman seems somehow to *be* the Australian guy. Yet how *could* she be? 'We should be having a glass of ouzo together, Spiro,' Dame Edna cooed at the Greek immigrant greengrocer's son, putting a bare arm round his shoulder. The former vice-president was nonplussed and not enjoying himself. 'I would like to describe our meeting today as the Agnew and the Ecstasy,' she went on, as the rest of us just went on laughing.

A message then came from reception that an *Evening Standard* photographer was outside, hoping to get a picture of Agnew and Dame Edna together. The great tax-evader knew it was time to take evasive action. He mumbled his thanks and made off down the stairs at an impressive pace (our dining-room is on the third floor). Dame Edna followed, waving her handbag and calling lustily for Spiro to wait for her; but he managed to get out of the building and into his car, unmolested by Edna and unphotographed by the *Evening Standard*. It was a pity about the picture, but we agreed it had been a very good lunch.

YOUR PROBLEMS SOLVED

Dear Mary . . .

26 October

Q. Every time I come to London I find other pedestrians bump into me in the street rather a lot. How can I go about preventing this annoyance from happening?
  – C.B., address withheld

A. Simply buy ten copies of the *Big Issue* as soon as you arrive in the metropolis. Carry these as you walk along. You will find that other pedestrians give you a wide berth.

DIARY

Barry Humphries

23 November

Approaching old age brings itself to my attention in small, irritating ways. Fortunately, aural whiskers have not yet sprouted, though I remember that my father started growing them at about my age. Instead, there are nasal daddy-long-legs to be attacked with increasing ferocity in the shaving mirror, and dried gravy to be occasionally scrubbed from the cuffs. This is caused by greedy reachings across the table. I have always wanted what I want when I wanted it. The other day I caught myself going out to lunch with a small bloodstain on the collar of an otherwise pristine shirt. Not very long ago I would have quickly changed, but this time I didn't, so I must have crossed an invisible line in my path to senility. An increasing tolerance of stains is another indication of that dwindling self-respect which finds its ultimate expression in death. However, my indifference to dribblings and damp patches is happily not total, so that I'm not yet like the old man in one of Ken Dodd's anecdotes who before departing the house in light-coloured Daks requires the attentions of his wife with a hairdryer.

I am certainly having a few small but vexatious memory problems. Perhaps I've always got people's names a bit mixed up, but they've been too polite to mention it. The first serious intimation of this occurred a couple of years ago in the Crush Bar at Covent Garden, during a performance of Strauss's *Die Frau ohne Schatten*. I bowled up to Sir Jeremy Isaacs, and asked him if he was planning to turn Hofmannsthal's melodrama into a movie. To my surprise he looked a bit blank, until I made a few casting suggestions and even furnished him with some hints as to how the story might be brought up to date. Only when he went away, chuckling politely, did my wife say, 'Who did you think that was?' 'Michael Winner, of course,' I replied, 'and he doesn't take too kindly to suggestions, either.' When she pointed out my gaffe, I made it worse it by rushing after the departing director of the Royal Opera House and apologising profusely that I was a bit jet-lagged (thank God for that elitist disorder) and had mistaken him for someone else. 'Who?' asked Jeremy, with a forgiving twinkle. My reply produced an astonishing change in his demeanour. Never before have I seen such profound affront and dismay published on the countenance of another human being. Of course, I shouldn't have said anything. My wife assures me that most of my blunders and solecisms are construed by people as jokes. This is one of the advantages of being a comedian. Even unbelievably bad behaviour is tolerated because most people assume they're just a bit slow on the uptake in the presence of such a legendary and often cryptic wag.

DIARY

Barry Humphries

14/21 December

I am a very good landscape painter with a style midway between that of Hitler and Churchill, only better. There is some evidence to suggest that Lavery put the finishing touches to Winston's better works, and Hitler's few successes are probably forgeries. I suppose my style is a kind of modified Fauvism. I am the Marquet of Melbourne. A couple of years ago, some Hampstead friends of whom I was, and am, deeply fond, admired one of my effortless efforts. It was a north Italian landscape in oils, and, flattered, I presented it to them. The gift was greeted rapturously, and I was pleased that a picture which would otherwise be stashed in a cupboard was now exhibited in the home of persons of taste and fashion. Months later, they held a party and I naturally scoured the walls for my masterpiece, so generously bestowed. Not a sign. Easing my way past the revelling guests – the Holroyds, Spurlings, Murdochs, Brendels, Warners and Drabbles – I peered up the stairwell. There were many more pictures hanging there, but not mine. With the air of a man seeking the lavatory, though not as a matter of urgency, I explored other less populated floors. A peep in the master bedroom, a casual glance into the nursery, a more feverish scrutiny of the maid's and children's quarters. Again I drew a blank. Finally, after a 15-minute search of the house from basement to attic, I discovered my little landscape in an ill-lit box-room, face against the wall and trailing a tendril of cobweb. I said no word to my hosts of this poignant discovery. Instead, a few weeks later, I brightly informed them that I had been offered, in Australia, a retrospective exhibition of my work – a rare honour for an amateur. Alas, it would mean, I explained, that I might have to borrow 'Umbrian Hillsides' for a month or two. The painting would perfectly represent the technical bravura of my middle period. 'Oh, we'll so miss it,' lamented my quondam hostess over the phone. All this happened two years ago, and I've never returned the picture. My intention was, and still is, to make a faithful copy of it and restore it to its place of honour in their box-room, but I just haven't got round to it. Now, this morning, I have a Christmas card from my friends, begging for the return of their treasure. What shall I do? What can I say? That my retrospective is now on tour – in Tokyo perhaps, or Peru? Who'd believe that? Or are all these questions better addressed to Mary Killen on your back pages? Are you reading this, Mary? Can you help me?

1997

Dear Mary; Barry Humphries

YOUR PROBLEMS SOLVED

Dear Mary . . .

15 February

Q. When I was married to my wife our social life seemed to just happen and we went each week to almost too many dinner parties. When we separated I was told that my new status of single, heterosexual, not impoverished man of 45 would ensure a constant flood of invitations. These do not seem to have materialised and I am wondering what I am doing wrong. How can I best pep up my social life, Mary? I am not sure how to go about organising things to do in the evenings as my wife always did it in the past.

  – Name withheld, London W8

A. Just as children take the roof above their heads for granted, many married men are under the impression that social life 'just happens'. In fact their wives must work tirelessly, making silent, unsung efforts or 'run-up' overtures at every opportunity. In this way they ensure that the basic frameworks and safety-nets are in place for a satisfactory social life and that the groundwork has been done and a display of friendliness taken place before invitations can be issued or received. You are now too old for retraining but you can still achieve a passive result. Stimulate the memories of your erstwhile dining companions by standing in your smartest suit at bus stops in places like Bond Street, Kensington High Street or Notting Hill Gate for up to an hour at a time. You should trawl in at least three people per hour per bus stop who have not seen you for some time and did not like to ring you in case you thought you were being exploited as a spare man. In no time at all the invitations will be being verbally issued and you can give out your phone number to facilitate these new encounters.

YOUR PROBLEMS SOLVED

Dear Mary . . .

1 March

Q. What should one do when one opens the door to find masked men on the doorstep who then push their way into the house Intent on robbery?
– D.P., Moreton-in-Marsh

A. Greet them by saying, 'Hello! You're first to arrive. The others will be here any minute. Such fun, fancy dress parties, aren't they?'

LETTERS

29 March

Sir: I am surprised that James Michie (Books, 22 March), as an old friend of Kingsley Amis, is perplexed by the title of Amis's new book, *The King's English*. 'The King' was a persona that Kingsley Amis invented for himself – a gangland leader who brutally enforced his own literary taste.

Amis imagined it thus: a hired thug goes to the door of a sensitive, aesthetic novelist called, say, Julius de Stoemp, and rings the bell. The novelist answers the door and the thug says, 'Julius de Stoemp?'

'Yes.'

'The author of *Trumpet & Shawms*?'

'Yes.'
'Don't do it. The King don't like it.'
Charles Moore
London E14

YOUR PROBLEMS SOLVED

Dear Mary . . .

29 March

Q. I am shortly to return from a most enjoyable six-week spell as writer-in-residence at Helsinki University. I am already worrying that I may bore or even alienate my friends in London by talking too much about Helsinki and Finland in general on my return. What would be the correct number of times I can mention these places on a daily basis?
— A.B., Helsinki

A. The average person engaged in normal everyday social interaction speaks some 30,000 words per day. If you limit your use of the words 'Helsinki' and 'Finland' to about a dozen times per day, you should run no danger whatsoever of alienating your English friends. Mentions of 'frozen sea' should be limited to five times a day; 'reindeer meat' only once a day.

LETTERS

17 May

Sir: David Fingleton's excellent review of the British breakfast overlooks two important components. There was no mention of kippers, nor any comment on either the variety or quality of the marmalades.

Montgomery of Alamein
London SW1

LETTERS

31 May

Sir: That Peregrine Worsthorne, once the ganymede of Stowe School, Bucks, should write an uncompromising attack on Sir Jeremy Isaacs for instigating a statue to Oscar Wilde is quite predictable. Nor is it a surprise to find it in *The Spectator*, that often diverting bible of reactionary provocation. In the ordinary way, despite having been accused in print by Peregrine of 'having expertly seduced him ... on the art-school couch' in our distant boyhood, I'd have smiled tolerantly at this tirade which, apart from being better written, could well have been signed, 'Disgusted, Tunbridge Wells', but so dishonest are his arguments, so false are his comparisons, that somebody surely must at least rap him across the knuckles and, as a great friend of the sculptor Maggi Hambling, commissioned to create the offending statue, it might as well be me.

The first bit of bad faith is the deliberate use, right at the beginning of the first paragraph, of the word 'paedophilia'. In Ancient Greece a paedophile was a lover of young men, and that Wilde certainly was, but in recent years it has come to describe almost exclusively a molester of small children, and that he could never have been. Nor, may I add, do an overwhelming majority of homosexuals have any sympathy for paedophiles in the contemporary sense. Still Worsthorne, an expert striker of cracked Pavlovian gongs, knows how to get his public's mouth watering. He describes Wilde as 'encouraging that vice'.

Then, suddenly, the implied small children have grown
up into 'working-class lads' whom Wilde sodomised. Less to
quarrel with here, although I don't know whether Wilde was
active or passive, but here again the language is carefully loaded.
These honest 'working-class lads' were in fact male prostitutes.
Admittedly, as in all prostitution, exploitation is involved, but it is
mutual exploitation. Wilde, like many gays, had a taste for 'rough
trade' or, as he put it, 'feasting with panthers', but he was hardly
unique in that. The statue is not going up because he handed out
engraved gold cigarette cases to 'stable boys' or stained the linen
at the Savoy, but because he was not only a great writer but also
a humane and lovable human being to whom a hypocritical and
savage injustice was done.

I don't suppose that even Sir Peregrine, with his proposal
to erect a statue of a homophobe, would advocate that it
should represent Wilde's destroyer, the repellent Marquess of
Queensberry.

It would be a tedious exercise to pursue and unmask all the
half-truths and distortions in this over-excitable piece, but most
of it is rubbish. Sir Jeremy, for instance, is shown as deciding to
suppress 'the plainly intolerable story of Wilde's sex life'. If this is
true, he's surely left it a bit late in the day. There have been two
films already (and another is on the stocks) which have made it
all pretty clear, while several full-scale biographies have left the
reader in no doubt at all.

Elsewhere Worsthorne admittedly condemns 'louts who
beat up poofters', but not those who offer verbal violence.
On the contrary, he makes out homophobes to be suppressed
but courageous martyrs, claims most of them to be 'devout
Christians' (at least he doesn't claim all) and prepared to be
shouted at in fashionable restaurants.

Well, elegantly as he writes, I am not won over. Nor am I
convinced that he is completely certain himself. He has always
been a self-intoxicating journalist, something he recently

admitted in a rather touching piece on earlier failings and misjudgements. Personally, too, he's both very courteous and rather lovable. Come back on the art-school couch, Perry – all is forgiven.

George Melly
London W10

LETTERS

21 June

Sir: I note with interest that both George Melly and Peregrine Worsthorne are now writing letters to your paper and it appears that they were both at Stowe together. I was also at school with them. Melly was in my House and Worsthorne was in the one next door. The latter's claim to fame, in my memory, was that instead of wearing a raincoat or an overcoat like all the other boys Worsthorne chose to wear a cloak! How we used to kick him! And he also had four Christian names!

Gordon Johnson
Vaucluse, NSW, Australia

DIARY

Barry Humphries

20/27 December

One of our Christmas rituals was always 'boiling the sixpences'. This was to sterilise them for incorporation in the pudding, which, in turn, was boiled. To this day, my sister still recycles the same old, now obsolete sixpences, some bearing the profile of King George VI, and spat out or choked on by at least two generations of the Humphries family. She is strongly of the view – which I share – that dollar coins and modern money clash with Dickensian ritual. No doubt there are devotees of Christmas reform and EU purists who might ridicule this old custom as anachronistic and even Eurosceptic. They may prefer to interlard their festive dessert with recently excised credit cards.

In New York recently I noticed beside the till in the city's best bookshop a fast diminishing pile of volumes recommended for 'holiday' reading. The title of this popular hardback was *Tips for Straight Women from a Gay Man*. A quick perusal of this daintily produced manual, nestling among coffee-table books on Bulgarian quilts, art deco cuff links and the unknown gardens of Nova Scotia, revealed a few arresting chapter headings, 'Dick Breath' being one of the more mysterious. It seems that straight America is turning more and more for guidance to the pillow-biting community. 'Wait for us!' cry the poor heteros to their trail-blazing, mattress-munching brethren. Merry Christmas.

1998

Dear Mary; Taki; Leanda de Lisle; Joan Collins;
Barry Humphries; Byron Rogers

EDITORIAL

Much surprise has been expressed at the adultery of the Foreign Secretary, Mr Robin Cook. Part of this is astonishment that anyone would wish to commit adultery with him. Mr Cook is undoubtedly blessed, but not aesthetically. He would seem an unlikely socialist sex symbol.

One answer is that his girlfriends are not sex symbols either. But Mrs Gaynor Regan, despite her churlish expression in front of the cameras, has something of the Pre-Raphaelite beauty about her. We can almost picture her lying down in a flower-strewn barge, floating down some quiet country stream.

Mr Cook's sexual detractors, as opposed to his moral ones, lack imagination. A handsome man has a certain glamour, but it is no more than the superficial splendour of a prancing animal. Only delayed adolescents or a desperate old maid or two would be foolish enough to believe that this is what true romance is all about.

If men fall in love through their eyes, more intelligent women have always succumbed through their ears. One of the most successful lovers in modern history was the eighteenth-century MP John Wilkes. Wilkes was hideous to look at, with a squint and a crooked jaw. But he managed to steal a girlfriend from Casanova. 'Give me half an hour to talk away my face,' he boasted, 'and I can seduce any woman ahead of the handsomest man in Europe.' It cannot take Mr Cook much longer, surely, to talk away his beard.

YOUR PROBLEMS SOLVED

Dear Mary ...

31 January

Q. How can I keep in touch with old friends of whom I am very fond without the nuisance of seeing and speaking to them?
 – M.A., London SW1

A. Simply hire an open-topped car or motorbike and, driving past their homes without slowing the vehicle down, shout 'Morning, Susan!' or 'Morning, John and Harriet!' It will soon sink into the householders that you have paid a friendly passing visit, but by the time they have rushed out you will already be several streets away.

HIGH LIFE

Taki

28 February

Last Sunday evening I took a much-needed break from the unending round of dinner parties – this is Gstaad in February, and the place resembles the American Embassy in Saigon *circa* 1975 – in order to see *Titanic*. I had read most of the reviews and was duly impressed by the terrific spectacle. It certainly brought back memories of transatlantic travel in the good old days, when the only NOCDs (not our class, dear) one encountered were the stewards, the officers and, occasionally, the captain.

Caricaturists are known for their ability to ridicule a person with a few strokes of their pen. This is what the writer and director have obviously set out to do. If any of you, dear readers, have not seen the film, do not let me deter you, just note the fact that the film has everything to do with PC and nothing with common sense.

Let's start with the villain of the love story, the beautiful Rose's extremely rich fiancé, played by Billy Zane. He is portrayed as an arrogant Nebuchadnezzar type, but better Nebu than nobody any day. In fact, the fiancé is a softy. He is practising affirmative action in taking a penniless young girl and her mother to share his fortune. Like Rick in *Casablanca*, under that cynical shell the fiancé at heart is a romantic and a liberal.

When he offers thousands to Murdoch, the officer in charge, to secure a seat for himself in a lifeboat, he shows what capitalism is all about: survival of the fittest. Just as Murdoch shows what fools old-type socialists are. He refuses the loot – in fact, he throws it back at him. Murdoch has absolutely no initiative, no drive. He could take the money and go for it, but, no, he dreams of paid company holidays and union get-togethers.

Predictably, the film hints early on that there's something wrong with the lifeboats. Not enough for everyone, it suggests rather pathetically. Yet there were enough boats for all the first-class passengers. Among the greatest outrages of this subversive and commie pinko film is the depiction of those poor stewards locking the steerage passengers below. Those stewards were performing their honourable duty. By making sure the steerage passengers went down with the ship, they not only improved the gene pool of the New World – badly needed even back then – they also saved those poor wretches from the miserable life that awaited them in the ghettos of the Big Bagel. (The Big Pizza in 1912.)

Bruce Ismay, the chairman of White Star Line, is my favourite hero. Ismay, however, is criminally libelled in the picture. Here is a man who could have easily done a Bob Maxwell and slid into an icy but painless death, yet he chose to live in order to sort out the paperwork and assist with the enquiries which were bound to crop up after the sinking. He chose a life of vilification and outrageous insult, all in the name of duty. The dastardly fink of a director portrays this unsung hero as a coward.

Finally, the plebeian hero of the movie, Joe Dawson, played by Leonardo Da Vinci DiCaprio. Early in the picture, he is invited to dine with the swells in first class. This is a horrid scene, full of cruelty. Just imagine how out of place young Joe must have felt. It must have embarrassed him awfully. I know for a fact that no swell worth his club membership would ever embarrass a pleb with such an invitation. This is a perverse film, dedicated to class warfare, a work worthy of Dr Goebbels. But worse was to come when it was all over. Ship owners, industrialists, arms dealers, bankers – even the conservative burghers of Gstaad – stood up and applauded. Jewel-covered peroxided women were openly sobbing. What the hell for? The rich guy made it. What was it that Lenin said about us selling them the rope they will hang us with? *Titanic* is a great film, and it could be an instructive one, too, as long as one sees it with the right perspective.

COUNTRY LIFE

Leanda de Lisle

14 March

I can't bear Robin Williams. It's not the cloying sentimentality or his hairiness. It's the two combined.

DIARY

Joan Collins

21 March

Some mornings I scoot off to my local supermarket for provisions *sans maquillage* and dressed down in a raincoat and a sensible dark headscarf – so like the ones worn by our own dear Queen. I appear suitably anonymous and consider that I blend in with the madding crowd of shoppers reasonably well. Last week, whilst I was browsing through the biscuit section in M&S, a woman similarly attired approached me. 'Salaam aleikum,' she said with conviction. I looked at her blankly. 'Salaam aleikum,' she repeated. 'I'm sorry, but I don't speak Arabic,' I said. She seemed surprised and stepped up for a closer inspection. 'You are Arab?' 'No. 'Fraid not.' I backed off into the custard creams, but the woman, obviously bonkers, came nearer. 'You look Muslim,' she said. She moved her face still closer to mine accusingly, and continued, 'You have Arab blood.' 'Alas, not a drop,' I said, now making a hasty getaway. I hailed a cab in the King's Road, gave the driver my address and whipped out my compact to inspect my face. To my surprise an Arabic countenance stared back at me. My headscarf had fallen forward, and was now resting on the bridge of my nose, giving me a distinctively Muslim look. Then the cabbie chirped up, 'Everything OK, then, Joan?' 'How on earth did you recognise me?' I asked. 'You can't fool me, luv. Saw you on *Parkinson* last week, I'd know that voice anywhere.'

DIARY

Barry Humphries

27 June

I have never had an operation in my life, though I've written constantly about illness and hospitals. As co-founder of the Prostate Olympics and Friends of the Prostate, I have long dreaded the moment when life, with a vengeance, begins to imitate art, but so far all clear. In the Sixties, a comic strip invention of mine called Barry McKenzie used to worry about his mother's veins back in Australia. Whenever his conscience stabbed him – and this was rarely – he would reflect: 'If this news gets back home, Mum's veins will be a write-off.' Well, I'm soon to go into hospital to have some purple spaghetti deracinated from my right calf, and I'm not looking forward to it, especially since I'll only be in hospital for 24 hours and unable to receive the condolences of many visitors. I come from a hospital-visiting community, and the morbidly caring people of

Melbourne rarely let a Sunday pass without visiting at least two infirmaries. If there is no one in hospital they know, it is not uncommon for them to visit total strangers, and the corridors of these institutions, which stand on almost every second street corner, are on Sundays thronged with the curious, the compassionate and the medically prurient dispensing crystallised fruit and acrid-smelling chrysanthemums to the bewildered patients. One small, enterprising private hospital actually sells special family packages to members of the public and their loved ones wishing to embark on a weekend sympathy binge. This entitles them to a tour of Casualty, Maternity, Pathology and a quick, supervised glimpse of Intensive Care.

LETTERS

27 June

Sir: I would like to join with Alan Clark's recent remarks defending the English soccer fans in France. We are a nation of yobs. Without that characteristic how did we colonise the world? And our fame as fighters is second to none. Now that we don't have a war, what's wrong with a good 'punch-up'?

The Dowager Marchioness of Reading
Chipping Norton, Oxon

LETTERS

4 July

Sir: Paul Johnson is quite right when he says (And another thing, 27 June) that 'lefties' are remarkably 'litigious'. I remember being sued for libel by the editor of the *New Statesman* many years ago. I can't remember his name, but he was an excitable chap with red hair.

Richard Ingrams
The Oldie, London W1

BOOKS

Byron Rogers

8 August

Memoirs and Confessions
by Ronnie Knight
(Blake, £16.99, pp. 227)

Ronnie Knight is a London gangster, or, as he would have it, a 'rascal'. Rascality in his case includes being charged with suspicion of murdering a man whom, he admits, he wanted murdered (he was found not guilty), and of handling stolen money (for which he is at present doing seven years). He was married to the actress Barbara Windsor for 20 years, and loved his mother, also his brothers (one of whom was murdered, and two others served long terms of imprisonment). His memoirs will thus for most readers be a step into an unknown world.

I have only met gangsters once. This was in a pub in south London and I was warned on no account to offer to buy any of them a drink; to do this, I was told, would be to betray a lack of respect. The result was that all night I was bought double whiskies by small, immaculate gentlemen dripping with gold and after-shave. Heaven, I thought, might be something like that.

The only thing was, a fortnight later one of them sent home to fetch an axe, with which he chopped up the bar and then, remarkably, the telephone box outside. I don't know why, except that it was something to do with respect. Someone had probably tried to buy him a Britvic.

Mr Knight, now 63, is hot on respect, the earning of it and the extension of it to others, like his cell-mate Big John, about whose crimes we are told nothing.

He's not only young but well respected. We'll all be lying about watching telly, and he'll ask, 'Shall I make a cup of tea?' and all us old geezers are saying, 'Yes, go on then, son', and next minute he's handing mugs round. We don't treat him as a gofer, he's just that sort of bloke – polite, quiet and respectful, which is why he gets respect himself.

These memoirs, ghosted for Mr Knight by someone who did a similar service for Reggie Kray, another rascal, read as though they could have been written by one of the Sioux, whose name for themselves was the Human Beings. No one else qualified for this title, so to these remarkable people the rest of humankind was somehow unreal and there to be preyed upon, because no respect was due.

The scene may have shifted from the Black Hills, but the assumptions are the same. To an East End gangster anyone outside the gang, or not in competition with it, is there to be robbed, smacked, to have his trousers drenched with lighter fluid and a match held near, also to have his wife and children threatened.

But when it comes to one of their own kind you could be reading Homer or any poem of the Heroic Age. In Shoreditch, not Cattraeth, ravens are glutted with blood and men go to sleep with the daylight in their eyes. This is Eric, a hero:

Eric was a hard man's hard man. To his friends, and I count myself to be one of that fraternity, he is a lovely guy and a gentleman. If, on the other hand, you're against him, God help you. In a now legendary battle with the Richardson gang, he carried on fighting even after suffering half a dozen broken bones. He was only stopped when his punching hand was pinned to his skull by an axe.

If you think that's the story of a man who lost a fight, you don't know how many men it took to get him to his knees. He lived through that horrifying incident and went on to fight again. Many of those battles he described to me in great detail, over a drink on the balcony of my home in Spain, the Villa Limonar, while I was in exile there.

We have heard the chimes at midnight, Master Shallow. Aye, that we have, Sir John. That we have. But the flip side of such nostalgia is that at no point is any sympathy shown for anyone who might have been at the receiving end of the gentlemanly Eric's attentions. No sympathy is shown at any point in the book.

Mr Knight is a thief from childhood, stealing from just about everyone who employed him. A café owner ('a lovely bloke') has his till rifled ('it was just the way of things'). A fruit and veg stallholder, for whom he worked, is robbed of his takings, but all this is just 'a liberty'. There is no gratitude in his world.

This, for example, is his detailed account, surprisingly detailed because he denied taking part, of a £7-million robbery from Security Express in Shoreditch. A guard, threatened with a shot-gun, is so terrified he asks to be allowed to write a last note to his wife and child. Of this Mr Knight notes:

Topping him was never on the cards. But while he couldn't be allowed to know that, at the same time he had to be calmed down in case he couldn't carry out his part in the scheme.

The robbers, his own brother Johnny amongst them (who got 22 years for it), do this, yet this is Mr Knight's one comment.

And there is one other. Living in Spain, he rings his ex-wife Barbara Windsor:

[I] asked her to do whatever she could to help them out [...] Diamond that she was, she agreed. No time to bear grudges.

In spite of this he is still prepared to portray her as a bald, nympho-maniacal dwarf:

Mind you, when she was down there using her mouth for her favourite game, and all I could see was a pile of blonde curls, I didn't give a monkey's what was on the top of her head.

He last saw her real hair in the 1980s, he writes ('it wasn't in the best of condition') and burying his nose in her various wigs was 'like making up to a piece of carpet'. She seems to have been loyal to him, bringing him meals when he was on remand, arranging bail, but this is not returned, for there is no respect:

> I often thought that if she hadn't always been so ready to discuss her bum and boobs at the drop of a hat, she might have gained a lot more respect over the years.

Yet he claims to have satisfied her sexually more completely than any man since their marriage broke up.

There are policemen, but they are corrupt and given to breaking down a man's door. There are journalists, but they are corrupt and tell lies. There are children, the children of his first marriage, but they disappear into thin air, only to reappear when they are grown up, at which point he writes that he is overjoyed to see them.

For in the midst of all this there is Ronnie Knight, 'a little friend to all the world', lovable, misunderstood, forever being fitted up for crimes he did not commit. Also a moral man, and an innocent one, who has to have it pointed out to him that some of his fellow inmates are homosexuals and rapists.

> Fuck me, I'm surrounded by pervs and nonces. I know I said I'll talk to anybody, but I meant whether they're a dustman or a duchess – it doesn't matter to me. But all that other business makes me feel sick. They want shooting. What they need is branding on the forehead with a red-hot poker, then decent rascals would know to blank them.

He has never had a bank account and never paid any income tax. Like Mrs Thatcher, he appears not to believe in society.

DIARY

Joan Collins

12 September

When I heard of the recent death of Akira Kurosawa, I was reminded of one of Billy Wilder's stories about him. In 1985 Billy, Kurosawa and a terminally ill John Huston had been asked to present the Academy Award for best picture, as a trio. Huston was to read out the nominees, Kurosawa to open the envelope and pass the card with the winner's name to Billy, who was to announce it and present the Oscar. All this had to be done at lightning speed to enable Huston to get off the stage and back to his oxygen mask. On the big night all went according to plan, until it was Kurosawa's turn to open the envelope. Having managed to open it, he couldn't seem to find anything inside, and was peering and fumbling for what seemed like an eternity. Billy, whose wit is still the greatest on the planet, said he had to use every ounce of self-restraint not to say in front of an audience of some 800 million, 'Pearl Harbor you could find.'

YOUR PROBLEMS SOLVED

Dear Mary . . .

12 September

Q. I am currently dating an attractive young lady and wish to ascertain her age before becoming more seriously involved. How do I do so without causing offence?
  – Name withheld, Sydney, Australia

A. Why not do what a woman would do in the same position and take your first opportunity to rootle through her personal belongings until you find the evidence you require?

BOOKS

Byron Rogers

19/26 December

Can Reindeer Fly?
by Roger Highfield
(Metro, £12.99, pp. 294)

Some years ago there was a television series on Welsh history which my mother watched, having become convinced that in the course of his excitable delivery the presenter's false teeth would at some point pop out. They never did, but at the end my mother, to her bewilderment, found she knew a fair bit about Welsh history. I have had a similar experience with Dr Highfield's digressions on Christmas, in the course of which, and in spite of myself, I learned a fair amount about physics, biology and all those other trap doors into which half my class at school disappeared silently a long time ago.

Take Santa Claus. For him to deliver all those presents in one night to the 2,016 million children under 18 in the world would mean a fairly disastrous collision on his part with the laws of science. The speed involved would subject him to forces 17,500 times greater than gravity, and the reindeer, encountering air resistance, would be vaporised within four thousandths of a second, creating deafening sonic booms. The absence of such booms enabled Richard Dawkins, a sentimental soul, to disprove the existence of Santa to a six-year-old.

Then there's Santa's weight, estimated by Dr Highfield to be around 30 stone, so the g force he will encounter is this times the necessary acceleration, which would be two billion times that experienced by any fighter pilot. And Santa has 4,212 million pounds of toys to deliver.

The message is clear: if you want to save on Christmas, talk to a scientist, especially in Britain where the spending on presents amounts to four per cent of an individual's annual income (and where eight per cent of the national economy is devoted to the production of such presents). With the help of a scientist Ebenezer Scrooge could have held off all the Spirits, kicked away Tiny Tim's crutch and died old.

Zoology comes in a rush with the reindeer. Rudolph's red nose, a chap at the University of Oslo wrote in *Parasitology Today*, was probably due to a parasitic infection of the respiratory system, reindeer being prone to such infections, especially when an effort like that involved in pulling Santa is added. This paper, the scientist recorded bemusedly, brought him more fame than anything else in his academic career.

For some reason Dr Highfield does not mention the one fact I know from direct experience, that it is impossible to get reindeer to work as a team, all the sleighs in Lapland being pulled by single animals. Dogs, yes, but then Santa would have encountered the bizarre slipstream of 12 small animals farting as one. Odd that no traveller should have mentioned that, but it is the one thing I remember about the Arctic, especially when compounded by the fact that the dogs get fed on rotting fish.

Rudolph would also have had to be castrated, Dr Highfield goes relentlessly on, to keep his antlers for Christmas. But then so might Santa Claus to preserve his own longevity, eunuchs living on average 13 years longer than intact males (according to a paper published in the 1969 *Journal of Gerontology*).

The business of his coming down the chimney may, according to an academic at Sheffield University, derive from the early yurts of northern Europe in which the chimney and the front door were the same. And Santa, he goes on, may be derived from the tribal shaman, usually high as a kite on magic mushrooms, which induced in him the conviction that he could fly. Snow is important as the shaman urinated in this, which was then eaten by tribesmen and surprise, surprise, the reindeer, all of whom got high as kites, hence the origin of the phrase 'to get pissed'.

This has to be the strangest book I have ever read, even stranger than Havelock Ellis, who introduced me to the anatomist Realdus Columbus who claimed to have discovered the clitoris in 1593, also to an Italian woman whose pubic hair reached her knees and was used to make wigs. Dr Highfield introduced me to a Miss X, 'a 34-year-old Episcopalian virgin, newspaper editor and lesbian', who considered the Christ child to be her rival for God's affection.

If like Cliff in the American TV comedy *Cheers* you have a weakness for bizarre facts, then this is the book you have waited for all your life. If you were a bore before, then, after reading this, you will be a bore on a superhuman scale. It is of course impossible to review satisfactorily. I loved it.

YOUR PROBLEMS SOLVED

Dear Mary . . .

19/26 December

From Sir Les Patterson.

Q. Recent unsavoury events in Washington have alerted the suspicions of diplomatic wives – including mine, God love her – to areas hitherto unexplored. The Lady Gwen used to confine her routine search for lipstick and powder traces to my collar and shirt-front, and I am proud to say I always passed muster. However, since Bill Clinton let the ferret out of the bag and spilled the beans, Gwen's inspections have travelled ominously south. Like any busy diplomat I am often forced to give some eager young intern a bit of rigorous after-hours dictation and I usually explain the odd incriminating stain on a hand-stitched Ermenogildo Zegna by blaming a research assistant for being reckless with her correction fluid, or citing an out-of-control advocaat-tasting at the Dutch Embassy. This morning the head of the War Office woke me up brandishing Y-fronts bearing unmistakable smudges of 'Luscious Lips' and demanding a sober explanation. Quick, Mary! How can a man explain a tell-tale touch of Max Factor in his diplomatic pouch?

A. The correct response is to express blameless bewilderment. Meanwhile you should swiftly and secretly remove a lipstick of similar shade from Lady Gwen's own cosmetic centre. Break the lipstick up and wedge pieces of it into the holes at the top of the drum of your clothes-washing machine. When the next load is emptied – you might even commission an emergency wash to speed up the reconciliation process – there will be luscious lips on every garment withdrawn and Lady Gwen will be forced to quite literally swallow her words.

1999

Dear Mary; Byron Rogers; Simon Barnes;
Charles Moore; Joan Collins;
Frank Johnson; Barry Humphries

YOUR PROBLEMS SOLVED

Dear Mary . . .

30 January

Q. Each night I drive from my office in London's Docklands to my home in Kensington. The other night I gave a lift to a colleague who horrified me by bringing out an apple and eating it, only inches away from my face. Am I correct in thinking that this was a breach of etiquette?
— I.B., London SE11

A. Indeed. Apples should never be eaten in such close proximity to another adult. Their flesh is too cold, the gnashing movements the teeth must make are too bestial; then there is the vapour apples exude. Your colleague might as well have gone to the loo inches away from your face. Preclude a recurrence by keeping a fruit-knife and paper napkin in your glove compartment and insisting he uses it, should he attempt the atrocity again.

BOOKS

Byron Rogers

6 February

Careless Love
by Peter Guralnick
(Little, Brown, £19.99, pp. 767)

The second volume of this authorised biography of Elvis Presley is a masterpiece of black comedy, although Peter Guralnick probably didn't intend this. The author of *Sweet Soul Music* and *Nighthawk Blues* wanted to portray the greatest pop icon of them all, to use words like 'riffs' and 'jams', and to convince us that the man and his music were worthy of serious academic study. All this, gloriously, got swept aside by eccentricity at its flood tide.

Few things are as depressing as the biography of a pop star, for what have you got? A small talent and the amplifiers, and the amplification does not end with the sound system. Once past that small talent you encounter the cynicism, and the suits, and the massed ranks of agents, publicists, accountants and lawyers engaged in the manufacture and the marketing of what until then had been a very ordinary human being. But two things make *Careless Love* unique.

The first is that this talent did not need amplifiers, it did not even need a musical accompaniment: the subject of this biography, virtually alone among pop stars, could sing. He could sing anything and you would have listened. The second is that in these pages you meet a supporting cast which includes a man with a pet anaconda he used to take swimming in the condominium pool, but even he and the snake get pushed to one side, for here they come, a tall, beautiful young man and a pop-eyed old con artist.

Elvis Presley and his manager, Colonel Tom Parker, were two of the strangest human beings ever to walk the earth. For all practical purposes they were astronauts, each occupying his own dream world, Elvis in reaction to fame and money and pills, the Colonel because he had had so much to make up, chiefly himself. Their own time, as for Don Quixote and Sancho Panza, was a mere backdrop to their curious adventures.

The Colonel wasn't a colonel at all, he wasn't even Tom Parker; he was a Dutch seaman called Andreas van Kuijk who had jumped ship and was therefore an illegal immigrant, which would explain why Elvis never went on an international tour. Had he come along, the Colonel wouldn't have got back into the country again. He had been so many things, a seaman, a municipal dog-catcher, a showman travelling with a dancing chicken act (the Colonel heating up a metal plate on which he then placed the chickens), and, having flown over all these, had finally settled into showbiz management, when he met Elvis.

He had little or no interest in music. All that was left to 'the boy'. The Colonel was interested in only three things: roulette, sunbathing and putting one over on as many people as he could, including the boy, getting him to appear in those embarrassing films and creaming off over 50 per cent of the take, which he then gambled away. A shameless cheapskate, he sold souvenirs outside concerts and, even though Presley was appearing on Frank Sinatra's show, charged one of Sinatra's friends a dollar for his autograph. He cultivated shabbiness, wearing a baseball cap, a loose-fitting short-sleeve shirt and seersucker pants, which, he said, saved time ('the big shots are afraid to be seen with me').

And then there was Elvis, who was fiercely against drugs, but carried the prescribable variety like Codeine around with him in half-gallon containers so that he had daily visions in which he took off in spaceships and believed that his thoughts could turn off the sprinklers in the Bel Air country club. He then got religion (from his barber), but saw the face of Stalin in the clouds over Arizona. He was fascinated by embalming and by childbirth, dropping in on funeral parlours and on delivery wards, where he cheered on the straining mothers-to-be. He was allowed to do this because he was Elvis, who, when he wanted a particular hamburger, summoned his private airliner and took off into the night. When the whim took him he bought Cadillacs for passers-by in the street he had never seen before.

He was a great patriot and cultivated police officers, though the laws of his country he never did understand. He set up house with a 14-year-old schoolgirl, whose father, a serving army officer, raised no objections, being assured that his daughter's honour was safe. So it was, although the underage girl who later became Mrs Presley noisily pestered the pop icon in bed to get on with it. But Elvis believed in virginity, sleeping with hundreds of women and in the morning congratulating those who had withstood his attentions.

He spent most of his time, when not on tour, behind closed curtains in his room, watching television and reading. Apart from the girls, his only companions were bodyguards recruited from old childhood friends, whom he equipped with guns, dark glasses and briefcases (one kept a single hairbrush in his). But the pills got him in the end. The doctors kept supplying them and he kept shovelling them in. He died taking a crap, and the doctors panicked. When the police got there they found nothing but teddy bears in his room.

But I remember where I was, and what I was doing, the night of his death, something I do not remember about anyone else, with the exception of immediate members of my family. Sad really. Only one letter from Elvis survives, that to a startled President Nixon, offering to help him solve the drugs problem. That Mr Guralnick has managed to assemble over 750 pages of biography from oral material is a tribute to his industry.

SPECTATOR SPORT

Simon Barnes

1 May

My father's best-ever shot at snooker was the time he smote off the head of the rest and, in a moment of surprised laughter, raised his cue from the table and caught the lightshade that hung above the table, causing it to fall from its moorings and pancake down on to the green baize.

I have never quite been able to emulate this stroke of genius, but watching the combination of dexterity and neurosis that make the world snooker championship such extraordinary television, I find myself thinking of the great pleasures of actually playing the game.

Snooker is one of those games that everybody seems to have played, and done so extremely badly. And everybody takes a mild but comparatively deep pleasure in it. This is real snooker: its rhythms are quite different from those of the pro game.

Last weekend, there was a considerable amount of tooth-sucking about a frame that lasted 43 minutes. Every frame of snooker I have ever played lasts at least that long: it takes an awful lot of tries to get the balls in the pockets, you see.

In the pro game, the reds are generally clustered at one end of the table, and the colours are on their spots. In a real game, the balls are all over the table, scattered to hell and gone: rebounding from the jaws of pockets, pinging off the cushions, colliding with each other in appallingly unpredictable ways, a table layout determined by the principles of Chaos Theory.

A regular feature of these games is the pocket-divider: a ball that strikes the cushion – generally quite hard – exactly halfway between the two pockets, so that it is impossible for your opponents to guess which pocket you were aiming for.

A break is any occasion in which the potting of a red is followed by a colour. A three-ball break is worth a round of applause, four balls is a lap of honour. The score generally moves up in increments of four, the penalty for a foul shot. A regular snooker partner of my past suggested that our games should be televised under the title *Pot White*, in honour of the number of times the cue ball was inadvertently propelled into the pockets.

And yet time and again I have pulled off shots that no pro would attempt: length of the table doubles, impossibly fine deflections, balls that run along the cushion for half a table's length. The reason pros don't play such shots is that even for a pro this is not percentage play. Control is the key to the pro game, chaos the key to the real one. If a pro makes an error, his opponent will punish him. In a real game, one gross error is generally answered by an error still more gross.

But snooker is a game of very real beauty: the colours and the sound and the nature of the ritual itself are wonderfully soothing. And indeed there is something soothing in the routine of quiet failure, punctuated by the occasional moment of competence and the odd miracle. Incompetence is a terrible thing in most aspects of life: at work, in attempting practical tasks, in trying to make the word processor do something you know it really ought to. But snooker exists as a safe outlet for incompetence: a world in which incompetence can be relished and chaos holds a mild and soothing pleasure.

LETTERS

29 May

Sir: I was distressed to read about Miss Jessica Mann's unfortunate
experience (Letters, 22 May) in being ejected from El Vino for
wearing trousers.

Having patronised the premises for 25 years when Fleet Street
was still Fleet Street (never with the intellectuals beyond the screen,
mostly with Denis Compton and sundry layabouts nearer the door),
I too found myself unwittingly involved in a similar dilemma.

My wife Sarah and her friend arrived to join me there before
going out to dinner. Being conformists, they sat down as required
before taking a drink. At this point a barman, a long-time friend,
approached and discreetly whispered, 'Sir, we have a problem:
your wife is wearing trousers.' Until then I had not noticed my
wife's clothes but a swift glance confirmed that, indeed, she
was wearing a pair of slacks, beautifully cut and probably very
expensive.

On relaying the predicament to my wife she replied, 'Where's
the problem?' Her friend was wearing a calf-length mink coat,
which Sarah borrowed and put on, then sat down again, wriggled
out of her trousers and finished her drink in fur coat and
knickers. This was entirely acceptable to El Vino's management
and no one batted an eyelid, least of all my wife.

Ian Wooldridge
London W8

YOUR PROBLEMS SOLVED

Dear Mary . . .

26 June

Q. I was walking near the Law Courts in the rain and could hardly see out of my glasses. A small, bald, elderly man greeted me by my first name. I thought he was a judge (I am a barrister) so I returned his greeting with a polite 'Good morning, sir.' On wiping my glasses I was horrified to see that he was my old public-school headmaster. It is now preying on my mind that he may think I respect him. How can I rectify this? A letter to the old-boy magazine explaining the error seems too heavy-handed.

    – H.C., Cheltenham, Glos

A. I have looked up your educational details in *Chambers and Partners Guide to the Legal Profession* in order to identify the headmaster to whom you are referring. I have passed on a copy of your letter directly to him.

THE FAT LADY SINGS

Charles Moore

14 August

One summer afternoon I was sitting in the garden of *The Spectator* when the sash from the top-floor kitchen shot up and Jennifer Paterson stuck her head out. 'Who's this Digby Anderson?' she yelled, brandishing the latest issue. I explained that he was to be our monthly food writer (at that time *The Spectator* did not run regular articles about cooking). 'If he can do it, why can't I?' shouted Jennifer. As was quite often the case in conversation with Jennifer, I could not think of a riposte to trump her, so I offered her the post.

Thus began, in her seventh decade, her rise from drudge in the kitchen to fame and fortune as a television cook. She died better known than anyone else associated with *The Spectator* in modern times.

Jennifer was appointed cook at *The Spectator* by Alexander Chancellor. He later made her office manager as well, which meant taking messages on her 50cc motor-bike. Alexander thought it also meant replacing the light bulb on his desk-lamp, but Jennifer disagreed and he remained in darkness for many months. She disliked any change, and when we finally had the decrepit office redecorated she screamed, 'The place looks like a cathouse.'

If you valued what is now called your private space, Jennifer was not the person for you. She would enter any office at any time saying anything that came into her head. In the mid-1980s, the paper was bought by Australians, and I was having my first, rather tense inter-continental telephone conversation with them when Jennifer barged in and started ruffling my hair, bellowing 'Darling little Editor' and smothering me with kisses. At the lunches which she cooked for the paper's guests, she would intrude her person and her thoughts upon all comers. Once, during a quarrel with Alexander, she came in and collected the remains of the first course. 'That was delicious, Jennifer,' he said, anxious to make peace. 'What was it cooked in?' 'Vitriol!'

Her television fame was particularly deserved and appreciated because she was a natural and, until then, frustrated actress. She loved singing and doing accents and striking poses. Before a big event she would have the equivalent of stage-fright. Once the Prince of Wales came to lunch and the palace let us know in advance that he did not like red meat. 'That bloody fusspot Prince will have whatever I give him,' she said. 'Your inviting him has given me a rash all up my leg.' (Here she offered to show me.) But when he did come she was charm itself and the food was halibut cevice. He and she later became friends, and he sent a letter to her hospital bed that touched her very much.

In all Jennifer's writing, the words came just as she spoke them – clear, funny, idiosyncratic. And the receipts (never say recipes) were excellent, so long as you made allowances for a certain carelessness. Some will remember the walnut and coffee cake introduced with the words, 'Here is a delicious and strange cake', in which she forgot to include the walnuts. I believe there was also a dish which required boiling a can of condensed milk: many readers wrote in to say that they had been injured in the resulting explosion.

Three weeks ago, I went to see Jennifer in hospital, but was told by serious-looking nurses that she was not well enough for visitors. Ten days later, I did see her, and explained that I'd been before. 'Ah yes, that was when I died,' she said. She was drinking vodka, and I said it was nice the nurses let her. 'I can do anything I like: I'm dying!' She had hundreds of kind letters and presents of caviare (requested in preference to chocolate), but there was one letter from a man who said her illness was her own fault for smoking. 'I've written back to him and said: "I'm 71, and you're a prat."'

She was very brave when she was dying. This was partly because the actress in her was determined to put on a good show, and partly because her Catholic faith was her strongest characteristic. If she's right, she's in Purgatory now. I think of her pulling her bad legs painfully upstairs, complaining noisily as she approaches the heavenly banquet.

YOUR PROBLEMS SOLVED

Dear Mary . . .

18 September

Q. Recently when visiting my new girlfriend's parents for the weekend, her millionaire father took me up in his helicopter, pausing before we set off to ask me whether I had ever been in a helicopter before. I was stumped for an appropriate answer to this subtle put-down. What should I have said, Mary?

  – P.D., London SW3

A. You could have smiled pleasantly and replied, 'Never one as small as this.'

DIARY

Joan Collins

13 November

I met President Clinton for the first time a couple of weeks ago. As we waited for him in the Oval Office an intern divulged, without a trace of irony, that 'the President uses the Oval Office mostly for business, but also for private matters'. Suppressing a smile, I was, however, suitably impressed when Clinton strolled in moments later, smiling affably and clutching a can of Diet Coke. The last American president of the twentieth century warmly greeted his guests, speaking to each of us as if we were the one and only person he'd been longing to see. This is an admirable quality, and a gift that precious few public figures possess. My two partners in crime, both sophisticated cynics, were greeted with great enthusiasm and were visibly entranced as Bill fixed them with his guileless blue eyes and chatted away. He gasped my hands firmly – he has beautiful and expressive hands, by the way, and enormous feet. In his gentle Arkansas drawl he asked all the appropriate questions. I must admit I was spellbound. The man has palpable sex appeal, and is much taller and slimmer than I'd expected. He also has wonderful breath, but not from a surfeit of mints or mouthwash. The White House photographer clicked away as the President pointed out a chunk of black rock that some astronaut or other had brought back from the moon. 'It's three and a half billion years old! Amazing, isn't it?' I surprised myself by answering, 'Almost as old as me.' After a further tour of the President's working offices we were next introduced to Buddy, the 'First Dog'. He turned out to be a frisky character, who instantly developed an uncontrollable passion for my right leg. Maybe it's something in the water there, or perhaps he just likes high heels.

SHARED OPINION

Frank Johnson

20 November

I met Mr Mohamed Al Fayed just once. I was entertained by him; entertained in both senses of the word. It was at a time when he was being much mentioned in these pages by several regular contributors. The mentions were all unfavourable. His famous public-relations man, Mr Cole, who has now left his service, would usually be the one who replied in Letters to the Editor, but on a couple of occasions a letter arrived signed by Mr Al Fayed himself. (I shall persist in including the 'Al' in his name. I realise that many deny his right to it, arguing that it is a Middle Eastern title which has to be bestowed by some higher authority, or inherited, and that he is entitled to it on neither count. But I believe in addressing people as they wish to be addressed. He could call himself King Fayed for all I care. I might draw the line at Duke Fayed, but even then the principle would be no different – as in Duke Ellington.)

We at *The Spectator* were especially delighted when the letters bore Mr Al Fayed's signature. It is no disrespect to Mr Cole's vast collected letters on his behalf to say that Mr Al Fayed writing, or at least signing personally, was an exceptional attraction from our point of view. After we printed a couple, I wrote to Mr Al Fayed to say that he had provided us with so much lively, free material that the least we could do was to ask him to lunch at *The Spectator*. He replied that he would be delighted to have lunch with me but would prefer it to be in the restaurant at Harrods. He added that the meal would, of course, be Egyptian or Maghrebian, with much couscous. But he quickly explained one sentence later that he was only joking, and that I would be offered the roast beef of old England.

Someone suggested that he had declined our offer of lunch on the grounds that he wanted to avoid being poisoned. I replied that our food was not that bad. Indeed, most of our guests admired it. No, really poisoned, it was further explained. He's rumoured to think that there are a lot of powerful people out there trying to poison him. I was, of course, flattered. It is always agreeable to be thought powerful.

The lunch duly took place at Harrods: Mr Al Fayed, Mr Cole and me. Very early in the conversation he dismissed a prominent British politician as a 'fuckhead'. I think it was the then prime minister, Mr Major. But Mr Howard, the then home secretary, was soon called a 'fuckhead' too. So were successive chancellors of the exchequer and foreign secretaries. Eventually even Lady Thatcher qualified. Then we got on to journalists. Quite a few of us were also 'fuckheads'. The worrying thought crossed my mind: at his next lunch, will I be one too?

After a while, I interrupted to say that, admiring though I was of his command of English, I thought the word he had been looking for, the word he must really have had in mind, was 'dickhead', not 'fuckhead'.

'So sorry, thank you,' he replied with impeccable courtesy, capping one side of his head with the palm of one hand, 'Thanks for correcting me.' His tone was as if I had put him right about a point of grammar or a line of English poetry: 'A host of golden *daffodils*, Mr Al Fayed, not chrysanthemums.'

I then mused to him that the term of abuse in question, 'dickhead', was of relatively recent usage. I had first heard it only about a decade before, from the lips of the young. In due course, I had heard Mr Tony Banks, a Labour politician who likes us to think that he has a command of the demotic, use it in the Commons.

'*Really!*' said Mr Al Fayed in a scholarly tone. It was clear that Mr Al Fayed also liked to keep up with the demotic, and I had contributed to his impressive command of this branch of our language. When we parted, he gave me a Harrods teddy bear. Back in the office, colleagues debated whether, in order to save me from myself, they had better perform surgery on it to ensure that it contained neither a tape recorder nor pound notes. A carving knife was fetched from the kitchen. I seized the beast and ran off with it into the night, presenting it eventually to a friend's child.

Later, in an interview, Mr Al Fayed, asked whether it was true that he tended to give his guests teddy bears, replied, 'Only if I think he's a good guy.' I do not know whether I come well out of this story.

NEW YORK DIARY

Barry Humphries

18/25 December

I'm living in a wonderful building overlooking the East River and Roosevelt Island, on which stand the romantic ruins of a lunatic asylum. On the horizon are LaGuardia and Kennedy airports, and I can see the Qantas jumbos landing after their long haul from the Land of the Hot Christmas. Dear, distant homeland, probably the only country in the world outside Iran whose intelligentsia live abroad. To the right of my vista is the imposing ziggurat of River House, where Lilian Gish and Ethel Merman once lived, and where now resides Henry Kissinger. Through my powerful Zeiss binoculars, from which no illuminated apartment window withholds its rosy secrets, I can watch the former secretary of state flossing, and much else. My building is among the few on the East Side which accepts tenants with dogs, so that it resembles a high-rise kennel, a Crufts in the sky. The lifts are crowded with Pomeranians, Labradors, chihuahuas, standard poodles, Yorkshire terriers, Afghan hounds, dachshunds, pugs and Rottweilers, all cleaner and better groomed than their shifty and anoraked owners. The other day a friend's cocker spaniel died, and he experienced extraordinary difficulty in arranging for its dignified committal. His vet was on holiday, the building supervisors unhelpful, so because of the prevailing heatwave he decided to place the body in a suitcase and take it to the park himself for surreptitious burial. However, while hailing a cab on the corner of East 54th Street and First Avenue, a black man leapt from the shadows, seized the suitcase, and made off with it into the night, deftly solving his problem.

2000

Wallace Arnold; Julie Burchill; Jeremy Clarke;
Dear Mary; Frank Johnson; Deborah Ross

DIARY

Wallace Arnold

1 January

After a most convivial dinner with very dear friends – beef on the bone followed by chocolate sponge on the bone, then a little bone on the bone to suck with coffee – our host invited each of us to pick the single word that, in our opinion, might best sum up the twentieth century. A thoughtful hush descended upon the assembled company, a hush broken only by the distinctive tick-tock of the grandfather clock. It was my own good self who broke the silence. 'The word is *tiresome*,' I piped up. 'We can all agree that it has been an immensely *tiresome* century.'

My choice was greeted with a murmur of approval. But what, asked our host – a regular panellist on the Home Service's *Round Britain Quiz* – what did we feel to be the single most tiresome aspect of this most tiresome of centuries? Suggestions came in thick and fast – the television, the 'Y-front', air travel, the portable toothbrush, 'jogging', public transport, the gramophone. But, once again, it was I who put my finger on it. 'Chewing-gum!' I exclaimed, pronouncing it in my humorous 'cockney' voice ('choowin' garm'). We all agreed that Mr Wrigley (dread name!) had much to answer for, though his answer would doubtless be inaudible, his mouth being chock-a-block with his stringy comestible.

This is not to say that all gum is to be abhorred. Far from it. Bubble-gum has long been all the rage in our great country houses. Historians date this to the days of King George V, for whom no week-end at Sandringham was complete until each of his guests had blown a handsome bubble: the King would measure the radius of each one with a pair of compasses before faithfully recording the statistics in his beloved game book. Paradoxically, one of the principal reasons why the royal family never took to Wallis Simpson was her inability to blow a properly rounded bubble; rumour had it that the bubble-blowing valve in her throat had been destroyed after too much casual use out East. Consequently, when the Duchess's wardrobe was put up for auction eight years ago, many potential purchasers were distressed to find that some of her finest frocks – by Givenchy, Dior and Balenciaga – had the tell-tale gubbins of strawberry-flavoured bubble-gum splattered over their necklines, testament to hundreds of botched attempts by Mrs Simpson to ingratiate herself with the King and Queen.

For 200 years the small Lancashire firm of Ritblatt and Son has produced old-fashioned sticky mints by dipping dead sheep's eyes in treacle, and jolly delicious they are too. But no more: the EC in its wisdom has decided that this contravenes health and safety guidelines. What price the euro now, Mr Blair?

Small wonder that our own Queen Mother, a stickler for tradition, so despised poor Wallis. She herself has, of course, always been highly gifted with the bubble-gum. Indeed, Noël Coward once remarked that she could blow a bubble the size of a small dachshund, its growth foreshortened by smoking, a common enough problem in those days. In the second volume of his journals my old friend and quaffing part-ner Woodrow Wyatt records in loving detail a dinner party he gave for Queen Elizabeth, the Queen Mother, on 23 May 1972, during the course of which a selection of hand-made bubble-gums by Bendicks of Mayfair was offered around. The Queen Mother took to them like a duck to water, discreetly popping a couple into her handbag for later. But Woodrow neglects to mention that this dinner party was a landmark in other ways, too. Roy Strong, the then clean-shaven director of the National Portrait Gallery, was also present, keen as mustard to prove himself in the upper reaches of society. Alas, his mother had always kept the young Roy at arm's-length from bubble-gum (it is one of those pas-times that unite the working class and aristocracy, bypassing what one might call the 'in-betweenies'), so when it came to a round of blowing, his attempts met with disaster, the livid vermilion gum splashing itself any old how across his upper lip. Amid much well-intentioned mirth, poor Roy ran from the dinner table in shame. Sadly, after half an hour with nail-brush and chisel in the men's cloakroom, he had come no nearer to removing the unsightly smear, so he decided to hotfoot it to the nearest all-night emporium of jokes and assorted ice-breakers. It was there that he came across the specs-nose-and-whiskers novelty mask that has been his trademark ever since, returning to the dinner table just in time for coffee, his distinctive new appearance gathering plaudits from all and sundry. A happy tale, with an uplifting moral for the new millennium.

DIARY

Julie Burchill

12 February

My mother died last month, and I do miss her. I miss her most of all because she was the only person I've ever known who was remotely like me. This is the curse of Teen: when our hormones kick in, all we want to do is get away from our parents and *be with people like us*. Too late we realise that, if we've been lucky enough to be blessed with good parents, they're the only people like us we'll ever find. All our roaming and search-ing was in vain, then, forsaking our heart's ease for a soft parade of straw dogs. For ages my writing hero has been Alan Bennett, so imagine my delight when I realised about 15 years ago that my mother was a living, breathing Bennett heroine, with all the spirit and eccentricity that implies. An incident that happened a few months before her death sums this up wonderfully for me. Walking the dog in broad daylight in the back lanes of our part of Bristol, my mother, a 70-year-old lady not in the best of health, espied what she called 'an old junkie' taking his solitary pleasures courtesy of a roll of Bacofoil and a ballpoint-pen case. I must point out that my mother, as anti-drugs as all of her generation, called anyone who took more than two Disprins 'an old junkie'. 'Come over 'ere, love!' called the junkie. 'I'll sort you out!' 'Get away!' cried my mother. 'I'll set the dog on thee!' The dog was only small, but it was enthusiastic and apparently saw the old junkie off handsomely. My mother walked on, her honour satisfied. 'And then I thought . . .' my mother mused. 'I had a roast to do, and I'd run out of Bacofoil . . . ' 'No, Mum!' I squealed, in the delicious agony of anticipation. 'Oh, yes! I went back and there was the roll of Bacofoil – ee'd 'ardly touched it. So I rolled it up neat and took it 'ome and did a roast in it.' Her eyes twinkled with glee. 'That roast you ate yesterday!' I loved the fearlessness and surrealism of this story, and started telling it to everyone who came to the house. My mum eventually told me to stop it, saying it made her look stingy and dirty. But I found it so funny that I didn't stop. After I returned from the hospital, less than an hour after her death, I went to the cupboard to get some biscuits for a neighbour who had called to commiserate. Something fell on my head, hard, really hurting me. 'Ow!' I picked it up. It was a roll of Bacofoil.

NO LIFE

Jeremy Clarke

19 February

One thing I do have in common with the ladies of our residential home is that we all love a nice fire. A log fire unites us and lends significance to our otherwise rather futile existences. 'Ooh, lovely,' comment the ladies when they see I've lit one.

I start to plan our winter fires during the summer. In the garden we have a eucalyptus tree that sheds its bark on the lawn all the year round. Before mowing the grass every week I gather up the long curling shards and store them in the shed for use as kindling later on. For lighting-sticks I smash up the unwanted furniture of those ladies who have passed away. (The home averages about two deaths a year.) On hearing about a death in the home I immediately think of lighting-sticks: lovely, clean, dry, straight-edged lighting-sticks of antique mahogany, pine and teak. When Miss Beryl Jarvis passed away last August, I had her dressing-table and wardrobe broken, sawn and split into pencil-sized lengths before she'd reached the crematorium.

Logs I buy well in advance of the burning season from a Mr Pine, a genial, ill-kempt old man who seems to be able to get his hands on a limitless supply of fallen timber. If I ask him for beech he brings beech. Or ash, he brings ash. If any of his beautiful ash logs are too big for the grate, and require splitting, they fall apart under the weight of my falling meat cleaver as whitely and cleanly as if they were green apples.

I lay the fire first thing in the morning, before the ladies are down. I use broadsheets to line the grate; tabloids don't get a fire going like they used to. On top of the lightly screwed-up balls of newspaper, I put a layer of eucalyptus bark; then a layer of tinder-dry pine branches saved from the Christmas tree; a layer of hardwood sticks from Beryl Jarvis's dressing-table; a layer of household coal; and on top of this lot I balance two or three of Mr Pine's wonderfully straight-grained logs. If I've been out for a walk on the beach already, I might put on a piece of seaweed, or a bit of old fishing-net, or a herring-gull feather, just to give the whole thing a nautical flavour. After lunch, when the ladies have tottered back to their respective armchairs for their afternoon nap, I light it.

When Violet Joint was alive, she managed to keep her eyes open just long enough to ensure that I lit the fire at the front of the grate, rather than shoving my lighted match in at random. Vi had very strong opinions on the right and the wrong way to lay and light a fire. One thing she told me that I didn't know – and she told me this on one of those very rare days when I had to apply a second match – was that if a fire burns unevenly to begin with, the house is in for a run of bad luck. Actually, there could be something in this superstition, because not long afterwards I was laying about Vi's bedroom furniture with the thick side of my axe. Hers was flimsy glued-together post-war utility stuff, mostly.

Once the flames have taken hold I stand a big metal fire-guard in front of the fire to prevent ladies from falling in on their way to and from the lavatory. Head-shaped dents in the fire-guard testify to the absolute necessity of this. The profoundest dent was made by the head of a gentleman, the only gentleman we ever had, a big, forgetful ex-naval officer who'd served at the Battle of Jutland. Early one winter's afternoon about five years ago, Commander wished us all good night, tripped over the coal scuttle and fell headlong into the fireplace, taking the clock with him as he went. Fortunately, Commander was always falling over and had taught himself to bounce. When he finally died, from natural causes, Commander's third and last wife took everything away except his pocket diaries. There were about 50 of them. Close examination of the minuscule writing revealed a catalogue of meals eaten, rounds of golf played, and of every passing shower between the years 1919 and 1971. I tried supplementing my lighting-sticks with them, but they gave off too much smoke.

And then Doreen Hume severely damaged the guard by trying to climb over it. Doreen was very confused, and sometimes mistook the fireplace for the door. When she finally died, the lighting-sticks I got from her old oak bureau lasted us nearly the whole winter.

I'm a bit worried at the moment. My stockpile of lighting-sticks is a little low and the ladies are all looking so well. Perhaps one or two of them might let me have a chair or two on account.

YOUR PROBLEMS SOLVED

Dear Mary . . .

19 February

Q. I will be taking the art critic Brian Sewell out to dinner the week after next. The last time I took this man to a fashionable restaurant his presence caused a considerable buzz and many of those present started behaving weirdly, one of them actually asking the head waiter if he could move to a vacant table beside ours. I am sick with worry that there will be further complications of this sort when Brian and I next dine together. How can I prevent the occasion from being ruined in the same way?

– I.P., London N6

A. Pick up the art critic from his home. Bring with you a loose-fitting rabbit costume complete with special aperture for the mouth and ask him if he would be kind enough to don this so as to prevent unwelcome attention at the restaurant you intend to visit.

YOUR PROBLEMS SOLVED

Dear Mary . . .

1 April

Q. I am the mother of the most enchanting 15-month-old girl twins. Part of my daily routine is to strap them into their large double pram and parade up and down the King's Road near our Chelsea home. This is quite a spectacle and numerous passers-by stop to admire my progeny, murmuring, 'Twins, how sweet', 'Such a lovely sight' or 'What beautiful babies.' Can you tell me please, Mary, what is the correct response to such compliments? Should I smile but rudely stride on, or stop to acknowledge their words and therefore feel obliged to engage in conversation regarding age, sex, identicalness, etc.?
– M.K., London SW3

A. Clearly, one is grateful for such gifts from God. However, compliments are bound to be excited every 50 yards or so during the display of adorable twins of the type you mention. Enforced boastfulness, and a halting of momentum which could enrage the twins, would be the result of responding to each compliment in full. The solution is to simply deter the well-wishers at source by donning a Romanian gypsy headscarf before setting out from home.

SHARED OPINION

Frank Johnson

6 May

One of the papers reported the other day that Sir Edward Heath will leave the Commons at the next election. At the time of writing, the report remains unconfirmed. We must hope that it is untrue. At this critical juncture in our island story, the nation cannot afford to lose from Parliament the Rudest Living Englishman.

The juncture is critical because of the decline of British bad manners. Once they were our glory. My generation was brought up on stirring and inspiring stories about Evelyn Waugh. I am slightly too young to remember it, but in our darkest hour – May 1940, 60 years ago this very month – his behaviour towards waiters, journalists and other defenceless servants must have inspired a generation. Nowadays, in contrast, one can hardly turn on the television without having to look at and listen to people being polite to one another. That is why viewers now hardly ever talk about *Question Time*, though apparently the programme still goes out weekly. Who wants to be subjected to, say, Mr Charles Kennedy being decent about asylum-seekers, answering his mild detractors with courtesy? We do not pay our licence fees in order to be exposed to that kind of language in our own homes. If my address was Tunbridge Wells, I would write a stiff letter about it for publication in the *Daily Telegraph*. Sir Edward comes from a different, more heroic age. In those days our politicians were not afraid to be disagreeable.

I took him to lunch only once. It was a couple of years after Mrs Thatcher became prime minister. As soon as he arrived at the table, I offered him champagne. He grunted, 'What's there to celebrate?' Magnificent. He was all I had hoped for. All anecdotes about Sir Edward are like that. He is never conventionally nice. He never lets people down.

I once asked Dr David Starkey to lunch at *The Spectator*. He had become famous by being rude to nearly everyone, especially his fellow panellists on that radio programme *The Moral Maze*. One of those Sunday-paper profiles had just described him as the rudest man in Britain. After our lunch, another guest, Mr Simon Hoggart, *Guardian* parliamentary sketchwriter and a *Spectator* television critic, complained to me, saying, 'I thought your friend Starkey behaved abominably.'

'What do you mean?' I replied, 'I thought he was perfectly charming.' 'Exactly,' Mr Hoggart retorted. 'That's the point I'm making. You do not accept an invitation to lunch on the basis of a reputation for being the rudest man in Britain only to be perfectly charming. It's sheer bad manners. Everyone else present wanted him to be rude. We could then go off and tell stories about his rudeness. No one wants to hear that the legendary David Starkey was perfectly charming.'

Mr Hoggart was of course correct. I remember that during the lunch Dr Starkey harrumphed with contempt and disbelief when I suggested that there was no evidence that a certain Tory politician was homosexual, but that was about the extent of his behaving in character.

Sir Edward is another matter. During the February 1974 election, a senior official of his Bexley Sidcup constituency association proudly told him, when he visited the constituency, that party workers had by now canvassed the entire constituency at least once. 'Then you'd better go back and canvass the doubtful wards twice,' he replied. He was always able to sink to the occasion.

It must be emphasised that the constituency official was senior. There is no evidence that Sir Edward has ever been rude to the weak, the junior or those who cannot answer back. In this a rude Briton differs from a rude American, still more from a rude German, though admittedly Evelyn Waugh was said to be rude to all classes. My observation of them suggests that rude Americans and Germans tend to confine their rudeness to secretaries, doormen and so on. They are seldom rude to their equals. But Sir Edward spent more than a decade being rude to a prime minister. In a sense it all comes down to self-confidence. In the old days, British public figures were rude because, unlike today's, they did not think that they had to make themselves agreeable and acceptable to everyone. Certainly not to the media. In the Boer war, Lord Kitchener greeted the approach of some British war correspondents with a cry of, 'Out of my tent, you scum.' So different from the public relations of our own Mr Blair.

Not that good manners are proof of a lack of self-confidence. There are politicians to whom good manners come naturally – we think of, say, the late Lord Home or Mr John Major. But much of what now passes for good manners among politicians is lack of stomach for conflict. I cannot say whether Mr Blair's good manners arise naturally or are a sign of fear of a fight. In the absence of any evidence to the contrary, it is only good manners to assume the former. But there seems to be much 'anecdotal evidence' that in private as well as in public he tends to tell nearly everyone what they want to hear. Right-wing visitors to No. 10 are assured of his devotion to capitalism; left-wing visitors are assured that he is an egalitarian too. Everything is subsumed into everything else. We can imagine him assuring President Mugabe that, in a very real sense, Bob, 'and I hope I can call you Bob' – Zimbabwe's land reform is very much like our council-house sales: a way of increasing owner-occupation. President Mugabe: 'Owner-occupation! I like that – especially the occupation.'

But nowadays Mr Mugabe's reception from Sir Edward would have been such as to lead to a severing of diplomatic relations. No British politician since Sir Edward has been as masterly as he was at conveying contempt. Whether the object of his scorn deserved it is another matter; most Conservatives now think he was wrong about most things. My point is to praise his uningratiating qualities, not his policies.

His political career, if it is drawing to its close, should inspire us all to be ruder to the deserving. I myself shall try harder to be so. I would wish my epitaph to be: fools did not suffer him gladly.

NO LIFE

Jeremy Clarke

27 May

Torremolinos is nothing like as horrible as we'd hoped it would be. Twinned with Stockport, Lancashire, and dating back to the 1970s, Torremolinos today has something of a quiet, historic feel to it and is favoured by the elderly. There are trendy little boutiques there now too, and I noticed two places offering tattoo removal by laser. So we pushed on to Benalmadena, a sprawling new development about five miles along the coast, hoping for something brasher, more loutish, and more in keeping with our expectations.

Three weeks ago there was a gangland shooting in one of Benalmadena's bars. A discussion became acrimonious, it was reported in the English dailies, and a man left the bar, returned a few minutes later with a gun, then calmly shot two of his interlocutors. The lady with whom I was travelling suggested it might be fun to find the place, have a few shants, and play Spot the Criminal. Unfortunately, neither of us could remember the name of the bar, so we parked in the Plaza Bonanza and asked around. Outside Barry's Place I interrupted the conversation an old cockney gent with long, nicotine-stained hair was having with a small boy about a pool cue.

'Excuse me,' I said, 'we are looking for an ex-pats' bar where they have been shooting at each other recently.'

'Oh, you mean the Grapes,' he said. 'Jimmy's pub. I don't know anything about a Pat, though.' The Grapes was the old geezer's local, as it happened. He not only told us how to get there, he told us the victims' names (they were friends of his), plus the name and current whereabouts of the man wanted in connection with the shooting (another friend of his). He also recommended the steak and kidney pie.

You had to be 'motored up', as he put it, to get out to the Grapes, which was, to be honest, a bit of a disappointment. Apart from Tina, the landlady, no one in the bar looked remotely thuggish. There were plenty of shaved heads and tattooed arms gathered around the bar, it is true, and everyone over 40 had bright, alcoholic eyes. But everyone was tremendously open and jolly, not threatening at all. The lady with whom I was travelling and I generally relish a hint of violence in the air. We've been in golf clubs with a more intimidating atmosphere than this place, however.

The bar of the Grapes was built of small glazed bricks and resembled a very large and elaborate fireplace. On a tiny stage off to one side, a fat skinhead with a kindly face was organising the karaoke. Catalogues of the songs in the karaoke machine's repertoire and some betting-shop pens to note down the numbers were scattered on the tables. Kids, mostly, were getting up to perform songs by Oasis or the Spice Girls. The fat skinhead tried to make them laugh in the middle of their songs by doing fruity, prolonged belches into his microphone.

Between songs he told jokes. 'Has anybody seen that new film about the life of Harold Shipman?' he said, pretending to look for a show of hands. 'It's called the *Old Dear Hunter*.' Also, we heard about a Buddhist hot-dog vendor who offered to make his customers one with everything. This went completely over everyone's heads, including mine, but the lady with whom I was travelling snorted so violently into her snakebite, several people looked over curiously at us.

The first adult to get up and sing whom we saw, was the owner of a hairdressing salon called Beau Locks. He had white shoes and a gold medallion and sang 'Three Coins In A Fountain', beautifully, with his hand on his heart, while behind him the fat skinhead took down his trousers and pants, bent over, and parted his cheeks. Then, to much applause, and stamping of feet, the landlady went on stage and did 'Your Cheating Heart', which seemed some sort of a Grapes anthem, because everyone turned to face her and bellowed out every word.

It took about five pints before I got up to sing. I sang 'I'm Going To Be A Country Girl Again (with an old brown dog in a big front porch and rabbits in the pen)', which went down OK. Then the lady with whom I was travelling got up and sang 'My Boy Lollypop', with actions, which went down an absolute storm.

Our getting up to sing made us accepted as part of the gang, or so we thought. But around one in the morning, when car-loads of men with wide shoulders and highly impractical shoes started arriving, and things livened up considerably, we were more or less chucked out. The next time I went up for a refill the barman said, 'Sorry, pal, el shutto,' to me, before turning to the bloke beside me and saying, 'Same again, Sammy?'

We didn't argue.

RESTAURANTS

Deborah Ross

23 September

First off, I think you should know that my preoccupation with Nigella Lawson has now shifted into full-blown obsessional mode. Isn't she beautiful? Isn't she sophisticated? Isn't she a total domestic goddess? Isn't she the new Marie Antoinette? What, no more bread at Sainsbury's? Well, let them have the number of that darling little patisserie in Notting Hill. I want to be her. I want to come home in the evenings and say, 'I've had a bloody awful day at work. I haven't had time to get anything in. I'm pooped. So, tonight, it's just going to have to be onion tart with bitter leaves, roast monkfish, pumpkin purée and mixed mushrooms, then almond and orange-blossom cake with red fruit. And if you don't like it, you can sodding well lump it.'

The only drawback, as far as I can see, is that if I were to become the next Nigella, I'd have to change my own name to the feminised – ella-ised – version of my father's name. I wouldn't mind, but my dad's name is Salman. Only kidding. It's Bonj. Got you again, didn't I? You lot are so easy to kid it's almost not worth bothering. OK, it's Denis. Denis? Does that mean I'd have to be Denise? Nah. I couldn't be a Denise. I'm not common. I've got a cleaner. I have fresh fruit in the house even when no one is poorly. I could be Denisella. Yes. That has a nice ring to it, I think. *How to Eat* by Denisella Ross. That would make it into the bestseller lists.

It would be full of useful tips, too, like: 'Just open your gob and shove it in. Easy-peasy pudding and Blakean fish pie.' Blakean? Yes, because the colour of this 'saffron-infused' dish reminds Nigella of 'Blakean sunsets'. I would describe my own fish pie as more Plathian. Depressing. Makes you want to stick your head in the oven alongside it.

RESTAURANTS

Deborah Ross

21 October

So, off to the newly-opened 'kosher gourmet' restaurant, Six-13, on Wigmore Street. Six-13? Yes, because there are 613 *mitvos*, or Jewish rules for living, which, I believe, start with:

1) If you can't find anywhere to park on Golders Green High Street, double-park.

2) If you can't double-park, triple-park.

3) If you can't triple-park, don't quadruple-park, because by that time you're practically on the other side of the road, which rather defeats the object, and you might have to do something awful like actually walk across it, which means using your legs, and this is said to be quite tiring.

Anyway, I go to Six-13 with my mother and my mother's cousin, Norma, who shares my fixation with Nigella Lawson – 'although she sometimes does things so unkosher that my hair stands on end' – and her husband, Harry, and their niece, Sima, who is visiting from Israel. Norma and Harry and Sima are all observant while my mother and I are rather lapsed. Still, we are *all* rather excited as you would be if, to date, the *only* Jewish dining-out experience has meant Blooms. Blooms! Where, as Harry puts it, 'the insolence of the waiters knows no limits'. He once asked for mustard to go with his salt beef. The waiter brought it but then whisked it away again almost immediately. Harry asked that it might be returned. 'What? For a *second* time?' asked the waiter. Still, I quite like Blooms for the way they serve chopped egg. Actually, they don't so much serve it as contemptuously shoot it at you from an ice-cream scoop. There is always this fantastic moment of tension as you wait to see if it is going to land on your plate or in your lap. Or the floor. 'Sorry, but my chopped egg seems to have landed on the floor.' 'So?'

Into the restaurant, where the decor upsets everyone instantly and, as it transpires, irreparably. It is very minimal. White tablecloths, pale-green walls, green velvet banquettes, bare floor. This is a mistake, I think, because 'Jew' and 'minimal' just do not go together. Jews need to see what they are getting for their money. Jews have never really got to grips with the 'less is more' philosophy. With Jews, more is more and a lot more is a lot more and, if you have a lot more, show it, wear it, drive it, dress the kids in it, dress the dog in it. 'It is very ... unadorned,' announces my mother, unhappily. 'A bit of patterned carpet would have been nice,' adds Harry. Later, when the bearded man at the next table introduces himself as a director of the restaurant, Harry repeats, 'A bit of patterned carpet would have been nice.' 'Do you know,' replies the director, 'what patterned carpet costs these days?'

2001

Dear Mary; Deborah Ross; Mark Steyn;
James Delingpole; Simon Barnes;
Barry Humphries

YOUR PROBLEMS SOLVED

Dear Mary . . .

3 March

Q. Some years ago in White's Club I found myself standing at the urinal alongside the late Sir Iain Moncreiffe of that Ilk. Seeing me washing my hands afterwards, he admonished me with the diktat that 'no gentleman washes his hands after using a urinal'. Urinals have been a source of disquiet for me ever since. It is a question of divided loyalties. My nanny always drummed into me that I should wash my hands after going to the loo, but Sir Iain was a great hero of mine. Can you clear up this matter once and for all, Mary, and tell me what is the correct protocol?
    – Name and address withheld

A. Use of a full lavatory exposes the discharger of waste to a range of unsavoury surfaces, after which hand-washing is *de rigueur*. As far as urinals are concerned, however, Sir Iain was correct, since the only 'surface' handled by the user is his own member. Historical evidence bears out this rule of protocol. A study of architects' plans for the Palace of Westminster reveals that, while lavatories in the Lords were always equipped with washbasins, the latter were only introduced to urinals – many of which were separate – during the last war. Their introduction coincided with the relocation of the bomb-damaged Commons into the Lords, thus bringing an element of middle-class behaviour into what had been previously a purely aristocratic domain.

FOOD

Deborah Ross

12 May

Oh dear! There I was, enjoying my Sunday, not doing very much, idly flicking through the papers, when I saw it. There it was, on page three of the *Sunday Times*, under the headline: 'Critics knock goddess off her pedestal'. It was all about the very lovely and gorgeous and beautiful Nigella Lawson, saying that her recipes don't work; the chefs have tried them and her flapjacks are difficult to remove from the tin, her blueberry muffins nosedive because of too much baking powder, and her cranberry upside-down cake collapses. Well, I was outraged. How dare they have a go at Nigella whom, as you know, I adore and worship and crave to be, what with her divine cashmere twinsets and hair as dark and glossy as a black Labrador's ears. OK, my own version of *How to Eat* (by Denisella Ross) didn't do too well but, as I can now see, the subtitle – *Just Open Your Gob and Shove It In* – might have done for it. Still, I am hopeful for the sequel, *How to Be a Domestic Slobbess*, which even comes with a free quiz to test how you score on this particular front:

1. Have yesterday's knickers ever fallen out of your trouser-leg while you were walking down the street?

2. When you're draining pasta, and your hand slips and the spaghetti plops from the colander into the sink, do you scoop it up and serve it anyway?

3. In Tesco, do you always march past the manky, dirt-covered, overpriced organic rubbish and head straight for the Ginster's pies, Dairylea Lunchables and jumbo bottles of Panda cola?

4 Have you ever made Nescafé by running the mug under the hot tap?

5. Would you do more tests like these, if only you could ever find a pen?

CINEMA

Mark Steyn

2 June

Those Krauts and Japs have all the luck. They may have lost the war, but they're getting a shorter print of *Pearl Harbor* (12): Disney execs have been busy snipping out bits of dialogue in order to avoid giving offence to German and Japanese audiences. To avoid giving offence to English-speaking audiences, they should have cut all the dialogue.

Connoisseurs will have their favourite moments. I greatly enjoyed the scene between Danny and Evelyn. It begins with a subtitle: 'Three months later'. Then Danny says, 'I can't believe it's been three months since I saw you.' But Evelyn also loves Rafe (and no, it's not pronounced 'Ralph'). She enters his room and sees him packing. 'Packing?' she says. Michael Bay then cuts to a close-up of the suitcase, with folded clothes inside. In its exquisite laboriousness, this encapsulates the picture's style more than any of the explosions. Bay's last blockbuster, *Armageddon*, was criticised for being fast-moving but shallow. So he's now made a film that's slow-moving but even shallower.

We begin in lyrical, cornpone Tennessee, where two little boys have two little toys. Gaily they'd play each summer's day, warriors both, of course. One boy is Rafe (Ben Affleck), who as the male lead has been given the designated trait: he's dyslexic, which may well be an advantage with a screenplay by Randall Wallace. Danny (Josh Hartnett) is The Buddy, so he has no trait. The years roll by to 1940 and Rafe and Danny are now flyboys playing chicken during training sessions on Long Island. Those nitpicky historians hung up on obscure facts and stuff will be reassured to know that Hollywood has an equally shaky grip on East Coast topography: this Long Island has spectacular mountains, presumably bulldozed when they built Alec Baldwin's place in the Hamptons.

Speaking of which, here's Alec himself as Colonel Doolittle handing Rafe his official papers immediately ordering him to England to fly with the RAF. Between 1939 and 1941, many brave Yank airmen volunteered as individuals for the RAF and RCAF but they weren't assigned to foreign air forces by their American commanders as that would have been in breach of US neutrality. Still, it does give Rafe's sweetheart, Evelyn, the opportunity to see him off at Grand Central Station: apparently, in those days, to get from New York to England, you took the train.

When it pulls in at Victoria, Rafe discovers that England is hell. Not only is it damp but, unlike back home, where the pilots have the healthy glow of a 1950s gay bodybuilding magazine, the local air aces are weedy, pasty, thin-lipped anti-hunks whose feeble Battle of Britain is sorely in need of a bit of Yankee derring-do. 'The German Luftwaffe relentlessly bombards downtown London,' intones the newsreel announcer, the authentic period flavour of his script matched only by the bass reverb of his Kiss-FM delivery, 'while Churchill's Royal Air Force struggles to maintain control of the British skies.' Fortunately, Rafe is there to save downtown London.

But half a world away Imperial Japan is preparing to attack Pearl Harbor to protest about the US oil embargo. Hmm. If you're doing a GCSE essay on root causes of the second world war, don't quote me on that one. Soon, Admiral Yamamoto (Mako) is going full steam ahead and cabling Tokyo with his own subtitles, translated from the original gibberish: 'The rise and fall of our empire is at stake!' Both the rise *and* the fall are at stake?

There follows 40 minutes of carnage that come as a welcome respite from the interminable triangle of Evelyn, Danny and Rafe. Evelyn (Kate Beckinsale) seems vaguely to resent the interruption. It's been difficult enough trying to deal with her feelings, she says irritably, 'and then all this happened', 'this' being the surrounding scenes of widespread devastation. The attack itself is played virtually in real time, à la *Saving Private Ryan*, but is completely uninvolving. Who's being bombed? Who's doing the bombing? I counted over 100 names in the cast list, yet the film has a total absence of humanity. On a Hawaii with no Hawaiians, anonymous Japs battle cardboard Yankees. Who cares?

Having wiped out America's Pacific Fleet, Yamamoto remarks, 'I fear all we have done is to waken a sleeping giant.' That would be me, I thought, waking with a start. So I got up to leave. But, amazingly, the movie hadn't ended, and suddenly lurched into what seems like an entirely separate film about the Doolittle Raid (it already is a separate film: *30 Seconds Over Tokyo*), in which four months after Pearl Harbor Colonel Doolittle led a couple of dozen bomber pilots on a crazy but morale-boosting raid. Hitherto in this movie, Danny and Rafe have been fighter pilots, not bomber pilots, and in reality there were no fighter pilots on the Doolittle Raid, but they're hand-picked for the gig anyway.

Bay's model was clearly *Titanic*: a love story set against the sweep of history. But, in *Titanic*, the love-across-the-classes romance sharpened the bigger picture. Here, the love story doesn't arise organically from the war, and doesn't illuminate any aspects of it: it's just a lame triangle. And Pearl Harbor and the Doolittle Raid don't really connect, either. The Americans are not temperamentally inclined to the Dunkirk Spirit, and those of us who wondered what Michael Bay and Jerry Bruckheimer were doing making a movie about a US military debacle are forced to the conclusion that maybe they only discovered it was a Jap victory halfway through shooting. In tacking a happy ending on to Pearl Harbor, they wind up missing the significance of the event: the only occasion in modern warfare when the US has been playing at home – when its own territory briefly came under the kind of assault that for Britain, France, Belgium et al. is par for the course. Pearl Harbor was, as they say, a 'defining moment', the end of American isolationism. *Pearl Harbor* the film testifies only to the new American cultural isolationism in which even the recent past is beyond the comprehension of Hollywood.

And why worry about Japanese sensitivity? Shortly after Pearl Harbor, the Japanese took Tarawa in the Gilbert Islands and arrested 22 British watchkeepers. The following year, they tied them to trees, beheaded them and burned their bodies in a pit. The Japs fought a filthy war whose depravities they've never been made to confront. It does 'em good to be reminded every so often. And, if Hollywood is too craven even to be jingoistic, then what exactly is it for?

YOUR PROBLEMS SOLVED

Dear Mary . . .

8 September

Q. When holding a glass of champagne at receptions where a speech is being given, I often wonder what one is supposed to do about clapping. It seems to me that you can either playfully pat the hand holding the champagne and thus risk spillage or even breakage, or else simply smile. Neither of these options seems adequate, and since I am usually one of the tallest men in any gathering I feel self-conscious about standing out in the crowd and being apparently unresponsive. What should I do, Mary?
  – A.B., London W8

A. With your free hand unbutton the bottom three buttons on your shirt. You will find that slapping the stomach will produce a very realistic clapping noise at the same time as helping to loosen up the proceedings.

DIARY

James Delingpole

29 September

May I lighten and lower the tone with a filthy, cringe-inducing true story? Tragically, I have been told that the operative word is just too rude for the Diary. So when I insert the euphemism 'molegriped', please try to think very, very dirty. OK, so this friend of my brother was at this druggy party where he didn't know anybody and he found himself in the garden sharing a joint with a group of strangers. For some reason, everyone was taking turns to reveal their sexual preferences. One girl rather shocked everyone by piping up, 'I like being molegriped hard. And when I say hard, I mean, really, really hard.' An hour or two later, this chap was back indoors, still knowing hardly anyone, when across the room he recognised a familiar face. He sidled up to the girl and tried reminding her, as politely as he could, of their earlier encounter. 'This is a bit embarrassing,' he said, 'but the only thing I know about you is that you like being molegriped really, really hard.' The girl blanched and looked back in absolute horror. At which point this friend of my brother realised: it was a different girl.

RESTAURANTS

Deborah Ross

6 October

I phone my older sister and ask her if she would like to go to Harvey Nichols for lunch.

'Oh, goody,' she says. 'I'll just dust off the Christian Lacroix.'

'Don't you mean,' I say, 'the British Lahomestores?'

'Oh, very funny,' she says, pointedly. 'Ha-bloody-ha.'

There is a certain edge to our relationship, which, yes, goes right back to when we were little. Gosh, she was magnificently bossy. It was do this and do that and don't step into my half (which was substantially bigger than my half) of the room or you'll have to be my slave for a week. If I recall rightly, which I'm sure I do, because I have neither the imagination nor the energy for false-memory syndrome, being her slave for a week meant much curtsying, much kneeling and much saying of 'O, worshipful princess, what is your bidding today?' Usually, her bidding involved a great deal of fetching and carrying, any number of Chinese burns, plus listening attentively while she convinced me that I was adopted. How cruel is that? Well, not very, actually, because I rather fancied being adopted. I minded much more when I discovered that I wasn't. Oh, the disappointment, not least because by that time I'd concocted a lot of fantasies, most of which had something to do with door-slamming and shouting, 'What do you care? You are not my real mother/father!' Also, when my real parents traced me, as they most certainly would, they would turn out to own a Cadbury's Creme Egg factory, to which my sister would one day come begging for Creme Eggs. But would I unpadlock the factory gates? No, I would not. 'Be off with you!' I would cry. 'And, anyway, I've got to go and feed my pony now.' What role did our older brother play in all this? Certainly, he wasn't as nasty as us, but he would write 'Up the Gunners' in laundry-pens on our foreheads while we slept at night. Indeed, should you ever have the misfortune of looking through our old family photograph albums, you will note that my sister and I always had hair-dos designed to incorporate very long, thick fringes. (Childhood. It's a good job it happens early on, otherwise who would ever survive it?)

SPECTATOR SPORT

Simon Barnes

10 November

You can say what you like about sport, but it tends to be a bit short on divas. Some of the women and quite a lot of the men do their best, but very few have what it takes. It's not something you can fake. Some can pout, but they can't strut. Some can do the tantrums, but not the bravura performances. Some can do the sulk, but fail to manage the killer smile.

Anna Kournikova has the face that launched 1,000 endorsements, but she can't play tennis terribly well, which takes the edge off her diva potential. She and Martina Hingis once had a fight with flowers, and vases, after an exhibition match: 'You think you are the queen, but I am the queen!' The two of them combined would make one perfect diva, but neither quite makes it on her own.

Marie-José Pérec, the French runner, did a fair diva impression with her tumultuous want-to-be-alone flight from the Sydney Olympic Games before the athletics had even started. But the real diva of track-and-field history was, of course, the great Flo-Jo, who is no longer with us.

We had Katarina Witt in skating, who combined artistry with an expectation (one based on hard experience) that any male she looked at in a particular way would either die or become her slave for ever. She once smiled at me twice in a single press conference; I survived, though it was a damned close-run thing. She has long retired, at least from skating.

But the greatest sporting diva now practising is Svetlana Khorkina, who last weekend won three gold medals at the world gymnastics championships in Ghent. Khorkina is the one who posed for Russian *Playboy* in order to demonstrate that real women do gymnastics. In order to serve the cause of sporting journalism, I inspected the results. Her case was altogether convincing.

Sydney was hell for Khorkina. The vaulting horse was set too low, and so she made a hash of her vault. By the time the error was discovered, she was so distraught – divas are good at distraught – that she had fallen off the bars and lost all hope. Lord, the tears, the agony, the sheer bloody tragedy of it all. 'If I weren't a sportswriter, I'd write 1,000 words about her face,' said my excellent colleague, Paul Hayward of the *Daily Telegraph*.

I found myself writing my own 1,000 on exactly that subject, largely because I hadn't looked at anything else that night. Khorkina, in tragedy or triumph: you're simply not allowed to look away. But, on my final visit to the gymnastics in Sydney, I was determined to be strong and write about somebody else. I was diva'd out.

Khorkina won a gold medal at the last gasp, giving us a million expressions of hope and fear, and finally joy. And then the podium pout.

What else could I do? In Ghent, she gave us an Olympic performance 12 months too late. Ridiculously tall for a gymnast – five-foot five, most of it leg – she must struggle to perform the moves that the prepubescent pixies perform with ease.

But when it comes off! And it all came off in Ghent, her whirling ascent to the beam being the unexpected high point of an incomparable performance to win the all-round gold. Once again, the podium pout. 'I like people to recognise me,' she said. 'From a distance of one kilometre.'

DIARY

Barry Humphries

15/22 December

Since the events of 8 November, my world has changed. At 4.20 p.m. on that day I was late for my Pilates class (Pilates, I believe, is Greek for a large room filled with rather attractive young and mature women in leotards, adopting concupiscent positions to the accompaniment of music by Erik Satie). I parked my car in Bryanston Place at meter 1707. I inserted a £1 coin. Nothing happened. A second £1 coin registered 25 minutes on the meter. I needed at least an hour. A third £1 coin bumped the meter up to 50 minutes. Still not long enough. So I inserted my last pound. The meter remained at 50 minutes. There was no sign of a parking assistant, and if I moved the car I had no more money for a functioning meter. So I ran to my class with an already accelerating heart-rate and my brow lightly mantled with the perspiration of rage. Returning to the car after an hour of gentle exertions I found a penalty notice which must have been affixed to the windscreen at the instant the meter expired. The fine was £80. I drove home and immediately wrote to Alan Clark (!), the head of parking for the City of Westminster, asking him to investigate other complaints against Meter 1707 Bryanston Place and waive the fine. He sent back a standard letter of acknowledgement explaining that there was a backlog of complaints and that I was in a queue. I'm now caught up in an elaborate correspondence with the Department of Planning and Transportation, which consumes hours of time and which is no doubt intended to make me regret ever having challenged the bureaucracy in the first place. I now walk to Pilates.

2002

Dear Mary; Jeremy Clarke; Deborah Ross;
Simon Heffer; Joan Collins; Lloyd Evans;
Michael Heath

YOUR PROBLEMS SOLVED

Dear Mary . . .

5 January

Q. I was given a box of Quality Street last week, a treat I have not experienced – for years – but where is the cracknel?
– G.W., Marlborough, Wiltshire

A. People who have returned to Quality Street following the anxieties of 11 September have found to their chagrin they cannot find cracknel and that a lot of the familiar wrappings hide unfamiliar contents. Why have they dropped cracknel? Its loss represents further subversive and unnecessary changes to the familiar icons of the middle-class world. Soon, no doubt, the military figure with the plumed helmet on the packaging will be substituted with that of a lap-dancer. For the moment, try to be grateful for the survival of the noisette triangle and toffee penny.

LOW LIFE

Jeremy Clarke

26 January

I've moved. On New Year's Day, after yet another row, I drove to the nearest town and rang up all the 'accommodation to let' notices in the newsagent's window. Now I'm renting this 1920s suburban semi from a Buddhist, Chris, and his wife, Edwina. It's a nice gaff, sort of tranquil, with buddhas great and small everywhere you look. And there's a colourful poster in the bathroom that says, 'Happiness, Peace, Joy, Serenity', sinisterly implying that these are all real, desirable, possibly permanent states of mind.

Chris and Edwina are staying in the Transvaal with an Afrikaner farmer. They've paid an agency £1,600 each to teach his labourers' children English. They sent me an email yesterday, saying there are lots of poisonous snakes, though they haven't actually seen one yet.

My boy came to stay at the weekend. He's 12, and a country boy, and was quite unprepared for the buddhas, and for the town itself, whose inhabitants have a reputation for living 'alternative' lifestyles. On our first outing to the high street we saw a middle-aged woman draped in diaphanous material dancing ecstatically outside the chemist's to the amplified song of the sperm whale. We were also confronted by a young man clutching his girlfriend in a kind of headlock. Could we give him 80p for a bag of chips because they were both 'starving', he said. He must have been a drama student because when I gave him a pound he said, 'Beggar that I am, I am poor even in thanks.' Not having been exposed to 'alternative' lifestyles before, my boy was disgusted and slightly disturbed by both beggar and whale woman. To the sound of bongo drumming, we selected and paid for ten sticks of incense from a stall in the market, took them home and cautiously lit one.

After tea we went for another walk around town. We often go for a walk after dark on Saturday night. There were no street lamps or pavements where I lived before, and we walked across fields and through woods to while away the evening. So it was a thrilling novelty for the both of us to walk along hard, brightly lit pavements for once, and to stop and peer through the lighted shop windows. In most of the shops we looked in, 'alternative' seemed to mean 'overpriced crap with spiritual overtones from India'. And why India, we wondered? We had to abandon our enquiry and hurry back, however, as the first spaghetti bolognese I'd ever made was having a disastrous effect on my bowel.

Back on the doorstep of our new home in five minutes, we looked at each other. I thought Mark Anthony was playing a cruel joke on his old dad at first. 'I thought you had the key!' I said, hopping up and down. Neither of us had it. We were locked out. Which didn't matter to me half as much as getting in and using the bathroom, where Happiness, Peace, Joy and Serenity were now more readily attainable than I had previously imagined.

A quick inspection of the windows and front door suggested that we couldn't break into the house without doing less than about £200 worth of damage. As a last resort we climbed over the garage roof and jumped down into the back garden, hoping we'd left the back door open. We hadn't. In fact, given my boy's neurotic, perhaps revealing, obsession with locking doors, it had been a long shot in any case.

With all hope of a quick entry now gone, the deliquescence in my bowel became insupportable. Apologising to my boy, and stumbling over an 18-inch-high earthenware buddhist, I made for a spot on the lawn near the hedge. I read a serious book once, written by an American, called *Crapping in the Woods: a Forgotten Art*. In it, the author suggested that many, if not all, of society's ills stem from the modern and unnatural habit of sitting bolt upright on lavatories. Far better for body and soul to squat in a natural setting, he urged his readers. I was taking him at his word when I was lit up by a beam of light from an enormous torch, or possibly a searchlight, and sharply challenged as to my purpose there in the garden.

It was the man next door. He'd heard us scrambling over the garage roof, he said. Unless we came up with a satisfactory explanation, he was going to call the police. From my squatting position on the lawn I told him that I was the new tenant.

He'd already heard rumours, apparently. 'The chap who writes for *The Spectator*?' he said incredulously. I was, I said. The beam was snapped off.

RESTAURANTS

Deborah Ross

16 March

It's Mother's Day and I've told my partner and my son to take me out for a nice surprise dinner. Or else. Truly, I deserve a treat. I'm a very good mother. I'm not one of those mothers who, say, steams the 'Bonne Maman' label off pots of strawberry jam so that, come the school fair, I can pretend that it's home-made. The fact that I know about this sneaky underhand technique which always wins sighs of admiration from other mothers (how do you have the time?) is neither here nor there or any-where else, and I'll personally take on anyone who suggests otherwise.

Certainly, I adore our son, who sometimes washes but mostly doesn't, and consequently smells rather, but who still manages to brighten our household, mainly because he never turns off any bloody lights. However, he's now nearly ten, which means that he is no longer quite as easy to fool, particularly at Scrabble.

'Mum, what does "qzwyxq" mean?'

'Qzwyxq. Well, dear, "qzwyxq" is what some naughty, slipshod mothers do when they steam the "Bonne Maman" labels off strawberry jam because they don't want to turn up at the school fair with a packet of Jaffa Cakes yet again. Now, it's on the triple, so that's 496 points to me, tra-la, tra-lee!'

Seriously, he does ask some pretty awkward questions these days.

'Mum, what's oral sex?'

'Haven't the faintest.'

'Mum, what's a paedophile?'

'It's a ... kind of potato.'

'Why don't people want to live near them?'

'Um ... because, darling, in the middle of the night, they gather on street corners and then come and suck your blood. The Paedophile is not like the Maris Piper. The Maris Piper is a fine, upstanding potato who will always babysit and feed your cats when you are away. The Desirée, on the other hand, is OK, but not as trustworthy on the babysitting front as she's at the Dubonnet as soon as you go out and probably gets the boyfriend round, too. Now, Duchesse potatoes are all very well, but they have airs and graces and expect you to curtsy ... ' Once I dig a hole, I certainly like to bury myself in it. I may even be quite like the King Edward in this respect.

FOOD

Deborah Ross

27 April

I love everything about my local Waitrose. I love the trolleys that seem to come with Volvo engineering, the wide aisles, the short queues, the staff (who actually look you in the eye), the ratio of 400 aisles of olive oil to none of Chocotastic Pop Tarts, the fact that it's beyond the means of most gaga pensioners, so you don't get stuck at the checkout behind a mad old lady attempting to buy a single lamb chop with milkbottle tops. I love it because there is no club-card scheme, which attracts the wrong sort of people. I love it because I recently heard a wonderful conversation between two trolley boys in the car park. School leavers, both of them, I suspect, but one was new and the other had been at the job a bit longer. The older hand kicked off the conversation.

'What d'you get for your dinners when you worked at Safeway, then?'
'Sausage 'n' onions. Cornish pasty.'
'Nice.'
'What d'you get here then?'
'Fish pie.'
'Eh. Nasty.'
'Nah. S'alright. Once you've picked the fish out.'

DIARY

Simon Heffer

20 July

Even 20 years ago it was quite usual to wear white tie to balls at Cambridge. Going to one at my old college last month with a contemporary and our wives, we were two out of what appeared to be only three men who were, as they used to say, properly dressed. The other was the Master, who for this rare example of someone in charge actually upholding standards deserves to be given his job for life. Black tie is perfectly smart for dinner parties, East End boxing matches and conventions of double-glazing salesmen, but on grand occasions it does look muted. Women make a vastly superior effort by comparison. Also, the original good idea of black tie has suffered from the development of absurd built-in limp wing collars, frilly shirts (for God's sake) and strap-on bow ties of the sort worn by Italian waiters. As with Ruskin's view of the Gothic, black tie has over the years become horribly debased. Perhaps this is why Gordon Brown refuses to wear it, though I fear not. As a statement against the decline in standards – and a judicious protest against our chippy, ill-mannered, middle-class-hating Chancellor – chaps should start wearing white tie again as a matter of routine. Some of you will think this simply snobbism, but, funnily enough, it's not. Nothing cheers us up like manufacturing a sense of occasion, which is why both the Jubilee and Queen Elizabeth's funeral went down so well. You do not need to be royal to do this either. No doubt *Vogue*, or some such publication, can launch this idea with a feature wittily entitled 'White tie is the new black tie'.

I sit, like all right-thinking people, fuming at the wickedness of the ghastly little tosser who decapitated Lady Thatcher's statue; my thoughts turn to the great woman herself. We were told she refused a hereditary peerage on leaving the Commons because of fear that its inheritance by her son might cause controversy. Now, of course, thanks to the constitutional vandalism of this government, inheriting a peerage confers no legislatory privileges at all. I continue to be offended that Lady Thatcher sits in the Lords in the same rank in the peerage as some of the failed local government officers and other deviants ennobled by Mr Blair. She should immediately be created Marchioness of Kesteven, Countess of Grantham and Viscountess Finchley in order to distinguish her further from this rabble. Given the Prime Minister's keen appreciation of self-interest, I'm sure he wouldn't lose too much sleep over the precedent this harmless but uplifting gesture would reset.

DIARY

Joan Collins

17 August

America's South West Airlines are now insisting that their seriously over-weight passengers must pay the price of two tickets when they fly, for which they will be entitled to sit on both seats. I believe all will benefit from this stance. On a recent flight from LA to NY, I was installed beside a lady of – to be kind – gargantuan proportions. Parts of her avoirdupois oozed on to my seat as I scrunched closer to the window in a desperate effort to avoid contact with her flesh, inappropriately clad in purple Lycra bicycle shorts and a sleeveless top. When the flight attendant enquired if we wanted a hot breakfast, I said yes, but my companion growled, 'No, thank you,' vehemently recoiling as if she had been offered a bowlful of asps. I devoured my scrambled eggs, croissants and jam (not bad for early-morning plane food) as my next-door neighbour sniffed disdainfully while delicately quaffing bottled water from a sort of baby's dummy, and, as she glanced at my repast, occasionally emitted a tiny sigh – whether of disapproval or hunger, I couldn't tell. 'Are you sure you wouldn't like anything, ma'am?' the FA enquired solicitously. 'I never eat breakfast,' barked my seatmate. 'Never.' I stuffed my croissant into my mouth and looked away guiltily.

At Kennedy Airport, after a stop off at the powder-room en route to baggage collection, I passed a coffee and doughnut shop, and there was my fat friend sitting at a table with a double-chocolate malt and a card-board box containing four doughnuts in assorted colours, which she was wolfing down as if it were her last supper.

LOW LIFE

Jeremy Clarke

24 August

Nanny is a full-time 'scrubber' as she puts it. She scrubs for a Mrs P and a Mrs R. She's not used to being on holiday. The inactivity is profoundly disturbing to her. She doesn't know what to do with herself. Most of the time she perches on our fixed caravan's concrete step, puffing unhappily on a succession of Superkings, and staring balefully at the passers-by.

Our caravan is at the entrance of the Valley caravan and camping park. Everyone entering or leaving goes right past our door. All day long the campers and caravaners come and go, surfboards and body-boards tucked under their arms. Those going towards the beach, from left to right as we look, are generally more cheerful, their heads held higher, than those coming the other way. Nanny hasn't been to the beach herself yet, though it is less than 100 metres away. She isn't inter-ested in beaches. Messy things, beaches. Too much sand all over the place. She would rather spend the week watching other people come and go to the beach, and pass comment on them, than go there herself. And that's how it's been. Nanny perched on the step, smoking and commenting; me inside the caravan asleep or watching TV; the boys out God knows where.

'Look at 'ee!' says Nanny, over her shoulder, to me. I look out of the door. An Afro-Caribbean man is going by. He is wearing a wet suit. 'Look at 'ee!' says Nanny. 'Black as a badger's tit!' Being a countrywoman, Nanny's similes are usually drawn from Nature. Some I find instructive. The suggestion that badgers' tits are jet-black has, I feel, enriched my imagination. A little later on she draws my attention to a family – mum, dad and a pair of toddlers in turquoise swimsuits. Their skin is extraor-dinarily white. In fact it is actually the colour white. 'Look at they!' she says excitedly. 'White as a dead pig's eye!'

From time to time the boys reappear briefly to demand money or food.

'What's for dinner, Nanny?' they say, or 'What's for tea?' 'Mutton rings,' says Nanny, to both questions.

When not drawn from Nature, her similes are based on familiar items in the workplace. This man trudging back from the beach in the rain had a face like a 'stewed broom'; another's looked like 'a dog's arse with a hat on'. The man with a face like a dog's arse with a hat on was also 'staring like a conger' apparently.

Nanny hasn't been entirely well for years. She's on 'stair-rods' for her asthma and currently taking a course of 'anti-bollocks' for a persistent tummy upset. Her tummy upset is characterised by loose motions, which fly out noisily, she claims, 'like a flock of starlings'. This perhaps goes some way towards explaining her reluctance to leave the concrete step, which she complains of as being ''ard as a dog's 'ead'.

Also occupying her attention this week have been the hourly developments in the case of the missing schoolgirls Holly and Jessica. 'I'd get hold of whoever was responsible and take it all off – the whole lot,' Nanny tells the boys enigmatically. 'But that's uncivilised!' exclaimed my state-indoctrinated son, not yet 12. 'What makes you think we are civilised?' I said. 'I didn't say we are,' said my boy. 'But we can at least try to be.' He had me there. I retired from the debate. 'An eye for an eye is what I say,' growled his Nanny. 'Slice it all off, like trimming a frosty turnip.'

YOUR PROBLEMS SOLVED

Dear Mary . . .

5 October

Q. I am a busy working mother with a number of projects on the go at any one time, and am constantly multitasking. Regarding vital things that I must not forget, I have always written reminder notes to myself on the back of my hand in black felt-tip. The unpleasant truth is that, although this system works efficiently, these days (I am almost 45), the back of my hand is not an area that I wish to draw to other people's attention, the texture of it becoming somewhat crocodilian. What do you suggest, Mary?

– H.R., Devon

A. Why not use the meeting point of your right thigh and kneebone as a scribbling pad? The average woman goes to the lavatory every two hours, a procedure which usually involves gazing at this precise area. In this way, each time you go to the lavatory or even think about going to it, the reminder image will flash into your head.

YOUR PROBLEMS SOLVED

Dear Mary . . .

9 November

Q. My 'partner' and I have a joint income of something over £500,000 a year. While not self-conscious about this, we sometimes worry about whether or not we are 'rich' and accordingly should feel rather guilty. Have you any criterion that can be applied to determine this question?

– Name and address withheld

A. The late Alan Clark and his friend Euan Graham coined the aphorism that 'one is rich only if one has a full complement of indoor domestic staff while one's parents are still alive'. This may be applicable to your predicament.

DIARY

Lloyd Evans

23 November

The most romantic place in London is the Tube. Romantic and frustrating. I fall in love on every journey. Several times, in fact, because each carriage I climb into seems to contain some mysterious goddess sitting a couple of berks along. There she is. My God (this is the kind of thing I find myself thinking), she's the one. Just look at her, beneath the advert for Leeds Castle, sitting demurely in her mac and make-up, engrossed in *Nicholas Nickleby* or the latest Wendy Holden. What a vision. Like an Egyptian queen, perhaps, or some enthroned divinity, a being carved from everlasting substances. (This goes on for several minutes between stops.) Her skin is flawless and supple; her glittering eyes skim the page; her moist lips disclose no secrets; the little doves of her hands clasp the book tenderly. I ache for her in silence (as we scream and rock through the tunnels). The purity and quietness of her attitude, her self-sufficiency and her obliviousness of me all intensify my desire. She's so close to me, this utter stranger, and yet I'm perfectly free to stare at her as if we belonged to each other. She's not a human being. She's an angel. She's a ... no, she's off. (We're pulling into a station.) I can't believe it, she's getting up; she's going. My sudden lust for her, my strenuous adoration, has counted for nothing. She's gone. Behind the doors whoosh shut and, as the train drags itself reluctantly away, I casually swivel my head to get a final glimpse of her before she disappears for ever into the world. A horrible pang runs through me. (Where do these longings come from? Why are they so intense?) And then some other divine slapper sits down in her place and it all starts again. Does anyone else feel like that on the Tube?

Life seems to be avoiding me at the moment. My female friends, meanwhile, are pushing babies out of themselves left, right and centre. When a new birth is announced, I always suggest a name. It's cheaper and more practical than some throwaway trinket, and if you choose wisely you'll stand a chance of being remembered. My current favourites are Herod, Bysshe and Kill Sin. So far the mums have ignored my advice, and I don't really like to ask why. Am I being too outlandish, or hopelessly unadventurous? I gather it's quite usual at kiddies' parties nowadays to meet three-year-olds called things such as Nimrod, Pythagoras, Helabja, Endorphin, Kilimanjaro, Saturn, Habitat and Big Bang.

DIARY

Michael Heath

28 December

This is the first Christmas in recent years that I haven't spent in traction or immobilised by glandular fever. You may imagine that I spend my days drawing and whistling in a carefree manner, but there are tears behind the laughter. Two Christmases ago I was invited to the *Erotic Review* party in a club in London's Soho. I had worked for the magazine doing dodgy drawings at fifty quid a pop, so they owed me a drink. Besides, I was eager to meet the *Erotic* staff who, I felt sure, writhed around all day on their laptops *sans* knickers and headaches. I found the club, walked in and was unable to see anything except a bar, far off in the distance, full of decadent, half-naked women and helpless men being used as sex objects. I leered towards them but found myself in mid-air, having missed the staircase. Then I landed on the dance floor and broke my feet. Not very sexy. I lay there in the dark, thud-thud music banging away in the background. I was panic-stricken. How was I going to get up the missed staircase and out into the street again? I suppose everyone thought I was drunk. I was not. A girl came over: was I all right? 'No, I've broken my feet. Get me some vodka.' After downing two large, anaesthetising vodkas. I stood up and walked out. This was the worst thing I could have done and I spent the rest of the evening in the casualty dept of UCHL. Eight months later. I could walk without crutches. My football-playing days are over, but that's OK as I've never played football.

2003

Boris Johnson; Dear Mary; Beryl Bainbridge;
Minette Marrin; Deborah Ross; Jeremy Clarke;
Charles Moore; Michael Vestey;
Barry Humphries

DIARY

Boris Johnson

4 January

If you are invited to one of these grand Indian weddings, you should jolly well make an effort. I enquired about the dress code, and was told that it would he all right for me to wear something called Kurta Pyjama. So I got the full bollocks. No mucking around. I went to the Delhi equivalent of Harrods, where the Suits-you-Sahib boys kitted me out, at some cost, in a green silk smock, an off-white silk waistcoat, and those funny drainpiped white pyjamas called churidars, not to speak of the agonising Jesus sandals called chaptals. And then there was the turban. Until you have had a turban wrapped around your skull, you do not appreciate what a socking great spinnaker of cloth it is. There's enough to make a bedspread, and when complete it significantly impairs your hearing. The final effect was a mixture of Nehru and Roy Hattersley canvassing in his local gurdwara. As the other guests started to roll up, it dawned on us that most smart young Indian men actually attend weddings in dark suits. They smiled broadly at me, and I beamed back, in a fixed sort of way.

The ceremony took place on a 'farm' outside Delhi, which is actually a kind of gentleman's estate. It is an Eden with waterfalls and lush lawns fringed with mangos, acacias and other strange and stately trees. The breeze whispered through the chains of marigolds that hung from the boughs and adorned the canopy in which we congregated. We all sat cross-legged while a bevy of bearded priests sang and thudded their bongos. I must have dozed off, but awoke in time to throw rose petals at the happy couple, and to receive Sikh communion, a sweet pudding called prashad. This is provided in quite generous helpings, so I was able to stuff it into the face of our youngest, to keep him quiet.

*

From time to time a Welsh-style silver band would launch into a crashing oriental polyphony, and people would dance, or cavort, across the lawn. If you want to look professional while doing Indian dancing, you raise your hands and rotate them as if changing a light bulb. Then you lower them and pretend to rev a motorbike. So it goes (squawk, honk, parp), light bulb, light bulb, motorbike, motorbike, all the while wreathing your features in Gandhiesque serenity.

The only real moment of culture shock, so far, was on the flight out. A couple of the children were in the seat next to me, gouging each other's eyes out, biting, pinching, and so on, and my eyes had closed in reverie. I awoke to find a sweet-faced Chinese air stewardess standing over me in my aisle seat. 'Prease, sir,' said the BA girl. 'Prease come with me. I have found a better seat for you in row 52.' Well, I began to say, wondering whether this was just a beautiful dream; well, that is really very thoughtful of you. It crossed my mind, in my groggy state, that this must be one of the world's favourite airline's popularity-building measures – to send gentle oriental girls, shortly before take-off, to separate fathers from their unruly children. As I unbuckled my belt and rose to go, the rest of the family started to protest. Why was I deserting them? I dunno, I said, but she wants me to move. 'It is the rule,' said the BA girl. 'We have a very strict rule that adult men are not allowed to sit next to young children. There have been incidents,' said the BA girl darkly. I was going to reassure her, and say how much I agreed with the policy, and that as far as I was concerned adult men should at all costs be protected from young children. But one of them gave the game away. 'He's our father!' said someone. 'Oh,' said the stewardess, flummoxed. 'Velly solly.'

YOUR PROBLEMS SOLVED

Dear Mary ...

18 January

Q. My husband and I will be entertaining a member of the royal family to dinner in the near future, and wish him to meet a female friend of ours, as we know that he will appreciate her sense of humour. Thinking ahead, however, we calculate that by the time everyone has been introduced there will be little time for the two in question to get to the point where they might start to have a laugh before we have to sit down. We have not yet sent out invitations, but can predict that we will be unable to seat our friend next to the Prince at dinner. Although she is an 'Hon.', she is bound to be outranked, and precedence will dictate that she be miles away from him at table. We know that he has to leave quite quickly after dinner. How can we get around this, Mary?

  – A.E., Wiltshire

A. You can confound the expectations of your titled friends by rethinking your guest list to ensure that all the other women present hail from ranks below that of 'Hon.', e.g., dental hygienists and mobile pet-groomers. In this way you can conform to protocol and still bring off the result you desire by seating the amusing 'Hon.' on the Prince's right.

DIARY

Beryl Bainbridge

1 February

I was brought up to pay little attention to vegetables, apart from beetroot, which was served every day, and carrots, of which we had two each on a Sunday, on the grounds that they enabled Spitfire pilots to see in the dark. And then last week I arranged to meet a friend in the bar of the Waldorf Hotel, and while waiting ordered a vodka-and-lime, no ice. After some time had passed, a small vase arrived with an enormous stalk of celery stuck in the middle and a radish floating alongside. Up until this moment, I had been feeling fairly gloomy – whether we are content or in a disturbed frame of mind depends, ultimately, upon the kind of thoughts that pervade our consciousness – but after half an hour spent sucking on the celery stem my mood altered, and I found myself humming. My friend having arrived, we crossed the road in the direction of Somerset House, and once there sat in a plastic tent watching the skaters glide and tumble upon the ice rink. A strange thing happened: the faces sweeping by, the outlines of the magnificent buildings, the small stars in the night sky became magnified, as clear as crystal. The radish I still held lay like a rose in my palm. Forget carrots. All one needs is celery.

Camden Town High Street could be mistaken for the set of a gangster movie. Down-and-outs swearing at you as you pass, police cars with sirens wailing speeding towards Kentish Town, bicycles careering along the pavements, large dogs sprawled across their owners outside the back entrance to Marks and Sparks. Last week my grandson became the victim of something called the Lebanese Loop. He had just put his credit card into the hole-in-the-wall outside the NatWest bank and tapped in his numbers, when someone clapped him on the shoulder. He turned round, and a man asked him where such and such a street might be. At that moment another man finished the transaction, grabbed the money but not the card, and they both ran off. The origin of the term hole-in-the-wall is rather interesting. In the nineteenth century the prisons had openings in the outer wall to allow relatives to pass food inside. Wasn't that kind, and ultimately so much cheaper than today's arrangements?

Once a week, more or less, I meet my friend Anselm for breakfast in El Sordido's down the road. It is the most excellent café in the world; their eggs, bacon, fried bread, sausage and tomato – you can have chips if you want, even at eight in the morning – are unbeatable. Many people of great intellect, though not quite the equal of Anselm, can be seen there in the early morning poring over books on philosophy, dictionaries at their elbow. Over the last few years we have seen many regrettable changes in the view from the window. Where once a sweet old lady could be seen doing a wee-wee into a paper bag, there is now a freshly laid pavement, and on the wall of the nearby building a mysterious sign, apparently made out of watercress, spells FARM. As there is not a cow or a hen in sight, nor any explanation, this remains a puzzle. We talk about many things of great profundity, particularly related to the happenings of the previous week. Anselm says that Pythagoras recommends we review each night the doings of the day. So I told him about the Lebanese Loop, and he was very curious and rather animated, until I got to the bit about the money being stolen, at which he seemed to lose interest. Turns out he thought I'd said Lesbian Loop.

LETTERS

1 February

Sir: I did enjoy reading Taki's unusually perceptive notes on the root causes of British thuggery (High Life, 11 January). I had no idea that social problems in the United Kingdom could be attributed largely to some people having dark skin. Actually, my grandmother regularly expresses similar views, but she is in a home where she lives mainly on soup.

Martin Foakes
Hong Kong

DIARY

Minette Marrin

15 February

I often think there is something very unfair and cheating about obituaries, which I read keenly every week. I know it's very aging to be interested in obituaries; I wish I weren't. I still have a schoolboy son at home, so I like to think that youth has not yet quite fled the house, but the truth is that, as time has worn on, obituaries have begun to interest me more than announcements of births and marriages. The end of the story is so very much more fascinating than the beginning, especially with famous people. But the trouble is that obituarists so often seem to get things wrong. Usually they're much too nice and uncritical – *de mortuis nil nisi bonum*. But how absurd. The only sensible time to kick a man is when he's not only down but dead. The obituarists were grovellingly, sickeningly nice about Roy Jenkins and Alan Clark, two of the nastiest men I ever met. It made me furious. Even journalists felt obliged to suck up to them post-mortem with laddish anecdotes and lunchtime reminiscences. Well, as the saying goes, if you haven't got anything nice to say, say it now.

Et in Arcadia ego; I, too, once had lunch with that Roy Jenkins, at a glittering party in a private house. My delight at being placed next to the great man was soon crushed by the experience. He was so insufferably pompous and patronising that if we had been in a restaurant I would have walked out. Our conversation turned to the discrimination against private-school children at some Oxford and Cambridge colleges – now universally acknowledged and even recommended by our government. 'It doesn't happen,' he told me flatly. I told him, politely I think, that I was convinced, both by talking to dons and by many individual accounts, that it did. 'Nonsense,' he said, really rudely. I persisted, whereupon he said, with magisterial disdain, 'You do REALISE I am CHANCELLOR of Oxford University? I know all about it. I can't help it if some of your friends' children didn't get into Oxford; they probably weren't as clever as they thought they were.' Vulgar, condescending ignorance! Later I worked out which character of fiction he reminded me of: it was Lady Catherine de Bourgh.

I wonder what my patron saint Jane Austen would have made of my encounter with Alan Clark. I met him at a political party in a private house not so long ago, for dinner and serious discussion. My motto has always been that any attention is better than none, so I didn't mind, at first, that he started flirting, though, since I was not an admirer, I did not flirt back. His style was certainly distinctive. After the usual overtures, he told me, staring into my face, that my eyes were absolutely dazzling, mesmerising. Then he said he couldn't work out whether that was because my eyes are too close together or whether it was because I have a squint. Despite this handicap, he pressed me more and more persistently to have dinner with him. I refused, very clearly, ever to have dinner or anything else with him. But he meant then and there. To leave the party at once. Apparently he thought saying no is a form of flirting; he pressed and pressed me, literally, as we queued to go into our hosts' dining-room. When at last he came to believe I was impervious to his charms, and would not rush off with him into the night, he turned to me with a peculiarly vicious look. And this is what this self-styled gentleman, this ladies' man, this intellectual, this flower of our civilisation then said: 'Well, fuck you, then. Fuck off. I'm not talking to you any more.' And he didn't, I'm glad to say.

In thinking about death and the dead, I find the tough and truthful approach much more comforting than conventional pleasantries. I particularly loved the lines the artist Lincoln Seligman included on the service sheet at the memorial service of his father, Madron Seligman: 'We are here on earth to do good to others. What the others are here for, I don't know.'

RESTAURANTS

Deborah Ross

22 March

I am writing this at home, on an utterly gorgeous spring day. The air is crisp, the sky is blue, and daffodils and crocuses and hyacinths would, surely, be out in our little back garden if only I'd ever been arsed to plant any. Oh, what a beautiful morning. Indeed, from my window I can see the sun bouncing delightfully off the council estate at the back where, almost nightly, we are treated to an absolutely first-class domestic.

'F*** off.'

'No. You f*** off.'

'No. You f*** off, you c***.'

My young son recently asked what a 'c***' might be. It's a biscuit from Germany, I explained, because, when it comes to these things, I'm a hopeless coward. My son will be off to secondary school shortly, where,

I recently learned, he'll be doing German in his first year. I am already thinking of ways to ban him from the school trip to Berlin in case he asks for one with his *Tasse Tee*.

LOW LIFE

Jeremy Clarke

12 April

At a nearby table, two speechlessly drunk dossers stood up to leave. One of them couldn't do up the zip on his coat. It was cold outside so it was an important issue. Then he stood patiently in front of his mate, like a little boy in front of his mum, while his mate had a go at doing it up for him. His mate couldn't do it up either. The project was abandoned and they set their faces towards the door. Listing heavily to port, the man with the problematic zip veered off at the wrong angle until he came up against a pillar, where he paused, then lit out again on a corrective course towards the door. 'The last time I saw anything walk like that,' said Dave, 'the whole herd had to be destroyed.'

RESTAURANTS

Deborah Ross

3 May

So, off to lunch with Anthony Horowitz, the author whose TV work includes almost everything with 'murder' in it – *Murder Most Horrid*, *Murder In Mind*, *Midsomer Murders* – and whose wonderful bestselling children's books include *Granny*, *Groosham Grange*, and the Alex Rider books, which are sort of James Bond romps and which my own 10-year-old son adores. Indeed, just before the latest Alex Rider book, *Eagle Strike*, was out in the shops, Anthony's publisher sent me a copy, as did Anthony himself, so I thought I'd pass Anthony's copy on to my son's friend Paul, another Alex Rider fiend, whose birthday it was. All well and good, until I picked up my son from Paul's party and asked if Paul had liked his present. 'Yes,' said my son. 'But he wondered why "I'm so looking forward to our lunch, Deborah" was written in it.' Since then, I have not been able to look Paul's mother in the eye, as I think she thinks I'm an old cheapskate, which I would be if I was, but I'm truly not. Listen: last year I bought my partner a bloody great piano for Christmas, while he bought me a plastic nose on which to keep my glasses because I am always losing them. Price difference? Only about £1,200, I would guess. But did I mind? No, it's the giving that counts, or so I told myself once I had stopped crying, which was round about April.

DIARY

Charles Moore

7 June

In his new book *At War with Waugh* – whose publication and the author's 90th birthday we celebrated last week – W. F. Deedes reproduces the *laissez-passer* for his Abyssinian journey of 1935. Addressed 'TO ALL WHOM IT MAY CONCERN', it was given him by his editor, H. A. Gwynne of the *Morning Post*, and states that Gwynne 'shall be obliged for all permissible facilities which may be granted him'. It bears an impressive seal. This explained something for me. When I was a young journalist on the *Daily Telegraph* and setting off for an infinitely less adventurous visit to India in 1982, Bill Deedes called me into his office. 'Here, dear boy, I think you'll find this useful. Your bona fides. The Indians like this sort of thing.' He handed me a 'TO ALL WHOM IT MAY CONCERN' document, bearing the Deedes family seal (with the motto, perfectly unsuitable for a journalist, *Acta non verba*). Sure enough, whenever I produced this talisman, I found that I jumped to the front of interminable Indian railway queues. Gwynne had been editor since 1911 and had reported the Boer war. The great Deedes became a reporter in the year my father was born and was my editor for the first four years of my career. I suppose that document is the nearest thing to an apostolic succession that a journalist can have.

DIARY

Michael Vestey

14 June

I was discussing with a friend this week the problem of remembering the Christian names of people one hasn't seen for some time, and was reminded of a social gaffe I committed some years ago. Bumping into a former flatmate and his wife in a London theatre bar, I struggled to recall her name so that I could introduce her to my then wife. An association began to form in my mind and I heard myself saying, 'And this is Fanny.' The woman stared at me and said, 'Pussy. He calls me Pussy.' 'Ah,' I replied in confusion, 'I knew it was something of the sort,' which, of course, only compounded the offence.

LETTERS

14 June

Sir: Stanley Baldwin was another prime minister who regularly used public transport (Letters, 7 June). Taking the train to his Bewdley constituency one weekend, he was confronted by a fellow passenger who asked, 'Aren't you Baldwin who was at Harrow in '84?'

'Yes,' replied the prime minister.

'I am in engineering myself,' said the passenger. 'Tell me, Baldwin, what are you doing with yourself these days?'

Gordon Rees

Leeds, Yorkshire

YOUR PROBLEMS SOLVED

Dear Mary . . .

2 August

Q. A few days ago I was in a flat belonging to one of my sister's friends, whom I do not know very well. On visiting the bathroom, I discovered a lavatory, no paper, a bidet and a neat pile of clean fluffy towels. Never mind what I actually did; what would have been the proper course of action?
 – Name withheld, London SW8

A. As a female, you were correct to be wary. This situation was less straightforward than it seemed. The first course of action open to you was to use the bidet and a clean fluffy towel, but the result would have been a 'used' towel with no obvious receptacle wherein to dispose of it. What if the person before you, equally embarrassed by the lack of a disposal option, had folded their used towel neatly back into the pile, complete with DNA samples? The second and better course would have been to exit the bathroom and discreetly search for some tissue or the like before re-entering. But if it was already too late, then you should have used the 'lettuce-drying method' on the affected body parts, simply whirling them hula-hoop style until all excess moisture had dissipated.

LOW LIFE

Jeremy Clarke

9 August

First thing Monday morning I was in court. No car tax. When I eventually found the magistrate's court, it was like the *Mary-Celeste*. No defendants hanging round the entrance smoking, no receptionist behind the glass in the foyer, no ushers, no solicitors briefing anxious clients in the corridor at the last moment, no cleaners, nobody.

Hearing muffled voices, I pushed open a heavy door and found myself in Court One. Inside, facing me, were three magistrates, two men and a woman, seated in a row. Below them, sitting at a large table, were a gowned lady prosecutor and a representative from the police in a dark suit. And that was it. No reporter, no solicitors, no witnesses, no other defendants, no stony-faced relatives. Just these magistrates sitting there like the last turkeys in the shop. They looked as glad to see me as I was glad to see anyone at all after coming such a long way.

Right off, I was warmly invited to stand off to one side in front of a solitary chair and introduce myself to the court by confirming my name and address. The magistrates beamed down at me from their elevated position while I did so. All smiles they were. Even the lady prosecutor was fixing me with this radiant grin. The head magistrate, male, nice tan, film-star teeth, tailored jacket, gold cuff links, wished me good morning on behalf of his bench, then he and his colleagues settled back, while the lady prosecutor got the ball rolling by reading out the details of the offence.

If I thought an account of my wrongdoing would send a small cloud across the magistrates' cheerful countenances, I was mistaken. On the contrary, the magistrate on the left wing, whose head, from his neck to the top of his bald pate, was scarlet with high blood pressure, leaned in towards his chief, and, shaking with suppressed laughter, whispered to him what I can only imagine was a very funny story.

He continued to whisper and shake with laughter, with brief intermissions to allow the head magistrate to pay attention when necessary to the case at hand, for as long as I was standing in the witness box. The head magistrate evidently found the story every bit as amusing as the narrator did. He became engrossed by it, returned to it whenever possible and soon he too was shaking with barely suppressed hilarity. My confident guilty plea went completely unacknowledged. When the time came for him to ask me if I had anything to say in my defence, he had real difficulty readjusting his face to more serious matters.

I wanted the thing over and done with as quickly as possible because my car was in the car park next door with no ticket on it and the tax had run out. In any case, I have absolutely no fictive imagination. I couldn't make up a coherent cock-and-bull story if I wanted to. And the truth will out anyway is what I always say. So I kept it brief and stuck with the truth. I told the court that basically I couldn't afford to buy any car tax at the time of the offence because I'd spent all my money on drink.

Even an admission of extreme moral turpitude such as this failed to depress anyone who happened to be listening. The lady prosecutor's encouraging smile, if anything, intensified. And the lady magistrate who was unfortunately too far away from her male colleagues to be party to the joke was clearly a woman of the world because her engaging smile never faltered.

Before passing sentence, the magistrate made a bit of a show of protocol. He turned first to his lady colleague and canvassed her for an opinion, then he went into conference with the scarlet magistrate, who made yet another amusing comment which made them both laugh.

Turning genially to me, he fined me £120, with £45 costs, and ordered me to pay £45 back duty. Then his face lost its cheerfulness for a moment. There was a debt of gratitude outstanding. 'Mr Clarke,' he said, 'I'm going to reduce the fine of £120 to £60 in recognition of the fact that you've turned up – which is more than most people do, I'm afraid. I'd like to thank you, Mr Clarke, very much, for coming.'

I stood down. Four broad smiles lit my way to the door. I gave a stiff little salute as I passed the bench. It wasn't till I got outside that I realised I'd been standing before the majesty of the law with my flies wide open. Black Levi 501 flies. All four silver buttons undone, fabric parted, no underpants.

DIARY

Barry Humphries

29 November

Ballet is an art form I could dispense with. With the exception of *Petrushka*, it's only interesting if it's sexually arousing and then you have to sit in the expensive seats in order to smell the dancers. I once went to a show by the New Zealand Ballet Company; very pretty girls, but all I managed to inhale was Tweed, an awful cologne that antipodean prancers and mincers used to douse themselves with. I prefer burlesque or striptease. The other night in Atlanta I took the Ednaettes – Dame Edna's comely satellites – to the Cheetah Club. These American theatre tours are long and arduous, and I had owed Michelle and Terri a social outing for some time. The Cheetah Club, a famous nightspot, seemed the obvious choice. We were shown to a comfortable, but – did I imagine it? – slightly sticky banquette from which we observed a cavalcade of Brazilian-waxed lubricity. The air was like the syrup from a cigarette stew – liquid dottle – but the show was better than *Swan Lake* by a mile.

In my youth, when I affected long hair in protest against the Australian short back and sides, a barber once said to me, 'You're a ballet dancer, are you, son?' I never understood why the other barber guffawed. In the Australian lingo of that far-off epoch a ballet dancer was a 'poof'. Still is, usually. It was also not uncommon for cars to slow down in the street so that the louts within could call out at any nicely dressed, if hirsute, male pedestrian, 'Where's ya violin?' There must have been a risible European fiddler with a flowing mane buried deep in the Australian racial memory. You never hear it now, but a rare and imaginative homophobic taunt was, in my memory, 'You've lost your lino, mate!' Again, this was not seldom yelled from a car at any man with the languid habit of sauntering hand on hip, as if transporting an invisible roll of linoleum. It's a phrase that I would like to revive. It would have come in useful in Atlanta, Georgia, a very nice city which, in spite of Cheetah's and its clientele, supports the largest population of lino-losers outside Sydney.

2004

Deborah Ross; Jeremy Clarke; Joan Collins;
Bill Bryson; Boris Johnson; Charles Moore;
'The Questing Vole'; Dear Mary; A. N. Wilson;
Simon Heffer; Mary Wakefield

DIARY

Deborah Ross

17 January

Hurrah! At last we get the MP3 player we bought our son for Christmas to work. Four adults, working in shifts, couldn't get it to work on Christmas Day. The same four adults, still working in shifts – very ill-tempered shifts – couldn't get it to work on Boxing Day. The instructions, provided by Hyuri Won Inc., and most loosely translated from the original Korean, were not of much help: 'Pause now you are in shortly, stop.' The internet site we bought it from had shut up shop until well in the New Year. We tried the people at PC World. Utterly useless, predictably enough. We waylaid anyone who had the look of a geek about them. (A well-thumbed copy of *Lord of the Rings* is usually a promising sign.) No joy. In the end, I had to wait for the site to open to be talked through it, which took most of a day, what with uploading and downloading, folders and sub-folders and sub-sub-folders of the sub-sub-sub-folder variety. I was thrilled when I got the first bit of music to play, and charged downstairs when I heard my son come in from school. 'I can work it! I can work it!' 'Great,' he said, 'but the thing is I think I've changed my mind. Can I have a mobile instead?' No, I didn't take it badly. 'What a joker you are,' I said, as I sold him to some passing gypsies. 'Also, your artwork is crap and I only put it on the fridge out of consideration for your feelings,' I added, as I waved him off.

LOW LIFE

Jeremy Clarke

24 January

Me and the boy are regulars at the weekly car auction near us. We never bid for anything. We just like to go and sit and watch the cars coming and going and seeing what they fetch. We don't even comment on an excessively high or low price. We talk only about the soup. We always sit in the same two seats at the back of the steep little indoor grandstand, and we always buy a cup of soup each from the mobile caterer in the car park beforehand. We've tried all the soups on sale, but I've now settled on the chicken and vegetable, and my boy generally has the minestrone with croutons. In addition to our interest in the prices fetched by the cars, and the soup, I also like to observe the second-hand car dealers' faces animated by greed.

Last week we were in our usual seats, sipping our soups, and watching the succession of Vectras, Puntos, Mondeos and Méganes passing from left to right just below us. It was uncomfortably cold as usual in the steel and concrete shed, and as usual I'd burned my tongue on the soup. But for me and my boy last week's car auction was an entirely different experience because for once we had cash on us − £150 to be exact. If we saw something we liked, we were going to make a determined bid for it. We were players, at last, in something higher than the soup stakes.

Because we'd been to the car auction so many times before, we were familiar with the situation and remained calm. Having stake money made us no more talkative than having no stake money. We sat and watched and sipped our soup. Many of those at the car auction, even the regular car dealers, find it difficult to suppress the excitement they feel when downwind of a bargain. They pace up and down drawing furiously on their cigarettes and bidding like demented Nazis. It is rare at that particular auction to see someone calmly bidding from a seat. The people stuck in their seats are invariably people like us who go to the car auction to be entertained. Players stand up or pace up and down.

Well, me and the boy knew we couldn't afford to get carried away with the excitement. We had to weigh up every car that came in before us as dispassionately as we had when we had no intention of bidding. My boy is taciturn, anyway, these days, having reached that peculiar stage of male adolescence when physical growth is phenomenal and the mind is a blank. And drunk or sober I have nothing much to say, anyway. So we were cool. We sat and watched and waited for the moment, if it came, to start bidding.

We were giving the bidding our full attention when a man wearing a postman's winter jacket came and sat next to me. Now and then he made a comment about the car under the hammer. As well as being very friendly, he seemed knowledgeable, too, At one point he said, 'See that Punto? It's been clocked.' 'How do you know?' I said. 'How can you possibly tell from here?' 'I clocked it myself, with a drill,' he said. 'It's my car.' When the bidding reached £500, he became scornful. 'More money than sense, some people,' he said. 'I wouldn't touch a Punto with a bargepole, anyway. Clocked or not.'

We watched the eventual buyer, a shuffling man of about 80, humbly present himself at the auctioneer's desk to arrange payment. The gavel had fallen at £650. It was the most overpriced car of the night so far. 'Mug,' said the postman. Then he stood up and sauntered away.

I refocused my attention on the matter in hand. The bidding for the next car, an M reg. Renault Mégane, started at £100. This was not out of our price range. I nudged my boy and tried to pass quietly what I thought was intestinal wind.

I hadn't exchanged a word with my boy for the last dozen or so cars. Now I turned to him and broke some distressing news. His attention stayed on the Mégane. He took a meditative sip of his minestrone with croutons. 'Whatever you say about the Mégane,' he said, 'they're a lovely shape.'

I limped down through the punters crowding around the Mégane and into the lavatory. The auctioneer's frenetic nasal voice was coming out of a loudspeaker attached to the wall. I went into a cubicle to assess the damage. It was more extensive than I feared. My Calvin Kleins had to be abandoned. When I regained my seat, my boy crossly informed me that the Mégane had fetched £140 and we'd missed what he reckoned was easily the bargain of the month.

DIARY

Joan Collins

28 February

Travelling in the United States is becoming more and more tedious, particularly the endless and intrusive security procedures. I'm often unlucky enough to be picked out for those euphemistically titled 'special searches' (due to my obvious resemblance to Mr bin Laden, no doubt) and I try to endure them with stoic indifference as I stand there, coatless, shoeless, hatless and sunglass-less, arms akimbo rather like a scarecrow while the officer wearing the grim, sadistic expression of an Alcatraz security guard runs what looks very much like a cattle prod far too close for comfort to one's private parts. It is not what I would term a good look, particularly if some sly soul who's just gone through the procedure sneakily takes a couple of snaps on his cell phone, which he'll invariably email to his mates. Nevertheless, refusing to do a Diana Ross, I close my eyes and think of England while the contents of every piece of carry-on are examined minutely. At one airport in the States recently, an amiable searcher, having examined the contents of my jewellery case in detail, remarked pleasantly, if a bit too loudly, 'You got some nice stuff there!' While his partner nodded in agreement, I yelped, 'It's all fake!' 'Looks good to me!' his partner said. I spent the rest of the flight imagining thieves under every seat.

LOW LIFE

Jeremy Clarke

28 February

We buried Uncle Jack in the family plot in the City of London cemetery, Manor Park, east London. He joined his parents, William and Constance, and his grandmother, Rachael, who died in 1916 aged 78. There wasn't much of a turnout to see the old bachelor off, I'm afraid. Congregated on the Astroturf around the hole were me (£10,000), my boy (£500), my mother (£15,000), two of Uncle Jack's nephews (£30,000 apiece), and an elderly female neighbour who used to take him in a hot lunch now and then (nothing at all). The vicar, who must have been frozen with only his billowing cassock between him and the Arctic wind, kept it short. The speed at which he dispensed with the committal and then the Lord's Prayer raised the interesting possibility that in a previous life he was a horse-racing commentator. The lack of a respectful pause between his final 'Amen' and the first mourner legging it unceremoniously for the car, however, was not his fault.

Afterwards we gathered around two tables in a nearby pub. One of Uncle Jack's nephews was Uncle Frank, whom none of us had seen since he'd been ostracised by the family for reading the *Daily Mirror* at his mother's deathbed. Neither had anyone yet met the young woman Uncle Frank had bought on the internet recently. We'd heard rumours, but disbelieved them. 'None of you have met Tanya, my Russian wife, have you?' he said, indicating the stunningly beautiful young woman standing beside him. That someone as young and attractive and apparently sane should leave Mother Russia to go to live with an aged reptile like Uncle Frank in a flat in Ilford was surprising. We goggled openly at her, while she looked humbly down at her glass. Even Uncle Frank looked at her as if he couldn't believe his luck. Someone had to say something, so my mother said, 'Do you like England, Tanya?' 'She likes my money, don't you, dear?' said Uncle Frank, patting the back of her head.

Although Uncle Frank has been excommunicated, it still behoved us to welcome his new young wife into the family, and to offer her our sympathy should she be aware of the enormity of her mistake. It wasn't yet clear, however, whether she could understand or speak English. 'So do you speak Russian, Frank?' I asked him. 'So far,' said Uncle Frank, 'I only know the Russian for "Get dinner pronto, otherwise punch up throat."'

This was too much for Uncle Jack's elderly female neighbour, who was a go–go dancer during the war, and who hadn't met Uncle Frank before. 'What sort of a pig are you?' she said. I felt sorry for this lady because she'd been cultivating Uncle Jack with hot lunches for years, thinking he had no one else to leave his money to. So she was rather gutted when, with the end in sight, an obscure branch of the family (us) turned up, sold his house, and whisked the golden goose off to the West Country.

For a while she bombarded Uncle Jack with letters, which I read out to him, reminding him of the various services she had performed for him over the years, and offering suggestions as to how he might recompense her. These letters were a great puzzlement to him because he'd forgotten who she was. Then she came to visit him. She stayed with us for a week and spent every day on the nudist beach at the foot of the cliffs. One day I allowed her to take my boy and his half-brother down there with her for an afternoon. Uncle Jack's neighbour is far from comely, and when they came back my boy and his half-brother were unusually quiet. To this day neither of them will speak about it and my boy adroitly changes the subject.

Uncle Jack's other nephew (£30,000) had flown in from the Algarve. He avoids England nowadays, he says, because he hates everything about it. Everything, that is, except the beer. English beer was the only thing he's missed in the 20 years that he's been living in Portugal. It was a pity, then, that the second pint of bitter he'd ordered was flat. (The rest of us were drinking lager.) Not one to take flat beer lying down, Victor marched back to the bar and presented the offending pint to the barman. 'I've come all the way from Portugal for this pint of ale and it's flat,' he said. The barman held the pint up to the light and squinted at it judiciously. 'Nah, mate, it ain't flat,' said the barman, handing it back. 'It's your rotten marf.'

DIARY

Bill Bryson

6 March

June. My first day back in Britain after eight years in America and I couldn't be happier. The sun is shining and I have a large cheque in my pocket with which to conclude the purchase of a nice house in Norfolk. Things could not be better. Setting off from Gloucester Road Underground station, I join a throng waiting for a Circle Line train that never comes. Silently we wait and wait – for ten minutes, then 15 – but nothing happens. 'I remember when trains used to go by here,' I remark brightly after a time to the man beside me. By chance he is a fellow American, but new to the country, and possibly to humour, and doesn't realise I'm joking. 'Are you saying there are no trains here?' he asks in alarm.

'Well, no, because then there wouldn't be people here, would there? I mean, we wouldn't all be standing here if there were no trains.'

'But we are standing here and there are no trains.'

This is not an easy point to answer. A voice comes over the Tannoy apologising for the delay, which it says is due to a shortage of rolling stock. 'You see, there are trains,' I explain to my new friend. 'They've just ... mislaid them.'

'This sure is a screwy country,' he says. 'Yes, it is,' I reply happily.

October. The first crack in my perennial equanimity appears. After discovering to our horror that we are the last people in England not to own a retro-look Roberts radio, we hasten to John Lewis in Norwich. Roberts radios, as you will know, come in every colour there is. Only five are on display at John Lewis, but a little sign says that all the others are available. 'We'd like a Roberts radio in this rather nice claret colour,' I say to the young man.

'We don't stock that one,' he answers, without looking up.

'The sign says you stock all of them.'

'Yes, but this is a smaller branch, so we don't stock everything.'

'Then why, pray, put out a sign that says you do?'

Mrs Bryson, recognising certain danger signals, is tugging me towards the lifts and fresh air, but I prevail upon him to take the little sign away.

'You're just provoking people and not all of them will be as constitutionally genial as I am,' I explain. Reluctantly, he removes the sign and puts it in a drawer. An hour later when we return to buy a radio (cobalt blue) the sign, I notice, is back.

November. An important cultural milestone has passed. It is now a million days since ITV has shown a television programme that anyone not on medication would wish to watch. We are now beginning to adjust to the idea that it is not necessary to search channels numbered higher than 2 on most nights, or higher than 1 when Jim Davidson is on BBC2. But we are still very happy. We spend a lot of time listening to our Roberts radio.

December. The Home Office orders my American daughter-in-law to leave the country. She arrived as a visitor with her husband, my son, and then applied to stay on. This, it turns out, is illegal – which is interesting because that is precisely what I did in June and they made me a commissioner for English Heritage. Anyway, although she is of impeccable character and properly married and takes up hardly any room, she is ordered to go back to Chicago until she can prove that she would like to live with her husband, which of course is what she was doing when they told her to leave. I am told that this new hard line on immigration is the fault of the *Daily Mail*. I don't really understand why, but I add the *Daily Mail* to the list of things I don't particularly like at the moment – the *Daily* and *Sunday Telegraph*, fly-tipping, Thomas Cook holidays, Microsoft (of course), people who send emails that ask for a receipt, the dollar exchange rate and George Bush's daughters. I do not, however, add the Home Office to my list, because they have the power to send me away at any time and I really wouldn't want that. So let me say here that the Home Office is wonderful. And it really is nice to be back.

LOW LIFE

Jeremy Clarke

3 April

Both of our upright vacuum cleaners broke down last week. I found a repair shop in *Yellow Pages* and took them along, and who should be behind the counter but Barry, my karate sensei. As well as being a friend, as my karate sensei Barry is also a sort of informal spiritual mentor. But I haven't attended his dojo for over a year, nor have I bothered to contact him. So my own pleasure at meeting him again was tinged with guilt.

I bowed and handed over the vacuum cleaners. We swapped news. It's been a bad year for Barry. He's been convicted of drink driving – he only had one pint of lager – and banned for a year. Then he had an emergency of some kind connected with his repair work, took a chance, got caught, and was given an extra six-month ban for driving while disqualified. He was also sentenced to 150 hours of community service on Dartmoor. On top of that, the day before he had to go to court his mum died.

Worst of all, his karate club has all but folded. He'd employed a 7th dan black belt to teach the senior grades, but this 7th dan's heavy-duty, X-certificate style of karate had frightened everybody away. Some nights Barry would turn up for training, he said, and he'd be the only one there. The only glad note in his *annus horribilis* was that his wife had run off with a brown belt. 'Peace at last,' said Barry. 'The only woman I've ever known who could put her lipstick on and shout at me at the same time.'

He asked me how I was keeping fit. 'Yoga, Barry,' I said. 'I've learned more about my body in a year of practising yoga,' I told him, 'than I have in ten years of kicking and punching the air in your poxy karate club.' Barry said he could well believe it. The crumpet was probably better as well, he said. I told him it was, and why, therefore, didn't he come and check it out one evening?

Barry has been teaching karate for 30 years. He is unusually short, and a kinder, more conscientious, more violent man you couldn't hope to meet. Of all the targets presented by a human opponent, in the first instance Barry generally goes for the throat. 'Because I'm small, see? It's always there, right in front of me.' But he didn't sneer at my invitation to try out a gentle activity whose ultimate goal is the merging of the individual consciousness with the universal. Going on what he'd heard, he said, it might even speed his recovery from a dislocated shoulder. So on Monday, Barry, puncher of throats, came to yoga.

He was late arriving and the class was full. The only available space was right in front of the teacher. Nicole is tall, slender (I've seen more fat on a butcher's pencil), graceful as a swan, and supremely 'fit' in both the traditional and the modern slang sense of the word. Barry, short, squat and his love of violence written all over his face, eyed her warily through eyeballs directly in line with, and about 18 inches from, Nicole's chest. Then away we went, stretching this way and that, trying to remember to keep what Nicole calls our 'tail bones' tucked in.

I tried not to look at Barry as one tries not to look at the results of a serious car accident. But one couldn't help noticing that a lifetime of shotokan karate had in no way prepared Barry for the one-legged 'tree' pose, for example. To begin with it looked as though his tree was going to topple over forwards. Then it was even money for it to fall over backwards. When it finally did go, it took everyone by surprise by crashing down sideways and knocking down almost an entire row of other trees in domino fashion.

Nor had all that kicking and punching prepared him for something as relatively simple as the triangle pose. For Barry to get anywhere near the required effect, Nicole had to straddle him and lever his shoulder around using her lovely knee as a pivot. His anguished cries were horrible to listen to.

'A-ha!' cried Nicole. 'Was that a click? Oh-oh, there it goes again!'

We finished up, as usual, lying in the corpse pose. After an hour and a half of gentle yoga, this was a pose at which Barry excelled. He lay there in a pool of his own sweat as if dead. And as usual Nicole turned out the lights and sang to us corpses, in Sanskrit, to the accompaniment of a sitar. I half opened an eye and saw her leaning over Barry and singing softly in his ear.

'You set me up you bastard,' was all he kept saying in the pub afterwards.

DIARY

Boris Johnson

17 April

It was our last day in Courchevel, and everyone was having a snowball fight by the lifts at 1850, when my friend Charlotte said in urgent tones, 'You know you've been looking for Posh Spice?' Too damn right I had. Le tout Courchevel had been hunting the maritally troubled superstar, who was rumoured to be somewhere on the slopes patching things up with 'the most famous Englishman since Nelson' (Rees-Mogg). One wife of a stupendously rich Goldman Sachs banker had pursued her so fast down Pralong, a blue run, that she had beaned herself with her own ski and needed four stitches. 'Well, don't look now,' said Charlotte, 'but she's standing about six feet away over my left shoulder.' I goggled and, by Jesus, there she was.

With the exception of Bill Clinton, all the celebrities I have met have turned out to be smaller than expected, but Victoria Beckham is minute. She was standing in a circle of gofers and parents and children, and sort of glaring at the world. Her eyes were invisible behind enormous Dior shades, but her lips were thrust out in her trademark snarl, like some rainforest chief. She was wearing a furry waistcoat and odd, low-slung baggy trousers, but the most interesting thing was her bottom. It was either the top of her bottom or the bottom of her back. It was plainly visible, and appeared to be tattooed with some inscription or device. I scrambled after her up the stairs to the ski lift, in an undignified attempt to read the message. What was it? 'Open other end'? 'If you can read this, you are too close'? It turned out to be four stars, signifying, apparently, the birth of her two children. One of these, Brooklyn or possibly Bronx, said loudly, 'I want to go home.'

All the women in our party said how stunning she looked, how those hair extensions, ripped from the heads of impoverished Ukrainian girls, were worth every penny of the £30,000 she paid for them. I must say, at the risk of seeming ungallant, that she was unquestionably beautiful but also a bit on the spotty side. Apparently these spots are never revealed to the public because she has some kind of deal with Jason Fraser, her favourite paparazzo. Wouldn't it be nice if famous acne-sufferers, such as Posh and Cameron Diaz, were more upfront about their affliction? Should they not agree to take part in an Acne Pride Week, and help to relieve the agonies of self-doubt endured by millions of teenage girls and boys?

THE SPECTATOR'S NOTES
Charles Moore
29 May

Tales from the Church of England. One bishop, known for the ambiguity of his sexuality, went to his doctor to complain of piles. 'It hurts near the entrance,' he told the medic. 'That's a curious way to put it,' said the doctor. 'Most people would call it the exit.' This story, by the way, is told by the bishop himself.

LIFE AND LETTERS
'The Questing Vole'
29 May

Earnestly interviewed for *Waterstone's Books Quarterly*, Philip Pullman shows pragmatism. 'As a former teacher, what responsibility do you feel to teenagers and other readers of your books?' he's asked. 'What do you want a teenage readership to think and feel after reading *His Dark Materials*?' Thus Pullman: 'What I want people to feel most fervently after reading one of my books is: "I must go out at once and buy his next one."'

YOUR PROBLEMS SOLVED

Dear Mary . . .

29 May

Q. I am very short of money but do not have much time available in which to work. Have you any tips, Mary, as to how one can generate a bit of pocket money without going to too much trouble?

– A.S., London SW8

A. Why not hire a commissionaire's uniform and stand around outside Harrods? Another of Dear Mary's correspondents, who lives next door to the emporium, reports that while idling some time away outside it the other day, waiting for a friend, he had a £50 note pressed into his hand by a Middle Eastern customer of the store who assumed from his appearance that he enjoyed flunkey status.

DIARY

A. N. Wilson

5 June

I was once naive enough to ask the late Duke of Devonshire why he liked Eastbourne, and he replied with a self-deprecating shrug that one of the things he liked was that he owned it.

DIARY

Simon Heffer

4 September

My wife has only been taken sailing twice in her life, and on both occasions the boat has capsized. The second of these incidents occurred last week in Brittany. Fortunately, no harm was done. However, a public-spirited German happened to be on the quay about 30 yards away when the boat my wife was in turned over, and he proceeded to jump in to help rescue the victims. As they swam to shore, the party noted that the German had insisted on taking every item of clothing off before jumping in. An Englishman would certainly have retained his underpants (and probably his socks), and so, I suspect, would all but the most exhibitionist Frenchman. Our brave German landed a long way from his clothes, and proceeded to stroll serenely back to them, stark naked, along a crowded quay without batting the proverbial eyelid. I am unfamiliar with Teutonic customs, but am reliably told that at the slightest provocation the Germans will take all their clothes off even in the most surprising places. I am sure they are not a nation of perverts and flashers. I prefer to think that their mania for public exposure is yet another way they have found of atoning for the regrettable events of 1933–45.

THE SPECTATOR'S NOTES

Charles Moore

16 October

Twenty-five years ago this week, I joined Fleet Street. And it actually was Fleet Street, no. 135, the offices of the *Daily Telegraph*, with its frieze of naked Mercuries rushing, presumably on expenses, to the four corners of the earth. I had seen Colin Welch, the paper's deputy editor.

He was friendly but held out no immediate hope of a job. Having only £14 remaining in the bank, I was desperate. Then I got a call from 'Peterborough', the diary column of the paper. Would I go and meet its editor, Mike Green, at 11.30? The Tube, which, contrary to popular belief, was much worse then than now, broke down on the way and I arrived, sweating and half an hour late, to be told that Mr Green was already in the pub. I hurried round and he asked me, without preliminaries, to start next week. The salary, he said casually, was £8,000, roughly double my best hopes. What was journalism like then, and how has it changed?

The pub. Mike Green was in the King and Keys, just down the street from the paper. The place was full of men and smoke. Beer often ran over every available surface. The staff of the *Telegraph* were very, very drunk. They would start drinking at about 11.30, stop at about 3, and then resume from 5 (pubs closed in the afternoons in those days). In my first weeks, a messenger 'boy' (he was over 60) got drunk and fell down the stairwell of the paper's offices to his death. No one thought of making the stairwell safer. Nick Garland, the cartoonist then as now, remembers going after lunch into an office which contained three journalists. All were asleep on their typewriters and all had expenses forms in them. Cheating on expenses was a recognised means of making up what were considered inadequate salaries. There was one leader writer, charming when sober, who became dementedly cruel when drunk. He sometimes drank with a man, unhappily called Armstrong, who had no hands. Once he turned to Armstrong and said, 'You know what you ought to do? You ought to go home and cut your ****ing throat, but of course you can't.' Nowadays the cruelty is one of corporate euphemisms about 'letting you go'. Then, it was a democracy of despair, the cruelty of people who mostly felt failures, made worse by drink and ...

Trade unions. It is impossible to exaggerate the greed and malice of the unions in Fleet Street at that time. Demarcations meant that if, after asking for a new lightbulb for six months, you finally installed it yourself, there might be a strike. The print unions controlled the printing floor, and managers could not go there without permission. The printers stopped the paper without warning, sometimes because they objected to something it was saying. They were clever men who often ran other businesses with the money they looted from us. Once, when I was a features sub, I went down to the 'stone' with a well-brought-up, left-wing fellow sub. 'Will I see you at the Greenwich Labour party meeting, Arthur?' she said to the head printer. 'Course you ****ing won't. I'm a ****ing capitalist.'

The journalism. The *Telegraph* was magnificent as a news-digesting machine. It crammed in enormous amounts of information, averaging about 14 stories on the front, rather than the three or four of today. On page three it related court reports of murders and sex crimes with prim gusto. Everything was done crisply, unshowily, permitting no ego on the part of the journalists. You never, ever wrote about 'media' (then a new word). But the trouble was that almost everything in the paper, apart from sport, was news. Features meant half a page about knitting patterns. There were no columnists at all, apart from Peter Simple. Arts were poorly illustrated and obituaries were tiny. The only difference between Saturday and any other day was that the leader page article used to be about flowers or historic houses rather than politics. The list for the leader page article was agreed weekly and would not reflect the news, so a piece by a Tory backbencher about pension reform might appear the morning after the Argentine invasion of the Falklands. The only news recognised as such was 'hard'. Thus a train crash in Bangalore would always trump, say, the fact that Jean Paul Sartre was no longer a fashionable thinker. The *Telegraph* told you very little about culture, love and marriage, health, death (unless violent), food, property, schools, soft furnishings, travel or ideas. It had great integrity, but it was narrow. On Peterborough, we wrote a lot about regimental reunions, everything typed with six carbons. One day, Lord Camrose, the proprietor's charming but drunken brother, rang us. Why had we done nothing about the 40th anniversary of the Free French? I apologised. After putting the phone down, I found that we had, about three days before, but neither I nor Lord Camrose had noticed it.

The people. At the apex stood the proprietor, Lord Hartwell. He was very shy and had two butlers upstairs but drove himself to the office in a Mini.

His wife was a great political plotter and hostess, and very demanding. The paper, I was told, had to appoint an airports correspondent so that there was someone to meet her at Heathrow. Lord Hartwell was roughly 70, and so were the managing editor, a man called Peter Eastwood, who controlled the news operation with his terrifyingly quiet voice, and the editor himself, W. F. Deedes. People kept saying that the dear old chap would have to retire soon. Twenty-five years on, Bill works for the paper every day and seems mentally even sharper now than he did then. There were several other old men. If you enquired what they did, you were told, 'Oh, he was one of the Few, you know.' There were hardly any women journalists and those there were tended to be given 'female' tasks like collating the weekly 'shopping basket'. The leader writers' department was the oddest. Jock Bruce-Gardyne was the Boris Johnson of his day in that he was an MP and a journalist and travelled between the two jobs on a bicycle. He used to sleep through leader conferences. T. E. 'Peter' Utley, the blind and sage guardian of the paper's soul, chainsmoked and, if he possibly could, gracefully passed the task of writing the leader to others. A very old man who had known Hitler well in the 1930s used to warn every day about the Soviet menace. Roderick Junor, son of the famed Sir John, wore a steel-reinforced bowler hat because he feared attack. I loved it all, especially the feeling that we were in a tradition and place continuous with Dr Johnson. But it must have been a sad time for any except the very young, because nothing worked. Mrs Thatcher changed all that.

DIARY

Mary Wakefield

6 November

On the Alitalia flight home, via Milan, I discovered an important difference between the English and Italians. I was having my usual snigger over the 'refreshing towelette' when I saw the Italian translation '*fazzoletto rinfrescante*' written on the other side of the packet. 'Is this a ridiculous phrase in Italian like it is in English?' I asked a nice air steward with a precision goatee. 'No. It is normal,' he said. 'It is an everyday word. Is it not in English?' No, I said. 'So I should not go into a London pub and ask for a refreshing towelette?' he said. Probably not. He looked confused. 'But what do English people ask for if they need a small wet wipe for their hands?' I turned to Angus for help. He was doing what British people do by instinct when confronted with a refreshing towelette or a hot flannel in a Chinese restaurant – attempting to have a bath in it. Having washed his face and scrubbed the back of his neck, I could see him contemplating an attack on his armpits. We looked at him in silence. Somehow, it seemed to answer the question.

THE SPECTATOR'S NOTES

Charles Moore

11 December

Back to class. When I did *Any Questions?* the other day in Yorkshire, I realised with a shock that it was 20 years since my first appearance. It remains a friendly programme to take part in, not least because it normally takes place in a small provincial town with an audience of people who actually want to listen. My first outing, back in 1984, was at Uppingham, the public school. At the dinner beforehand, my fellow panellist Esther Rantzen asked me if I had been to Eton and what it was like. She wanted to know because she had put her son down for it. I said I thought it was a good school, and she seemed enthusiastic. On air, there was a question from the floor about boarding schools. Oh, said Esther, she wouldn't have any truck with them: she didn't believe in 'delegated parenthood'. I was only 27 at the time, nervous and inhibited by the vestiges of the courtesy which my education had taught me, so I did no more than gaze open-mouthed (not an effective tactic on radio). Today, I hope, my Fleet Street education would triumph, and I would shop her.

YOUR (CELEBRITY) PROBLEMS SOLVED

Dear Mary . . .

18/25 December

From John Humphrys:

Q. In my line of work I often have to talk to politicians. Some of them are very unpleasant to me and it can be most hurtful. I am rather a timid person who dislikes confrontation. How should one deal with this?

A. Please explain these problems to your local GP who, although the waiting lists may be long, can probably get you on to an assertiveness training course.

2005

Jeremy Paxman; Dear Mary; Sam Leith;
Jeremy Clarke; Leanda de Lisle; Nigel Farndale;
Marcus Berkmann; Simon Heffer; Barry Humphries

DIARY

Jeremy Paxman

8 January

As it happens, I had a bit of time on my hands over the holidays, since being dropped from the New Year edition of *Woman's Hour*. One of their producers emailed a few weeks ago; the suggestion was to have something called *Man's Hour*. Great idea, I said, and thought of how one could be true to the spirit of the show. Well, obviously, one should have a cookery spot: I thought something on how to brew your own beer sounded promising. And something about men's bits, probably on the horrors of circumcision. There was great potential. For a start, there are the jobs we're all expected to be able to do just because we're men. Across the land over the Christmas holidays we were handed the carving knife and told to get on with slicing the turkey. By what mysterious, osmotic process are we supposed to have learned how to do this? Being a beast which looks as if it was invented by Edward Lear, the turkey is actually easy enough. But how on earth are we supposed to know how to deal with a shoulder of lamb? No one admits the apprehension which overcomes men on these occasions. Personally, I can't even be confident of sharpening the knife properly.

It was clearly a productive seam. It's time someone tackled the stomach-churning anxiety of being pointed at a car and told to get it started, or the frisson which passes through you when you've rewired an electrical appliance secure in the common sense conviction that brown is the colour of the earth wire. (It is not – *Spectator* Health and Safety rep.) But my role in *Man's Hour* came to grief on the question of circumcision. How often have listeners sat through similar items about female genital mutilation, including one in which Jenni Murray declared in supremacist tones that the clitoris has twice as many nerve endings as the penis? I do not suggest – mainly because I don't know – that there is any equivalence. That was what we wanted to find out. The producer began beavering away and discovered an organisation called 'Reclaim the Foreskin', which evangelises for the little bit of maleness that so often (although less and less frequently, apparently) gets discarded soon after birth. There was even a doctor who was happy to explain his technique for regrowing the missing bit. All was going swimmingly until the editorial hierarchy got to hear about plans to discuss the foreskin. While, in the usual way, protesting their liberal credentials, they were worried about making it 'relevant and interesting to the audience'. I have been around the BBC long enough to know what this means, and that was the end of my role on *Man's Hour*. The antediluvian assumption behind *Woman's Hour* is that all the other programmes on the radio are designed by and for men. I don't think so.

YOUR PROBLEMS SOLVED

Dear Mary . . .

22 January

Q. I am shortly to attend a fancy dress party. Following the furore of Prince Harry's choice of fancy dress outfit and his SS armband, I would like to seek your advice as to whether my own proposed choice of costume could possibly give any offence. I am planning to go as Sir Edward Heath.
– A.T., Dorset

A. You have chosen well. In spite of his somewhat exaggerated Europhilia, Sir Edward is remembered as a former prime minister with wide-ranging interests in classical music and sailing. I guarantee you will cause no offence with this choice.

BOOKS

Sam Leith

12 March

The Insider: The Private Diaries of a Scandalous Decade
by Piers Morgan
(Ebury Press, £17.99, pp. 512)

Early on in Piers Morgan's memoir of his career as a tabloid editor, there is a very funny incident. It is a Saturday in 1994 and Morgan, then editor of the *News of the World*, knows that the *Sunday Times*, his broadsheet stablemate, has bought the serialisation rights to Jonathan Dimbleby's book about Prince Charles. Its editor, John Witherow, declines to tip Piers off about what's in the book. So Piers decides to get one over on his snooty rival.

He gets his colleague Rebekah Wade to sneak into the *Sunday Times*'s offices dressed as a cleaner. She hides in the loo for two hours waiting for the presses to roll, then jumps out, snaffles one of the first copies to be printed, and legs it back to the *NoW*. 'I had a copy of the *Sunday Times* before Witherow did, and it was sensational stuff.' Morgan gets his staff to 'crash all the text straight into the paper'. 'Theft isn't journalism, Morgan – you bastard!' Witherow shrieks.

Zoom forward to the end of the book, and Morgan, now editor of the *Mirror*, is having a drink with Wade, now editor of the *Sun*, on the eve of the publication of the Hutton report. He becomes aware that the document she has face down in front of her is a leaked copy of the report, and that the *Sun* is about to scoop him by publishing. 'All I had to do was get my hands on it, run out of the restaurant and file it to my newsdesk, and we would just about catch the first edition.' When Wade's attention lapses, he makes a grab for it. She's just quick enough to see him coming, gets the other end, and the two newspaper titans are tugging a sheaf of A4 back and forth across a restaurant table.

"'Give me that," she said firmly. "Bollocks," I shouted back. "You've nicked it, anyway, so why can't I?'" Wade wins the tug of war and spends the rest of the evening 'smirking' at our hero.

Nothing much changes across a career, does it? Of such stories – funny as hell and as morally discriminating as a rutting polecat – is the best of this extremely enjoyable book made.

Like the BBC's Gavin Hewitt, Piers Morgan apparently takes the view that there should be a statute of limitations on private or 'off the record' conversations. You honour confidences until you get a big enough book deal. He addresses these concerns head on. 'As for those who will inevitably squeal that I have breached confidences,' he writes, 'I would respond that I have not.' Well, that's all right then.

You need to know what you're getting. This is a memoir presented as if it were contemporaneous diaries, so it will be little use historically. Private conversations are imaginatively reconstructed – as betrayed in some very weird dialogue. Many of Morgan's judgements and even predictions in the text, we have to assume, have been made with hindsight. It works, rather, at the level of gossip.

Even the gossip is partial. Absent from index and text alike, for example, is Marina Hyde, the younger journalist with whom Morgan is widely believed to have had an affair (I know Marina a little, and she has always resolutely denied it to me; I don't call her a liar) and whose firing from the *Sun* is an important part of the background to Morgan's feud with David Yelland. She appears only in the acknowledgements, by first name: 'Marina, my best friend ... unpaid but razor-sharp proof reader'. Did she help with the text? She's a very good writer and *The Insider* is, intermittently, better written than Morgan's column in the *Standard*. At one point, Morgan writes, 'My computer messages amused.' That fey, intransitive use of the verb 'to amuse' is a Hyde hallmark both in conversation and in print.

But I digress. In book reviewing, as in Morgan's beloved football, the theory is that you play the ball, not the man. But here, the ball is the man.

Morgan is occasionally compared to *The Office*'s David Brent (scholars of the programme will identify Kelvin McKenzie as Morgan's 'Finchy').

There is a certain Brentishness in Morgan's sense of humour. He constantly repeats, very pleased with his wit, some 'cheeky' crass remark he has made to a celebrity, or a boorish practical joke he has played. And, as you do when watching Brent, you wince along with the victims. Only joking, mate! When Morgan affects to laugh at himself, it's through tightly clenched teeth. He's touchy. As with Brent, you get the sense of real nastiness underneath.

Morgan affects not to know the name, for example, of 'some little runt from *Sunday Business*' who had the cheek to doorstep him over his dodgy share-dealing. The little runt was my friend Conal Walsh, now of the *Observer* – as Piers knows fine well, having hurled threatening abuse at him when they subsequently met at an awards ceremony.

Morgan claims to have been surprised by the view that his appearance on *Have I Got News for You* was humiliating: 'It all went quite amusingly as far as I was concerned ... I was bemused, I was just having a laugh.' Anyone who saw the programme will remember the ugliness of the way Morgan lost his temper. He was not having a laugh.

His vendetta against *Private Eye*'s editor Ian Hislop, too, was ugly. (Not that Hislop's campaign in the *Eye* against 'Piers Moron' was a picnic.) But this spat, too, he feels obliged to insist, was 'a good laugh ... I'm just doing it for fun.' Bollocks.

Morgan is obviously stung by Cherie Blair's view that he lacks a 'moral compass'. Reading this book, you realise she's not quite right. Piers does have a moral compass, but it is one on which the needle spins wildly around; a compass beset with powerful magnets labelled Self-Interest, Self-Pity, Self-Righteousness and so forth. None is labelled Self-Knowledge.

At one moment, Piers proudly confesses to having taken a private revenge on Rosie Boycott, then editor of the *Daily Express*, with 'an invented little news story saying EXPRESS EDITOR FACES THE AXE'. At the next moment, he's whining about 'lawless' and 'invented' stories about him in other papers.

One moment, he's sniggering at the 'unethical ... but very handy' arrangement his *News of the World* has with the Crime Correspondent of the *Sunday Mirror*, who he pays to leak him their scoops in advance. Once he's at the *Mirror*, he arranges (after, he tells us, giving him 'a month to stop') to have the poor man fired. He delights in stealing John Witherow's scoop, but throws a tantrum when Alastair Campbell does the same to him, passing to the *Sun* an exclusive article by Bill Clinton ghosted for the *Mirror* by its political editor. 'Hypocritical', here, is as often a term of self-congratulation as it is of abuse.

But this is the stuff of which red-tops are made. We pretend to disapprove of them, and they pretend to disapprove of each other, and they make gross intrusions into people's lives, and we devour them. Piers Morgan was a brilliant tabloid editor. His *Mirror* spanked David Yelland's *Sun*.

However self-serving his account of his tenure may be, the scoops he and his staff got were spectacular (Ryan Parry infiltrating Buckingham Palace as a footman; Andy Lines finding the fireman Mike Kehoe after 9/11; Divine Brown, Trevor Rhys-Jones and Paul Burrell telling all), the stunts entertaining, the cock-ups even more entertaining.

His memoir is historically negligible, analytically null, morally rudderless, sloppily edited, hopelessly written, boastful, whining, sentimental, thuggish and with all the fascination of a horrible accident. Just like a red-top newspaper on a good day.

Anyone who is interested in knowing how tabloids work and what the people who write them are like – anyone interested, in other words, in a culture in which the Prime Minister lends his support to a campaign to get a character from *Coronation Street* out of prison ('Free Deirdre Rashid!') – should read it.

LOW LIFE

Jeremy Clarke

12 March

'Swim, please,' I said. 'Member.' The receptionist swiped my card and looked at her computer screen. Optimism, surprise, puzzlement and finally despair swept across her pretty face. The usual story, then. Every time I try to pay to enter my leisure centre, the insanely cheerful minimum-wage (lower band) receptionist has to summon the permanently angry manager to show her how to circumvent the new computer programme's quibble about letting me in.

This time it had accused me of not renewing my membership, an accusation savagely nullified by the manager's right forefinger. I paid him and received change. But I wasn't out of the woods yet. The manager gazed intently through the window separating the reception area from the pool. He snatched up a pool timetable and studied it. Public swimming periods are restricted to times when special-interest groups aren't using the pool. Often I've turned up with my rolled-up towel under my arm, only to be told I couldn't go in. Which sacrosanct special-interest session was keeping me out this time, I wondered. Canoe Club? GP Referrals? Asbo Hour? It was Pool Aerobics, which had been cancelled, said the manager, so I could go straight in.

If most of your swimming is done in noisy, choppy, council-operated baths, there is something almost transcendental about breaking the surface tension of a large becalmed swimming pool. I slipped in silently and, loath to ruffle the surface of the water, swam breaststroke lengths underwater. For ten minutes, before the public swim session officially began, and the regulars had turned up, I had the pool to myself. It was bliss.

On the stroke of the hour, however, a serious swimmer emerged from the changing room and the spell was broken. You could tell he was a serious swimmer by his hat, goggles and minimal trunks. The narrow shoulders and bulging thighs said he was a front crawler. I hate front crawlers. These aqua-fascists intimidate other pool users with their velocity and turbulence. They bat up and down in straight lines without deviating. Everyone else – children, the elderly, namby-pamby breast-strokers like me – must make way for these lords of the creation, who, when resting, lean back against the shallow end admiring their own tits.

He slipped into the water beside me, pulled his goggles down over his eyes and kicked off. His front crawl, I hate to say it, was perfection: powerful, rhythmical, economical and barely a splash. Instead of struggling against the water, like some of them, he embraced it lovingly, breathing to the right every fourth stroke. At either end he flip-turned beautifully under the water.

Next out of the changing rooms were two ladies, mid-forties, swim hats decorated with three-dimensional plastic flowers, come to chat as much as to swim. They chatted as they strolled out to the pool, chatted as they lowered themselves into the water at the shallow end, and chatted as they pushed off, side by side – and all without a moment's loss of eye-contact.

I recognised one of them. I hadn't seen Sandra for 20 years. I went out with her once, for about a fortnight. She was lower-middle class then, but looking to change, either upwards or downwards, it didn't matter. For a long time she could have gone either way. Then she met and fell in love with Jim, a council worker, a lovely chap, and she consciously became a working-class woman. She got being working class off to a tee more or less straight away. You'd think she'd been born into it. As they paddled off towards the deep end, I heard Sandra say to her mate, 'So I said, "Oh!" And he said, "So it's 'Oh!', is it?" And I said, "Yes it is 'Oh!'" And he said, 'Well, you can shove your "Oh!"'

The serious front crawler had flipped over at the far end and was powering towards Sandra and her friend like a torpedo. I watched and waited for the inevitable collision. But without hesitation or deviation he simply powered his way between them. The gap was small, too small, certainly, to swim through without causing offence. The manoeuvre was part pragmatism, part arrogance, but mostly intimidation. This is my lane, it said. Go away.

Sandra and her mate stood up and staggered apart. The front crawler had already flip-turned at the shallow end and was pounding towards them again. He tried to force his way between them as before, but this time received a knee in the head from one side and a well-aimed punch in the head from the other. This time he stood up, furiously rubbing his head. 'Sorry!' chorused Sandra and her mate.

The next time I looked he'd sensibly chosen another lane, and Sandra and her mate were swimming complacently by, and Sandra was saying, 'So I said, "Where's it all gone?" and he said, "Where's what all gone?"'

DIARY

Leanda de Lisle

14 May

I don't know why it is, but a lot of people seem to assume that writing a book doesn't require any work. I began my book about James I and VI four years ago, and I have only just finished it. The other day when I told someone I was a writer they replied, 'Oh, that's a nice hobby.' Hobby! It was not a hobby that turned my bottom the same shape as my chair or turned me into a gibbering wreck. Awaiting my book reviews, I have called my agent and asked her if she would mind giving me her home number in case of 'emergency'. The best news thus far is that my Peruvian mother-in-law, who has spent the past four years telling me how boring my book sounds, has loved it. But who knows how others will feel? My husband Peter won't put up with my hyperneurotic outpourings, and the children's mantra, 'Chill your beans', isn't at all what I want to hear. My agent, however, is always there for me … I think. She appeared to give me her number happily, but then she told me a cruel story. An American colleague of hers was going off on holiday when a client rang demanding to know what he should do in an emergency. 'Call the doctor,' she replied.

DIARY

Nigel Farndale

28 May

An actor friend and I were worried that we were not being good role models to our sons, of which we have three apiece. It was all very well taking them around National Trust properties, teaching them chess and explaining to them the difference between native and Pacific oysters, but what they needed were fathers who took them to football matches – especially the eldest, who are now pushing eight. As my friend lives in Chelsea, we decided Stamford Bridge would be the place. 'Do you just turn up?' he asked. 'I'm pretty sure you have to book,' I replied. 'Right. I'll get on to it,' he replied. 'This Saturday?' 'Yes, this Saturday.' We steeled ourselves to the prospect of having to chant on terraces and drink lager from cans. Then my friend rang back and, sounding rather sheepish, said, 'Um, apparently the football season ended last Saturday.'

My day job is writing interviews for the *Sunday Telegraph* and top of my wish list of subjects at the moment is the governor of California, Arnold Schwarzenegger. I particularly admire his use of the phrase 'economic girlie men'. I'm not quite sure what it means but I imagine he thinks most men are girlie men, compared to him. My actor friend and I no doubt qualify.

I've been 'postal stalking' Arnie for months now and I'm beginning to suspect that it is my request to do the interview at his house that is putting him off. I always try this on, and am surprised how often people agree. The 'at home' interview has thrown up some fascinating insights for me over the years: the walls of Gore Vidal's *palazzo* in Italy were covered with photographs ... of Gore Vidal; an entire wall of Joan Collins's apartment in New York, meanwhile, was taken up with a mirror; Ann Widdecombe's fridge was full of tiramisus; and in the downstairs lavatory of Dave Lee Travis's farmhouse in Tring there was a stack of jokey books about flatulence. I request the interview be 'at home', then, because I feel it important to see interviewees in their own contexts, surrounded by their own ephemera. And because I am very nosy.

I have a friend who paints portraits and he is given much greater access to his subjects – Tony Blair, George W. Bush and Rupert Murdoch among them. As Murdoch was too busy to do formal sittings, my friend had to fly around the world doing preliminary studies wherever he could. After a few weeks he became invisible, always quietly sketching in the corner. I pleaded with him to keep a diary but, alas, he is far too discreet. I did manage to prise one endearing story out of him, though. Only once did the mogul come to the studio where my friend works. As it happened, that day the place was also being used to film one of those lookalike commercials, and waiting in the corridor outside were 'Posh and Becks'. Murdoch was bemused. 'Wasn't that . . . ?' he asked after walking past the two lookalikees. The director of the commercial was equally puzzled: 'Did we order . . . ?'

LOW LIFE

Jeremy Clarke

18 June

The morning after the students' summer ball they told me that, just beside the entrance, a girl, naked except for red striped knee-length socks, was lying on her back on the clipped lawn, staring up at the stars, as if she'd been ravished. Her clothes were strewn about, also the contents of her handbag, as if she'd been robbed as well. She was an art student, they said, and her lying there like that was a work of art, an installation, intended for the intellectual stimulation of those queuing to have their ticket checked and their hand stamped.

My friends also told me that halfway through the ball they'd gone to look for me and found me unconscious outside, flat on my face on the lawn, next to the naked girl. Someone had taken off my shoes, arranged them neatly side-by-side and set fire to them. Overheard suggested titles for my rival installation were 'The Oldest Swinger in Town' and 'The Death of Icarus'. My shoes burned merrily, they told me. I said I didn't think one could set fire to one's shoes as easily as all that. One of my friends, a physics graduate, reminded me that leather, shoe polish and Odor-Eaters were all highly flammable. 'Well, obviously you're the expert,' I said tetchily, embarrassed that I couldn't remember going to the students' ball, let alone making an installation of myself while there.

POP MUSIC

Marcus Berkmann

13 August

It's always delightful to welcome a new star to the pop firmament, if only because it means that there's someone else to take the mickey out of. James Blunt's emergence increases the number of old Harrovian army officers currently making hit records to one, and this is therefore the only thing anyone wants to know about him. It's an interesting career path – Harrow, Sandhurst, Radio 2 – but it shouldn't be a surprising one. I think we have to blame the Beatles here.

The notion that pop music is a purely working-class activity, which has greater credibility when created by the poor and dispossessed, wasn't actually theirs: like a few things, they stole it from poor, dispossessed American blues musicians. But in their sweet, chippy, Liverpudlian way, the Fab Four made the absolute most of what used to be called humble origins. Paul McCartney has made the best part of a billion dollars, and the other three didn't do too badly either. And this was when middle-class kids cottoned on. It's great fun to rebel against your parents by playing viciously loud music with guitars, but when there really are pots of gold at the end of the rainbow, pop starts to turn into a sensible career option.

I have always wondered how the parents of Peter Gabriel, Tony Banks and Mike Rutherford reacted when their sons announced they were forming a band and calling it Genesis. That's not why we sent you to Charterhouse! And yet their career was launched by another Old Carthusian, Jonathan King. This may be the first reported instance of the old boy network operating in rock 'n' roll.

But Genesis weren't the first public-school boys to make a career in pop music, and James Blunt won't be the last. (Incidentally, note that it's 'James', not 'Jim' or 'Jimmy'. And somehow, to his parents and friends I bet it's really 'Jamie'.) True, some public-school pop stars suffer credibility problems. Chris de Burgh will never be cool, although I suspect this is more to do with his appalling songs than with the fact he went to Marlborough. Nick Drake also went to Marlborough, and no one seems to mind. Mick Fleetwood of Fleetwood Mac was at Sherborne, and his father was a wing-commander. Stewart Copeland of the Police went to Millfield, although tragically not at the same time as Tony Blackburn. David Gilmour of Pink Floyd was at the Perse School in Cambridge, but his palpable poshness has never been seen as a disadvantage, except by anyone who really hates Pink Floyd.

When I was at Highgate in the mid-Seventies, we were all rather proud that top progressive rockers had similar backgrounds to our own. If only we had known that Freddie Mercury was an old boy, but for some reason this piece of information was brutally suppressed by the authorities there. Still, we were not to be deterred. Boys at Highgate went on to play drums for Culture Club, bass for Wang Chung and guitar for the Weather Prophets, among many others. No doubt their efforts are now commemorated on a plaque in Big School.

These days schools seem rather prouder of their musical alumni, and vice versa. To judge by its website, Tonbridge is almost indecently pleased by the success of weeds and wets Keane, who named themselves after a tealady there. Radiohead famously all went to Abingdon, where Thom Yorke was nicknamed 'Salamander' on account of his 'weird, wonky reptile eyes'. Chris Martin of Coldplay went to Sherborne and has been known to use the phrase 'house colours' in interviews.

Perhaps this is as it should be. I always felt embarrassed for Joe Strummer of The Clash, who had been to City of London and felt the need to apologise for it for the rest of his life. Bob Geldof was very funny about this in *Mojo* recently. 'Excuse me? The Clash? A load of middle-class geezers dressed by Jasper Conran and living in Regent's Park! Their first gig? In a small room for invited journalists! Very revolutionary.' But before learned critics with beards start writing books about the bourgeoisification of rock 'n' roll, let's not forget that, on occasion, the public-school system simply doesn't work. After all, Shane MacGowan of the Pogues went to Westminster. 'Brush your teeth, boy!' they probably said to him, but to no avail . . .

LETTERS

3 September

Sir: Among the public-school pop stars not mentioned in Marcus Berkmann's amusing article (Arts, 13 August) were Michael ('Mike') d'Abo of A Band of Angels, which largely comprised Old Harrovians like himself, and later of Manfred Mann; Lord David Dundas, another Harrovian, of Jeans On fame; the Old Etonian Jeremy Clyde of the duo Chad & Jeremy; and Peter Asher and Gordon Waller, the Old Westminster boys who became Peter & Gordon. Waller went on to play the Presleyan Pharaoh in *Joseph and the Amazing Technicolor Dreamcoat*, written by Tim Rice (Lancing) and Andrew Lloyd Webber (Westminster). I seem to remember that one of Dusty's early cohorts in the Springfields claimed to have gone to Eton and that there was an Etonian called Pilkington-Miksa in the group Curved Air (led by the Old Westminster Francis Monkman). But Craig Brown's suggestion that Marc Bolan may have been Captain of Boats at Haileybury appears to have no foundation in fact.

    Hugh Massingberd
    London W2

DIARY

Simon Heffer

17 September

An opinion poll showed the other day that cricket is a more popular sport than football. Football is not, in my view, a sport: it is somewhere between a business racket and a mental illness. Like many Britons, I associate it with all the worst aspects of our society – violence, drunkenness, drugs, racism, exploitation, greed and stupidity; and that's just for starters. As a lifelong cricket obsessive, my main fear now, following our Ashes triumph, is that cricket becomes the new football. I trust our players are too sensible for that, though I am not sure about their cash-obsessed employers at the England and Wales Cricket Board. To reassure us, the ECB should take two immediate measures: discouraging players' wives from appearing in the media, and banning our boys from wearing vile multicoloured sponsored clothing – especially preposterous baseball caps – when off the field. I like to think there is no danger of a man in a blazer and flannels, blessed with a demure wife, ever having his head turned by fame or riches, at least not since the late Captain Robert Maxwell MC fell off his yacht.

LOW LIFE

Jeremy Clarke

24 September

Six for Sunday lunch. Me, my boy, my mother, my mother's boyfriend Dr Lovepants, my sister, and this poised, well-groomed, long-haired chap, billed as the new man in my sister's life. Me and the boy are a bit late and everyone else has started eating.

The new man in my sister's life's hair is receding at the front and long at the back and he's got a pointy beard. I'm dying to discomfit him with searching questions. New men in my sister's life, as a group, are normally among the most unserious people in the world. But this one looks like he's treating the occasion with at least as much earnestness as my sister. The mien is essentially polite. The price tag on the bottle of French wine he's brought says a whopping £6.50.

A man of immense intellect and apparently no emotional intelligence whatsoever, Dr Lovepants has already launched into his customary meal-time monologue. He's a compulsive talker, and an ideal candidate, I tell him, for the compulsive talkers' self-help association On Anon Anon. His failing memory means that sometimes we have to listen to a monologue that was broadcast earlier.

He and my mother have been visiting National Trust properties in Kent. At Chartwell they were shown around Churchill's garden studio by an official guide, who kindly shared his favourite Churchill anecdote. It was a marvel, frankly, how this guide managed to get a word in edgeways. The story involves the great man himself (Churchill) and a small boy, one of Churchill's grandchildren. Dr Lovepants acts both parts with a high standard of mimicry that is his main saving grace.

Churchill has shut himself away in his studio to study the newspaper. Timid knock on door. Snort of irritation concedes that the Lion's Roar is indeed at home. Enter small timid grandchild. 'Grandfather,' he says. 'Is it true that you are the most famous person in the whole world?' Newspaper lowers, revealing face of the old warrior, on which pugnacity is only slightly tempered by kindliness. 'Yes. Now bugger off.'

We laugh. But all eyes are on the new man in my sister's life to see if he's laughing. He is, but not sycophantically, in spite of our framed portrait of Churchill that he must have noticed hanging in the hall. But before anyone can fire off a 'So what do you do for a living, then?' Dr Lovepants has moved seamlessly on to a description of Down House, former home of Charles Darwin. (Seamlessly, I should add, except for the lumps of food that come tumbling out of his mouth every so often.)

Dr Lovepants tells us how he and my mother followed the circular garden pathway that Darwin walked every day. Darwin used these walks, said Dr Lovepants, to give voice to his interior conversation. Does he mean in the same way that he, Dr Lovepants, uses his visits to articulate his own, I ask him? But he affects not to hear. Maybe in monologue mode it's only himself he can hear.

Throughout the first course, which is roast beef, no one else can get a word in. Over the apple crumble, Dr Lovepants fixes the new man in my sister's life with his eye and he ratchets up the intellectual ante. His monologue goes from the garden path at Down House to Darwin's theory of evolution to the absurdity of creation theory to Jewish history. And then a flurry of Jewish jokes, the punchline of the last of which has Jehovah tinkling a bell and calling out, 'Two teas, please, Mohamed!' And then on via eugenics to Francis Galton and Oliver Wendell Holmes.

Dr Lovepants leans forward and says to the new man in my sister's life: 'You've heard of Oliver Wendell Holmes, I take it?' We hold our breath. A direct question. The new man in my sister's life is being permitted to speak – to say whether or not he's heard of Oliver Wendell Holmes. Has he or hasn't he? The way Dr Lovepants puts it, it sounds crucial in some way. None of us has, of course. But then again none of us has ever heard of anyone outside the Bible or the Premiership. If you ask me, Oliver Wendell Holmes sounds like a housing association.

The new man in my sister's life says, 'Do you mean Dr Oliver Wendell Holmes or his son Judge Oliver Wendell Holmes?' He says it with warm familiarity, as if both are personal friends. My sister, who only reads menus, looks at the new man in her life with awe and reverence.

After lunch my boy consults his *What Car?* guide to second-hand car prices and reports that the new man in my sister's life's Mercedes is worth £4,600 trade price and £5,600 to a dealer. Again, impressive. Clearly this new man in my sister's life is going to be one to watch.

LETTERS

1 October

Sir: In his recollections of the wrestler 'Judo Al' Hayes (Sport, 24 September) Frank Keating didn't mention the man's finest hours – his historic series of duels with the dreaded Doctor Death. This battle of the titans had its beginning when, in the very early 1960s, the wrestling promoter Paul Lincoln started to feature a new star in his squad – a masked hero known as the White Angel. The White Angel always fought minor villains, and always won all his bouts with courage and chivalry.

This was in sharp contrast to Lincoln's other big star, another masked man, who gloried in the title Doctor Death and always fought minor heroes, and always won all his bouts with spite and chicanery. When would these two anonymous warriors meet? We grappling fans waited with bated breath.

Finally, after a series of gallant challenges from the White Angel and a lot of bad-tempered shouting from Doctor Death, the match was made. Thousands packed an outer-London wrestling venue. The two masked colossi fought ... and fought to a draw. Thousands went home in an agony of frustration and relief. Things couldn't be left like that, of course. A rematch was scheduled. Thousands again found the entrance fee. And the result was another draw.

Professional wrestling was, and is, proof that you can fool some of the people all of the time, but clearly the promoter decided he was in danger of overstretching his luck. At the third meeting, before even more frenzied thousands, the White Angel and Doctor Death met again, and Doctor Death won. The White Angel was ceremonially unmasked, and seen to be, as many of us had already guessed, 'Judo Al' Hayes himself. And we all went sadly home, having learned the bitter lesson that life is not a fairy tale, that evil must sometimes triumph over good. But in retrospect White Angel Al never stood a chance. Because if we had seen beneath Doctor Death's mask, we'd have recognised him too. He was Paul Lincoln. The promoter himself.

Colin Bostock-Smith
St Leonards on Sea, East Sussex

YOUR PROBLEMS SOLVED

Dear Mary . . .

3 December

Q. As part of his mid-life crisis my husband has bought a brand-new Maserati. It is his pride and joy, but the trouble is that, so far, he has been unable to show it off. We live in the country and invitations to large parties, which should provide a perfect opportunity, have to be ruled out because they invariably involve parking in a muddy field. He does not like to drive it on wet roads because he worries it will get dirty and then rusty underneath. Unlike some of his fellow mid-life crisis friends, he does not have a carpeted garage with underfloor heating. How, therefore, without being so coarse as to openly boast, can he let people know that he owns a Maserati in the first place and thereby bask in the admiration of his peers?

   – A.E., Pewsey, Wilts

A. This is a perfect time of year to drive the Maserati to a concert or play at one of your children's schools. With a careful selection of parking position your husband can be confident that an official will need to address the assembled company over a microphone to make the request: 'Will the owner of the silver Maserati, registration number such-and-such, please move it since it is blocking important access.' As your husband stands up and picks his way through the auditorium, mouthing 'sorry' towards the stage, his peers will certainly get the message.

DIARY

Barry Humphries

17/24 December

I have been reading the autobiography of the second most loved of all Australian divas, Dame Nellie Melba, who writes vividly and well. She describes her mixed feelings on first meeting Oscar Wilde: 'I had never seen anything in the least like Wilde before,' she writes. 'We did not seem to breed that type in Australia.' Dame Nellie would be obliged to revise this view were she to visit modern Sydney, where no pillow goes unbitten.

2006

Dear Mary; Dot Wordsworth; Jeremy Clarke;
Alexander Chancellor; Beryl Bainbridge;
Charles Moore; Barry Humphries;
Lloyd Evans; Joan Collins; Paul Johnson;
Deborah Ross; Taki; Ferdinand Mount

YOUR PROBLEMS SOLVED

Dear Mary . . .

7 January

Q. A friend in the fashion world telephoned me to say that she was sending round a handbag worth £400 for my Christmas present. She told me frankly that she would not normally spend £400 on me but she had been given this bag by a public relations person representing a certain designer and did not want it for herself. She added that, if by any chance I did not like it, she would prefer me not to sell the bag on eBay since the designer would inevitably get to hear of it and recognise the provenance of this 'one-off'. The bag duly arrived. It is a very beautiful object in its own right, but not capacious enough to be of use to me or any of my friends. Clearly I cannot return it to the shop. What should I do, Mary? It seems such a waste.

– Name and address withheld

A. Beautiful small handbags such as the one you describe make stylish doorstops when filled with a heavy substance such as sand. Put to such use, this present will be a joy for ever – either to yourself or to someone you pass it on to, and you can give heartfelt thanks to your friend.

MIND YOUR LANGUAGE

Dot Wordsworth

21 January

It would be the luck of Sir Menzies Campbell, known familiarly as Ming, to reach a height of fame just when *minging* and *minger* have become voguish terms of opprobrium. The earliest known occurrence of *minger* in print comes from 1995, in a magazine advertisement reading, 'Jade . . . seeks like-minded love warrior for spanking nights out, mingers need not apply.' The *OED* (online, since the word is too new for whatever paper version supersedes the second edition of 1989) defines it as 'An ugly or unattractive person, esp. a woman.'

The word is still new enough for users to get it wrong. A nickname for Anne Robinson, the popular quiz-game hostess, is 'the ginger minger', but I have heard broadcasters pronounce *minger* to rhyme with *ginger*, as if *minger* were connected with *minge*, a word of unknown origin meaning 'the pudenda muliebris'. (It is found in Joseph Wright's *Dialect Dictionary* in a quotation dated 1903.) There are still some people with the surname Minger, though it is much rarer than Smellie.

Where does it comes from? There is a dialect word *ming* from Scotland, attested from 1920, meaning 'human excrement; something smelling unpleasant'. One can understand the later development in this sense. The unconnected seventeenth-century word *minge*, meaning 'urine', comes from Latin *mingere*, 'to urinate'.

Quite independently from all this, a character appeared in 1934 called Ming the Merciless. That was in the first adventure of Flash Gordon, the cartoon-strip space hero. Flash had landed on the planet Mongo, where Ming was Emperor. When not attempting to finish off Flash Gordon with death-rays, Ming was developing a soft spot for Flash's female companion Dale Arden.

Sir Menzies Campbell was born in 1941, but was not named after the alien emperor. Indeed his first name was Walter. His second name,

Menzies, was pronounced to rhyme with *sing-is*, as the way is in Scotland.

In origin, the zed in Menzies was a letter called *yogh*, in form like a '3' descending below the line, or like a long-tailed 'z'. It was used in Middle English to represent a slightly coughing sound, the guttural and palatal unvoiced spirant, as in *enouȝ* (enough) or *niȝt* (night). Caxton used the yogh, but then it fell out of use, only being retained by Scottish printers. So it became conventional, even when printers only had one letter for yogh and zed, in names like Dalziel and words like *capercailzie* or *gaberlunzie*. In Scotland weird-looking spellings such as *zer* (*year*) and *forzet* (*forget*) survived for a while, but proper names are more tenacious of oddities.

LOW LIFE

Jeremy Clarke

11 February

I wanted to get from the youth hostel in the centre of Dartmoor, where I was staying, to a town on the outskirts where my brother lives. My brother has a subscription to the Sky Sports channel. I planned to pop over and watch the second half of the midweek match and be back in time for evening prayers and the ceremony of the shutting of the gates, or whatever the form was at youth hostels. Unfolding my Ordnance Survey map on the dining-room table, the warden and I leaned across and studied it. 'Now, we're here,' said the warden, pressing his forefinger against the youth hostel symbol. And, doing my best impression of a second world war English army officer, I added, 'And Jerry . . . is here, here, here, here and here.'

Ignoring my levity, the warden suggested two possible routes. I could go the long way round via the main roads (or what passes for the main roads on Dartmoor), or maybe I should consider a short cut, which he traced out with his forefinger. This route was marked on the map by a microscopically thin line, straight at first, then wandering this way and that, then, losing confidence in itself altogether, becoming a dotted line among a diffuse matrix of other dotted lines that mostly went nowhere or perhaps passed into another dimension. If this was a viable short cut, I surmised, it was probably known only to the warden and itinerant pedlars. Which route did he recommend? Whichever route I chose was entirely up to me, emphasised the warden, clearly anxious about what he was going to say at the inquest.

DIARY

Alexander Chancellor

25 February

The story goes that my great-grandfather Murray Finch Hatton, MP for Lincolnshire in the 1880s and later 12th Earl of Winchilsea, shot an African tracker in the leg while big-game shooting in Kenya. Mortified by what he had done, he rushed forward and gave the tracker a golden guinea. The man limped off, but soon returned. He had consulted his wife, he said, and wondered if his lordship might kindly oblige by shooting him again.

DIARY

Beryl Bainbridge

4 March

The changes in attitudes to sex could be likened to advances in science. Anything is possible and almost everything permissible. The other night, by mistake, I twice prodded the number 9 on that box attached to the TV and observed several naked young women being rude with each other. It only lasted a few seconds before a notice came up saying I had to send £58 somewhere or other if I wanted to see the rest. This reminded me that I was expelled from school, aged 13, after my mother found a slip of paper in the pocket of my gym slip and took it straight to the headmistress. I was called a rotten apple in the barrel; it was a verse about having sex against a wall. More than 100 years ago a Madame Fontaine was pilloried in the press for riding in her birthday suit upon a heifer attached to a balloon drifting across London. In her defence she pleaded that she was only trying to earn a few bob depicting an airborne Lady Godiva, and that she had been too high up for her intimate parts to be properly viewed. Today Madame Fontaine would be instantly hailed as a celebrity and asked to present children's television programmes.

THE SPECTATOR'S NOTES

Charles Moore

22 April

Although Nick Griffin went to Cambridge, one is unlikely, in educated middle-class circles, to have friends who vote for the BNP. The only person I have ever known who said he did so was the late Alan Clark. While he was a Conservative minister, he told me that he voted for the National Front (as it was then called) at council elections. I never knew whether or not to believe this. Alan's desire to shock was so great that it frequently overthrew the truth. Besides, voting BNP would have been inconsistent with his stated views. I once asked him if he minded being labelled a fascist. 'Yes, I bloody well do,' he said. 'Fascists are shopkeepers who look after their dividends. I'm a Nazi.'

DIARY

Barry Humphries

13 May

When the gifted Australian actor Russell Crowe threw a telephone at an American hotel desk clerk, I sent him a letter of congratulation. As one might expect in a wonderful but barmy country like America, the desk clerk became an overnight millionaire. I have just completed a 15-week theatre tour of the US, so I have been in a lot of hotels and been tempted in nearly all of them to maim, and possibly even disembowel, arrogant illegal aliens loitering behind computer screens at the front desk, or impersonating waiters, or gender non-specific 'servers', as waiters quaintly prefer to be called. The stupidity and 'attitude' of most receptionists in designer boutique American hotels would test the sanity and patience of Prince Charles, who is, without doubt, the best-mannered man in the world.

Most hotels now have 'spas', a fancy name for a swimming pool and an often whiffy steam-room. To make it seem more oasis-like, loud New Age muzak relentlessly percolates, and one can't have a massage without having to listen to pan pipes, gamelans and exotic bird calls. Not seldom, each swimming pool contains a lone Band-Aid adhering to its turquoise bottom. The other day I was lolling by a pool in Arizona, reading yet another irresistible Venetian mystery by Donna Leon, and sure enough, staring at me from the depths of this 'infinity' pool and magnified by the glassy surface was yet another undulating Band-Aid with a sanguine and saffron blob on its gauze. This unwelcome submarine garnish is now as ubiquitous as that inexplicable fleck of blood on the bedside lampshade, and the faint but unmistakable hieroglyphs on the bed-head engraved by the toenails of enraptured honeymoon couples and adulterous conference delegates.

Starbucks, incidentally, is on my list of the grossly overrated, along with Bruce Chatwin, Cézanne's 'Bathers', French onion soup, Bob Dylan,

Niagara Falls, *Citizen Kane*, the Caribbean, the novels of Patrick O'Brian, Pilates, lobster, *The Lord of the Rings*, and most sculpture.

THEATRE

Lloyd Evans

8 July

If I could make a wish, I'd choose to be Sam Shepard for an afternoon, or however long it takes him to write one of his plays. I'd put on my dungarees, sit at my typewriter and get started. 'Scene One. A squalid shack in the Midwest. Threadbare carpets. Crippled plumbing. Drowsy flies buzzing around a three-day-old corpse. In a rocking chair sits an obese lunatic, who hasn't shaved since 1973, muttering about his ex-fiancée and drinking lighter fuel.'

I'd give the bearded drunk an incoherent rant lasting 17 minutes, then I'd bring on his ex-fiancée, and the happy pair would exchange *fortissimo* insults for about an hour. Then they'd kill each other. Curtain. The End. Having written a new Sam Shepard play, I'd be immediately inundated by calls from Hollywood superstars begging me to let them play the lead roles. The show would run for a year, earn a stackload of royalties and win an important prize sponsored by a rich East Coast newspaper. Despite all this acclaim I would never smile.

DIARY

Joan Collins

22 July

Princess Margaret's grand car-boot sale at Christie's last month reminded me of my own souvenir of PM. Several years ago I had decided to collect silver boxes, and a mutual friend asked if I would be interested in a couple belonging to her. 'She's having a clear-out,' the friend explained. 'Wants to get rid of a lot of junk. Would you be interested?' He brought over a beautiful, and rather large, embossed square silver box for which I cheerfully coughed up £600. The following month PM had another clear-out and I bought another smaller but equally attractive box. When I opened the first box, I was fascinated to discover hidden under the velvet a small engraved card announcing, 'Presented to HRH Princess Margaret and Antony Armstrong-Jones on the occasion of their visit to _____.' (I shan't reveal the name of the country to save international embarrassment.)

That Christmas I gave my annual party and the friend declined my invitation because of a previous engagement with PM. However, at 11 o'clock, he rang to ask if he could bring her over for a nightcap. 'She'd really like to see you. She loved you in *Private Lives*.' Flattered, I told him to bring her right over. As the princess regally entered my hallway, I suddenly remembered the giant silver box sitting front and centre on the coffee table. I tried to stop her coming into the room by persuading Roger Moore to engage her in spirited conversation (which worked). A few Famous Grouses later – in a tiny glass because 'my hands are too small to hold a large one' – the princess was as happy as can be and, except for a small glint of recognition which I quickly doused with more FG, the silver boxes went completely unnoticed.

LOW LIFE

Jeremy Clarke

22 July

My boy left school at the end of last term, aged 16. He can read and write after a fashion, and he knows something about the rise and fall of the Nazi party and how to make delicious scones, so all in all a good result.

AND ANOTHER THING

Paul Johnson

12 August

And that reminds me: what did Jane Austen and Bill Clinton have in common? A corridor. During most of her writing life, poor Jane had no room of her own and had to write in a corridor, convenient when the house was silent, but a passageway at other times, so that she had to cover up her manuscript when she heard someone approach. Oddly enough, the couplings of President Clinton, such being the public nature and geography of the White House, also had to take place on a corridor, similarly (if rarely) subject to interruption. Hearing noises, the President was forced to zip up his trousers, just as Jane had to conceal the pages of her current novel. Jane once memorably observed, 'Follies and nonsense, whims and inconsistencies do divert me, I own, and I laugh at them whenever I can.' *Ceteris paribus* and allowing for the standards of different epochs, Clinton's awkward interruptions were precisely the 'follies and nonsense' that would have made Jane Austen laugh.

LOW LIFE

Jeremy Clarke

23 September

As far as I'm concerned, global warming was proved to be an incontrovertible fact last week in the beer garden of my local pub. The scepticism of scientists and academics no longer washes. For about the past five years I've been noting the warning signs. The sun has felt hotter. The winters in the south-west have felt consistently wetter. In summer, the horizon, seen from my window across miles of open sea, is rarely unobscured by air pollution. And mountaineering friends returning from abroad swear that snow lines everywhere are retreating.

Until last week, though, I reserved judgement. What do I know? Maybe the sun feels hotter because my skin and hair are thinning as I get older. Maybe the horizon is less sharp because my eyesight isn't what it was. Perhaps my mountaineering friends aren't truthful or fail to take account of changing seasons. And in any case, if popular anxiety is justified and the planet is heating up slightly, so what? Everything changes except the avant-garde – and thank goodness for that. And there's always the nudist beach at the bottom of the road to fall back on if it gets a bit hot and sticky.

We were lounging around a wooden table in the beer garden in the middle of the afternoon: bare chests, bare legs, sunglasses; drinking tall frosted glasses of ice-cold lager and feeling like kings. Wafting across from the next table was the sweet smell of skunk from an extended family of young New Age-type travellers, six of them, all nicely stoned and inclining towards the horizontal, plus two young lurchers and a contented baby.

Suddenly, one of them, this skinny, sinewy, tattooed guy, also shirtless, jumps to his feet, goes over to a flowering fuchsia bush and studies it intently. Then he goes nuts. 'Guys! Guys! Quick!' he yells, and frantically beckons to the others to come over. One of them raises himself to his feet and ambles across. And as soon as he arrives at the bush, and focuses on the exact spot his mate is pointing at, he too seems to take leave of his senses. Now both of them are holding their heads with both hands and hopping about, and yelling 'Man!' and 'Jeez!' and 'Far out!' and suchlike. And soon all six of them are there, exclaiming and hopping about and pointing whatever it is out to the baby.

'Come on. Let's see what the freaks are going on about,' says Trev resignedly. (There are two main identifiable constituencies in the pub: alternative hippie types, and good ole country boys and girls. The latter tend to dress conservatively, even if they don't act particularly conservatively. Each regards the other with amused condescension.) We get up and mosey over.

And no wonder they're excited. Industriously grazing from flower to flower, and oblivious to the commotion it is causing, is what looks like a miniature hummingbird. Well, I knew some of them were small, but this one is ridiculously small, perhaps an inch and a half long including the long, probing beak. And the colours! Straight out of an LSD hallucination! The feathers were a surreal pattern of red, brown and orange and it had a band of white spots on its tail. It was hovering like a hummingbird does and its wings were humming audibly. You couldn't have made it up.

'What the hell is it! What do you think it is, man?' said one of the travellers. 'F***ing bee,' said Trev authoritatively. 'It's got to be a hummingbird!' says someone else. 'It's got a long beak. Bees don't have beaks!' 'Some of them might,' says Trev, for whom confounding the experts is a matter of policy. Whatever it is, one of the travellers pulls up a chair and sits and watches it closely for 20 minutes, occasionally groaning with astonishment, as if it were a scene from *Fantasia* come to life.

A week later we're celebrating my brother's 40th birthday in the garden and more or less the same thing happens. Someone sees another one, can't believe their eyes, and starts squealing. And soon all 19 guests are clustered around a flowering bush, babbling with astonishment. So I go inside and log on and discover that they're moths; hummingbird hawk moths, to be precise; over here briefly on a working holiday.

So after I've spread the news, everyone then troops indoors and gathers around the laptop to view the web-page. There's 19 of them – aunts, uncles, grandparents, cousins – craning forward as I try to relocate the page. And for some reason beyond my control, this picture of a naked woman posing provocatively on a deserted tropical beach pops up. She looks well over 16, fortunately. 'There,' I say. 'Hummingbird hawk moth.'

CINEMA

Deborah Ross

14 October

The History Boys (15)

I love Alan Bennett. I seriously do. I once saw him in Marks & Spencer (Camden) and it was all I could do not to throw myself worshipfully at his feet. I had to hang on to the chiller cabinet until the moment passed. I even felt a little faint. I might have blushed. He is certainly the man I would most like to marry. I know, I know, he bats for the other side, but I wouldn't be overly demanding. Perhaps on my birthday, as a treat.

HIGH LIFE

Taki

14 October

The telephone rings and a downmarket voice greets me with a cheery hello. 'This is Peter McKay, your old friend,' says the bubbly one. 'We hear that *Vanity Fair* paid for your party.' For any of you unfamiliar with McKay, he is a scandal-purveyor of talent, malice and unparalleled mischief, who writes under the pseudonym of Ephraim Hardcastle in the *Daily Mail*. My first reaction, needless to say, is to wonder why *VF* should pay for my party. And I tell him so. 'No, *VF* did not pay for my party, but Graydon Carter, the editor, and his wife Anna, as well as Dominick Dunne, a *VF* columnist, were invited as they are old and good friends of mine.' McKay obviously read this as an affirmation because the next day he led off with an item which stated that 'the shindig, which lasted until 5 a.m., was planned in consultation with Graydon Carter, editor of *Vanity Fair*, which flew its society editor, Dominick Dunne, to London, berthing him at Claridges, to report exclusively on the bash. Columnist Taki often rebukes vulgarians whose parties feature in celebrity magazines. Did *VF* buy up his birthday bash?'

The mind boggles. The English language provides words only up to a point when one wishes to answer in the negative. If one goes on too long, one tends to protest too much. So, what to do? Hang up is one way, but it will be taken as affirmation. Make sure gossip merchants do not have one's telephone number is another, but that, too, will be seen as an affirmative answer to their non-posed question. Kill all gossip columnists seems to be the only solution. But then I might have to commit suicide myself.

BOOKS

Ferdinand Mount

11 November

The Life of Kingsley Amis
by Zachary Leader
(Cape, £25, pp. 996)

What is it about fruit? There is no more searing passage in the memoirs of Auberon Waugh than the bit when three bananas reach the Waugh household in the worst days of postwar austerity and Evelyn Waugh places all three on his own plate, then before the anguished eyes of his three children ladles on cream, which was almost unprocurable, and sugar, which was heavily rationed, and scoffs the lot. So in all the 900-odd pages of this marvellous *Life of Kingsley Amis* there is nothing that chills the blood more than the moment when Hilly Amis's eight-year-old son Jaime reaches for the one peach in a fruit bowl otherwise containing only oranges, apples and grapes and Kingsley shouts, in a voice described by his son Martin as 'like a man hailing a cab across the length of Oxford Circus during a downpour on Christmas Eve', 'HEY! That's *my* peach.'

Behind the sacred monster's mask lurks a monstrous baby, an insatiable craving machine. There is a line that appears in *Take a Girl Like You*, but also uttered by Kingsley himself as he and some friends pulled up at a fried-clam joint on the way to the Newport Jazz Festival: 'Oh good, I want more than my share before anyone else has had any.' Just as Kingsley would later tell the 'That's *my* peach!' story against himself, so he was constantly working his own episodes of unbridled selfishness into his fiction. In his last book, *The Biographer's Moustache*, the novelist tells his biographer, 'These days the public *like* to think of an artist as a, as a *shit* known to behave in ways they would shrink from.' To which the biographer, maddened by his subject, retorts at the end of the book, 'You're not a reluctant shit and certainly not an unconscious shit, you're a self-congratulatory shit.'

CINEMA

Deborah Ross

18 November

Casino Royale (12A) has pulled it off on all counts. It delivers the basic goods – the chases, the fireball explosions, the lavish glamour, the Aston Martins – yet it is also intelligent, moving, involving and sexy. You will be shaken, stirred, left to settle and then shaken and stirred all over again. I'm still shaking and stirring as I write. Why? Daniel Craig. He is stunning: a serious actor who not only takes the part seriously, but does so with astonishing presence, an athlete's grace and an almost animalistic power that he manages so skilfully to temper with a softer soulfulness. When he is on screen you cannot look at anything else, not even the back of Mark Kermode's hair. Craig's face shouldn't work, really. It looks like a pumpkin someone has taken a hammer to, but teamed with what are, surely, the most thrilling blue-blue eyes ever, it really does. [. . .]

In what amounts to a lovely, clever and not-before-time reversal, Bond himself is, I think, the sex object. When Vesper first meets him she compliments him on his 'perfectly formed arse'. There is even a scene where he emerges from the sea – a homage, I would guess, to Ursula Andress and Halle Berry – in baby-blue trunks. I agree it's a little bit camp but, boy, does it hit the mark all the same. I doubt there's a woman who, after seeing this film, doesn't then get into bed with her husband or partner, look over and go, 'Oh s**t.' I know I did.*

---

* We're still not talking, by the way.

2007

Jeremy Clarke; Boris Johnson; Sally Emerson;
Taki; Lloyd Evans; Kate Chisholm; Simon Hoggart;
Deborah Ross; Gyles Brandreth; Rod Liddle;
Joan Collins; Toby Young; Emily Maitlis

LOW LIFE

Jeremy Clarke

13 January

Winston Churchill's secretary John Colville records that one of the first signs that the great man's phenomenal memory was beginning to fail him, and that dementia was setting in, was when he made the intriguing faux pas of addressing a man by the name of Brownjohn as Mr Shorthorn.

A sure sign that the mental ebb tide is in full flow of course, is when you can't remember your own name. Nursing homes are packed to the rafters with people who've forgotten what they're called. It's said that US President Ronald Reagan, making a visit with Nancy to a residential home for the elderly, was led up to the oldest resident and, to the woman's obvious delight, embraced her warmly. 'Do you know who I am?' said a coquettish Ron, bending over her. 'No,' said the woman, 'but if you ask at reception, I'm sure they'll be able to help you.'

Until recently, our house was a residential home for the elderly. The title of Resident With The Least Idea Of Who They Are went easily to Jim Eliot, an ex-naval Commander who'd served at the Battle of Jutland. This delightful man had lost his memory and virtually his entire vocabulary, and yet retained the perfect manners of a between-the-wars British naval officer. I've read somewhere that, as it dies, the mind deteriorates in reverse order, with the most recent acquisition of human evolution, language, going first; then reasoning, then the instinct for self-preservation, and so on, until the only thing left is sexuality. Commander Eliot did not conform to this theory. His exquisite good manners were so ingrained that neither senile dementia, nor even his week-long death, made the slightest inroad into it.

I was sitting one sunny afternoon in the conservatory reading the paper, half obscured, well, hiding actually, behind some geraniums. Also enjoying the sun that was pouring into the conservatory was Eva, one of our residents, a resolutely working-class Lancashire woman in her early nineties who was nearly blind. In comes the Commander, a large man still at 95, spots a lady sitting on her own and pulls up a seat. They sit there, facing the sea, in companionable silence, the Commander exuding a kind of humorous gallantry and gentlemanly lack of ego far beyond anything ever preached by a holy man or Greek philosopher.

After a bit he ventures an amiable comment. 'Most extraordinary!' he says, raising his walking stick and aiming the rubber tip at the exact centre of a small passing cloud. (The natural world intensely interested the Commander because his memory was so shot to pieces that at every moment he was seeing it as if for the first time. Clouds, in particular, amazed him.) No comment from Eva, who hasn't seen a cloud in years. Loath to bore anybody with anything as tedious as his personal enthusiasms, Commander lets the subject drop. His conversational gambit appears to have failed. Eva might be blind, but she's not unsociable. 'And who might you be, love?' she says, in spite of them both having inhabited the same house for more than a year. Commander rests his wrist on the handle of his walking stick and thinks long and hard. Nothing doing. He hasn't a clue. 'Do you know, I don't know,' he says.

This from the Commander is verging on the verbose. Usually his valiant attempts to articulate the words in his mind result only in a strangulated gurgle. The only complete sentence I've heard him utter before this was when I woke him with a cup of tea on the morning of the first Gulf war. 'Commander, we're at war!' I said, placing the cup and saucer beside him. 'Oh, what a nuisance!' he said, and giggled.

The Commander hauls himself to his feet and totters away. Eva, who is also deaf, opens her watery blue eyes and looks this way and that, like a wary tortoise, trying to discern whether the man who addressed her is still there. About five minutes later, Commander hobbles back into the conservatory clutching an envelope. He's made the laborious journey upstairs, located his room and found an old envelope bearing his name and address. He stands before Eva and presents it to her. She starts with fright. He presses the envelope into her arthritic claw.

She hasn't a hope of reading it, not even if it were the right way up. But she cranes forward and holds the envelope closer and closer to her face until it's pressed right up against her eyeballs and she's wearing it like a mask. 'Sorry, love,' she says. 'I can't read it.' Commander tries to say something, but the power of speech has once again deserted him. He resumes his seat and looks out at the sea. I shut my paper and solemnly wonder at the transient nature of empires.

DIARY

Boris Johnson

27 January

The other day I was giving a pretty feeble speech when it went off the cliff and became truly abysmal. It was at some kind of founder's dinner for a university, and I had badly miscalculated my audience. I thought it was going to be a bunch of students, and when I saw the elite group of retired generals, former *Telegraph* editors and Nobel prize-winning economists, all in black tie, with their wives, I desperately tried to extemporise something profound. There were some musty sepulchres set into the wall of the ancient hall, so I started burbling about social mobility in the eighteenth century and widening participation in universities today. Frankly, I thought my sermon was more or less ideal. I began some guff-filled sentence with the words, 'I am sure we all agree ...' It seemed to go well, so I did it again. 'I am sure we all agree we need world-class skills ...', I said, or something equally banal, at which point a man down the table shot to his feet and shouted, 'Well, I don't! I don't agree with what you are saying at all. It seems to me to be quite wrong for you to claim that we all agree when I don't agree.' And blow me down, he appeared to be wearing long purple vestments. It was, of course, Britain's most turbulent priest, the Bishop of Southwark. I realised I was being heckled by a blooming bishop, and from that moment on my speech was irretrievable. I told a long and rambling story about sheep, in the hope that the man of God would be appeased, and sat down. I did sniff him later on, and though there was an aroma of hot cassock he didn't seem notably drunk.

*

Just up there, I said to the taxi driver. Just turn right at the Belisha beacons. A few seconds later I looked up and – what the hell? He'd scooted
right past them. There! I jabbed. There at the Belisha beacons! 'The
what?' said the cabbie. 'Oh you mean the pelican crossing. No one calls
them that any more.' I was dumbfounded, like Simon Heffer on being
told that the 'wireless' is in fact called the radio. And I was sad. Is it not
time for a Tory transport secretary to turn back the clock and insist that
whenever we speak of these lollipops we continue to commemorate his
predecessor, Sir Leslie Hore-Belisha, who served in that office from 1934
to 1937? If that isn't Conservatism, I don't know what is.

DIARY

Sally Emerson

10 February

Since my two children have dispersed to Hollywood and gap-year Sydney, I
spend a great deal of time at home with the individual who needs me most: my
house – mean, moody, magnificent, prone to upsets if left. Its tanks conven-
iently overflowed when we went away to Los Angeles at Christmas. That'll
show me. Today yet another painter came to inspect the damage and I thought
I heard the pipes gurgle a little, as if with laughter. This house used to be the
Chinese military attaché's, and we still receive letters trying to persuade us to
buy used fighter planes. Once we had an invitation to a party on a Thames
river cruise to discuss buying submarines, but I didn't think I'd get away with
turning up and getting out my cheque book. In the attic we discovered a
menacing picture of Mao, and the neighbours relate stories of the lawn being
mowed by a row of Chinese in suits, one pushing the mower, the others
walking beside him in a regimented row in the spirit of old communism.
We also had various soundproofed rooms. God knows what they were for.

I see the Blairs have been increasing their property portfolio. The first
house my husband and I ever sold was to Tony and Cherie Blair, in

Highbury near the new stadium; Number 10 Stavordale Road, in 1986. That house played its tricks too. We'd never had any problems with our boiler or roof, but they did. Indeed, when we saw them some years later, during their first visit to 10 Downing Street when Bill Clinton was visiting and John Major was prime minister, Cherie's first words to us were 'F***ing Stavordale Road'. Sweet.

HIGH LIFE

Taki

10 February

I am seriously thinking of suing Silvio Berlusconi for plagiarising many of my lines. I love Berlusconi, but while he was crooning on board a liner long before he made his billions I was using lines such as 'With you I would go anywhere . . . especially to a desert island . . .' or 'I would follow you anywhere, even to the loo . . . I feel so possessive and jealous . . .' and other such corny lines. Uncool as they may sound now, believe me they used to work, and sometimes they still do.

All seductions begin with flirting. Flirting is the key which turns the engine on. It is as simple as that. Without flirting, you cannot seduce, and without seduction the race becomes extinct. The British newspapers used the term 'playboy antics' to describe Silvio's badinage with young attractive women. But not everybody who uses chat-up lines is a playboy, otherwise you'd have 50 million Italian playboys and ten million Greek ones. Show me an Italian or a Greek man who doesn't flirt and I'll show you a pervert. Flirting has never ruined a marriage or driven a wife to drink. Coldness does that. Men who flirt usually service their wives regularly, and everyone else they can get hold of. Nothing wrong with that; we Europeans need more people and less immigration.

About two years ago Rachel Johnson rang me and asked me for some tips while researching her novel *Notting Hell*. Basically, how to handle a wife, a mistress and – hopefully – a few girlfriends. I wrote ten basic rules which were originally published by her in an article about her novel. So here, at last, are Taki's ten rules for playing away, straight from the horse's mouth: (1) Always remind your wife that you love her and will never leave her for anyone else, ever. (2) Always remind your prospective lover that, if she gives in, you will never leave her and that you love her more than your wife. (3) Always promise marriage. Promising marriage has served me well these last 50 years, although if one is past 60, one should promise that the last will and testament will look very kindly upon anyone who has had carnal knowledge of the soon-to-be deceased. (4) Never raise your voice or show anger. Always fake jealousy with both your wife and lover, and especially with your mistress. (5) Deny, deny, deny. Never admit the slightest indiscretion. Confessions are for amateur adulterers. (6) Be very generous before and after the affair. Women talk, and word that one is generous gets around quicker than bad news. (7) Marry a beautiful woman, preferably upper class and sure of herself, and cuckold her with lesser, uglier beings. She won't mind and they will be flattered to cuckold someone superior to them. (8) Be romantic. Whisper, write notes to both the wife and the lovers. (9) Make love to everyone concerned regularly. Well-serviced women do not go looking for trouble. (10) Always be in a good mood and always make them laugh. Show me a man who makes women laugh, and I'll show you one who gets laid a lot.

THEATRE

Lloyd Evans

24 February

Just over a week ago the death was announced of Sheridan Morley, my predecessor-but-one in this job. He was a distinguished broadcaster and theatre historian and a superb raconteur. He had one of the most attractive speaking voices I've ever encountered. People complained that he sometimes fell asleep in the theatre. He wasn't sleeping. He was remembering the play done better elsewhere. At *The Spectator* we heard of his death with great sadness.

RADIO

Kate Chisholm

24 February

Listening again to *Just a Minute* I could see exactly why children love it. The topics on which the contestants have to pontificate for 60 seconds without hesitation, repetition or deviation are much more abstract and obtuse than they used to be – The End of the World, A Secret I Will Never Tell and The Bee's Knees, for instance. But this only gives Paul Merton, Clement Freud and their fellow competitors the chance to indulge in the kind of wordplay and off-the-wall thinking that kids love when they are at primary-school age but which we lose as soon as we enter the adult world, chastened by the torments of hormone-induced self-consciousness and seduced by the persuasive power of normative thinking.

'In order of magnitude,' ruminates Clement Freud, with 33 seconds left on the clock, 'bee's knees are not very large. Gnat's knickers are even smaller. But nit's knackers are the tiniest of all things.' Roars of laughter from the studio audience, glimpsing momentarily a view of the world with which they were once familiar.

TELEVISION

Simon Hoggart

3 March

I used to write a few political profiles in my time, and the one thing I always hoped was that the subject would refuse to co-operate. You had to offer to interview them, naturally, otherwise there might be legal difficulties. But you prayed they would say no. That rarely happened. When I did see them, I would try to concentrate on the sort of detail that can be hard to come by – where they spent their honeymoon, why they had that row with X, favourite television programme and so forth. What I usually got was the elder statesman in relaxed and contemplative mode, casting his wise, benign eye over the political scene at great and tedious length.

The good stuff invariably came from friends, colleagues and enemies. Take Denis Healey's splendid riposte to the Prince of Wales during a lunch at Chequers. The prince had been chuntering on about his life, how dreary and demanding it was, you really wouldn't want to be me, and so forth, when Healey interrupted him: 'It's yer own fault. You didn't need to take the job,' which was, as my informant said, a perfect Denis remark, being very rude, quite funny and totally untrue.

TELEVISION

Simon Hoggart

17 March

The News Quiz on Radio 4 gives its participants a direct line to Middle England. We forget that a decade ago Princess Di was losing her popularity rather fast, thanks to her high living and a succession of partners who did not – how can I put this? – snugly fit her public image. Earlier a joke at her expense would have been greeted with a sharp intake of breath and even hissing from the studio audience, but by 1997 such lese-majesty was welcomed. At the time she was campaigning against landmines, leading Alan Coren to say, 'I don't know much about landmines or Princess Diana, except that you'd be mad to want to poke either of them.'

There was a short 'did-he-say-what-we-thought-he-said?' moment followed by a huge shout of laughter. Somewhat to my surprise (and pleasure) this excellent gag survived the edit and was broadcast at lunchtime on a Saturday. That night there was the car crash in Paris; the producer came in on Sunday and locked the tape in a safe so it could never be broadcast again. If it had, I assume that a furious nation would have reintroduced hanging, drawing and quartering exclusively for BBC executives.

LOW LIFE

Jeremy Clarke

24 March

At Cheltenham this year I was once again a guest of racing tipster and bon viveur Colonel Pinstripe. The Colonel is famous for his rambling, gossipy, sexist, often libellous telephone tipster line, the avowed goal of which (seldom attained) is to send callers home with 'bulging trousers'. Serious, high-rolling gamblers who ring up his tipster line must be surprised to find themselves invited by the Colonel to repeat solemnly after him, as if it were a mantra, the words 'bulging trousers', having earlier learned, at a pound a minute, about the Colonel's obsessive passion for the wife of Irish trainer Willie Mullins.

In chalet 47, a nomad-style tent within a tent full of other nomad-style hospitality tents, Colonel Pinstripe hosted his annual party of lords, knights, politicians, bankers, venture capitalists, racehorse owners, trainers, gamblers, agents (football and literary) and journalists, all of us qualifying for our invitation by virtue of being, in the Colonel's words, either a 'rogue' or a 'funster'. 'Rogues and funsters! Rogues and funsters!' piped the Colonel throughout the afternoon.

It's an education, chalet 47. By circulating and saying how-do-you-do, you can learn more about how this country functions in a single afternoon than you can by studying the newspapers for the rest of the year. (By all accounts, we're presently a bit like Zaire under Mobutu.)

As well as a free bar, there was a sit-down lunch and afternoon tea for those on solids, and three waitresses anxious to satisfy our every whim, almost. There was a television set in the corner to watch the races. And to save everybody the trouble of walking the 20 yards to the Tote, a dead ringer for Michael Caine, both in looks and sardonic wit, was personally taking bets. So, in theory, one didn't have to leave the table. Parvenu that I am, however, I preferred to trot along to the Tote because Zara Phillips was often to be found there placing the royal tenner, and, elevated by Mumm champagne to the point of insanity, I fancied my chances. His Royal Highness Prince William could also be seen among the hospitality tents. Tall and slender and blushing continuously, he seemed to spend the entire afternoon marching purposefully between his chalet (no. 48) and the Tote, anxiously pursued by three detectives, the largest and slowest of which had the facial expression of a man who has committed every sin in the Decalogue.

After luncheon, fairly squiffy by now, I went outside the tent for a breath of fresh air with a football agent. You could hardly move for people, so the football agent suggested we go into the parade ring to stretch our legs. He showed the men on the gate his badge, which easily did the trick for both of us, and in we went.

The horses were parading before the first race. About 5,000 people were pinned behind the rail, straining to see. But on the lovely circular sunlit expanse of bright green there were only a few isolated groups of owners and their associates, plus BBC sports presenter Clare Balding and a camera crew. The football agent and I stretched our legs on the turf, then we spoke to a couple of the owners who were friends of his. Neither rated their horse's chances of winning much. The second owner was positively, perhaps even clinically, depressed about them. After about a minute's conversation with him, we began to get depressed as well, so the football agent suggested we talk to Clare Balding to cheer ourselves up. So over we trotted, and she must be an old mate of his or something because she was genuinely pleased to see him. The football agent introduced me as 'Low life'.

By no stretch of the imagination, even in a society as democratic as ours, was I either suitably dressed or eligible for the parade ring at the Cheltenham festival. I know nothing about horses except that I'm frightened of them. My charity-shop clothes were unco-ordinated. The buckle on my trousers had given way and they were open to about halfway down the fly. I was seeing double. I'd been watching Crufts all week, however, and was thrilled to be seeing not one but two of Clare Balding in the flesh.

But she's one classy lady is Clare Balding. Her astonishment at being introduced to what must have appeared to be an inquisitive tramp was momentary, tinged with good humour and immediately suppressed. 'Do you know,' she said, pointing to two startlingly beautiful black horses being led around the ring, 'I quite fancy that horse over there, number nine.' Back in the tent I invested a tenner on number nine with Michael Caine. (Colonel Pinstripe was singing, 'Funs and Roguesters! Funs and Roguesters!') Number nine won the first race at 20–1. 'Can I owe it to you, chief?' said Michael Caine, when I accosted him for my winnings.

CINEMA

Deborah Ross

28 April

The Painted Veil (12A)

Readers, I cried. And I cried a good deal. True, I'll cry at anything, and I don't just mean *Seabiscuit* or *The English Patient*. I cried, for example, when Rachel returned to Ross in *Friends*. I cried when Dr Green died in *ER*. I will cry during *Animal Hospital* if a hamster has to be euthanised, even though I think hamsters are horrid and ratty and should just be stamped on. So my crying has nothing to do with whether anything is any good or not. A high score on The Ross Cryometer, in short, cannot be taken as an indication of quality. It might even be an indication of cheap, sentimental crap. But I don't think this is the case here, unless I am kidding myself, which I am good at, too. (I always, for example, weigh myself while holding on to the sink, which is actually a good idea as otherwise I'd probably be fat.)

DIARY

Gyles Brandreth

5 May

The telephone rang at 7.45 a.m. It was a journalist I know. She sounded tense. 'Gyles,' she said, 'do you want to come out?' 'It's a bit early, isn't it, darling?' I replied. 'I mean, "come out",' she said with emphasis, adding, with a little laugh, 'Everyone knows you're gay.' 'Do they?' I asked. 'Am I?' 'Oh, come on,' she persisted, 'Frankie Howerd made a pass at you once, didn't he?' 'Yes.' 'And you knew Ted Heath?' 'Er . . . yes.' 'Well?' she said. I put the phone down. What is this bizarre obsession we have with the sexual orientation of others? Frankie Howerd was certainly promiscuous (and, oddly, in the habit of propositioning straight men – perhaps rejection was his bag?), but if anyone manages to turn up hard evidence that Ted Heath walked with a squeak, I'll be surprised. Of course, if it does transpire that there was a touch of the Tommy-two-ways about our Ted, it just shows you what a truly modern Tory he was.

LIDDLE BRITAIN

Rod Liddle

9 June

There's been quite a fuss about the official new logo for the 2012 Olympic Games in London. People are aghast at the fact that it is a) hideous and b) cost £400,000. A child, a blind man, an ape let loose with a paintbrush could all have done better, the argument goes. Well yes, of course. The jarring amalgamation of irregular shapes does indeed bring to mind the sort of graffiti one finds on walls near a home for the educationally subnormal – and there is the faint aftertaste of Adolf Hitler, too. Squint a little and the logo turns into a swastika; stare at it head on after a glass or two of schnapps and you can make out the bold letters SS. The logo is supposed to emphasise the 'inclusive' nature of the games. I suppose the Nazis were inclusive, in a fairly bad sense of the term.

But this public carping neglects two very important points: first, all corporate logos are hideous and necessarily stupid, doodles dreamed up by some ghastly little marketing rebranding monkey who feels himself infected with zeitgeist. And second, they are always, always, hideously expensive and a blind paraplegic ape etc. could do better.

The truth is, we've all got off rather lightly with an outlay of just £400k, as I daresay the executives at Wolff-Olins, the people responsible, are angrily muttering to one another at this very moment. After all, Wolff-Olins are the people who almost destroyed Abbey National with what was described as the most catastrophic rebranding in corporate history – and they charged the company a large fee for the privilege of so doing. Out went that pale red logo with the folksy umbrella sheltering people from an unforeseen shower, immediately recognisable by everyone. Out went that awful word 'National' – a big, bullying beast of an adjective. And in came a logo where the word 'Abbey' was written in crayon by a spaced-out imbecile, followed up by some seriously bad TV advertising.

The aim of all this, Wolff-Olins insisted, was to 'demystify' money, but those of us who discovered how much they had been paid for this farrago ended up all the more bewildered by the quixotic nature of the stuff. I seem to remember that Wolff-Olins also created that prancing, homosexual piper who now adorns the BT corporate masthead. They also did Ikea and the job there was to 'democratise interior design'. That's one way of describing what Ikea does, I suppose.

If I'm honest, I don't object hugely to the 2012 logo, or at least no more than I had expected to. It has been argued that the design tells you nothing about London, that it fails to capture the spirit of our capital city. But the same was true of Athens in 2004: if the Greeks had wished to capture the spirit of their capital city they'd have depicted an asthmatic kebab-shop owner choking to death on traffic fumes against a backdrop of the Acropolis, but they didn't. And similarly Peking next year – never mind this androgynous bloke dancing in ecstasy, what's wrong with the interior view of a prison cell, maybe with a subtle rice-paper overlay?

DIARY

Joan Collins

18 August

The shiny new 'Vodka Palaces' lie scattered across the bay of St Tropez like the discarded toys of a spoiled child. Each year they seem to grow bigger, as do the gorgeous girls who cluster on deck and throng the boutiques and clubs – taller anyway. Many of the boats are owned by Russian billionaires – how did they become so rich so fast? – and it seems that three or four dazzlers hang on the arm of each stocky oligarch. What did the Russian government feed their pregnant women and toddlers two decades ago that made these women sprout into tall and skinny beanstalks? And why is it only the girls who seem to have inherited that giant gene? All the men are pretty ordinary both in looks and height; maybe their massive wealth makes up for their massive bellies. At Cave du Roi, the local dive where a jeroboam of Cristal can set you back €10,000, I stood with two girlfriends, primping in the powder room, our mouths agape at these giraffes. None of them was under six foot, and they sauntered about in tiny mini-dresses and five-inch stilettos, idly tossing waist-length locks. Either the government gave them hair growth supplements in infancy or Russia is making the most realistic extensions since Lady Godiva! Feeling like three of the dwarves from *Snow White*, my girlfriends and I sat in the club becoming more hysterical as each Amazon tottered past: truly a scene from *Attack of the 50ft Woman*.

LETTERS

25 August

Sir: Joan Collins (Diary, 18 August) makes an interesting point about the abnormal height (and hair growth) of 'Russian' women aged about 20. I wonder if they are Russian? I met a similar long-haired slender giantess (complete with five-inch stilettos) in Brussels a few years ago and I asked her where she came from. 'Ukraine' was the answer. And what happened in Ukraine about 20 years ago? Chernobyl. I understand strawberries nearby grew as big as footballs.

Mary Clark
Cumbria

LOW LIFE

Jeremy Clarke

8 September

'So. Jeremy. Why do you want to learn about eating seaweed?' said Ingrid as we trooped down the leafy farm track to the beach. Ingrid, our leader for the day, was a spry woman in her early fifties wearing a hand-stitched buckskin Hiawatha tunic and possibly little else. She was going to show us how to identify, harvest, prepare and cook a four-course seaweed 'feast' over a driftwood fire. I was preparing myself for the collapse of civilisation, I told her. 'When we're all eating each other,' I said, 'I'm hoping that a side dish of seaweed will vary my diet a bit.'

A dozen of us had responded to the flyer pinned to the vegetarian café noticeboard advertising Ingrid's day of instruction. My fellow punters were all foot soldiers of the New Age and they all had that air about them of holy children treading lightly upon the earth. They couldn't work me out at all.

My pessimism about the future of Western civilisation compensated though, I hoped, for my numb-nut 'Hammers on Tour in Cardiff 2006' T-shirt.

As we passed down the lane Ingrid identified a flowering wild-mustard plant, a clump of wild sorrel and a bed of watercress, from which we harvested garnish for the seaweed salad. Ingrid was very strict with us about pinching off only the tops of the watercress plants 'to ensure their blessed continuance'.

Finally, we descended via a zigzag path into a narrow secluded cove. The tide was right out. It was one of the lowest tides of the year.

We gathered a pile of driftwood, then Ingrid gave us a team talk. Our primary consideration, she said, as we harvest the seaweed with our scissors and knives, is that we avoid dishonouring the beauty and the community of the seaweed. As we cut it away we must ask permission in our hearts and thank it for giving itself up for our nourishment. Then she stepped out of her Hiawatha tunic and stood stark naked before us.

Her pubic hair was unbelievably profuse. It was a map of British India, roughly speaking, including what later became Pakistan, Bangladesh and Kashmir, with parts of Burma, Tibet and Afghanistan added on. I couldn't take my eyes off it. All of us except two then followed her lead and stripped right off as well. Opening her arms in supplication to embrace rock, sea and sky, and tilting her map of India at the horizon, Ingrid intoned, 'This is all a miracle and a gift to us all. Thank you, Mother Ocean, for welcoming us here, your children.' Then with her eyes closed in ecstasy she led us in a sung chant. 'O-cean! O-cean!' we sang. As chants go I've heard better. After a good two minutes of that, we picked up our scissors, buckets and carrier bags and Ingrid led us forward, a line of hobbling nudists, over the sharp rocks. 'Out we go!' she sang. 'Out we go among the rocks and the sea, our brothers and our sister!'

Squatting on the slimy, seaweed-fringed rocks at the water's edge we snipped away at whatever Ingrid advised. The seaweed, once you started to take notice of it, was remarkably varied in shape, colour and texture, and, seen floating beneath the surface of the rock pools, not unattractive. We harvested bright-green sea lettuce; long strings of sea spaghetti; flat, shiny brown strips of kelp; and pretty florets of purple sea dulse.

There were just three casualties during the afternoon. One woman slipped and scoured the skin from both buttocks on the jagged edges of a rock. On Ingrid's advice she lay on her back on a thick bed of kelp, which is reputed to have healing properties. On learning that it also nourishes the skin, this woman asked to be buried up to the neck in it while she was lying there, and I was first on the scene with a slippery armful.

Another casualty was the loss of a pair of glasses into the sea. They fell off a young woman's nose and dropped out of sight in deep water. She was blind as a mole without them but remained cheerful. Being unable to see for the rest of the day wouldn't be such a bad thing, she said, as consciousness of one's external reality can become such a distracting chore at times.

And sadly there was one death. While I was tending the fire I allowed a sand-hopping insect to burn alive while Ingrid, issuing me with cooking instructions, was crouched over the fire.

'Ah! Ah!' she wailed. 'He's burning! Ah! Blessings! Blessing on your journey, dear Mr Sandhopper!' It could have been worse, though. One stray spark and we could have had a forest fire on our hands to match the recent tragedy in Greece.

STATUS ANXIETY

Toby Young

22 September

One of the occupational hazards of being a journalist these days is that, sooner or later, you'll get a call asking if you want to be in a reality show. The reason is simple: we're just about the only people left in the country who are likely to say yes. It is not just that we're complete publicity whores – we're hardly alone in that respect – it is also that we have the perfect excuse: we can pretend we're just doing it for 'journalistic reasons'.

I don't think I've ever turned down the opportunity to appear on a reality show. Indeed, earlier this year, I agreed to fly to Kenya and take part in a marathon alongside Les Dennis, Michaela Strachan and Ruby

Wax. Unfortunately, I had to pull out when I realised it clashed with another reality show I had already agreed to do in a railway arch in Bermondsey. I'm thinking of changing my answering machine message so it says, 'Whatever it is, the answer's yes.' (For years, this was the outgoing message of John Leslie, the ex-*Blue Peter* presenter.)

I've now done so many reality shows that I've had to abandon the journalism excuse. These days, I pretend I'm just doing it for the money – and, in fairness, you can earn a decent living as a reality show contestant. I don't wish to be unkind to Jade Goody, whom I regard as a sort of role model, but I think it's unlikely she'd have a net worth of over £2 million if she had never appeared on television.

Of course, the real reason journalists always say yes is because we cannot resist the allure of television. Cathode rays act like a tractor beam, sucking us all in, no matter how high-minded. The last of us to hold out was A. A. Gill who, for years, maintained that he simply didn't do telly. Then, in a day that will live in infamy, he popped up as a judge on *Project Catwalk*, a Sky One knock-off of *Britain's Next Top Model*. Whatever it is, the answer's yes.

You can imagine my excitement, therefore, when I received an email from an ITV executive asking me if I wanted to be on *Hell's Kitchen*. This wasn't in my capacity as an occasional food critic, but as a full-blown contestant. I and ten other 'celebrities' would receive a crash course in cooking from Marco Pierre White, then compete for the public's affection while working in the restaurant equivalent of the *Big Brother* house. 'This would be approximately a two-week commitment,' the email concluded. Would I be interested in meeting with the show's producers to discuss it further? You bet I would.

The conventional wisdom about how to impress television producers is that it's like seducing a beautiful lover: you have to play hard to get. While this may be true of *Question Time*, it isn't true of reality TV. Being shy and retiring isn't an asset on, say, *Celebrity Love Island*. What the producers of these programmes want are people who are 'interested in new experiences', 'willing to have a go' – or, in other words, slags.

After making a very favourable impression on the producers of *Hell's*

Kitchen – 'I want to go on a journey of self-discovery' – I thought it was in the bag. I even made the mistake of bragging about it to Giles Coren, *The Times*'s restaurant critic, who immediately informed me that he'd turned it down. I don't know if he was telling the truth – he may have been – but whenever a fellow journalist tells me that he's about to appear in a reality show I always tell him that I turned it down. The number of hacks who say they've forgone the opportunity to appear on *I'm a Celebrity . . . Get Me Out of Here* is at least as great as the number who claim to have seen the Sex Pistols play at the Screen on the Green in 1976. (I was invited to that gig, by the way, but I turned it down.)

Then, just before *Hell's Kitchen* was due to be broadcast, the ITV executive called and said that they'd decided to make me 'the first reserve'. 'If any of the contestants drop out, you're the first person we'll call,' she said. I duly explained this to all the people I'd already told I was going to be on the show, such as my parents-in-law, and then had to deal with a deluge of enquiring phone calls when not one, but two of the contestants dropped out and neither of them were substituted. I didn't even get summoned to give my verdict on the dishes of the two finalists – that honour fell to Giles Coren. My humiliation was complete.

Ah well. There's always the next series of *Extreme Celebrity Detox*. Whatever it is, the answer's yes.

DIARY

Emily Maitlis

15/29 December

It has been that sort of week, really. A lot crammed into a smallish space. On Monday I dashed from the Policy Exchange Christmas party to the re-re-re-relaunch of Duran Duran. In the seats behind us were Bob Geldof and Tara Palmer-Tomkinson, which safely gets my Weird Pairing of the Week award. It was groupie heaven, crowned with a kiss from Simon Le Bon. My cheek is now on eBay.

2008

Tim Rice; Hugo Rifkind; Deborah Ross;
Dear Mary; Toby Young; Rod Liddle;
Marcus Berkmann; Beryl Bainbridge

DIARY

Tim Rice

5 January

My daughter has just got married and a beautiful and lively event it was, moving from her local church in St James's Gardens to the Dorchester via Routemaster buses. I took the opportunity in my speech to thank many for their efforts to be present but reserved my principal praise not for those who had journeyed from Australia, America and South Africa, but for those who had travelled just a few miles from other parts of London. When you have flogged through hideous traffic at the end of another ghastly working day to attend a wedding in your home town it is always extremely annoying to sit through praise showered upon those from foreign parts who are having a terrific holiday, away from everyday pressures, with a lavish wedding and numerous other social freebies thrown in. I hope my words redressed the balance on behalf of all those who endured the hell of a journey from one postal district to another rather than the thrill of flying from one continent to another.

I was determined not to give guests the opportunity to reject the food on offer, at least before they got there. It is quite extraordinary how hosts now seem to be required to cater for every dietary whim of those they are generously entertaining. If you are not prepared to take a chance on the nosh offending your health, environmental or religious quirks, then don't come, or at least be quite happy to push the obnoxious items to the side of your plate and chew bread or your napkin. Whenever I get a form asking for my dietary requirements I always put 'large helpings', which request is unfortunately (but quite correctly) rarely acted upon.

SHARED OPINION
Hugo Rifkind
22 March

It is social awkwardness, I have always thought, that prevents Britain from being properly corrupt. Reading about these allegations of bribery against a potato supplier for Sainsbury's, I found myself almost awestruck. Imagine having the balls for that. I find it hard enough to tip.

I bribed a policeman once, in a remote bit of southern Africa. I really wasn't very good at it. I was in a car with my girlfriend, and we were motoring merrily along, and then there were suddenly police, everywhere. They waved a clearly decrepit speed camera at us, cited some implausible speed, and then showed us a handwritten chart that appeared to mean I had to send the government the local equivalent of £500. Then they just stood there, waiting.

It took me a while. The sun beat down, the policemen stared at their shoes. On the verges, cattle yawned. And even when, really after ages, it finally dawned on me what they were after, I still wasn't entirely confident. So in a sentence laden with terrified double meaning, I suggested that I might be interested in paying a smaller fine, if I could pay it now, and they weren't to write it down.

'Eh?' said the policeman, and above us, vultures cawed.

'Do you want a bribe?' I blurted.

'Yes,' said the policeman. So I gave him a tenner.

CINEMA
Deborah Ross
22 March

Lars and the Real Girl (12A) is a comedy which tells the story of an introverted, emotionally backward loner (Ryan Gosling, in bad knitwear and anorak) who believes a sex doll is real and introduces her to the local community as his girlfriend. It all sounds gorgeous, as if it is going to be wonderfully distasteful – how could it not be? – but, disappointingly, it just isn't nearly distasteful enough. This is a shame, particularly if you have been waiting a long time for a decent film featuring bad knitwear and a sex doll, as I have.

YOUR PROBLEMS SOLVED

Dear Mary . . .

17 May

Q. I have caught a cold from a senior member of the royal family. I feel sure there must be ways in which I can turn this to my social and/or financial advantage and I admit that I have deliberately been sleeping in a draught in order to prolong the symptoms. What do you suggest, Mary?

  – Name and address withheld

A. There are very few socially acceptable ways in which one can market such a condition or even use it to boost one's status. For example if anyone said 'Bless you!' when you sneezed, it would be quite wrong to then remark on the provenance of your cold. Where charitable fundraising is concerned, however, it is a different matter and, if you act quickly, you could offer your services at some *Tatler*-y party. You could charge £50 a time to allow snobs eager to have this sort of rare intimate contact with royalty by baccillae to join you in a claustrophobic overheated booth within the party. The takings could then go to charitable causes and tongues would wag as to how you were in a position to catch the cold in the first place. Naturally you would refuse to be drawn on this issue.

STATUS ANXIETY

Toby Young

14 June

Did my wife really mean it when she said I didn't have to be present at the birth?

By the time you read this, I will be the proud father of another baby. That is the plan, anyway. My wife has had enough of being pregnant and has booked herself into hospital to be induced. The actual due date is 19 June, but her midwife says it is perfectly acceptable for the baby to come out a week early.

When Caroline informed me of this I was a bit put out. 'But darling,' I said. 'I've got a lunch date with an important television executive that day. It could take months to reschedule.'

'In that case, why don't you keep it?' she said. 'I honestly don't mind if you're not there this time.'

'Really? Are you sure?'

'Absolutely.'

I was cock-a-hoop. To be honest, I did not care for being present at the birth of my first three children. I know it is customary these days, but there is still no proper role for expectant fathers in a delivery suite. My wife doesn't go in for hand holding and, being a grown woman, she does not need to be told when to 'breathe'. On all three occasions I had the sense of being an interloper at a secret feminine ritual.

Part of the problem is that I simply have no grasp of delivery-room etiquette. For instance, after the birth of our first child I spotted a young black baby in the adjacent bed and suggested to Caroline that I photograph her holding this baby instead of our own. My plan was to email that picture to all our friends. No explanation, just the words: 'Marcellus was born at 6.15 this morning. He weighs 7lb 15oz.'

Needless to say, this suggestion went down badly – so the prospect of not having to worry about sticking my foot in it again was very appealing.

Then I spotted a fly in the ointment. If Caroline did not want me at the hospital, would I have to rush back from my lunch and single-handedly take care of the children? Suddenly, being in the delivery suite did not seem so bad.

'Don't worry,' she said. 'I've arranged for my mother to come over.'

The news just got better and better! Friday was shaping up to be something of a holiday. After dropping Caroline off at Queen Charlotte's, I could go back to bed with a cup of tea and actually read the paper for the first time in five years. After that, I could catch up with some of the Euro 2008 highlights backed up on my Sky Plus and then, when my mother-in-law arrives, head off to my lunch, followed by a trip to the Shepherd's Bush Vue. Has *The Incredible Hulk* opened yet? If not, there is always *Iron Man*. Presumably, this is exactly how expectant fathers behaved in the Good Old Days.

It was not until the following day that my reverie was shattered. I was at the opening of a new alfresco restaurant at Fulham Palace called The Lawn – lovely, by the way – and bumped into Clare Margetson, the former women's editor of the *Guardian*. I boasted about how 'enlightened' my wife was, not holding with the politically correct view that husbands ought to be present at the birth of their children.

'She didn't mean it, you idiot,' said Clare.

'What? No, no, no, I'm sure she did.'

'Are you insane? Of course she wants you to be there.'

'But then why—'

'Women say that sort of thing all the time. It's a test. She doesn't want you to be there under duress – she wants you to be there of your own free will.'

'Are you positive about this?'

'Believe me, if you're not there, she'll hold it against you.'

A quick straw poll of the other young mums at the party confirmed that Clare was correct. Having got into trouble before by taking things Caroline has said at face value, I decided to listen to their advice. In these situations, men are expected to be metro-sexuals, not red-blooded heterosexuals. *Iron Man* would have to give way to Ironing Man.

My father-in-law, a wise old bird called Ivo, telephoned to tell me I was doing the right thing. He recalled that a friend of his had been unable to attend the birth of his youngest daughter because of a 'business dinner' and he still had not heard the end of it. 'That was 33 years ago,' he said. 'I think you've made the right decision.'

SHARED OPINION

Hugo Rifkind

23 August

White Van Man to White Dog Man. Or rather, Tintin. You may have heard how, on the Continent, an adult, updated version of the adventures of Hergé's famous boy reporter-detective has been withdrawn from shelves. According to the estate of Georges Remi, who was to Hergé what Eric Blair was to George Orwell, *The Pink Lotus* 'perverted the essence of the personality' of Tintin himself. In it, we apparently see Tintin as an older, unhappy, unethical tabloid hack; a borderline alcoholic and a womaniser.

This does, indeed, pervert the essence of his personality. The Tintin I loved was inseparable from a bearded sea captain, and always carrying around his tiny hound. They spent their life gallivanting around the globe, and were seemingly unhappy in the constraining embrace of home. Their only female friend is a blowsy opera singer, but they prefer the company of professors, butlers, and a pair of chaps called Thompson and Thomson who, despite being unrelated, wore the same clothes, had the same moustache, and were never seen apart. Hack, maybe. Alcoholic, possibly. Womaniser, no.

LIDDLE BRITAIN

Rod Liddle

27 September

Apparently, David Miliband's speech to the Labour party conference was deliberately low-key because he did not wish to have a 'Heseltine Moment' – that is, he did not wish to be seen as being too obviously a threat to the Prime Minister, too openly desirous of his job. What a fabulous strutting little cock this man truly is. Flying around the world in the Queen's private jet to deliver fatuous or anodyne pronouncements to the media at an extortionate cost to the taxpayer, all the while considering himself the heir to the leadership of a great political party which in better times would have considered him a smug, jumped-up, risible little wonker who was maybe suitable for a very junior role in the Department of Work and Pensions, at best. And of course, heir to the leadership of a great country; come on, Britain – that simply cannot be allowed to happen. Do you remember all those leftie rumours of how a coalition of the secret service, the army, industrialists and hard-right Tory politicians were about to take over the country in a coup towards the end of Jim Callaghan's premiership? I assume quite a few of you *Spectator* readers were actually part of the coup – in which case, can't you get something up and running for the day Miliband takes over? I'll help. Just say the word. At the very least I could sit by the guillotine, doing some knitting.

The remarkable thing is the extent to which Miliband clearly believes that leadership of both the party and the country are sort of his by rights, that his qualities are so self-evident that his elision to power should be unquestioned. So much is apparent by his willingness to compare himself favourably to a politician 500 times his worth, Michael Heseltine. It is like me comparing myself favourably to Goethe. To be sure, the mop-headed, mace-wielding Europhile who, unforgivably, buys his own furniture had one or two faults – a certain arrogance, perhaps hubris. And like Miliband, he was not without ambition. Unlike Miliband, however, one could understand why he had ambition, even during his most infuriatingly imperial moments. Heseltine was a Big Beast; David Miliband, by contrast, is – at best – a stumpy little Muntjac deer and his brother Ed something much smaller still, perhaps one of those nematode worms which stab themselves to death with their own penises.

Mr Ed the Talking Horse was on *Newsnight* this week, in fact, demonstrating why some pro-Blair party munchkins think he is preferable to his brother: more human, less aloof, you see. In his interview with Jeremy Paxman he said nothing whatsoever. Now, I know politicians are famous these days for not saying anything; but Ed really did divest himself of absolutely nothing. He began every single answer with the words: 'Surely, Jeremy, you can't expect me to answer that.' And then didn't answer it. The questions weren't impertinent, personal or irrelevant; Paxo didn't ask him if he masturbated regularly. He just asked, politely, in the most general terms, what a more relaxed spending policy might entail and what strictures might be brought to bear on the running of our financial institutions. 'Surely, Jeremy, you can't expect me to answer that,' came the reply every time, a smirked 'f*** you' to both Paxman and the electorate. The nerve we have, expecting to be told stuff, expecting politicians to engage. Mr Ed and his brother do not comprehend the extent to which this astonishing hauteur offends the public – because, I suspect, they have never really been members of the public themselves. They have always been politicians or wonks, developing in total isolation from the real world, rather in the manner of those weirdly well-spoken alien creatures in a John Wyndham novel.

POP MUSIC

Marcus Berkmann

6 December

It all started earlier this year, when my friend Chris managed to get four tickets for the first of the Leonard Cohen concerts at the O$_2$. 'There's one for you if you want it,' he said. Well, obviously I wanted it, but cash was a little short at the time – in fact, not so much short as entirely absent, avoiding me as though I'd said the wrong thing. And I do have an ongoing tinnitus problem, the result of reviewing too many awful Tin Machine gigs for a certain crazed mass-market newspaper in the early 1990s. Earlier this year I went to a friend's book launch held in a seedy West End dive where they played chart tunes at ear-splitting volume, and for a week afterwards I thought my head was going to explode. So I said no to Chris, with the greatest reluctance, and slight relief in the knowledge that the £67 I didn't have, I still didn't have, rather than having £67 less than that.

But the Leonard Cohen concerts, as everyone will tell you, were life-changing events, not least for Leonard himself, whose money problems outclass my own in every way. A few weeks later Chris rang up again. 'I've got four more tickets for 13 November. There's one for you if you want it. And it really wasn't that loud. The sound quality is so good it doesn't have to be loud. Go on, you'll regret it if you don't.'

So, obviously, several months later I find myself on the Thames Clipper, surrounded by slightly worn-looking middle-aged people all buzzing with anticipation, or coffee. As we shall see at the O₂, Laughing Len attracts a pangenerational audience – young people accompanying aged parents, with the occasional grandparent hobbling along behind, who bought Len's first album in 1967, or might have slept with him. There's also a glorious preponderance of attractive young Jewish women milling about but, overall, this is the crumbliest and most bourgeois audience for a gig I have ever seen.

The O₂ itself is strangely reminiscent of Stansted Airport. Do you do your shopping before or after you go through security? One of our number had the lid of her bottle of water taken away by a Customer Safety representative, as the bouncers are now called. With its lid, apparently, the bottle could be used as a missile. Not that many of this audience could throw anything more than three feet.

We take our seats, noticing that many of the executive boxes are empty: presumably the people who would have filled them have all been sacked. A man three rows in front of us looks astonishingly like Andreas Whittam Smith. Is it he? Would the priestly founder of the *Independent* be seen in public drinking a pint of Beck's Vier from a plastic glass? Maybe it's his raffish younger brother. The black sheep of the family. Ken Whittam Smith.

The stage, of course, is miles away. The musicians look like Oompa Loompas. Len himself looks gaunt and tiny, with a natty hat. 'Thank you for climbing these dizzy financial and architectural heights to get to your seats. It's much appreciated. Thank you.' This will be the single most courteous gig I have ever attended. And Chris was right: the sound quality is astonishing and the volume is bearable, even for my ruined ears. Cohen's band is quite something. Javier Mas, on mandolin and 12-string, is virtuosity in a dark suit. But none of the players showboat. They solo from time to time, but their skills are always in service to the songs, not the other way round. The backing singers are Sharon Robinson, who co-wrote 'Everybody Knows' and the whole of the *Ten New Songs* album, and the Webb Sisters, two young Englishwomen I had never heard of, who will contribute a heartstoppingly lovely version of 'If It Be Your Will', accompanying themselves on guitar and harp. There will be an amazing live album to be created from all this.

The gig, it has to be said, is half an hour too long. During 'Take This Waltz' the bankers all leave, looking at their BlackBerrys importantly. As Leonard launches into 'So Long, Marianne', representatives of the insurance industry depart, their bald heads gleaming in the arclights. It seems extraordinary that these shows are only happening because Cohen's manager ran off with all his money. Was it a blessing in disguise? How must it be to feel all that love? It seems like the natural culmination of a unique career, and we feel honoured to be there to witness it. On the boat back, we say what can't really be said, that these might be his last concerts, without saying what is even more apparent: that this might have been the last one for a good proportion of the audience too.

DIARY

Beryl Bainbridge

20/27 December

The days leading up to Xmas are such fun, aren't they? All those cards and presents to buy and all those charity requests reminding one of starving children, crippled adults and abandoned dogs. Over the last few days I've been trying to concentrate on more important things, such as Sight and Time. Obviously the two go together, for both determine a view of the world. In regard to Sight, my bathroom ceiling fell down because the house next door put up scaffolding and the chap in charge stepped on to my flat roof and put his foot through it. He denied doing so, of course. When I now get into the tub there's a bloody big hole up above and the rain comes through. I'm not too upset because I was brought up to believe that, owing to the cost of heating water, one only needs a bath once a fortnight. All the same, the hole annoys me. As regards Time, I find it odd that it flies when one is young and drags when old. If the laundry man is due to come at ten o'clock and I get up at seven, months pass before he arrives.

2009

Deborah Ross; Dear Mary; Rod Liddle;
Hugo Rifkind; Miriam Gross; Lloyd Evans

CINEMA

Deborah Ross

16 May

Angels & Demons (12A) is based on the book by Dan '*Da Vinci Code*' Brown and is directed by Ron Howard and stars Tom Hanks and all I can really say about it is this: if there is one movie you don't see this year, do make it this one.

YOUR PROBLEMS SOLVED

Dear Mary . . .

4 July

> **Q.** An old friend summoned me to a black-tie dinner at the Cambridge college of which he is master. On arrival I found I had forgotten cuff links so I threaded a shoelace through each cuff and tied them together that way. Knowing that I have about 20 pairs of cuff links at home, I could not bring myself, in the current financial climate, to go out and buy another pair. I felt my response was imaginative but my host raised his eyebrows in a pompous way and made me feel small. Who was right, Mary?
> – C.S., Worcs

> **A.** It really depends on how the laces looked. Might they have looked a little bit Sir Les Patterson? Might your host have felt the omission was symptomatic of a general lack of respect for himself? Next time this happens why not take a tip from Edward McMillan-Scott, vice president of the European parliament?

When, on a recent occasion, he found himself similarly caught short, he employed a pair of polo mints with standard-issue brass butterfly clips plunged through them. The result? Understated elegance for less than five pence.

LIDDLE BRITAIN

Rod Liddle

15 August

It's been a grim summer for news, all things considered, what with Afghanistan and flying pig flu and the rain and now Harriet Harman squatting over us all like one of those terrifying smallpox deities the Hindus have. So I thought I'd share with you a story which, in the midst of this gloom, cheered me up enormously. It is the story of a little ginger and white pussycat called Wilbur, who lived in Bristol with his owners, Martin and Helen Wadey. Martin and Helen loved Wilbur a lot. His purr was, according to Martin, 'like a dynamo'. He was the family pet and suitably adored.

Anyway, one day Wilbur set off in pursuit of that familiar and engaging leisure option for our millions of domesticated cats – killing wildlife in a neighbour's garden and then taking a massive dump in the middle of the lawn. Off he went on his pitter-patter little paws, over the fence, across the flower bed (pausing briefly to urinate on a rose bush) to check out what creatures he might harry to death – look, over there, a vole scampering with fright beneath the hedge! Or that fledgling mistle thrush obliviously looking for its mum. Wilbur thought about it for a moment, then devised a plan of action: start with the thrushling, then have a dump just by the patio and finish up spending a bit of time tracking down the vole – worth the effort because they're endangered, apparently. But then Wilbur caught a first whiff of something quite unexpected: a rich, exotic, luxuriant smell he did not recognise – beguiling and yet somehow carrying a sleek, sinuous harbinger of danger. What the hell is that, Wilbur wondered to himself, in those last few seconds before he was eaten by the python. Wildlife 1, Pussycat 0.

Not just eaten, mind, but – according to the press reports – 'crushed, asphyxiated and consumed whole'. I don't know what the *Daily Telegraph* would have preferred the python to do – maybe stun Wilbur humanely with some sort of electrical device before flambéing his liver for a light supper, accompanied by a glass of Chablis. Whatever, Martin and Helen heard 'blood-chilling cries' emanating from their neighbour's garden and immediately suspected that it was Wilbur. They were right! The RSPCA turned up and with some piece of hi-tech equipment detected the cat's ID chip inside the python's bulging stomach and the faintest, defeated, plaintive miaow. Laugh? At this point of the story I was paralytic with mirth and jubilation – but then I read on and a familiar irritation began to settle on my shoulders.

First, the Wadeys' bizarre and unjust reaction in complaining about such an outcome. Like all cat owners they seem utterly without any notion of responsibility, either to their neighbours or indeed to the wild-life which surrounds them. Some 80 million wild birds and animals are killed by domesticated cats each year and this may well account at least partly for the rapid decline of some of our garden songbirds – the thrush, the dunnock, the starling, the house sparrow. Not to mention the water vole. But cat owners could not give a monkey's – that's nature, they argue, that's what cats do, they decimate wildlife.

Well, sure – and that's what pythons do, they eat cats, given half a chance, so stop whining. Cat owners also do not care that their creatures wander over all the gardens of their neighbourhood, leaving behind their toxic ribbons of noisome defecation and the bodies of dead birds and mammals on the back steps of their neighbours' houses. Wilbur was doing precisely this when he was eaten by the neighbour's civic-minded Burmese python; if the foul creature had stayed in its own backyard, it would be alive right now to rub itself up against its owners in the manner of a sexual deviant released on parole several years too early. The snake was minding its own business in its own terrain and had not expected to be disturbed by an agreeable late afternoon snack blundering through the undergrowth, believing itself – mistakenly, as it turned out – to be top of the local food chain. Tough, puddytat. And yet when the RSPCA was called the focus of anger was directed at the owner of the python, who was issued with a written warning about keeping his snake indoors, safely locked away. Why? Why wasn't the same warning issued to Mr and Mrs Wadey, to the effect that they should not be allowed another cat unless they could guarantee that it would not invade their neighbours' gardens? At least the python stayed in its own backyard. And didn't the RSPCA have a device to see what was lurking in Wilbur's stomach?

SHARED OPINION

Hugo Rifkind

17 October

Karl Lagerfeld is one of those rare individuals who has managed to look like his own desiccated corpse without first having died. Whenever I see pictures of him, rocking that Nazi-zombie-meets-waiter-from-Strada look that he does so well, and clutching a small and emaciated dog, I always wonder if the poor dog is on a diet, too. And then I wonder whether it eats more or less than he does.

As such, Lagerfeld's views on the desirable weight of models should probably be taken with what you or I would call 'a pinch of salt', but which he and his goblin dog probably call 'a five-course meal, oh my, I feel so bloated, pass me the patent leather sick bag'. Still, he's been speaking out this week against people who say models are too thin. Or, as he puts it, 'fat mummies who sit with bags of chips in front of the television saying that thin models are ugly'.

Some analysis here. The 'bags of chips' bit is initially confusing, seemingly suggesting that the real power in fashion lies with characters who might be played by Kathy Burke, lolling around on their sofas with a fish supper, somewhere in the North. I suspect he actually means 'crisps'. Easy mistake to make, if you never eat either. No, the 'chips' bit isn't the real insult here. And nor, actually, is the 'fat'. The bit with bite, the bit where you really feel the hate, is 'mummies'.

Finally, I think I get fashion. I never understood how an industry so dominated by women could seem to hate them so much. Now, I see. Fashion isn't anti-women. It's anti-human. A model, for people like Karl Lagerfeld, should be a coathanger with a face. To be human – to eat, to smile, to give birth, to have visible eyeballs – is to be base and disgusting and worthy of contempt. To look like a mummy is the worst thing in the world. Unless you mean an Egyptian one. He's probably all in favour of that.

DIARY

Miriam Gross

14 November

Not long ago, I astounded the men sitting next to me at a dinner party (yes, dinner parties still take place here and there) by saying that I thought Gordon Brown was handsome, and indeed had sex appeal. The men exclaimed that I had gone off my rocker. But the women within earshot immediately chipped in to support me. They agreed that the Prime Minister was an attractive man: he exuded an aura of manliness, of reticence, of depth of feeling, all qualities which are very attractive to women. There then followed one of those enjoyable conversations about who among our leading politicians did, and who did not, have sex appeal. As it turned out, no one round the table could think of a single man on the front benches who had 'it' – not David Cameron, not George Osborne, neither David Miliband nor Ed, not of course Ed Balls, not Alistair Darling, no, not Alan Johnson, not Nick Clegg or even Vince Cable. Not Tony Blair. There was only Gordon Brown. However, in the last few days, whenever I've seen the Prime Minister on television, he's looked increasingly puffy and pasty. This is hardly surprising given the painful publicity he's received over his letter of condolence, but it occurred to me that he'd better call an election soon before he loses his last remaining asset and with it, perhaps, a large number of women voters.

HOW VODKA CURED MY FEAR OF FLYING

Lloyd Evans

19/26 December

I've discovered a brilliant way to cure my phobias. It's so easy, so ingenious and so cheap (it cost me nothing), that I want to share it with as many people as possible. My technique will work its magic on any trivial or unreasonable fear you suffer from. Mine happens to be flying. Or it used to be. Until 28 July this year I hadn't travelled in a plane, or even visited an airport, for 16 years. I was perfectly content as a flightless species, but my wife likes to flit off to the Med whenever possible and enjoy a week of sunstroke and food poisoning, so she booked us a holiday in the island paradise of Gozo, a tuffet of volcanic rock near Malta. I wasn't keen to go but I felt I owed my wife a thank-you present for rearing our lusty little lad to the age of three without offering a single murmur of complaint – at least not while she's asleep.

I researched our destination. In July the temperature of Gozo is about the same as the temperature of a forest fire. Photographs indicated that the island's chief attraction (apart from eating couscous and watching jet-ski accidents) is a collection of poorly repaired churches. Gozo's residents express themselves in Italian and Arabic, languages I don't speak, so my conversational sallies would be limited to package-tour English. Sun hot. Tummy painful. Doctor quick.

I had a higher motive too. Spurred by manly pride, and a modicum of social embarrassment, I was determined to do battle with my fear of flying. The swiftest way to disempower a phobia, as we all know, is to embrace it and assimilate it by a simple process of habituation. Our flight was at noon. At 8.30 a.m. my wife was upstairs filling three suitcases with an edited version of her life's complexities while I was down in the kitchen with little Isaac, searching for the perfect pre-flight stiffener. I poured half a litre of vodka into a plastic bottle and added a spoonful of orange juice. And there it was. A 'screwdriver', I believe it's called. Fluids aren't permitted on aeroplanes these days, apparently, so I necked the lot as our train bowled through south London towards Gatwick.

Reaching the terminal, I knew I wasn't quite 'there' yet, even though I'd taken the additional precaution of having a glass of Valpolicella for breakfast. Luckily, I'd secreted a can of Special Brew in my jacket, just in case, and having downed the super-strength wonder-beer while trundling along a travelator I began to feel absolutely tickety-boo, as they used to say in Bomber Command. Climb aboard a 737? I'd have flown the damn thing if I could have found it. But I couldn't. And it's at this point that my holiday memoir becomes a little hazy. Not only could I not find the plane, the plane couldn't find me. Nor could the flight attendants. Not could my wife who, temporarily beguiled by some overpriced sunglasses, had failed to spot me ambling towards an unmarked stairwell. For two hours the full deployment of Gatwick's locate-and-detain team scoured every inch of their patch and failed to discover me. (Note to SO19 – if you can't identify one paralytic holiday-maker, what chance do you have against waves of highly trained terrorists?)

Resigned to her status as an abandoned party, my wife wiped away her briney mascara and boarded the plane with my son and our luggage. But as soon as the on-board bureaucracy registered my absence she was chucked straight back off. 'Security' was cited. Obviously it's standard practice for a terrorist to put his family on a plane, smuggle an exploding knapsack into the baggage-hold, and then toddle home to watch the fireball on the news.

I returned to our house, somehow or other, and settled down to a well-earned snooze. My wife showed up a few hours later. After some interesting discussions we decided to try again. Noon, next day. Gatwick. As we returned to the check-in, little Isaac had a flashback which emerged in a burst of merry chatter. 'Mummy crying,' he trilled. 'Lost aspen, lost aspen.' I chuckled nostalgically. My mood this time was sober and serene, bordering on positively radiant. That's because I wasn't getting on an aeroplane. My task was merely to wave goodbye to the Evans duo from the safety of the good sweet earth. Terra never felt firma.

Six days later my understrength family returned from the sub-tropics, faces glowing like lumps of uranium, intestines bubbling with toxic bacteria. A perfect holiday all round. Mind you, I couldn't help noticing I didn't get a present.

It didn't matter. A far greater prize was now mine. I had trounced my demons. I had conquered my fears. Never again would I be afraid of flying, because never again would I take to the clouds. Simple as that. Phobia dispatched. Now at this point you'll be thinking I've cheated. I haven't cured my phobia. I've surrendered to it. And that's not allowed.

Well, here's the fascinating thing. A phobia is a two-pronged beast. One prong is the phobia itself. Prong two is the fear of social disapproval if you treat your phobia in unorthodox fashion. Phobics are under invisible pressure to adopt the correct procedures. A good phobic enlarges on his panic attacks and feverish sweats. He bores his peers with tales of mantra-chanting and crystal-fondling, of psychic refits and soul overhauls.

All that stuff's acceptable, even glamorous. What's beyond the pale is to junk the therapy cult altogether and sign an unconditional surrender pact. I've tried telling people I'm scared of flying and I'm not going to do anything about it and they're appalled. They look away in disgust. They cross the room. It's like telling them I've taken up bear-baiting. Or shooting orphans in the sewers.

It's not as if I've turned into a xenophobic little Englander. The world is still my oyster. A ferry to Dieppe and I can penetrate the farthest crannies of Africa and Asia in my hiking boots, and if the Bering Straits stay frozen, my overland range extends to the tranny-shacks of New York and the scrublands of Tierra del Fuego. Travel is possible. Over-rapid, transcontinental travel isn't.

The outrage I've encountered must be a form of religious abhorrence. I'm a heretic, a denier of the orthodoxy that science and its first ministers, analysis and technology, are an invincible force making our lives ever happier, richer, longer and more enjoyable. Every problem can be solved by the application of sophisticated thinking.

But it can't. Fear of flying, I've discovered, isn't confined to a handful of neurotics. Nor is it widespread. It's universal. The most seasoned traveller is apprehensive during take-off and landing. And when the plane lurches into a thunderstorm, even the pilot grips the controls a little tighter. That's common sense. To hurtle through the sky at 600 mph in a sitting-room made of tin is inherently risky. It's unnatural too. And those who refuse to do it, or who openly fear it, are classed as 'phobics', as sufferers from a form of lunacy. To me that's the oddest thing of all. Some readers will agree with my family and conclude that I'm a head-case. I'm mental. Suits me fine. Bring a strait-jacket. I'd rather be strapped into that than into economy.

2010

Rod Liddle; Dear Mary; Rory Bremner;
Jeremy Clarke; Melissa Kite; Charles Moore;
Toby Young

LIDDLE BRITAIN

Rod Liddle

2 January

It is very difficult, watching a *Thomas the Tank Engine* DVD with your young children, to escape the suspicion that the Reverend Wilbert Awdry was anything other than a thoroughly vindictive and authoritarian old scrote, with a spiteful streak the width of the Fat Controller's stomach. You would not leave your kids with him in person. The errant rolling stock are subjected to ghastly punishments and humiliations – including one engine being bricked up in a tunnel for months on end while the others laugh at him.

As the Canadian academic Shauna Wilton pointed out recently, the programme does indeed 'promote(s) a rigid class system that stifles self-expression', as well as being sexist: the only females on Sodor – Annie and Clarabel – are carriages and are pulled by the males. None of the engines are poofs, although Henry's livery seems to me a little camp and you can imagine the unctuous Thomas doing a spot of cottaging in his spare time, unwisely propositioning policemen, asking for his funnel to be polished and so on. They have mad, smug, spooky faces, the engines, and they rattle along through scenery dredged from a 1940s comic book to the accompaniment of a clunking piano motif written by a refugee from the 1960s Beatles wannabes The Marmalade – a chap called Junior Campbell. I know of no parents who like the programme. 'Take your idiotic chubby eyebrow-less face and your inane little stories and go jump . . .' one Canadian mum wrote on a website, summing up the view of most of us. As I say, I know of no parents who like it. And I know of no young kids who don't.

In this, the Revd Awdry is a little like that other whacko and bitter purveyor of dross to the kiddies, Enid Blyton: despised by parents, loathed by academics, adored by children. From the same generation, both writers were ultra-conservative, patrician and had no truck with changing mores or indeed literary artifice. Blyton at least allowed girls to intrude into the action in the *Famous Five*, whether as the perpetually simpering Anne or the scary proto-diesel dyke George, but it was Julian – en route to the Bullingdon Club and the Tory front bench – who ran the show.

Attacks upon Blyton are not new, of course – I remember them vaguely from when I actually read her stuff, back in the mid-1960s. But the usual thing to say about her writing then was that while she was an appalling stylist and clearly possessed of the most reprehensible political sensibilities, she could tell a good story and it was this that the kids enjoyed, in spite of her ideological shortcomings.

Much the same has been said recently about *Thomas the Tank Engine* – but if you think about it, this is very hard to argue. There aren't really any stories in *Thomas the Tank Engine* apart from various engines being humiliated and punished as a consequence of their misdemeanours or their hubris. And that's the conclusion you should reach, I reckon, in both cases: the kids like these stories not in spite of the narrow conservatism of the writers, but precisely because of it. Children feel most comfortable in an ordered and clearly demarcated world, a world divided into hierarchies. They have a Manichean view of good and evil and they like to see the baddies get punished, preferably in a thoroughly unpleasant manner. They may also identify with gender stereotypes which conform to the roles they have already been assigned or, more controversially, have worked out for themselves from a very early age. Children, and especially little boys, are conservative, when they are not actually fascists.

Maybe this is why the most popular children's books tend to come, however unconsciously, from the political right. *Wind in the Willows*, with its class warfare against the uppity stoats and weasels; *Winnie the Pooh* with its gentle hierarchy of stupidities. When I was 11 or 12 I recall being mesmerised by Richard Adams's *Watership Down*, a book from the centre right if ever there was one, militaristic and paternalistic and in which both females and stupid foreigners were assigned strictly marginal and purely instrumental roles. I even remember the *Guardian* complaining about this at the time – much as, 25 or so years later, it complained at the sexism and racism of *Harry Potter*, the lack of disabled access ramps in Hogwarts, discrimination against the house elves etc. J. K. Rowling may herself be a charming and impeccably liberal woman, but the ideology of the *Harry Potter* books does not reflect this mindset, no matter how often she tries to tell us that Professor Dumbledore is, to use the old-fashioned vernacular, as bent as a butcher's hook.

She knows what kids like – as did, of course, Roald Dahl, perhaps the most successful children's author of the last 50 years and a man who did not remotely even pretend to be liberal; hard right, Roald was, with an abiding affection for Margaret Thatcher – and it shows in his work. Today the coolest and most captivating books for boys in the ten-to-twelve age group, and adored by both of my two lads, are Charlie Higson's young James Bond confections, which sort of pre-imagine the spy's childhood at Eton. Is it possible for a scenario to be any more right-wing? Ian Fleming plus fagging?

Higson's stuff, I suspect, will endure, and has already done astonishingly well; Blyton and Awdry's stuff has of course already endured. But what of the progressive opposition? The counterbalance to *Thomas the Tank Engine* is most of the rest of the stuff on toddler TV, epitomised by the execrable *Balamory* – a colourful fictional seaside town in Scotland where every second person is gay, black or disabled, where girlies take the lead role in each episode and where nothing bad ever happens to anyone.

My daughter found it witless and vapid even when she was two years old; she yearned, I think, for certainties and retribution, for the reflection of reality which she was beginning to experience, however gently, in the non-fictional world around her. 'Put Thomas on,' she would demand, clambering down from the sofa in abject disgust as this rainbow coalition of ineffably friendly and inclusive people began helping one another in a friendly and inclusive manner. And I would accede and slip a disc into the machine and hear the lugubrious Scouse tones of Ringo Starr begin to relate the tale of a bad-tempered crane called Cranky which eventually got smashed in half and all the engines came to laugh at it and tell it that it had received its just deserts. Not a nice man, that Revd Awdry, but he rocks.

YOUR PROBLEMS SOLVED

Dear Mary . . .

2 January

Q. Lucian Freud is a friend of mine but I could never afford one of his paintings. He often comes to dinner and I always leave out paper napkins in the hope he might do a doodle but no luck so far. What do you suggest, Mary?
   – Name and address withheld

A. Why not serve a thick chocolate pudding on a square white plate? Just as Lucian concludes his dish, having scraped an inadvertent pattern onto the plate, whip it away from him and photograph it quickly before spraying on a sealant. With correct marketing this could yield up to £100,000.

DIARY

Rory Bremner

13 February

The posher middle classes – the people who absolutely love Bird and Fortune's dinner party sketches and laugh at the characters without the slightest recognition that they might be watching themselves – are an endless source of unintentional humour. One of John Fortune's neighbours once sympathised with the relatives of a hostage taken prisoner in Iraq. 'It must be dreadful for the family . . . just the not knowing. Mind you,' she went on, 'it was the same for us. We had to wait weeks before we got our planning permission.'

   I was reminded of that when my wife, never one to do things by halves, put her back out while exercising. On the school run, we asked around if anyone knew a good local osteopath. One man's face brightened visibly. 'We've got a wonderful chap who did reiki on our dog.' As I burst out laughing, he seemed a little surprised. 'No, no,' he insisted, 'he was really good – we got another year out of her.'

LOW LIFE

Jeremy Clarke

13 February

Choosing frames for my new varifocal lenses was like choosing a new personality. Each pair I tried on projected something slightly different. What kind of person should I pretend to be from now on? Philosophical? Whacky? Left-leaning? Post post-modernist? It was an unexpectedly exciting moment.

The young assistant stood with me at the display and offered her professional opinion. In quick succession I popped on a couple of dozen different frames and looked into her eyes and tried to be serious. She knew immediately whether or not a particular pair of frames suited my face. If they did, and she liked them, she shook her fingers as though she'd just burned them on a hotplate. Presumably this meant they were 'hot' or, perish the thought, that they made me look 'hot'. If she thought the frames suited but were boring, she let her eyelids droop, as if she were about to fall asleep on the spot. If she didn't like them, or they suited me not at all, she pretended to have a mouthful of vomit and to be frantically casting about for somewhere to throw up.

Only one pair left her in a quandary: the ones I kept returning to, the heavy black retro frames. I'd seen them in newspaper obituary photographs taken in the 1950s of the faces of colonial administrators. The disgraced Conservative Chancellor of the Exchequer Reginald Maudling wore something very similar. And Ronald Kray wore a pair when he was allowed out for the day from Broadmoor to attend his mum's funeral at Chingford cemetery. The designer frames were theatrical without being

ridiculous, but only just. The personality projected was one of assidu-
ous depravity. In a British film, they'd be the kind of glasses worn by a
sadistic paedophile.

The assistant wasn't sure about these. She sucked in her lips and gave
me the level, downward-facing, wobbling-palms gesture. (It was like
going shopping with Marcel Marceau. Had she been deaf at one time in
her life? I wondered.) Well, it was either these, I said, or these – and I took
off the Reginald Maudlings and put on my second choice, an oblong,
hyper-serious, ultra-light, It's-Grim-Up-North-London kind of a frame.
She took one look at the latter and started to nod off again.

The opticians was a large, bustling, city-centre shop. The assistant led
me around the floor canvassing opinion on my Reginald Maudlings.
Everyone we asked immediately dropped whatever they were doing
and gave their considered opinion. Far from being annoyed about being
interrupted, they were all glad to be asked. Working in an opticians
might be, by and large, a repetitive job, but it seems that pandering to a
customer's foolish vanity, by giving his chosen pair of spectacle frames
either the thumbs up or the thumbs down, never stales. On the whole,
the verdict was favourable.

For a final decision, the assistant said she'd go and fetch a colleague
who could always be relied on to 'tell it how it is'. Then she disappeared
through a 'staff only' door at the back of the shop. She was gone for a long
time. I assumed it was because honesty was such a rare and controversial
commodity these days that the colleague was confined in an obscure
room, possibly manacled, and that numerous forms and waivers had to
be filled out before she could be allowed into the public arena to unleash
another of her devastating judgements.

Finally she reappeared through the 'staff only' door with this famously
truthful colleague. I was expecting to be presented to some hatchet-faced
old graduate of the school for hard knocks. But this woman had a kind,
untroubled face. She was of an older generation than anyone I'd met so
far. Perhaps anybody born and raised before the political-correctness
revolution, and still working, will inevitably have a reputation for
outspokenness.

The assistant led her over and introduced me to her. Then she retreated a step, screwed up her eyes and raised a protecting shoulder, as if expecting flying debris. I snapped on the Reginald Maudlings and stood erect. The colleague with the reputation for telling it like it is looked appraisingly at my face. I watched her mild eyes follow the outline of my features and come to rest finally on the frames. 'With a big conk like that, he might be better off with brown,' she said. 'But the style suits him well. In fact, he might look almost handsome,' she added, 'to someone galloping by on a horse.'

YOUR PROBLEMS SOLVED

Dear Mary . . .

20 February

Q. My new boyfriend was on his own for years and developed some bad habits, such as eating with his mouth open. He is so lovely otherwise and quite happy for me to kick him under the table when we are out with others to remind him to shut his mouth, but I wonder if there is some very quick way of retraining him.

– J.L., London W8

A. Why not start with a dog-training collar of the type which allows the owner to deliver small electric shocks when the dog is naughty? This Pavlovian method of retraining can be conducted in your own home and should bring very swift results.

REAL LIFE

Melissa Kite

20 March

How much screening does a person have to go through in this country to obtain a rabbit? Being recently lagomorphically bereaved – and newly single – I am in desperate need of new pets. I always adopt a stray after a break-up. It's how I came by the legendary giant black rabbit BB, now passed on, God rest his soul. He was the creature I brought home to make myself feel like living again after the wedding I called off. No wonder he grew to the size of a dog. It was a big job.

Oh, and by the way, to anyone thinking of consoling me, please do not even think of telling me in a squeaky voice that my beloved BB has gone to 'bunny heaven'. Just because I am 38 and let rabbits run loose in my house does not mean I am retarded. (Am I even allowed to say that word any more?) I may be a fool for a fluffy ball of fur but I am perfectly sentient. I know that when rabbits die they go where all the other pets go. To proper heaven. To be with Jesus and grandma and Elvis.

Anyway, I have just tried to register on a rabbit rehome charity website and have filled in a form which I am sure is longer than the form I would have to fill in to adopt a child. 'Have you kept rabbits before?' Hard to know where to start with this one. I would have loved to have given my long and colourful rabbit-whispering history. But as there was only a yes/no box for an answer I ticked yes and moved on.

'Do you have rabbits now?' Yes, I explained. A recently bereaved male rabbit called TT. I know you're not meant to put two boys together but my friend found him in a box by the side of the road and he really took to BB, in fact, a bit too well, if you know what I mean. But I'm a modern mother and whatever my pets turn out to be is fine by me.

'What sex of rabbit do you prefer?' As I say, either will do, although I have a feeling TT might actually like to try a girlfriend. Not that I'm trying to pressure him. I just think he wouldn't mind finding out. On the other hand, maybe that would confuse him. He's been through a lot lately and he is used to being with a man.

'How many rabbits would you like?' I think just the one. I've nothing against three rabbits in principle, I just think it would take way too much ethical deliberation to decide whether to go for a girl, girl, boy combination or a boy, boy, girl combo.

'Where will the rabbit be living?' In the house.

'What sort of cage will you be providing?' As I said, the house.

'How big is it?' Two bedrooms, living room, large kitchen/breakfast room.

'What bedding will you be providing?' They tend to fall asleep in front of the TV most nights, but they can sleep on the bed if they prefer.

'What chew toys will you be providing?' I've got a big Fortnum's hamper and a cane sofa. BB ate most of the sofa but there's still a bit left which the new one's welcome to. Otherwise, carpets, curtains, shoes, clothes, phone chargers, computer equipment, etc.

'What sort of litter tray will you be providing?' They get microchipped and I train them to use an electronic dog flap into the garden.

'How old are the children who will be looking after the rabbits?' Thirty-eight.

Then there was a lot of jargon about facilitating a home visit to be properly vetted by one of their qualified rabbit-rehoming experts.

I submitted the form but heard nothing back. So I tried another pet-rescue centre in Surrey. They told me that of the 25 rabbits featured on their website, most were reserved and of those 'available' only one sounded 'suitable for my needs' and she had a waiting list of people interested.

I felt like saying: are you insane? The world's overrun with rabbits. There is no rabbit-shortage crisis. Whoever heard of reserved rabbits or waiting list for rabbits suitable for individual needs? How come whenever I'm sitting at home minding my own business the phone never stops ringing with people begging me to take in stray rabbits but the minute I decide I want to offer a little mite a home they're all playing hard to get?

Thankfully, I've now found a rescue centre where they're not demanding a degree in rabbit husbandry and are offering me and TT an 'appointment' next week, which sounds exciting. If this doesn't work, I'm going to have to apply for a baby.

THE SPECTATOR'S NOTES

Charles Moore

5 June

I recently met a New Yorker who said he had been testing his eight-year-old daughter's knowledge of geometry. 'What's the shortest distance between two points,' he asked her. 'A taxi,' she replied.

LETTERS

12 June

Sir: There is no storyteller more delightful than Claus von Bülow, but I must correct his version of the one quoted by Taki (High Life, 29 May). Claus may have been at the launch of Leni Riefenstahl's memoirs, but I definitely was and Ronald Fuhrer was not, for being at the apogee of his shortlived fame as a London host, Ronald was giving a swagger dinner party that evening. I asked Riefenstahl to inscribe a copy as a present for him. 'So . . . Herr Ronald?' she said, pen poised. 'Fuhrer,' I answered. Her gnarled hand trembled as she wrote the word.
  Nicky Haslam
  London

LIDDLE BRITAIN

Rod Liddle

17 July

What on earth is the government going to do about all these deranged northerners running amok shooting people? The more callous among you might well argue that it doesn't really matter, as these madmen are only shooting other northerners, and so it is therefore none of our business. Perhaps. But there is no guarantee that the next deranged northerner will not get on a train, if he can afford it, and start shooting at us, instead. This is the thing; you simply cannot tell with nutters, there is no logic to their mayhem. There is a case to be made for employing the consensual, democratic approach adopted by the Cumbria and Northumberland police, which is to let each respective deranged northerner shoot several people – to get it out of his system – before the law is brought in to constrain him. Some people have criticised the police for this, but it seems to me as good an approach as any other.

One thing, though, is for sure – until a week ago, Cumbria's Derrick Bird thought he was odds on to win the much coveted Mentally Ill Northerner of the Year Award, to be presented by Yorkshire's Karen Matthews – who, if you remember, hid her young daughter Shannon in a drawer beneath a friend's bed for a month or so and claimed she'd been abducted – at a glittering ceremony at Batley and Spen Working Men's Club in December. And then suddenly Northumberland's Raoul Moat has snuck in, snatching the commemorative pig-iron beer tankard from Derrick's hand. Derrick must be gutted, as well as dead.

You think this is all in bad taste? Believe me, this is nothing. This is *nothing*. The Raoul Moat affair has uncovered a sort of seething pit of madness which well exceeds anything achievable by even the lowest form of satire. I do not mean Mr Moat himself – who, hereafter, will be referred to as 'Moaty', which is the name given to him by his thousand upon thousand of supporters in the north-east of England, including the former England football international and drunkard Paul Gascoigne, of which more later – but the others, the people online, the people in the streets, the people. And the queuing up to put flowers upon his 'shrine', which is situated next to a storm drain where he once lived. These lumpen-shrines are a comparatively new thing, a Diana thing, or post-Diana thing, I suppose; the garage flowers tied to the railings in what is known as a 'Catford Bouquet', after the south London suburb where people get stabbed to death. It is said that these sorts of bouquets and wreaths, together with attendant illiterate textspeak notes (RIP Monger luv u xxx lol) were left in a Liverpool backstreet on the site where a 'body' had been found, even though later it was discovered to be the carcass of a chicken. Maybe that story is apocryphal, but I wouldn't bet on it. Shrines: once to Mary or Jesus, then just to people who had died suddenly and unfortunately, then to domestic fowl, now for murderers.

Moaty was undoubtedly mad as a box of frogs: paranoid, hobbled by an insurmountable tide of self-pity, thick as a block of mince, possessed of that strangely warped sense of maleness which sees everything as a direct challenge to his very existence, to his essence, and as a consequence convinced that vengeance must surely be wreaked against everything. Banged up for minor assault 'against a relative', as the courts put it – or for 'brayin' his bairn' as they might more accurately say in Newcastle – he came out of prison not full of remorse or contrition, but seeking redress. Like a sort of extreme version of *Viz* magazine's pisshead loser 8-Ace – lachrymose, self-obsessed and ineffably stupid. He shot his partner; he shot dead his partner's boyfriend; he shot a policeman – and then, this being not enough, declared war against the world, convinced that he had been transgressed. Implacably convinced that he was the real victim. And the magical thing is that there were plenty of people to agree with him on this point. Like Gazza.

Something strange is happening with our lowbrow celebrities; stuff is occurring which should not occur. You expect them to display their non-talent, milk it for a few years, talk rubbish and then disappear for ever. Yet in the last two weeks a woman who became very famous for having large breasts, Samantha Fox, was reported as having contracted rabies.

And then it transpired that the attractive 'singer' Cheryl Cole, another emissary from Geordieland's untermensch, apparently has malaria. There is something biblical about all this. What next, we wondered – Geri Halliwell to get leprosy? Simon Cowell to be beset by a plague of locusts? But no, it was Paul Gascoigne, slurring his words, pissed out of his head, telling a local radio station that he was driving to Rothbury to meet up with Moaty (© Paul Gascoigne) and had brought him some 'chicken' and a 'dressing gown' and a 'fishing rod', in case he wished to do a spot of, uh, fishing. The radio interviewer took the mickey out of him, quietly and lethally. Gazza thought Moaty had been misunderstood and, yep, transgressed. 'Top fella,' said British football's greatest wastrel since Bestie.

And now the shrine and the Facebook campaign. More than 18,000 people have signed up to it, at the time of writing. There's one man, for example, saying: 'All down 2 women. A man has 2 fight 2 hurt u a woman just has 2 press that button 2 fuk with your head.' Even so, there are plenty of women signed up, such as this one who wrote: 'He did wrong yeah but he was let down. He was a legend mainly for proving wat a poor society we live in yeah.' Well, yeah, you may have half a point there. Lol. And then there's 'you have won the hearts of reall people – totally understand your feelings' and 'police=scum' and another really long one which ends 'PS – take care of Sir Bobby' – a reference to Sir Bobby Robson, the former manager of Newcastle United and England who died of cancer not so long ago.

From the sobbing queues along the Mall and Green Park some 13 years ago to the wreaths by that storm drain, there is a section of the public which will mourn anything, and become angered by it, desperate for a chance to emote and show its anger, fabulously – almost inconceivably – stupid, illiterate, ill-educated but incredibly sure of their rights. Next time, incidentally, some newspaper tells you that 18,000 people have written in online to complain about something, or demand something, remember the 18,000 who signed up in support of Raoul Moat.

STATUS ANXIETY

Toby Young

24 July

It's the summer and that means the festival season is upon us. I say that as if I'm a veteran of the festival circuit when, in fact, the last one I went to was Hood Fayre (sic) in Totnes in 1980. That was the year I took my O-levels and I remember sitting in a tent, sucking on a Camberwell Carrot, when I bumped into my History teacher. 'Shouldn't you be revising?' he said. It won't surprise you to learn that I failed everything apart from Eng Lit.

Some 30 years later, I decided to dip another toe in the water. Caroline and I were offered a free day pass to Latitude last Sunday, the annual Suffolk music festival, and since we were going to be in East Anglia anyway it seemed like a good idea. Consequently, at 11 a.m. on Sunday morning we strapped the four kids into our red minibus and beetled along the A12 to Southwold.

'This is your sort of music,' said Caroline as we emerged from the car park, referring to the noise in the distance. By that she meant at least 50 years out of date, i.e., classic rock 'n' roll. 'Hang on,' I said, straining my ears. 'It can't be . . . it is. It's Tom Jones!' I immediately placed a toddler under each arm and started running. This was too good an opportunity to miss. Tom Jones! I had no idea he was still alive, let alone performing. Things were looking up.

Unfortunately, before I was allowed into the main arena I was under strict orders to get the children some lunch. That wasn't a problem for the boys – they were happy with burgers and chips – but six-year-old Sasha wanted a vegetarian crêpe. (She's her mother's daughter.) That meant standing in a queue for 20 minutes, by which time the septuagenarian sex bomb was into his first encore.

I probably would have caught the last five minutes had not Freddie, my three-year-old, demanded a wee. I sprinted towards the Portaloos clutching him like a rugby ball, only to be confronted by another queue.

When our turn arrived Freddie took one look at the toilet bowl and refused to go anywhere near it. 'Yukkie,' was his verdict.

Having missed Tom Jones, we made our way to the children's area. As I schlepped along behind carrying two-year-old Charlie I was overtaken by a man pulling two children in a cart. 'Where did you get that?' I asked. 'We brought it with us,' he replied. 'It's a bit of a pain in the daytime but it really comes into its own at night.'

So that's what festival-going couples do with their children at night. They pull them along in a cart. Caroline and I, being avid devotees of Gina Ford and her *Contented Little Baby Book*, were shocked. Shouldn't small children be tucked up in bed by 7.30 p.m.? Not for the first time that day, we felt very square.

The children's area was rather sweet. Charlie and Ludo, our five-year-old, engaged in some *Women in Love*-style mud wrestling in the Greenpeace tent, while Sasha coloured in a card and mailed it to her best friend at the Pixie Post Office. Caroline sent me into the woods with Freddie, instructing me not to come back until he'd relieved himself. Easier said than done considering there were CCTV cameras everywhere. Indeed, no sooner had I pulled his trousers down than a couple of security guards appeared and ordered me to pull them up again. In the end we found a suitably secluded ditch, but Freddie's attempt to do a 'standing-up wee' resulted in both of us getting rather wet.

For a 46-year-old man, the most depressing thing about Latitude was the sheer quantity of beautiful young women. Wherever you looked there was some long-limbed goddess dressed in little more than a handkerchief. Insofar as they noticed me at all, I was the starey-eyed bald bloke with a wet patch on his trousers. ('I couldn't borrow that handkerchief for a second, could I?') It didn't take long for Caroline to pick up on this. 'Stop perving,' she said, as my head swivelled left and right like a gun turret.

Not sure we'll be going to any more music festivals this year. Like Latitude, several of them are billed as 'family friendly', but most of the other dads looked at least ten years younger than me. The Last Night of the Proms is more my speed. And I'll be leaving the kids at home.

REAL LIFE

Melissa Kite

21 August

'Ring us when you get lost and we'll come and get you,' was the reaction of the gamekeeper at the farm where I keep my horses when I told him I was going on a trail ride with three female friends. 'Really,' I said, 'just because four women are going off on a riding holiday does not mean we're going to get lost and need a man to rescue us. We can read maps, you know. We've got a compass. And a TomTom.'

'Right you are,' he said, giving me one of his deadpan looks. Which was unfair, I thought, because we were very well prepared. We packed all the required elements in our saddlebags, including the map and directions from the trail-riding company.

The problem with maps, however, is that they really can't do much for you if you don't look at them. Call it exuberance, call it a moment of blondeness, but as we cantered off across a field at the start of our first day we all assumed that someone else knew why we were cantering in that particular direction. Sadly, no one did.

And it wasn't until we got three miles further on that someone thought to ask, 'Where are we, you know, on the map?' Things can change pretty quickly from idyllic to nightmarish. One minute we were riding happily along the Ridgeway in bright sunshine, the next minute we didn't know where to turn because the map no longer coalesced with where we thought we were. And that was when the skies turned black and a torrential rainstorm came crashing down on us.

It is at times like these that people's true characters come out. Friend number one was thoroughly inspired by it all. 'What an adventure!' she kept exclaiming. Friend number two developed an addiction to the compass, which she hung around her neck and consulted ceaselessly: 'We're facing north ... we're still facing north ... we're facing north-east ... we're facing south ...' All of which was impressive but, as we didn't know where we were on the map, the fact of whether we were pointing north or not was utterly without consequence. Friend number three came up with all sorts of extreme suggestions for cutting through woods and jumping fences in order to right ourselves. As for me, I proclaimed that the end was nigh. 'Oh, no, it's like *The Blair Witch Project!*' I wailed. 'We'll never get out of this alive!' But somehow we managed to right ourselves and rode on to our pub stop.

We had gone horribly out of our way and so by the time we reached the Queen's Arms at East Garston it was 4 p.m. We had to rest the horses for two hours before we could start out again and by that time we only had a few hours before dark. The friend who claimed to be enjoying herself declared the threat of sundown a huge excitement, while the girl with compass addiction resumed her endless search for north.

Just when we thought we were nearing our B&B, we asked a dog walker where we were and instead of telling us we were half a mile from Woolley he looked at our laminated map and said, 'Oh, I see you've got the Queen's Arms on your route. Well, that's just down there.' Yes, we had ridden for two hours in a complete circle. Which of course, was straight out of *The Blair Witch Project*, as I predicted.

So I flagged down a farmer driving by in his tractor and garbled hysterically, 'You've got to help us! We're four stupid women and we've been riding around for eight hours and we're going insane and I don't know how you're going to do it but you've got to get us to Woolley!' The poor man explained exactly where we had to go but I wasn't having it. 'Do you have a mobile number?' He nodded at me with his mouth open. 'Give it to me. When we get to the next bridleway junction I'm calling you to make sure we're taking the right turn.'

I must have convinced him of our utter incapability because we had only gone a few paces when we heard him coming up behind us in his tractor. He waved us to the side of the track, put the tractor in front of us and gave us an escort through his fields all the way to the point where we could actually see our destination. I trotted happily behind our knight in shining Massey Ferguson, enjoying myself for the first time that day. When we were safely installed around a farmhouse table eating home-reared beef I sent him a text. 'We couldn't have done it without you,' I said, and I meant it. The gamekeeper, as always, was right.

STATUS ANXIETY

Toby Young

2 October

I'm a pack rat. I can't bring myself to throw anything away. When Caroline first moved in with me she couldn't get from one end of our bedroom to the other because every inch of floor space was taken up with piles of old newspapers and magazines. I have lock-ups full of stuff, some of them in New York. At one point, I asked a friend if I could use the space under his stairs to store a cache of second-hand coats I'd bought at a jumble sale. When I wanted to retrieve one five years later, he gave me a blank look and told me he'd moved two years earlier. I haven't spoken to him since.

Our present house is blessed with two large attics – or 'storage spaces', as I prefer to call them. (It was one of the reasons I bought it.) As you can imagine, they are stuffed to the gills with junk and a couple of weeks ago Caroline announced that she wanted me to clear one of them out so the children could use it as a 'den'.

'But what shall I do with all my stuff?'

'Throw it away,' she said.

'Are you mad? There are heirlooms up there – some of them worth hundreds of thousands of pounds.'

'In that case, why not sell them?'

With great reluctance, I agreed to a car boot sale and on Sunday we drove to a playground in Battersea and I set out my wares. Pride of place was given to an antique lamp that I'd inherited from my maternal grandmother.

''Ow much d'you want for that?' asked a middle-aged man in a sheep-skin coat.

'I can see you've got a good eye,' I said. 'That's a very valuable piece.'

'I'll give you fifty pee for it,' he said.

'FIFTY PEE?'

'We'll take it,' said Caroline.

Seconds later, Granny Ann's bedside light was gone. I couldn't believe it. I told Caroline that Arthur Daley had got the bargain of the century. There was just no way it was worth so little.

'Go and have a look around,' she said. 'You'll quickly discover that fifty pee is the going rate for an old lamp.'

I followed her advice and it wasn't long before I came across our friend in the sheepskin coat. He was standing behind a trestle table with his wares laid out in front of him. Slap-bang in the centre was my grandmother's antique lamp.

'Hang on a minute,' I said. 'I didn't know you were a stallholder.'

'Oh, yeah. Been coming here for years.'

'How much are you asking for my lamp?'

'Five pound.'

'Five pounds?!? But I just sold it to you for fifty pee.'

'No law against making a profit is there?'

He explained that he always made a point of getting to the car boot sale early and combing the stalls for bargains that he could then sell for a mark-up. It was how he made his money. He pointed out that they still hadn't let in members of the public. All the people buying and selling at this point were other stallholders, hoping to turn a quick profit. When you paid for a pitch, you weren't just paying for the opportunity to sell, but to be allowed in early so you could get first pick of the merchandise.

I ran back to my stall where I'd left Caroline in charge. Clearly, the right strategy was not to sell anything until the public had been let in. Too late. By the time I got there she'd sold everything apart from four exercise DVDs.

'How much did you make?' I asked.

She counted up the money in her pocket.

'Twenty-seven pounds fifty.'

I was crestfallen. I recalled all the years I'd spent lugging this stuff from house to house – in some cases, country to country. I'd thought nothing of hiring removal companies to pack it up into boxes and ship it overseas. Twenty-seven pounds fifty would barely cover the cost of one box.

'Where are you going?' she asked.

'Nowhere,' I said. 'I just want to check something.'

Seconds later I was standing in front of Arthur Daley again.

'I'll give you two pounds for it,' I whispered.

'Four quid and it's yours,' he said.

We settled on three pounds fifty.

THE 'C' WORD USED TO BE THE ONE THING YOU COULD NEVER SAY. HOW TIMES CHANGE.

Rod Liddle

11 December

The kids are all asleep, the wife is in bed reading feminist propaganda, from outside in the darkness I hear the shocked *keewick* of a Little Owl. Otherwise, all is silent and at rest. This is the time of evening when I make my way very quietly to my study with a glass of wine 'to do some work'. I don't want anyone to catch me at it, so I put my hand over the computer's little loudspeaker when that annoying Windows ident music comes on. She caught me at it, once, my wife. Came downstairs for a glass of water and saw me hunched and furtive over the laptop, tapping away and making guttural noises. She just looked disappointed and went back to bed, but it was a bit embarrassing.

Anyway, it's the same procedure every night. Open the computer, bring up the internet and tap into Google those three crucial words ... 'Rod Liddle c***'. How many will it be tonight? The anticipation, let me tell you, is intense. Tonight it's only 831. That's pretty poor. I need to write something nasty about the Welsh, or cats, pretty quickly or I'll be down at the level of someone on the *New Statesman*. As it is, even my best scores pale before someone famous like John Humphrys (3,800). And journalists, as a group, don't do as well as you might imagine. Unpleasant world leaders get quite a few – Kim Jong-il had 17,600 just after he'd shelled that South Korean island. But even that pales before your mega celebs – Simon Cowell, for example, who is one of the judges on that awful programme *X Factor*, scored 93,000 c***s on Google last Saturday evening, which is hugely impressive.

But who, exactly, is the most c***ed man alive in the world, I can hear you ask? Who is it that provokes more people to call him a c*** than anyone else on God's earth? This never changes, it is always the same answer, a man in a c***-class of his own. It is always Bono. And he is way out ahead, with 154,000 the last time I checked, and I check regularly. Respect to the Irishman. Perhaps now, at last, he has found what he was looking for.

2011

Rod Liddle; Dear Mary; Jeremy Clarke; Melissa Kite; A. A. Gill; Deborah Ross; Mark Mason; Tanya Gold; Joan Collins; Ozzy Osbourne; Tom Hollander

FROM HERE UNTIL THE ROYAL WEDDING IT'S SEWAGE ALL THE WAY

Rod Liddle

1 January

I hope you are looking forward to the tsunami of industrial effluent which is coming your way in the first quarter of the new year. You will not be able to avoid it, unless you are Helen Keller. One way or another, Wills and Kate are going to get you.

Or, more properly, their agents of misrule are going to get you, the meeja, with their telephoto lenses and their hacked mobile phone accounts, and their rubber gloves for rummaging through dustbins and their long sharp noses for filth and discord and their deep gullets and unquenchable thirst for vapid, pointless liquid excrement. If you were being charitable you might argue that the principal victims in this deluge of unmitigated bollocks are the happy couple – which is true, of course. But they have legions of courtiers to assuage the worst of it, to reassure them, to hide the papers. You and I are alone. We have nothing to look forward to except for 30 April or the gentle, emollient embrace of the grave, whichever comes quickest. It will be a wonder if, by the end of it, we are not all republicans.

I do not mean the Royal Doulton china plates or the photo spreads in *Hello!* magazine, or any of the other paraphernalia aimed with cynical precision at thick working-class monarchists. That's fine; we all need to make a bob or two. I mean the rest, the stuff supposedly imbued with greater resonance, or with cattiness and spite. Here's a selection from 45 seconds looking through the papers:

- The shrieking, horse-faced congenital idiot Janet Street-Porter has taken Kate Middleton to task for wearing a cheapish (£60) blouse from Whistles and a dress from the high-street store Reiss. High-street shops are boring, says Janet. She advises Kate to dress like herself, i.e. in the manner of an eight-year-old with a strange bone disease who has just failed an audition for *Rainbow* on account of a dodgy CRB check.

- The celebrity hairdresser Nicky Clarke has said that Kate's hair is 'unadventurous'. I hadn't been aware that hair possessed a capacity for adventure. I thought it just sat there, on your head. I suppose I am a poor judge, but I always rather liked Kate's hairstyle. Nicky, meanwhile, has the carefully teased and dyed blonde locks of a young woman from Basildon who has just been shagged in the doorway of Dolcis. At midnight, after a kebab.

- Kate Middleton is to be trained by 'coaches' in how to wave at poor people. She will also receive lessons in 'beach behaviour'.

- The historian Andrew Roberts is to give Kate a lesson in the history of the House of Windsor. 'Mainly German and not terribly bright' should do it, I would have thought.

- One of Kate's 'friends' from school has revealed that she was a bit of a munter when she was younger, not half as sexy as her sister, and had braces on her teeth. But she was a '100 mph kind of girl', despite being hideous.

- One of Kate's uncles is apparently a fat coke-sniffing slob who lives on the 'party island' of Ibiza. And her brother James is milking his new celebrity (although quite how, we are not told). But apparently when he goes to nightclubs and is not recognised he becomes 'quite upset'.

- Kate's mum and dad run a mail-order company which sells the details of its customer base 'for money!' Just like every other mail-order company, in fact.

- The Queen's dogs will be barred from both the wedding and the reception because Kate finds corgis 'distressing'. The canine retinue will remain at Buckingham Palace, where they will be entertained by equerries.

- The orchestra at the wedding will be comprised entirely of disabled Austrian musicians. It is not revealed if they are disabled now, or will be rendered so especially for the event.

- The *Daily Mail* columnist Quentin Letts will be advising the happy couple on how to deal with the media. Here's a tip, Quentin – tell them to do what the singer Lily Allen did and sue the *Mail on Sunday* for invasion of privacy and inaccurate reporting at every available opportunity. Good for Lily.

- Posh and Becks will be at the wedding. So will Elton. You won't.

- Kate is on a 'gruelling weight-loss programme'.

- As if having Quentin Letts as an adviser wasn't enough, Kate also has to read this sort of fabulous drivel from Quentin's queer-bashing *Daily Mail* colleague Jan Moir: 'Now she [Kate M] is Hermione in *Harry Potter*, a plucky innocent who has passed through the Chamber of Secrets to the royal Goblet of Fire.' Imagine the mentality of someone who can write that, look back at it and think: 'Yep, I've nailed the story there. The *mot juste*.'

That, as I say, is from 45 seconds of trawling through the sewer. Only one of the above was made up – you can choose which. Because it doesn't matter terribly. To be honest, the trivia doesn't bother me much, one can ignore it, or laugh; it is the nastiness of much of the coverage that appals and will continue to appal these next few months. The frantic digging of dirt about Kate Middleton's family, the desperation with which the press will search for anyone who has ever had anything bad to say about her, or her parents, or her uncles, or a friend of her uncle's. The readiness of us columnists to stick the boot in as if she were not a person at all, but a commodity.

The media, on these occasions, behaves like a deranged dog determined to gnaw off its own back leg. They have this story, but it is not good enough for them; they want more and more, and they want filth, if possible. So much filth that, in the best of all worlds, the wedding is called off – although they would not admit to this if you put it to them.

YOUR PROBLEMS SOLVED

Dear Mary . . .

1 January

Q. My life has been transformed by my new hearing aid but, due to its visibility, I am constantly being asked by people 'Was it shooting?' As it happens, it was, but I slightly resent the assumption that I can be stereotyped in this way. What should I say, Mary?
  – B.G., London SW1

A. Why not throw them off their stride by replying, 'No, it was helicopters.'

LOW LIFE

Jeremy Clarke

8 January

The registrar opened a screen and clicked and typed her way down a list of questions. I was 'giving notice' of our intention to be married after a statutory 15 days had passed. It was the day before Christmas Eve.

'Has either of you been married before?' she said. (She was tired and distracted. So many elderly people had died in this recent cold snap, she'd told me earlier, she was run off her feet.)

'No,' I said.

'Your partner's full name?' she said, fingering her mouse. For a split second, before it came to me, my mind was a blank. The registrar eyed me speculatively as she touch-typed.

'And her date of birth?'

Cow Girl was Pisces, I knew that much. I knew because I'd checked in an astrology book to see whether Pisces women are compatible with Aquarian men. (It's a recipe for disaster, apparently.) I picked a date in March at random.

'And do you have £33.50 with you?' she said. 'I do,' I said.

She oscillated the mouse and settled the cursor on the completion button. Before she made the final click, she looked at me, her face wearied by death, and said kindly, 'You're both sure you want to go ahead with this?'

I stared at the carpet.

Nearly 600 emails had passed between us, 400 before we'd seen each other. We'd met three times, each time at the same spa hotel. Before our first meeting, I'd told her to feel free to straighten me out with criticism. I'd been on my own for too long, I said, and might not be entirely fit for purpose. But I hadn't expected the litany of complaint and derision which followed, and which intensified on each subsequent occasion.

Bed was fine. No complaints there. Well, there was one thing, actually. My kissing technique was rubbish. 'No tongues!' she'd exclaim crossly, even when she was tied up. And why did both my public and private kisses always have to culminate in a mauling frenzy? We weren't teenagers, were we?

But when we were up, dressed, and out and about, everything about me annoyed her. I had to start a list and keep a pen handy. I smell – usually of body odour, though occasionally of chip fat. That was top of the list. I'm deaf and blind. I can't remember anything. I'm lazy. I lack ambition. My jeans are too short. I need a haircut. I talk too much. I talk too little.

At breakfast at the hotel one morning, I'd strolled back to the table from the buffet with a mini-croissant sticking out of my gob. She didn't like that. That went straight on the list. And there is that silly little dance that I do when I see her – think Hitler's jig outside the railway carriage in France in 1940. That's on there. Then she didn't like the way I greeted the women on the reception desk. My voice was too high-pitched, she said. It had made her cringe with embarrassment. So that's on there, too.

When I asked her why the criticism was so biting, she said it was because of her disappointment at the difference between my writing voice in the emails, which she'd loved, and my real self, which she liked hardly at all. I was rougher than she'd imagined. She'd pictured someone more civilised and articulate.

I looked at the carpet and thought about the list of criticisms I'd started about Cow Girl. A mild objection to her using my electric toothbrush to clean out her navel was all I had written down so far. Oh, and the bloody cats, Bobby and Sammy. Bobby Cuddles and Sammy Jack are Cow Girl's sun, moon and stars. She has a selection of clips on her mobile phone of Sammy and Bobby play-fighting, or of her disembodied hand tickling Bobby's tummy. (Sammy doesn't like having his tummy tickled quite so much.) She's played some of them to me in bed. When we are living together, she says, I'll be able to tickle Bobby's tummy too. If we go through with it, I expect her 'boys' will be there at the marriage ceremony, cradled in her muscular lap-swimmer's arms.

Finally, the one and only Sufi proverb I know entered my mind. It says: If two horses come galloping by, the first called Happiness, the second called Unhappiness, why not leap on to the back of the latter?

I looked up at the registrar's exhausted face. 'No, I'm not sure,' I said. 'But what the hell.'

She clicked the mouse. My notice was given. 'That'll be £33.50, then,' she said.

REAL LIFE

Melissa Kite

2 April

One of the joys of spring is my annual nose around other people's houses. Or it used to be. It seems things have changed in the house-hunting world. Estate agency has become automated.

I had spotted a nice three-bedroomed place near Tooting Common and had rung the agent to ask them to show me round.

'Are you registered with us?' said the perky voice at the other end, sounding suspiciously like a call centre operative. There then followed an inquisition I can only liken to getting through security at Tel Aviv airport when you've got a stamp on your passport from Iran.

It started with the utterly baffling question: 'Why are you looking to move house?' Why? I can get my head round an estate agent asking me the what, how and when of my house-moving ambitions. But why? 'Why do you need to know why?' I asked, feeling the Kafkaesque red mist descending. 'Because it's part of the registration process,' she said. Clever, clever. These people never diversify from the circular logic of their crib sheet, which is indestructible.

Of course, I didn't want to tell the disembodied voice of a person known to me for 30 seconds the story of last year's abortive attempt at getting hitched to the world's most unpromising candidate for a husband and now finding myself alone and wondering whether I ought to invest in a larger property anyway. But you can't argue with someone filling in a form, so I had to tell her.

'Oh, I see,' she said. 'Yes,' I went on, warming to the honesty of my theme. 'And then I saw that house and I thought, I'd quite like to buy that because it's got a big pile of logs in the breakfast-room hearth.'

'Right,' she said, 'and is your flat currently on the market?' 'Nope,' I said, positively emboldened by the joy of honesty now. 'I'm probably the worst potential buyer you have for this property because I've not even thought about putting my own property on the market. I would be a nightmare to deal with because I don't have the finance in place and it would probably take ages to arrange the sale of my flat, which is in the middle of a lease extension. And then there'd be a chain, and the fact that I'm naturally indecisive and make a drama out of everything, which will hold things up further. In fact, I wouldn't blame you if you didn't want to show me round. Waste of time, in all likelihood.'

'Well,' she said, undeterred from her primary purpose, 'I just need to take some more details.' Ravenously, she swallowed up my name, address, three telephone numbers and then demanded an email so they could send me updates on other properties. 'Look,' I said, 'if it's all the same to you, I'd rather not give you my email. I just want to look at this house and if I like it I might buy it and if I don't I won't.'

'But we have to take an email,' she said. 'It's part of the registration ...'
'... process, yes, I know.' We argued back and forth for a bit and then, sounding exasperated, she blurted out emotively, 'It's because of Suzy Lamplugh!'

This floored me. For a second I nearly gave in. Then I thought, hang on a minute. 'But you've got my name, address and phone numbers. What's an email going to prove?'

'It's for our security,' she said in grave, outraged tones, before adding, 'I remember it like it was yesterday. We all remember it.' Oh, dear. If I wasn't careful this phone call was going to end in me being written up as a person of insufficient ability to be moved by a tragedy. So I said, 'I'm really sorry about the difficulties faced by the estate agent community. Perhaps I could just narrow down the issues outstanding to the following proposition: can I look round this house without giving you an email?' 'No.' So I gave her my email and we made an appointment for me to view the property and I put the phone down.

A few minutes later, the first message arrived. 'Dear Kite,' it said, rather impertinently. 'In order to comply with the latest directives from the EC on privacy and electronic communications we are sending you this email on an automatic basis.'

In other words: 'Here's some junk mail that could contravene some junk regulations prohibiting junk mail that doesn't announce that it's junk mail.'

Ten minutes later my email box was swimming in unsolicited messages, including ones from other estate agents who were also now warning me that unless they warned me they were sending me junk mail they would be contravening EC regulations.

And they tell me I'm a nuisance.

DIARY

A. A. Gill

23/30 April

Two men on a first date get chucked out of the John Snow pub in Soho for kissing. There's a whole lot of issues here, not least the recurring heterosexual jealousy of gays who manage to get a proper snog on a first date. And then, how can anyone have a pub in Soho and be surprised by men kissing? And how can anyone be a landlord anywhere and be shocked by anything that happens in a pub? Customers regularly wet themselves, vomit down each other's necks, have hysterical crying jags, queue up to inseminate each other in fetid toilets and read the *Daily Express*. The faux prudery and front-parlour morality of your average England landlord is something I'd forgotten about, and not having to listen to it is one of the bonuses of not having picked up a drink for 25 years. But I do think that one of the pleasures of going to European cities is seeing people kiss in public. Not for any prurient reason, but just the vitality, the excitement and the joy of it. The person who occasionally kisses me with intent takes a sterner line. She insists public kissing should be restricted to stations and airports, and only then when one of you has a ticket. And to very attractive people – apparently the cut-off age is 25. The John Snow pub is named not (as you'd imagine in Soho) after Channel 4's newsreader, but after the father of epidemiology, who proved that cholera was spread by germs and not miasma. The source of the epidemic was the water pump in Broadwick Street.

LETTERS

7 May

Sir: A. A. Gill (Diary, 23/30 April) is way off beam when he states that Londoners who do not realise that the John Snow pub is named after the epidemiology pioneer believe it to be named after the Channel 4 newsreader. Right-thinking Londoners have always assumed it was named after the great Sussex and England fast bowler of the 1970s. I am still inclined to cleave to this view.
Tim Rice
London SW13

CINEMA

Deborah Ross

14 May

As *Attack the Block* (15) is being touted as 'the new *Shaun of the Dead*' I expected a light-hearted romp rather than something quite bloody and nasty, although this does, at least, come in at a highly manageable 88 minutes. (Next week's fourth *Pirates of the Caribbean* film is 140 minutes, can you believe, but don't worry, I'm already in training for the boredom. I paired socks all morning, will be watching paint dry this afternoon and, just to make sure, I'm setting off tomorrow for a camping trip to Wales.)

LOW LIFE

Jeremy Clarke

28 May

After the Cow Girl debacle, I went straight back online with another dating site. I was working on the same principle as those eager to get behind the wheel again as soon as possible after a serious accident to regain confidence.

I signed on with a dating site designed for people wanting to have sex with as many people as possible and posted a photograph of myself with no clothes on, just my glasses, and smiling confidently and a little suavely at the camera, as though clothed or unclothed it was all the same to Lord Tangent, as I called myself. I also indicated, by ticking boxes beside diagrams of little stick people making love in various positions, the positions I preferred. Three of the ten I hadn't considered before and one looked well beyond my capacity, but I ticked all of them. I also ticked yes to ten questions about my sexual habits, likes and dislikes, including one asking whether I 'like it if it hurts a bit'. The wider I cast my net, I reckoned, the greater the harvest. In the space where I was invited to say something about myself, I said I was single and looking for someone who didn't mind getting muddy.

BOOKENDS

Mark Mason

11 June

It is 1979. You are a 15-year-old boy starring in a hit US television show. You've seen the crowds of screaming girls outside the gates as you arrive for work, and are therefore very excited to have received your first fan letter. You open it eagerly and begin to read: 'Dear Mr Rob Lowe, You are a great actor. Can you please send me an autographed photo of yourself? If possible in a bathing suit or in your underwear. Sincerely, Michael LeBron. #4142214 Pelican Bay Prison.'

Anyone who thinks of Lowe as Action Man made flesh (blandly handsome, zero personality) will be pleasantly surprised by his autobiography, *Stories I Only Tell My Friends*. You don't swap the Brat Pack for *The West Wing* without a certain amount of nous, and in this very well-written book (no ghostwriter) we learn a lot about the movie and TV biz. For example, big names in a pilot episode guarantee nothing: you can still 'arrive like the *Hindenburg*'. Flagging studio audiences are given free candy so they'll 'cackle like hyenas, high on sugar'.

Lowe may occasionally bathe in Lake Luvvie – he wants his son to be called John, his wife wants Owen, they go for 'Johnowen' – but overall the book is engaging and revealing. A nurse leans over Lowe's just-dead grandmother to ask for an autograph. An entire cast refuses to publicise a film, so the producers send out a parrot that appeared in it instead. The light sabres in *Star Wars* were broomsticks. Welcome to Hollywood.

FOOD

Tanya Gold

9 July

Rules is the restaurant where Edward VII ate himself to death and, in a way, it looks like him. It is spacious and regal and covered in velvet. His personal dining room upstairs is a cocktail bar now, with a lump of Stilton as focal point and memorial. Downstairs there are stags' heads and a painting of Margaret Thatcher as Britannia, with pointy breasts. From a distance, it looks as if she is topless.

The customers are the sort of people who like to watch powerful women topless. That is, they are powerful men, in groups or, quite often, alone. Rules has single booths for these lonely creatures – well, they can accommodate two small people, or one very fat man, and it is always one very fat man who is there, wiping the blood from his mouth with a blinding white napkin. They all have grey hair and grey suits and grey newspapers. But the waiters are camp, and this leavens the atmosphere; should a psychotic customer attack you, a melodramatic waiter would throw himself in its path, screaming 'No'. There are also tourists who have lost *The Lion King* and seem bewildered, and toffs, who come here because the menu, with its lumps of meandering cow, reminds them of home.

Rules has been here since 1798. I once tried to calculate how many cows had been slaughtered for its kitchen, but when I got to 77,000 I gave up. They specialise in British Food. Not Crappy Modern British Food with its insincerities and collusions and fears – yes, I'm comparing Rules, though very subtly, to Nick Clegg, who I would quite like to eat, and fiscally speaking, may soon have to – but proper, earthy, beastlike BRITISH food. The type of food that would, were it still alive as it came to the table, eat *you* and then lick its own face, bellowing and snorting like a newspaper editor.

So, here we have the Disney Pantheon – hare, deer, woodcock, pheasant and pigeon. It is solidly but not thrillingly done – too much flair and we wouldn't be in England. We'd be in France and that would be awful.

My beef on the bone is dense and pink; the blood explodes in my mouth. It is not brown, which is good, because people who like their beef well done should be made to eat tyres. It comes with a Yorkshire pudding so tall I can't really see the restaurant beyond it. It is like going blind but eating the blindness. The blindness is soft, light, crunchy; a meringue without sugar, the size of a phobia. The potatoes dauphinoise are gurgling with butter and cream. The carrots are plain and steaming – proper carrots, not pretentious ones, because some vegetables just need to be left alone.

My friend Paul, who is a comedian, eats a woodcock. It comes on a silver platter, and it has a head. It looks completely revolting and he turns it over and fillets the organs, because he is half mad. He says he loves it. I have never been afraid of him before.

Pudding is saner, because I am not chewing my bones, like Jeffrey

Dahmer, and Paul is not eating a liver, like Hannibal Lecter. Is there a connection between the love of kings for this restaurant and the way we devour living things here? It feels tyrannical and visceral. I have golden syrup pudding – a dome of sponge doused in custard; pure sugar, uncut. Paul has a too-big slab of lemon meringue pie and we can almost smell the flame-thrower that burned the meringue. They leave the food alone here, which is why it comes to you almost snarling; it feels more like death than eating, as Edward VII would know.

Do I recommend this restaurant? From a pool of blood I say – yes.

DIARY

Joan Collins

3 September

My three adorable grandchildren are nothing if not outspoken. I've had them and their parents staying with me for the past three weeks in the south of France, like some bizarre episode of *The Waltons*. While discussing with seven-year-old Ava Grace her plans to become a movie director, I suggested that she might cast me in one of her films. She replied, laconically, 'If you're still alive then.' Out of the mouths of babes.

YOUR PROBLEMS SOLVED

Dear Mary ...

17 September

Q. I have recently had two youngish builders working for me, and in a rare spell of sunny weather they asked if it would be all right to remove their shirts. I naturally agreed. One of them had a religious pastiche on his upper torso: the Virgin Mary, sundry cherubs and what looked like a scene from the *Kama Sutra*. The other inclined more to the Garden of Eden, with a snake heading with forked tongue down towards his lower abdomen. Could you let me know what the correct reaction to this artwork is? Ignore them completely? Say something inane like, 'Ah, *vita brevis, ars longa*'? My young (early thirties and definitely middle class) niece has a tasteful swallow on her left shoulder. Where are we on all this?

– H.A., by email

A. Tattoos are never tasteful – they are not what nature intended. Their only use is their ability to signal someone with no capacity for thinking ahead. Consequently they are best ignored.

FOOD

Tanya Gold

17 September

Oslo Court is the Jewish mother birthday party venue, or lunch if the Jewish mother must be home in time to be medicated – a convention, a summit, a trough for Jewish mothers. And so, when you telephone for a reservation, they will ask you, having as yet no idea who you are – do you need a cake? You should always say yes. Because who doesn't need a cake?

It inhabits the ground floor of an expensive but ugly apartment block in St John's Wood. But that just adds to its lustre in Jewish mother circles. It is a restaurant that has been disguised as the home of your cousin. Weave past Jaguars – also called Jew Canoes – and you are in. It is decorated in snarling pink; they say that Dame Barbara Cartland came here once, and disappeared into the decor. It has pink walls, pink tablecloths, pink customers, pink napkins, pink food. It is like being in a Jewish mother's bedroom; no, without wishing to be vulgar, it is like being inside a Jewish mother. If Jewish mothers had a national flag, this restaurant would fly it. Everyone has big hair, even the men.

It's not Jewish food. Jewish food is horrible, and who knows that better

than Jews? Jews have given plenty of wonderful things to the world –
monotheism, communism, psychiatry – but cuisine is not one of them.
Why the early church fathers left this off the list of our crimes, I know
not. Deicide, well-poisoning, trying to make people eat mashed herring?
The last time I made matzo balls my boyfriend said, 'Is that why the Jews
of the Warsaw Ghetto held out so long, baby? They threw matzo balls
at the Wehrmacht?'

It is, instead, historical re-enactment cuisine, from May 1976 – steak,
liver, veal, fish and anything that butter will stick to. It does seafood too,
which the Jewish mothers don't mind, because it feels edgy to have a lobster in the kitchen. And it is the only way they know they are not at home.

The staff are all male and in black tie. They are well versed in Jewish
mother needs. They love indiscriminately and unconditionally. Their
response to irrationality, or even violence, is more love. This makes me
wonder if they meditate. They bring steak diane (for mother), wiener
schnitzel (for me) and calves' liver for my boyfriend. It is all fat and
warm, and it expands inside you, to begin that other Jewish mother
hobby, which is developing heart disease. Jewish mothers, like anacondas,
expand to fit the food available. I watch a tiny woman at the next table
swallow a Dover sole that is bigger than she is.

Pudding is a West End show. (Not *The Sound of Music*. That is a musical
about the Anschluss.) The pudding waiter, who is a star in front-of-house
circles, has been waving at me all evening, with the promise of crème
brûlée and other depravities. I would like to say that Oslo Court has
wrought the tablets of the Ten Commandments in sponge, or rebuilt
the Second Temple in lemon drizzle cake, but it has not. (They would,
though, if you ordered in advance, and said it was an 80th birthday.) But
his trolley is from a fairy tale.

He tells us what we are going to eat. 'I love you,' he says to Mother
and, to prove it, he brings a chocolate sauce for her ice cream that is
almost all hard alcohol. My boyfriend is not told he is loved (he is not
Jewish) but he does get a piece of cheesecake. I get pastry, oozing cream
and, as I eat it, I watch Mother get blind drunk on dessert. 'You must
give Oslo Court,' she says, 'a thousand stars.'

DIARY

Ozzy Osbourne

15 October

Speaking of my Ferrari – I just got a new one: a 458 Italia. I wanted it to look like one of those stealth fighter aircraft: completely black, with no shine on the paint. But the guys at the dealership said it would scratch too easily, so I ended up getting it in silver, and they put these matt-black stickers over every panel, which you can wash regularly, then peel off and replace whenever they get too messed up. Now all I need to do is persuade somebody to get in the car with me. Whenever I reach for the keys, people run for the hills, screaming. What's so scary about me driving a 600-horsepower supercar around LA? So far, the only time the car's been driven is when my assistant pops down the shops for milk.

It looks like my son Jack might be about to tie the knot. Already, people are coming up to me and asking, 'What advice are you gonna give him, since you and Sharon have been together so long?' All I can say is that I'm still very much in love with Sharon. It's no more complicated than that – I just am. Having said that, when you've been on a 40-year-long bender, your memory tends to suffer, so cheating isn't a practical option. It's all very well when a natural-born con man decides to play a few away games. If I tried it, I'd forever be in the wrong house at the wrong time, calling some poor woman by the wrong name.

TOP GEAR

Tom Hollander

15 October

The exciting thing about showbiz is, you never quite know where you are. I thought of a good test some weeks ago. I phoned Denee, my agent's assistant.

'Can you ring Audi and see if they'll give me a car. But for goodness sake be discreet.'

I know it sounds grasping, but I'd been forced to it. Orlando Bloom had an A4 3.0 TDI when we did *Pirates*, which he let me drive up Regent Street because he was worried about his carbon footprint; Kate Winslet was in a Q7 last year in Cornwall when I got lost following her because I couldn't understand her directions; and Michael Gambon has an R8, but he probably paid for that. He also has a Ferrari. Fair enough. But when I saw the charming and talented Benedict Cumberbatch filling up what looked like an S5 at a service station near Oxford, something inside me snapped.

'They'd be happy to.'

'What? Really?'

'Yeah, they said they love you.'

'Fuck, that's amazing. I can't believe it. Wow.'

'Yeah, and they pay for everything except the petrol and any fines you incur.'

'Unbelievable. Seriously, what do I have to do?'

'Nothing.'

'Really? Brilliant.'

'They said they're having a polo match next weekend which they'd love you to go to, but no pressure.'

'Oh no. Do you think I should go?'

'Probably you should, if you want a car.'

'Yes of course, I must go ... but will they pick me up?'

I went. In a chauffeur-driven A8. Benedict was there. And Nick Mason of Pink Floyd and Prince Harry and Charlize Theron. We all laughed and drank Pimm's in the sun. There were lots and lots of different kinds of beautiful new Audis. And a really delightful woman from the Audi press office called Tabitha. She was warm and mischievous and funny and clever, and she was giving me a car. It was hard not to fall in love with her. I asked her out to dinner.

'You don't have to take me out because I'm giving you a car, you know.'

'No, no, I'm not, that's not the reason, it's because I really like you, of course it is.'

I phoned my parents.

'Mum! Dad! Audi are giving me a car!'

'Really, darling, that's wonderful. Why?'

'Well I don't know, I think it's a form of recognition in a way, for, you know, having achieved something.'

'For *Rev*?'

'Well I suppose so, and also other stuff in the past, maybe. *Pirates* probably.'

'And they're just giving it to you?'

'Um, I think it's on an indefinite sort of semi-permanent loan.'

'Well, how exciting!'

'Yes, and when I get it, I mean when it's delivered, I'll come down and we'll drive around in it . . . I'm going to ask for a convertible.'

In questioning my motivation for dinner, Tabitha had alerted me to the danger of the situation. It was tricky. Lovely though she was, I must be careful not to drink too much and make a pass at her, because that might go badly and could jeopardise the car. On the other hand, if it went very well and she liked it, then we'd probably have to do it again, and again, or for at least as long as I wanted the car, which was, well, forever. I couldn't risk that. What if she tired of me? Or, God forbid, me her? What if there was some mechanical work that needed doing and I couldn't get it done because we were going through a difficult patch? So it was clear: at dinner don't flirt too much and don't talk about cars at all. Less fun as an evening, but the sensible way forward. And definitely the most honourable.

The evening arrived and we had a jolly time. We talked about the food, the wine, and the merits of the BlackBerry over the iPhone, while I firmly established my credentials as a genuine friend. We were each in our own bed by about 9.30.

Unfortunately, for a few days afterwards I was unable to stop myself from sending her quite a few texts and emails about which model of Audi I thought might be appropriate. Eventually I settled on a supercharged six-cylinder black S5 cabriolet. I had my car space slightly enlarged to accommodate it.

In due course, the car arrived. I felt a stab of disappointment. It was a pale hairdresser-blue four-cylinder diesel. But it was convertible, and had an iPod dock, and pretty lights in the footwells.

My nieces loved it. We listened to Rihanna with the top down and they waved their hands in the air.

Mum and Dad liked it as well. 'It's great,' said Mum. 'It's fine,' said Dad.

'Yeah, no, it's fine for now. I'll just keep it for a few months then ask for something a bit more me.'

'Quite right,' said Dad.

Several weeks later I emerged from a long swim in Ibiza and stretched out on to my towel. There was a missed call from Tabitha. I felt a twinge of guilt. I hadn't spoken to her since our dinner.

'Hello, Tom, long time no speak, hope all's well, are you in? One of our drivers is outside your house to take the car back, but he says you're not there. Can you call me back as soon as you get this?'

'Hi, Tabitha. Hi, um, what do you mean? – there's a repo man outside my house?! I don't understand, I thought the car was for me to use, you know, on a kind of semi-permanent basis . . . '

'Oh no, we always said we'd take it back this week . . . didn't you get the text message?'

'No! What message? No,' I spluttered. 'I mean I'm in Spain on holiday. Did I do something wrong? I mean . . . is this . . . is this . . . because of, y'know, dinner . . . is it because I haven't been in touch since dinner?'

'No, it's because we always lend cars out on a temporary basis. When are you back?'

'Late Thursday night, but I thought some people have them, y'know, semi-permanently?'

'Only in very exceptional circumstances . . . someone'll be outside to collect it at 7.30 a.m. on Friday, OK?'

'But what's Benedict's arrangement? Hello? Hello?'

When I next arrived to visit my parents, it was in my old Golf. I explained I'd given the Audi back because it wasn't the right model and I'd prefer to wait for the right one.

'Oh very good,' said Dad. '"Take it away!"' He laughed and waved his hand like an aristocrat.

'Ha! Yes,' I said. 'Sort of.'

A STAR AT CHRISTMAS

Joan Collins

17/24 December

Walking swiftly through a major Beverly Hills department store, I was constantly accosted by the eager wide smile of sales assistants who oozed into my path with reptilian intent. 'How are you today?' they trilled as if they gave a damn. 'I have the flu – highly contagious,' I replied. Dodging sprays of ill-smelling scents that they wish to douse me with, I negotiated my way through the overcrowded cosmetics department. During recessions, lipstick sales surge.

2012

Rod Liddle; Camilla Long; Toby Young;
Tanya Gold; Deborah Ross; Brian Sewell; Dear Mary;
Craig Brown; Tom Hollander; Joan Collins

IS IT EMPOWERING FOR WOMEN TO HAVE THEIR BAPS INFLATED?

Rod Liddle

7 January

I wonder what explanation will be found for the mysterious discovery of a woman's body tucked behind a hedge on the royal estate of Sandringham? The obvious answer – that she was murdered and partially eaten by a senior member of the royal family, or perhaps a number of royal family members operating as a pack – is, I think, too easily arrived at, too pat. It is true that the Queen and Prince Philip, along with the Wessexes, were in situ over the Christmas holidays. And one might add as corroborating evidence that the royals have been publicly criticised for shooting raptors on the estate and so perhaps diverted their bloodlust towards the pursuit of humans, suspecting that this might occasion less opprobrium.

But I still do not quite buy it. Even less, the other so-called 'obvious' answer – that this unfortunate was one of the legions of mentally deranged royal women whom the Windsors have kept hidden from us for years, in cellars and outhouses and secret asylums around the country. I have never bought into this theory, though; it is hard to think of anyone being madder than Princess Margaret or the Duchess of Kent, and they were allowed out and about in full view of the public.

My suspicion is that the dead woman is a commoner and that her death had nothing to do with the royal family. Statistically, it seems almost certain that she was a woman who had recently undergone a cut-price breast-enhancement treatment and was out for a walk when one, or perhaps both, of her breasts exploded causing mortal injury. According to the newspapers, between 40,000 and 70,000 British women have availed themselves of this French cheapo boob job procedure, pioneered by a firm which has now gone bust and whose principals are now being investigated by the police. The 'rupture rate' is said to be anything between 1 per cent and 15 per cent, so they will be popping off all over the place. If you are thinking of going someplace where there are likely to be vain women with unfeasibly large breasts, I'd wear protective outer clothing, if I were you.

The now somewhat discredited Poly Implant Prosthetic treatment involved bunging stuff into the implants which differed a little from the medical norm: from what I can gather, tile grouting, crunched-up sour cream 'n' chive flavour Pringles, carpet underlay etc., anything that came to hand, really. You may if you like criticise the women for being so gullible as to expect that the cut-price service they were getting would match the sort of thing which costs double the price. In which case you might also criticise the National Health Service, which availed itself of PIP for women who required reconstructive surgery after a mastectomy.

If the women were gullible, so too was (in effect) the government. There are now debates as to who should pay the bill for the expensive surgery which will remove these globes of purulent landfill from thousands of women, at a cost which has been estimated at £150 million. The shadow health secretary, Andy Burnham, has castigated the cosmetic surgery industry and suggested that it should somehow pick up the bill.

Much of what he said about plastic surgeons seems to me absolutely right, but still, I cannot see why they should pay for the mistakes of others. Nor do I understand why the women should have to fork out. Morally, the worried women are in no different a position to those of us who smoke or drink or consume fast food and then expect to be treated on the NHS when the consequences of our foolhardiness reveal themselves in gravely tumorous form. When eventually I am admitted to hospital gasping like a beached whale and with glutinous black lung stuff hanging out of my nose, I would not expect Wills or Imperial to pick up the bill for my treatment. Indeed, my position is arguably less deserving than the women who had cosmetic surgery: I know precisely what I am in for; they did not. Further, the PIP treatment had received the imprimatur of the NHS, so they were entirely within their rights to assume it would be fine and dandy. All roads lead to death or injury, in any case, be they the road marked 'vanity' or the road marked 'smoking allowed'.

But why do so many women wish to have their tits monkeyed with? According to the British Association of Aesthetic Plastic Surgeons (yup, that's BAAPS: who says the quacks have no sense of humour?), the number rises rapidly each year, despite an economic climate which would freeze the nipples off an Eskimo. An opinion poll some years ago suggested that two thirds of women would contemplate plastic surgery and that they were, on the whole, depressed about their bodies.

Once upon a time, cosmetic surgery was something one kept quiet about in the hope that nobody noticed. Nowadays, though, it is something women proclaim proudly, as if it were a human right long denied to them by men, as if having your baps inflated were a form of gender empowerment. It is an odd consequence of feminism that women now feel it is politically right-on to have themselves mutilated in order to look better ('for ourselves – not for you!') and even more right-on to accede to requests for sexual intercourse with men or instigate such activities themselves. I suppose one should not complain too much.

Still, we should foot the bill for the remedial surgery and do so quickly, maybe hoping that this present health scare will dissuade women from having their bodies sliced up by men appealing to their vanity.

A YACHT? WOULDN'T THE QUEEN PREFER A REALLY NICE SOAP?

Camilla Long

21 January

Gove, a man so unsuited to the satanic machinations of high office that he looks like a permanently startled guppy, made a really strange boo this week by suggesting a collection of rich monarchists buy the Queen a £60 million yacht for her diamond Jubilee.

Really? A yacht? Men just can't buy presents, can they? Quite aside from the fact that a floating shagpad with a 12-person crew, a Jacuzzi, an indoor gym, and four on-board jetskis is the last thing anyone should spaff cash on right now, why did Gove think she actually wanted a yacht? That she wouldn't prefer a really nice soap, or a charming footstool? A toy for the corgis, or a *Learn How to Paint Watercolours* step-by-step guide? Yachts are only ever hideous, from the 100-foot penis extension owned by Aristotle Onassis – complete with bar-stools made of whale foreskin – to the grim supertankers that run aground off the coast of Italy.

And even if the Queen really loved *Britannia* – her single tear at her decommissioning in 1997 certainly suggested this – she is unlikely, at 85, to want to spend any more time slurping around northern waters now, sitting, grim-faced and damply blanketed in a dripping, darkened hull, on a two-week holiday with 22 relatives and only one set of Boggle.

The whole thing reeks of a crazed panic buy. Gove clearly woke up in the middle of the night, thought, the Jubilee's only months away, we still haven't done anything, no one ever gets her anything really good, let's get her a big flash boat! So off he rushed, and now he looks like the man at a 50th wedding anniversary who's turned up with a massive leg of pork.

STATUS ANXIETY

Toby Young

21 January

On Saturday my wife and I finally succumbed to the combined pester power of our four children and bought a hamster. They've been nagging us for over a year to buy them a pet and this seemed like the least hassle. We opted for a six-week-old Syrian with reddish-brown fur and white patches. We decided to call her Roxy on account of her being so pretty. It's short for Roxana, the Bactrian princess that Alexander the Great fell in love with.

I quickly realised that hamsters are a bit like printers, in that you think you've got a bargain until you realise what the running costs are. Roxy herself was only £10, but the cage set me back £65 and her food is so expensive that I'd be better off taking her to the Savoy Grill every day.

When we got home, we had to lay down a few ground rules to prevent her escaping. On no account were the children to take her out without adult supervision and once she was back in her cage it was absolutely vital to ensure that the door was firmly shut. To ram this home, I stressed that she was very unlikely to survive if she got out. Either she'd find her way into the garden, where she'd be eaten by a fox, or she'd scramble up the chimney, in which case she'd be burned to a frazzle next time we lit a fire. 'Her best hope would be getting stuck beneath the floorboards where she'd slowly starve to death,' I said.

The children looked suitably horrified and swore up and down that they'd never leave her cage open.

Fast-forward to last Saturday night. Everyone had gone to bed and I was settling down to watch *Match of the Day*. Before it started, I decided to look in on Roxy, who was clinging anxiously to her bars, looking lonely and desperate. 'Poor thing,' I thought, and carefully lifted her out of her cage and placed her in the Perspex exercise ball we'd been persuaded to buy by the owner of the pet shop (£25). I then put her on the floor of the sitting room where she happily rolled around for the next 90 minutes. Afterwards, I put her back in her cage and went to bed.

I was woken at 6 a.m. the following morning by my eight-year-old daughter in tears. Sasha had come down to discover the door of Roxy's cage had been left open overnight and there was no sign of her. 'It's all my fault,' she wailed. 'I was the last to play with her. I'm a terrible person.'

Rather foolishly, I immediately pointed out that I was the one to blame, at which point she stopped crying and narrowed her eyes. 'I hate you,' she said. 'You're the worst daddy in the world.'

Before long, the other children were up and my attempts to reassure them that Roxy would be OK – 'Plenty of rodents survive in the wild' – fell on deaf ears. 'What if she's been eaten by a fox?' asked Sasha. Six-year-old Ludo ran to the kitchen and reappeared with a large breadknife, at which point he started trying to jemmy up the floorboards. I was powerless to stop him. 'What if she's under there, Daddy?' he said. 'She'll starve to death.' Needless to say, I have not been allowed to light a fire since.

At the time of writing, Roxy has not rematerialised and I'm still in the doghouse. Sasha is a drama queen at the best of times, but the hamster's disappearance has propelled her to new heights. 'I feel as though I've lost a sister,' she told me on Sunday night, her little body convulsing with sobs. I managed to avoid pointing out that we'd only had Roxy for eight days and filed the comment under 'funny stories to tell at her wedding'. But the truth is I feel pretty bad about it.

Every night I set a trap, which consists of a piece of Hot Wheels track leading up to a bucket full of hamster food. So far, no Roxy, but on Monday night I did hear a faint scratching sound coming from the cupboard under the kitchen sink. Ten minutes later I was on my hands and knees peering into the cupboard with a torch having emptied the entire contents on to the kitchen floor. Again, nothing. My latest wheeze is to borrow the next-door neighbour's Manchester terrier, but knowing my luck he'll probably ferret her out and then swallow her in one gulp. The only solution may be to get a dog of our own. At least you don't have to buy them a cage.

FOOD

Tanya Gold

25 February

The Grand Hotel, Brighton, is the most beautiful hotel in England. It is bright and shiny like Simon Cowell's teeth, surrounded by something very ugly, like Simon Cowell's face.

THE MEANING OF NADINE DORRIES

Rod Liddle

28 April

[Nadine] Dorries is on the Jesus-saves-born-again-Tea-Party right of the Conservatives. I don't know what her views are as regards capital punishment, but if asked, my guess would be that she feels strongly that people should be hanged regardless of whether or not they have committed an offence.

CINEMA

Deborah Ross

28 April

Avengers Assemble, my lovelies, is 'the superhero event of the year',
And if this gets you all excited, you probably have nothing to
    fear.
But if big action so big it's humongous just isn't really your thing,
You may find, as I did, it drags, with its surfeit of CGI bling.

The fact is the earth is in peril, you won't be surprised to learn,
As there's a villain afoot called Loki, as played by Tom
    Hiddleston.
Loki purrs and taunts and is well camp, with a mullet plus helmet
    with horns,
But don't be deceived, my lovelies, as he's the most evil baddie
    ever born!

Loki has stolen 'The Tesseract', a glowing cube that can do cool
    stuff;

It can supply the world with unlimited energy but, as if that
    weren't enough,
It can also open a portal, a portal to – gulp! – 'outer space',
And Loki plans to summon an alien army, one that'll kill off the
    human race.
(Yes, my lovelies, you've spotted it: global domination is what has
    him in thrall,
Rather than, say, something a bit different, like free dentistry or
    aromatherapy for all.)

Now Loki must be defeated, but by who and how, where and
    when?
This is the question for General Fury, as played by Samuel L.
    Jackson.
And he knows the answer – yes, indeedy; knows exactly who'll
    make it all fine,
And it's a quintet of Marvel superheroes, coming together for the
    very first time.

So we have Scarlett Johansson as the Black Widow who, in her
    leathers, is phwoar!
And Chris Evans as Captain America, plus another Chris
    (Hemsworth) as Thor.
Meanwhile Jeremy Renner is Hawkeye, Robert Downey Jr is
    Iron Man again,
And Mark Ruffalo is The Incredible Hulk who, when he gets
    cross, splits his pants and goes all green.
(I know, doesn't rhyme. Give me a break here.)

Now, like I said up top – did you pay attention to what I wrote? –
This is an effects-driven movie, so you'll like it if this floats your
    boat.
It's a 3-D bonanza with battleships, iron dragons, explosions
    galore.

But frankly, my lovelies, I could have done with less action, and
    the back stories? Rather more.

The Hulk is the best character by a long shot, as he gets his own
    tragi-comic arc,
And Ruffalo's lovely performance hits the ball right out the park.
Also, Captain America is quite funny, so uptight and nerdy and
    old-fashioned,
But as written and directed by Joss Whedon, I don't think
    character is his passion.

Indeed, just when any banter gets going – which is what I liked
    most of all –
Another bloody battle would commence, as if battles can never
    ever pall.
Well, I can assure you they can – and so do – all this
    bish-bosh-splat!
And as the outcome is rather a given, where is the jeopardy in
    that?
(All I'm saying is if set-pieces
Are not to your liking,
You may get rather fed up
Of all the gratuitous fighting.)

This will be loved by genre fans, when all is said and done,
But at two hours forty, you may find it numbs your bum.
Seriously, more attention to character could have made it a lot
    more fun.
And now I have said all that, I believe my poem is done.

PS: You'll never get this kind of thing from Lloyd Evans, or
    Delingpole, aka Jamie. Which is why I am paid four times as
    much and get to sit on Fraser's knee.

DIARY

Brian Sewell

12 May

Lose weight is the advice of my cardiologist: 'It will make everything easier.' I see his point when I visualise a stone as 14 lb of shopping, but losing it is difficult when my only exercise is on the damned crutches and I am as tempted by strange cheeses as was St Anthony by naked women. On encountering – there is no better word for the event – a Mont d'Or in Waitrose, I succumbed in a split second. It looked evil. Its odour was that of a man on a long pilgrimage. An alien from the Haut-Doubs, it is circular only because it is shaped by a shaving of dark pine and trapped in a wooden box. Removed from this support it collapses, its leprous skin cracks, and its oozing innards creep in all directions, as mobile as a heavy syrup and as elastic as a fondue. In me it induced a state of ecstasy; my dogs it drove quite mad.

Why is there no English cheese to match it? In Hexham (like Doubs, border country) for an undeserved literary event, I wandered the market place where there were local cheeses on a dozen stalls, pretty enough, but so mild as to be tasteless. Embarrassed at having tried so many, 'Which is the strongest cheese you have?' I asked a big strong bloke, and he commended one clothed in a mould as blue as a small bird's egg, claiming it to be blue inside this party dress. And so it was, but its flavour was as strong and interesting as a sugar-free marshmallow.

But if the cheeses were a disappointment, the local tonic water was not. I am addicted to tonic (the quinine in it is a prophylactic against cramp) and Hexham, to my great surprise, produces a version infused with herbs and fermented. It is astonishing. I could compose for it a panegyric of the ilk written by Christie's for investors in fine wines – 'impulsive and forthcoming, sweet despite its tannic grip, honeyed with fragrance, a touch of balsamic character with rich and lingering aftertaste'. I would much rather drink it than champagne, even Laurent-Perrier.

STATUS ANXIETY

Toby Young

7 July

Roxy Mark II is dead. I hoped I'd never have to write those words, but there's no doubt about the matter. I don't mean our replacement hamster has escaped like the first one (current whereabouts unknown). I mean she's expired. She's not resting. She's passed on. She is no more. She has gone to meet her maker.

I first learned the news when I was travelling in East Africa a couple of weeks ago. Caroline called in a state of panic to say she 'thought' Roxy was dead.

'She's not moving,' she said. 'I forgot to feed her. D'you think she's died of starvation?'

'Oh Jesus,' I replied. 'Not another one?'

'Sasha's right, isn't she? We're pet serial killers.'

That was my eight-year-old daughter's verdict after Roxy II went AWOL last month. Coming on top of losing our cat and then losing Roxy Mark I (I left her cage door open), this was her withering conclusion. A little harsh, but these tykes are merciless when it comes to handing out moral judgements. I managed to win a reprieve when I recaptured Roxy II in the downstairs lavatory – 'You're the best daddy in the world' – but she had now been proved right.

My first instinct was to blame Caroline – 'Nothing to do with me, gov. I wasn't even in the country' – and she must have suspected as much because she quickly followed up by telling me we'd have to stage the 'discovery' of Roxy's corpse after my return. 'I just can't deal with this on my own, babe,' she explained.

I agreed, not least because as long as Caroline remained convinced she'd 'murdered' Roxy I would earn vital brownie points by covering up for her. In fact, it's inconceivable that Roxy II starved to death. She was so fat she looked like an over-sized stuffed toy. Died of over-feeding, more like.

On the morning of my return, Caroline shot me a pointed look over the breakfast table: 'Have you checked on Roxy since you got back?' I dutifully trudged into the playroom and, seconds later, came back into the kitchen, having composed my features into a mask of gravity.

'I've got some bad news,' I said. 'Roxy II is dead.'

'No,' said Sasha, her face crumpling. 'How? How did she die?'

I let the question hang in the air for a few seconds as Caroline looked at me imploringly.

'Wet tail,' I said. This was the cover story we'd agreed on. It's a fungal infection caused by poor personal hygiene, something Roxy II was definitely guilty of.

'Why did you let her tail get wet?' asked Sasha, tears streaming down her face. The question was specifically addressed to me.

'No, no, you don't understand, it doesn't literally mean—'

'PET SERIAL KILLER,' she screamed, and then stamped out of the room.

Given the truth of this accusation, the comment she made when she reappeared was somewhat surprising: 'I think we should get a dog.' She pointed out that the reason we'd bought a hamster in the first place – or, rather, two hamsters – was because she'd wanted a dog and we'd persuaded her that this was a more suitable pet. Turned out, hamsters weren't so easy to manage after all. So why not get a dog? At least a dog might have a chance of surviving more than a fortnight in the Young household.

'Mummy and I will discuss it.'

I quite like the idea, but Caroline has never been keen. There's something about dogs that brings out her inner Jewish American Princess. 'They're so dirty,' is her standard objection. When I look at a dog, I see a loyal, undemanding friend – a foot-warmer on cold winter nights – whereas Caroline regards all dogs as miniature poo factories. The very thought that a dog might sniff another dog's bottom and then lick her face makes her shudder with horror. Cats are barely any better because they lick their own bottoms.

'Can't we just not have a pet?' she asked. 'I'm not a pet person.'

I would go along with this, but the thought of having wasted all that money on the hamster cage is deeply upsetting. My plan now is to try and capture a mouse – there are plenty in our garden – and stick it in the cage. I will then put Sasha in sole charge so if she wakes up one morning to find that her mouse has ceased to be she won't be able to call me a 'serial killer'. I'm worried that if this idea takes root in Sasha's head it's going to cost me a fortune in psychiatry bills.

THE FINAL VICTORY OF MIDDLE-CLASS FOOTBALL

Rod Liddle

21 July

John Terry – the gift that keeps on giving. It is not enough that this stoic and rat-faced footballer should have provoked the most absurd and hilarious court case I have yet seen. Now it looks like there'll be another one, perhaps even funnier, predicated upon a reaction to the fact that he wasn't convicted of racially abusing another footballer, Anton Ferdinand, as everybody seemed to wish. Some chap 'tweeted' that Ashley Cole, who gave evidence on behalf of Terry, was a 'choc ice' – and of course now the police are involved. They had to be: it is deeply racist to liken black people to items of confectionery or popular snacks.

Interestingly, in a semantic sense, it is the 'ice' bit of the description which is considered offensive, not the 'choc' bit. It is a term which implies that Ashley is black on the outside, which I think is OK, but white on the inside, which is definitely not. In other words he is a traitor to his race. There are many similar terms – Oreo, Bounty, coconut and so on – all of which suggest the same thing, that the subject is an 'Uncle Tom'. I must say, 'choc ice' would not be the comestible I would choose to represent Mr Cole, if asked to do so. I've always thought of him as more of a Double Decker – a crisp layer of biscuit topped by a moist and sultry nougat. I am not sure if this is racist or not, but I daresay I will find out soon enough.

CINEMA

Deborah Ross

15 September

Hope Springs (12A) is a comedy-drama about a long-term marriage that has effectively stalled, and is one of those films that is only as good as its stars. Luckily, in this instance, the stars are Meryl Streep and Tommy Lee Jones. Meryl, we know about. I once had dinner with Meryl, and have talked of little else since, until I realised it got on everybody's nerves, but have gaily continued nonetheless. She is the greatest film actress of her generation, our generation, any generation. She could play my left shoe, if she put her mind to it. She may even be playing my left shoe right now. How would I know? But Mr Lee Jones? (I don't feel matey enough to call him by his first name.) He has a face like an old-style leather football that's been left out in the rain, year after year. He usually plays those remote, taciturn, weathered *No Country for Old Men* types. But, in this, he is adorable! So cute! I'd bring him home and ravish him, if I didn't have my own dead marriage to think about. Although, as it simply lies there, we could just step over it, I suppose.

YOUR PROBLEMS SOLVED

Dear Mary . . .

15 September

Q. I am divorced and now share a flat with a great male friend who is also divorced. Because we get on so remarkably well everyone assumes that we have become gay. How, without being heavy-handed, can we signal that this is not the case?
 – R.W.-J. and A.W., London W1

A. I have discussed your issue with a mutual friend who assures me that you have no need to worry. He pronounces: 'No one will think they are gay when they see how dirty their flat is.'

DIARY

Craig Brown

6 October

This week sees the 30th anniversary of the death (or 'untimely death', as death is now invariably known) of Glenn Gould. The fame of most classical musicians tends to wither when they die, but Gould's seems to grow and grow: his grave is the most visited in Canada, he has appeared on *The Simpsons*, and not long ago in its apparently straight-faced list of The 100 Most Important Canadians in History, *Maclean's* magazine ranked him the No. 1 artist in the world. Such posthumous blossoming makes him rather closer to a rock star, which is, in all but the most literal sense, what he was. In fact, he makes most of today's rock stars look doggedly conventional. He hated Mozart, sunshine and Italian opera, and loved tomato ketchup, overcast skies and Petula Clark. He was a rabid hypochondriac, taking a briefcase of pills, a bottle of disinfectant and a blood-pressure kit with him wherever he went: he once hung up the phone when he heard his friend sneeze on the other end of the line.

When he still performed in public – he grew to hate audiences, describing them as 'a force for evil' – Gould refused to wear the customary white tie and tails, preferring to appear in scruffy clothes and mismatched socks, his shoes held together by rubber bands. He would then play his piano from his special low chair, sitting just 14 inches from the ground, so that his knees were a good deal higher than his buttocks. Thirty years on, his fame has increased but for some reason his influence hasn't. Classical musicians remain studiously starchy. One might have expected Gould's influence to have liberated them, but far from it: the pious aura of the Sunday school still hangs over classical concerts. We should be grateful, though, that in at least one area his influence has been so negligible. He was a rotten driver, generally driving with his legs crossed whilst singing and conducting from a score open on the passenger seat. He couldn't see what was wrong with it. 'It's true that I've driven through a number of red lights on occasion,' he once protested. 'But on the other hand, I've stopped at a lot of green ones and never gotten credit for it.'

Jack Straw certainly wouldn't approve of Glenn Gould's grubby, rubber-banded shoes. In his autobiography, Straw confesses to what he calls 'a clean-shoe fetish', incessantly brushing and polishing his shoes whenever he has a spare minute. In a footnote, he outs Ernie Bevin and Neil Kinnock as fellow Labour shoe-polishers, and names Tony Blair as the owner of 'the most extensive shoe-cleaning kit I'd ever seen'. Jack or Glenn? Smart or scruffy? On the great shoe divide, I'm firmly with Glenn. Shining shoes is as loopy as washing cars, or cleaning trees. People with well-polished shoes generally have something to hide, just like those with ostentatiously firm handshakes, and those who spend too long looking you straight in the eye. If in doubt, think what Lord Archer would do, and do the opposite.

STRANGERS ON A TRAIN

Tom Hollander

6 October

If I subtracted from my life all the time spent either thinking about sex, or engaging in behaviour calculated to achieve it (by which I mean most of my social life and career choices); or dealing with the consequences of having achieved it (by which I mean all of my romantic life), well, I don't know how much of my life I'd actually have left. Childhood. The useful bit.

Fifteen years ago, in August, I boarded a train in New Orleans bound for New York. The journey time was 29 hours. What to do? Write postcards? Read a book? Try to have sex with someone?

It was a sultry afternoon: Spanish moss dangled in a sensuous manner, the edges of things were blurry in the heat. And we passengers would be packed together for a really long time going in and out of tunnels. I didn't actually set out to do it. It was more of a daydream. It would be a wonderful thing. To meet someone lovely and to pass through every stage of an affair, within the same journey. First meeting, seduction, consummation, farewell. Like station names.

I drifted into the smoking carriage. The place where everyone has at least one vice in common. So a good starting point if you were actually going to try and seduce someone, which I wasn't, but since we had 29 hours I could at least flirt with the idea. Before I read my book.

The most attractive woman in the carriage was small, dark-haired, bright-eyed and talking animatedly to a big black soldier. But I wasn't trying so it didn't matter. And because it didn't matter, somehow he drifted away, and I found myself talking to her, and we got on, and in a way that I really can't remember there was a seamlessness with which we made our way, over a few hours, from smoking carriage to bar, and from bar to restaurant car, and over dinner we told each other our life stories, and in the narrow section of corridor on our way back to our seats we were forced close together and I turned and kissed her. Or did she kiss me?

Her name was Pamela Reed and she was travelling back to Atlanta, Georgia, to meet her parents. She had been forcibly estranged from her crack-dealing boyfriend who was now in jail. Her father was a colonel in the army and her mother was a schoolteacher. She was the apple of their eye and the source of all their pain. To me she was compelling. Obviously. And Atlanta was about two hours away. I remember her hand reaching behind her and holding mine and then we were in a bathroom. Quite a big American one. And in there we reached the consummation stagepost of our journey. And it was so wonderful that I was only slightly irritated at the noise of the guard hammering on the door yelling 'Excuse me! Excuse me!' You can go to the devil, I thought, because we are utterly alive and free and you are just a wage slave with a bunch of keys and a little whistle.

I said, 'Your nipples are surprisingly dark.' She said, 'I'm a quarter Cherokee.' I said, 'Wow.' And I felt love for her, because it was all so simple. She wanted me and I wanted her and I was the guy. I was the Marlboro man.

As we sidled past the guard back to our seats I was only half-listening when he said: 'Young lady, I've told you about this before . . .'

We sat in silence with our hearts racing. It was late at night now. A kid threw a piece of screwed-up paper at us. And the train hooted as it slipped into Atlanta.

And then we said goodbye and lovely to meet you and there was no exchange of addresses or telephone numbers. No guilt. No expectation. No blame. Farewell.

What a girl.

I felt a pang of something as she stepped down on to the platform. I stood slightly back from the window and as the train moved away I watched her meet her parents. Before she kissed them she wiped her mouth with the back of her hand.

I spent the next 18 hours reading, sleeping, looking out of the window and thanking God for his munificence. For once, my uncomplicated, all-pervading desire for womankind had been met by its opposite. Everything had come together, so to speak. I leaned back in rare contentment and the bounteous American landscape drifted past in Amtrak Panavision. There was only a nagging disquiet about that comment of the guard's.

'I've told you about this before . . .'

Surely he didn't mean that. Surely it was a general moan: 'I (Mr Boring Jobsworth) have told "you" (plural, you lot, all you customers) about "this" (generally being in the bathroom too long and other petty infringements) "before" (on a daily basis, as part of my boring job, and this complaint is like a daily mantra).'

Surely he couldn't have meant: 'I, the long-suffering guard on this train, have been watching for months now as you, Pamela Reed, compulsive sex addict and notorious Amtrak bicycle, have taken a succession of strangers into the bathroom and screwed them without protection just before greeting your traumatised parents.'

If that was true, then I was not a total stud, Pamela Reed was mentally ill, and our romance on the train was simply the meeting of two deranged people.

I resolved to put such thoughts out of my head. This was classic Groucho Marx ... if it had happened to me, then there must be something wrong with it. No, the whole thing was magnificent. No point thinking anything else. I looked forward to telling my friends.

Over the years, my attitude has matured. I'm more accepting of the notion that all experience is flawed. So what if she was a sex-crazed psychopath? If your desire is to meet a complete stranger on a train and couple with her almost immediately, then what do you expect? Look at that horrid Sylvia in *Parade's End*. I reckon I got off lightly.

No, it was still beautiful. I still love her, wherever she is. Even if she's on her knees in a bathroom stall. I love her for the dream of it.

And I hope she's OK.

(Pamela Reed's name has been changed.)

LETTERS

24 November

Sir: I very much enjoyed the excellent piece by Harry de Quetteville about Hugh Montgomery Massingberd (as he then was, when I worked for him at the *Daily Telegraph* from 1987 to 1989). He transformed the obituary pages with his fine wit, his disdain for pomposity and his fascination with the unusual aspects of people's characters. I was rootling through the 'obituaries in waiting' one day when I came across the obit of H. Monty Mass, as we called him, and was surprised to find he had written the whole thing himself.

It began thus: 'Hugh Montgomery Massingberd, who has died aged ?, was a very fine writer who never achieved the literary acclaim of which many believed him capable.' After some detail, the obituary went on to say: 'Tall and well-made in his prime, he sacrificed his fine physique in pursuit of the most alarming gluttony, but he retained his titanic capacity for work and his fatal attraction for the opposite sex.'

It was I who printed the obituary and distributed it on the desks about the office. It was swiftly deleted from the computer system (which in those days was woefully insecure) and to my knowledge never appeared in print. He was a lovely man and I think would not begrudge me, then a young journalist, my small excursion into the world of mischief.

Mary Gold
Aldington, Kent

AMERICAN NOTEBOOK

Joan Collins

15/22 December

I bumped into Steve Martin dining with Eric Idle at a Beverly Hills boîte, as one does. 'I really enjoy your *Spectator* diaries,' said Steve. 'And I,' said Mr Idle. 'And you and the roller-skating nuns were the best thing in the Olympic finale,' I chirped back. Hollywood folk love to give each other compliments. I buttered up George Clooney at the Carousel Ball, where he was being honoured for his charitable work in Haiti and the Sudan, by telling him how much I adored *Argo*, which he co-produced, and that same night I told Shirley MacLaine how much I liked her in *Downton*, even though I'd gladly have maimed her for the part. I was impressed by my self-restraint.

At an Academy screening of *Hitchcock* (in which Anthony Hopkins was brilliant) some patrons sitting behind us told me how 'great' I looked. A few minutes later a very haggard-looking actress, much past her prime but trying hard, was hailed by these same punters with cries of 'Great to see you again' and 'You look sooo beautiful!' After she left they turned to each other and hissed, 'God she looks terrible.'

2013

Charles Moore; Rod Liddle; Leah McLaren;
Melissa Kite; Tanya Gold; Giles Coren;
Marcus Berkmann; Dear Mary; Toby Young;
Roger Lewis; Tristram Hunt; Sebastian Faulks

THE SPECTATOR'S NOTES

Charles Moore

5 January

My autistic nephew has a young friend, with learning difficulties but of high intelligence. Recently, she was asked who Narcissus was. 'He fell in love with himself,' she answered. 'Yes, and then what happened?' 'The relationship didn't work out.'

IF THE MICE HAVE TO FACE MY WIFE, THEY'LL HAVE ONLY THEMSELVES TO BLAME

Rod Liddle

5 January

I was in bed by one o clock on New Year's Day. We did the countdown thing, for the kids, and then hung around for a while looking tired; it was only later, when my wife and I were upstairs in bed, that the real fun began. A long and corrosive argument about the mice, probably the fifteenth we've had on this subject since we moved in back in August. We could both hear the mice downstairs, whooping it up, holding some sort of shindig of their own; the relentless skittering across the stone floor tiles or the parquet wood blocks in the living room. I was tempted, at one point, just to shout downstairs: 'Keep it down a bit will you, we're trying to get some sleep up here.' My wife, listening to the sounds of revelry – just wait until they work out how to use the CD player – turned over and said, full of contempt: 'So much for your bloody entente cordiale.'

She has a point. I thought I'd struck some sort of deal with the mice but it now looks like I was as deluded as Chamberlain. You cannot deal honestly with these sorts of creatures. The deal was that they were allowed in and out of the house, especially in very cold weather, and were entitled to crumbs and stuff they found down the backs of things. But they had to keep out of sight and not gnaw at any of our food; in return, the doveish clique in our marital coalition, i.e. me, would hold sway – and so poison and those horrible traps which snap the creatures in two would not be deployed. Only humane traps have been used so far, the ones in which a mouse enters a tilted black tunnel at the end of which I have deposited some Green & Black's organic fair-trade cocoa powder; when it reaches this bourgeois manna, the trap snaps shut. The captive mice can then be released a couple of miles away, near where the gypsies live.

NEWBORN NOTEBOOK

Leah McLaren

5 January

At some point in the last decade it became customary for women my age to greet each other by commenting on our appearances. 'Darling, you look AMAZING!' we say to each other now at parties. 'Nice hair!' 'Great shoes!' 'Have you started running again?' This social tic never really bothered me until I had a baby. The fact is, after you have a baby you do not look amazing. You look like someone who has been stretched to bursting and then suddenly deflated, a person kept awake for weeks on end while the miracle of life chewed, sucked and mauled you before lumbering off leaving you for dead. In other words, you look exhausted and a little bit fat. But you don't mind, not really. Because here's the thing: a person just came out of you. A real live person who is now, somehow, able to stay alive with the help of nothing but your own magically occurring fluids. It's utterly banal and yet nothing short of miraculous and sometimes when you think about it, your brain starts to tingle and you want to run down the street shouting the incredible story of what has happened to every person you meet. So when someone says, 'You look AMAZING!' you kind of just want to smack them.

My NCT group never contacted me after the course ended, which I thought was a bit odd. Then I did a search on Facebook and found out they'd formed a club and been meeting every Thursday afternoon in Chiswick for the past three months. I racked my brain for reasons why they might have blackballed me and came up with a number of plausible ones: 1) They were threatened by the fact that I'd attended the classes alone, even though I'd been careful to explain that Rob had refused to come because he'd already done a course with his ex-wife and found it to be 'a complete and utter load of hippy bollocks'; 2) They were put off by the fact that I was planning a home birth; 3) They noticed I wasn't wearing a wedding ring; 4) My new fringe was too edgy for Chiswick. I fretted about the situation for weeks, nattering on to Rob, who in exasperation finally reminded me that I'd scoffed at the whole notion of 'mummy friends' in the first place. While this was true, I pointed out that the whole point of an NCT group was that I should decide whether I wanted to hang out with them, not the other way around.

REAL LIFE

Melissa Kite

5 January

'They all have very distinct personalities,' said my friend Hannah, as she invited me to come to her house and pick a bunny. In truth, I hadn't given much thought to the preferred personality of my forthcoming rabbit.

I confess I wanted a quick fix of a bunny, a companion for Tinkerbell Butch Cassidy, so called because she started life as a girl and then morphed into a boy when, upon closer inspection, I panicked and declared the vet's earlier pronouncement misguided.

Tinky had been bought as a companion for TT, the two-tone bunny I found in a box by the side of the road. They had been happy when I thought they were boy and girl, and just as happy when I declared them boy and possible boy. To make it a bit more glamorous, I subtitled them Butch Cassidy and the Sundance Kid. Tinky Butch was pretty stoical when TT Sundance passed away last year and living in the kitchen she wasn't exactly lonely. But I never could shake off the worry that all animals in captivity should be with their own kind. It wasn't important to me what the personality of the new rabbit was, therefore. All that mattered was what Tinky thought.

And so Tinky and I pitched up at Hannah's house where her big rabbit Bow was sprawled out on an armchair in the living room, a weary look on her face as daddy rabbit hopped around the back of the television chewing cables and clearly taking the responsibilities of fatherhood very lightly indeed.

Hannah went out to the garden and came back carrying a tray full of wiggly grey fluff, which turned out to be three tiny lionhead bunnies. She put them down on the floor and we took Tinky out of her carry case and let them all run around. 'By the way,' said Hannah, picking up Tinky and turning her over, 'this is definitely a girl.'

'Wow!' I said, delighted to have the mystery solved at last. 'How do you know?'

'Because if it were a boy, by now something, some things, would have, um, appeared ...'

'Oh yeah ...' I said, feeling like a total fool.

After a few minutes of fluffy chaos it was clear that Tinky was hanging out most with one of the girl bunnies, who had just been sexed by the vet and so had a blob of bright pink nail varnish in her ear.

'Well, I guess it's that one then,' I said, scooping them both up. 'Come on, Tinky and Pinky.'

'Is that what you are going to call her?' said Hannah, looking downcast at my lack of imagination.

'Well, I could give her a longer name, of course. Perhaps something to chime with Tinkerbell. How about Wendy?'

'Cute,' said Hannah, looking somewhat reassured that her bunny was going to a home where her distinct personality would be nurtured. 'Now, I'm fairly sure you've got sleepy bunny,' she said, earnestly. 'The other girl is adventure bunny. She gets up to everything. This one is more timid.'

'That'll do fine,' I said, reaching for my bag and taking out the agreed £20 before she got into a longer discussion of Wendy Pink's educational and social needs.

The bunnies snuggled up in the carry case all the way home and when I put them in their big cage in the kitchen they seemed very happy. Cydney the spaniel was excited too. She is used to Tinky but the arrival of a new fluffball sent her running round in circles yelping ecstatically.

I shut her out and let the pair have a run round the kitchen, then after dinner popped them back in their house and shut the door. They were munching from their bowl, locked safely behind bars, when I let Cydney back into the kitchen and turned away to do the washing-up.

Suddenly, there was a terrible commotion. Cydney hurtled across the kitchen and threw herself at the fridge, behind which, by some incredible feat of escapology, the new bunny was crouching.

Hannah's face flashed into my mind as I imagined saying: 'Yes, yes, very happy ... no, I don't have any pictures, because, er, my camera's broken and so is my phone ...'

Thank heavens Cydney has done enough gundog training to have the restraint to desist from swallowing live furry things when they are flying around her and so my screams of 'leave it!' did just save the new bunny from being recycled as spaniel supper.

Luckily, the Builder Boyfriend is always at hand for such emergencies. He has fashioned a wooden guard around the bottom of the cage where adventure bunny had been squeezing herself through a two-inch gap.

The important thing is that Tinkerbell Butch Cassidy thinks Wendy Pink Houdini is the best thing since sliced hay. And that's what counts.

FOOD

Tanya Gold

26 January

It is, as far as I can see, the only pub in Kensington that still contains natives, that is, people born within the district, who have never cried inside a branch of Foxtons.

CANADA NOTEBOOK

Giles Coren

16 February

In downtown Quebec City, where we are staying, it is minus 26. I can't help wondering if this is cold enough to achieve that longed-for dream of all English prep-school boys: a wee that freezes solid on contact with the air and can be snapped off and waved around. I will never know, though, because from the brittleness of my fingers and toes I am worried about what else might snap off if I tried. Instead, I settle for a sneeze which solidifies into buckshot on leaving my nose and tinkles on the pavement like falling coins. And also for a go at 'tire sur neige', in which one flings boiling hot maple syrup into the snow and then eats the resultant amber lolly, thus breaking the first survival rule of the Mounties: 'Don't eat the yellow snow.'

POP MUSIC

Marcus Berkmann

9 March

I haven't heard the David Bowie album yet, but the Amazon order is in and Postie has been alerted as to the importance of the delivery. How often these days do any of us feel so excited about an imminent release? The ten-year gap between Bowie albums might have something to do with it, but the 30-year gap between decent Bowie albums is probably more relevant. And all this is down to the excellence of the single. Gary Kemp of Spandau Ballet wept the first time he heard 'Where Are We Now?', and I was blubbing well into the song's third or fourth week on Radio 2.

Nostalgia for lost youth isn't exactly a new theme, but the song's grandeur and strange fragility seem to speak directly to the slightly melancholy middle-aged male, which is pretty much all of us. Convention would demand that after the second chorus you would get a third, which would edge the song perilously close to anthem territory. But, no, we cut straight to the coda, so after a long, slow build-up and a peak that is over before you know it, the song actually seems to end too quickly. Anyone who sees a parallel with life itself may already have celebrated their 50th birthday.

YOUR PROBLEMS SOLVED

Dear Mary . . .

6 April

Q. I am absolutely fed up with the non-arrival of spring. Is there anything that you can do to help, Mary?
– A.B., London W8

A. Based on the 'carry a heavy umbrella and it will not rain' principle, go out and buy thermal underwear, gloves and a winter coat up to the value of £500. If funds will stretch, invest in a sledge. Spring will follow in a couple of hours.

YOUR PROBLEMS SOLVED

Dear Mary . . .

13 April

Q. May I pass on a tip to readers? I left it too late to order antibiotics from my GP surgery before the four-day Easter break and could sense a chest infection developing. What to do? I rushed out and bought a brace of intensively farmed broiler chickens and ate my way through them over two days. There were obviously enough antibiotics within to effect a cure and I sidestepped the need to ring for an emergency prescription.
  – G.W., Wilts

A. Perhaps this explains why chicken soup has long been credited as 'Jewish penicillin'.

FOOD

Tanya Gold

20 April

The Ritz Hotel is a cake on Piccadilly made of stone; inside this cake, Lady Thatcher died. Some think it is tragic that she died here in the cake of stone; I do not. It has Italian men in tailcoats, a gifted pastry chef, and views of Green Park; she chose, I suspect, the ultimate free-market death.

STATUS ANXIETY

Toby Young

25 May

When are you truly middle-aged? 'The years 20 to 40 are what you might call the fillet steak of life,' said Philip Larkin. 'The rest is very much poorer cuts.' Some might dispute this and put the turning-point at 45, while others will maintain it's all about how old you feel rather than your biological age. To my mind, the critical factor is when you go through a particular rite of passage. I'm talking about a colonoscopy.

I've been trying to avoid having one for years, but a recent visit to my GP convinced me I could put it off no longer. After I'd told him about various stomach ailments (I won't go into details), he asked if any members of my family had ever suffered from bowel cancer. I was shocked. Aren't doctors supposed to avoid using the 'c' word unless it's absolutely necessary? As it happens, my father did have bowel cancer so I immediately began to worry. My GP advised me to have a colonoscopy as soon as possible.

I then made two mistakes that I'd urge readers not to repeat. The first was to ask for a gastroscopy at the same time. This is when a scope is shoved down your throat so a doctor can examine your stomach. The specialist looked at me a bit oddly when I made the request, as if to say, 'Are you quite sure?', but it was too late to change my mind at that point. 'In for a penny, in for a pound,' I said, cheerfully.

The second was to elect to have both procedures – the endoscopy and the wrong-end-oscopy – without sedation. Not quite sure what possessed me to do that. I think it was partly because I didn't want to waste time sobering up in a recovery ward afterwards – I'm far too busy, doncha know – and partly because I feel competitive with my wife. I reasoned that if she could give birth to four children without any pain relief, I could dispense with the sedation.

When I told the specialist about this plan she was quite surprised. 'I don't think anyone's ever requested not to have sedation before,' she said. 'The procedure can be quite uncomfortable.' As any fule kno, 'uncomfortable' is doctor-speak for 'excruciatingly painful', but again, I didn't feel I could back down. It didn't help that the doctor was quite pretty. It's one thing being thought a coward by a man, but even worse by an attractive woman.

The gastroscopy was horrendous. I'd fantasised about being able to control my gag reflex through sheer willpower alone, but it wasn't to be. I was choking almost continuously, like a terrorist suspect being water-boarded by the CIA. My only consolation was that at least the procedures were being carried out in the right order. Better to stick the scope down my throat and then up my bum rather than the other way round.

The colonoscopy wasn't quite as bad, although it did take the best part of an hour. The worst part was when the doctor had difficulty getting the scope to 'turn the corner', something that happened three or four times. This is when the long, metal tube gets stuck at one of the U-bends inside your colon and a nurse has to press down on your tummy to help the doctor move it forward. At that point, I experienced some sharp stabbing pains that had me whimpering like a little girl. So much for wanting the doctor to think I was a real man.

During one particularly unpleasant episode, the male nurse asked me what I did for a living. I was about to answer when the doctor said, 'Don't feel like you have to respond. He's just trying to distract you.'

'Thanks a lot,' I thought. 'He might have succeeded in distracting me if you hadn't pointed out he was just trying to distract me. As it is, I'll just have to remain focused on this gut-wrenching pain.'

Afterwards, I was getting dressed in the recovery ward when another male patient was wheeled in and parked next to me. He, too, had had a colonoscopy, but unlike me he'd been sedated. He looked quite groggy, poor chap, and I felt a surge of triumph when a nurse told him he'd have to wait an hour and a half before he was allowed to leave.

I haven't yet had the results back from the various biopsies the doctor took, but she told me everything looked fine. My GP says that men who are 'at risk' like me should have a colonoscopy every year. That's something to look forward to, then.

Welcome to middle age.

BOOKS

Roger Lewis

22 June

*What Fresh Lunacy Is This?: The Authorised Biography of
Oliver Reed*
by Robert Sellers
(Constable, £20, pp. 500)

Midway through this startling book, Robert Sellers asks himself a question with such apparent seriousness I barked with laughter: 'Was Oliver Reed an alcoholic?' A more pertinent enquiry would be: 'Was the man ever capable of drawing a sober breath?' *What Fresh Lunacy is This?* is the monotonous chronicle of a nasty drunk whose 'explosions of pissed aggression' filled every waking hour, culminating in a deranged session, while filming *Castaway* in 1986, when he attacked an aeroplane.

Reed would gulp 20 pints of lager as a way of limbering up. He'd then switch to spirits and the cycle of fighting and carousing would begin. It's a miracle he survived to be 61, dropping dead in a Maltese bar after 'drinking copious amounts of rum and arm-wrestling with 18-year-old sailors'.

Myself, I find no amusement in dissipation, but Sellers seems always to be impressed and tickled by Reed's nasty pranks: sticking a lit candle up his nose for a bet, chewing light bulbs or putting cigarettes out on his tongue. He loved to climb up a pub chimney and leap into the grate as a demonic Santa Claus. He liked to beat up waiters, hoteliers and chauffeurs. 'He was always trying to test a person to see how scared they were of him.' He would dangle people over balconies or insist on swordfights. He said to a restaurant manager in Austria, 'I'm coming back tomorrow night. If you haven't got a Union Jack by then, I'm going to trash this place.' They hadn't. So he hurled chairs through the window.

There was real violence in him. On location, there'd always be 'knife wounds, hospital visits and stitches'. Reed urinated on foreign flags, on Mercedes limousines and on anyone standing below him on the stairs. He vomited over Steve McQueen, and Bette Davis said that he was 'possibly one of the most loathsome human beings I have ever had the misfortune of meeting' – a wide field in her case. Of the directors he worked with, Reed put laxatives in Michael Winner's coffee, head-butted Terry Gilliam and on numerous occasions threw Ken Russell across the room in judo tackles.

The Neanderthal behaviour – or riotous horseplay, as Sellers would have it – was present in childhood. Reed was born in Wimbledon. His grandfather was Herbert Beerbohm Tree. His father's brother was Carol Reed. He was always being expelled from school for his angry outbursts, and he flourished as a bully. He threw a pet dog over the banister, broke his own brother's nose, and hit a neighbour with a garden hoe.

Though Sellers tries to argue that Reed was dyslexic and insecure, 'with a low boredom threshold', it is surely simpler to say the man had a fascist mentality and was a crackpot. He clung to his instinctive belief that 'the strongest succeeded, while the weak got abused and ignored'. He particularly enjoyed National Service because of 'the atmosphere of bullying. He was in his element.' Promoted to corporal, 'his men came to despise him utterly'. He never stopped being 'the macho army lout', and tried to volunteer for active duty during the Falklands. (He made *Fanny Hill* with Alfred Marks instead.)

Reed started out in show business as a male model ('There was a mystery and a roughness and a sort of animal element to him'), graduating to bit-parts in Norman Wisdom films and Hammer horrors. His defining role was as a werewolf. He was also notable as Gerald Critch in *Women in Love* (1969) and as Father Grandier in *The Devils* (1971), the latter 'a tirade of masturbation and flagellation'. He was meant to be making a comeback in *Gladiator*, but because he'd dropped dead in the middle of filming, the role was assembled from out-takes, reverse-angle shots using a stunt double and computer-generated trickery. (I couldn't tell.)

What's clear from Sellers's biography is that Reed didn't like acting, never discussed it and perhaps rather despised himself for being so good at it – for the camera did capture a unique, brooding, sinister stillness. What a Flashman he'd have been, or a Richard III or Mussolini. Even Kurtz in *Apocalypse Now*. He is unnerving as Bill Sikes in *Oliver!* directed by Uncle Carol – and during the shoot he spiked the young Mark Lester's orange squash with vodka. 'Looking back on it, it's quite amusing really,' says Lester unconvincingly.

With the proceeds of the junk he appeared in – six films with Michael Winner! – Reed was able to afford an Edwardian mansion near Dorking, where he was very much the dissolute lord of the manor, filling the halls with road diggers, carpenters, builders and 'people he'd meet in pubs' – people he could easily dominate and from whom he did not have to fear intelligent conversation. His best pals were Hurricane Higgins, Keith Moon and a bruiser and personal bodyguard called Reg, whom Reed pushed off a wall for a laugh. Reg broke his back in two places.

Such was Reed's 'warped notion of masculinity' and his compulsive need 'to prove he was a man', it comes as no surprise to learn he didn't like women much – or children. 'He was hard and he was hurtful,' says his son. Reed's idea of romantic chivalry was to say to one of his wives, 'Loves yer? Course I loves yer. Fucks yer, don't I?' When he met Gayle Hunnicut, then the wife of David Hemmings and later of Simon Jenkins, he thought he was being charming by announcing, 'Give me a kiss, you fucking lovely Texan whore.' Thora Hird's daughter, Janette Scott, was terrified: 'I really didn't know what to do with him and I was afraid.' Reed stalked her and tried to run her car off the road.

Women were wenches consigned to the kitchen – their lovingly prepared meals often flung in their face or at the wall: 'I can't eat this shit!' Sex to Reed was a sort of rape or assault – but luckily, owing to his drinking, his libido vanished in his thirties. His last wife (and widow) was 16 when he began courting her. He'd meet her off the school bus. 'He treated her like a doll, always adjusting her hair or clothing.' Creepy.

Only one possible conclusion may be reached after reading this book and examining the evidence: that despite his homophobia ('You're a poof. You're a fucking poofter,' he said to Ian Ogilvy), Reed was homosexual, or crypto-homosexual, or deutero-homosexual. He was always stripping off in male company and couldn't wait to expose his penis, which was tattooed with the design of an eagle. His kitchen cupboards had handles shaped like penises. His door knocker was a brass cock and balls. In pubs he thought it amusing to indulge in two-men kissing contests and, according to Sellers, was 'unable to resist anyone in uniform'.

If he remains 'a cultural figure in our nation's psyche' – a large claim that I somewhat dispute – then it'll be for two things. First, there were his drunken, boorish appearances on late-night chat shows, which may now be watched with dread on Youtube. Secondly, he is remembered for the nude wrestling scene, before the roaring drawing-room fire, in *Women in Love*. 'He's got a bigger donger than me!' Reed had complained of Alan Bates. I cherish the remark of a pensioner, seeing the film with her friend in an otherwise empty cinema. As the grunting and grappling proceeded, her critique was succinct: 'Nice carpet.'

FOOD

Tanya Gold

29 June

Scott's is owned by Richard Caring. I have been rude about Caring restaurants in the past: J. Sheekey is too cramped, 34 is called 34, Le Caprice looks like Joan Collins's head. Scott's, however, is so lovely that I hope my one-sided feud with the orange restaurateur can be brought to a conclusion. [...]

We are invited to wait at the bar; instantly, I see Roger Moore, leaving in a small, very dignified procession. I am reminded of a slowly cruising, benevolent Bentley Continental; A points out that this is because our satnav is programmed with Roger Moore's voice. Later, when reading the

Daily Mail, I will learn Moore has been at Michael Winner's memorial service, which adds to the sense of dining in BBC Television Centre 1973 and Monaco at the same time. I am also (fairly) certain that the actress Lesley Joseph, who played Dorian in *Birds of a Feather*, is in a booth, as overdressed as only an actress can be. She is dressed, in fact, as a dress; and like many Jewish women, she can prowl while sitting down.

MY 50 WEDDINGS

Marcus Berkmann

21 September

A couple of weekends ago, I went to my 50th wedding. Everyone I have mentioned this to has pulled a rather strange face, as though to say, 'You count the weddings you go to? What unhinged variety of cross-eyed lunatic does that?' But like so much of lasting value in life, this began with a conversation in a pub. Back in 1997, I was moaning to my old friend Terence about how many weddings I was having to go to. People I knew simply wouldn't stop getting married. So how many in all? asked Terence. I don't know, said I. It could, and probably should, have ended there. But the freelance career was passing through one of its periodic dips, and I had slightly too much time on my hands, so I went through old diaries, made some calls, studied my cheque book stubs and compiled a list. Aged 37, I had been to 38 weddings. I rang Terence up to tell him the happy news. Hmm, he said, deep in thought. When the invitation arrives, has it ever occurred to you simply to say no?

Once you know you have been to 38 weddings, you can't help but count. If your mind works in a certain way, a list can be a thing of beauty. (I have long toyed with writing a book called 'The Joy of Lists', complete with drawings of a naked woman and a man with a beard making some very interesting lists.) Each subsequent wedding has gone on the list, although the flow quickly abated to one or two a year. As middle age takes root it's important that we set ourselves new targets, define new goals, in order to keep the intellectual juices flowing. For me, that target became the 50th wedding. Marooned for a year on 48, I was saved by an old friend's slightly rushed second wedding this spring (bride gloriously big with child), and earlier this month, when the eldest daughter of an old American friend of my long-time girlfriend married an English banker in the leafiest Kent village imaginable. The half-century! In my mind's eye I raised my bat to the cheering crowd.

I will admit: I do like weddings. Even if you barely know the protagonists – I knew no one at the one two weeks ago – you feel honoured to witness this public celebration of what is essentially a private and intimate act. At weddings, irony is suspended for the day. Even the brutal sarcasm of former boyfriends and girlfriends of the happy couple, who may have been invited just to rub their noses in it, can be placed in context. Just as a funeral frees you to weep and wail and gnash your teeth, so a wedding encourages you to look kindly upon humanity while drinking free champagne. Later on there will be loads of food and the opportunity to dance ineptly to hits of the 1970s. Wedding togs are unique in that almost everyone looks good in them, except when dancing, when everyone looks ridiculous. In this sense, at least, it's the most democratic of our great social rituals. And as we let our guard down, almost anything can happen. I myself began at least one long-term relationship at a wedding, although she did watch me rather carefully when we subsequently went to others.

After 50 weddings, though, some trends become apparent. Of the 50, six were people I barely knew at the time or have lost touch with since. Of the remainder, only eight have ended in divorce, while a ninth is in the process of crumbling horribly. One more was cruelly abbreviated by the wife's death, and the other 34 couples are still together. Either the people I know are a particularly faithful and uxorious bunch, or (as I have long suspected) many of them simply can't afford to split up and so are stuck with each other, at least until the children move out. Only the very rich and the very poor can afford to divorce now, the very poor because they have nothing left to lose.

Most of them, also, were first marriages. I have been to a couple of seconds (including my mother's) but many of these seem to take place at a secret location, i.e. I am not invited to them. Twice have I been to both first and second weddings and on each occasion I was one of very few people who had been to both. You feel proud but a little anxious, for you realise that statistically you have little chance of being invited to the third wedding, in however many years' time.

Certain things, though, never change. When the priest asks if anyone knows of any just cause or impediment why these two people should not be joined in holy matrimony, at least one person will titter audibly and around a quarter of the congregation will look round at the door, expecting Hugh Grant to burst in. Similarly, it is widely considered a miracle if the best man hasn't mislaid the ring. Such is the baleful influence of TV sitcom on our lives, although worse still is the priest who thinks he is a stand-up comedian. A notable recent development is the so-called groovy priest who thinks it's hip to make repeated references in his address to the couple's sex life. In a just world, such lapses in taste would be punished with medieval acts of violence.

The best man problem remains acute. You will never get a friendlier, more supportive audience for a speech in your life, so most best men never begin to realise how disastrously their speeches have failed. Many grooms attempt to solve the problem by appointing as their best man someone who barely knows them and so cannot embarrass them unduly. One monomaniac of my acquaintance chose himself for the job. There was no one he trusted more and it gave him the opportunity to make two speeches. We all knew the marriage wasn't going to last, and his wife might have had an inkling by the end of the evening.

As it happens, I was best man myself not so long ago, for my friend Terence, who finally got married, aged 53, to an Australian woman of high intelligence and impeccable good taste. The speech went well and I didn't lose the ring. He has said he will be happy to return the favour one day, whenever the call comes. Because that may be the strangest thing about all this: I have been to 50 weddings, but not one of them has been my own.

WINE

Rod Liddle

21 September

Ah, this all started out so well, and with such good intentions. This attempt of mine to write seriously and informatively about wine. Well, to write about wine, full stop, really. There was always going to be a problem with someone who rather likes retsina, I suppose. My chief criterion for judging wine is quantity.

The many bottles of Spanish wine arrived. My wife and I sat in the courtyard, at the little iron table. I had a notebook on the table, and there was a bucket beneath the table, so that we could spit out the wine, like I've heard they do. It was a warm and scented summer evening; earlyish – the rabbits were hopping around in the field, the bats were still asleep. The bottles were lined up. We had Manchego cheese, and olives. We kicked off with an Allende Rioja 2009, a yellowish confection. I suspect readers of *The Spectator* would probably prefer a Pinochet Rioja rather than an Allende Rioja, but never mind. I swilled the stuff around my mouth, Alicia did the same. We spat into the bucket, via my trousers. I picked up the pen. 'Quite a ... BIG taste, I think,' I said. My wife nodded. 'It's very oaky,' she said, 'and I like it.'

What does she mean 'oaky'? She's never tasted any oak, to my knowledge – so how would she know? Maybe she just meant it's okay. We kept drinking and, for a while, spitting, until my wife said that we don't usually drink decent wine, we just buy that £4.99 Pinot Grigio from Morrisons, buy it by the lorryload, isn't it sort of a waste to be spitting good wine out into a bucket? And that, really, is when the rot set in.

We finished the Allende and opened the Placet Rioja, with a corkscrew. We had to hunt up and down dale to find the corkscrew. It's not something we're accustomed to employing. Our usual wine doesn't need a corkscrew. Anyway, the Placet wasn't as BIG as the Allende, but it slipped down very nicely. I wrote 'citrus flavours' in my notebook, an observation with which my wife disagreed. 'I'd say it was the opposite of citrus,' she said, 'whatever that is. Peach, or something.' I ventured that people often said that wine had overtones of passionfruit, perhaps this is the sort of wine they mean. Alicia said she couldn't taste any passionfruit at all, and there were none of those pips.

The bats were out; the olives and cheese and rabbits were gone. I think I saw the Perseids overhead, but I may have been mistaken. Alicia put some music on, loud music hammering out of the annex, and we opened the next bottle, the El Quintanal (that's 'Five Arses' in English, I think) Verdejo. Do you know, one minute it was there, the next minute it was gone. This was definitely our favourite, probably because it was the closest to the sort of stuff we're more accustomed to drinking. It was a very pale colour, the colour of rainwater running down a slightly dirty window, and its taste was not describable as BIG at all. I tried to write down 'small' in my notebook, but was having some difficulty.

The nights draw in so quickly in August, especially in the country. It's all downhill, really, from 21 June, isn't it? We kid ourselves that there's a whole summer to come. I get forlorn and lachrymose when drunk; my wife gets exuberant and loud. She'd taken her top off and was dancing to the music in a bra, dancing to some growling noise from the Drive-By Truckers. 'I'm too old and too decrepit to dance,' I moaned at her. 'Sit down.' Normally she complains about the mosquitoes biting away at her, but right now she didn't appear to notice them; they were lined up on her arm, chewing away. We moved on to the next bottle, which was something called Viña Gravonia. It was a deep and poisonous-looking yellow, clearly intended for palates more discerning than our own. This definitely had a very BIG taste, I remarked. I don't think Alicia heard. She was sat down now and her neck seemed to have lost the ability to support her head properly and there was a thin line of drool on her chin. 'Itsh got a strange short of afterburn,' she said.

'I don't think that's the wine, love ...'

Too late, too late. I tried to get her to come back to the table to finish the Gravonia but she couldn't, so I joined her on the floor of the bathroom with the bottle and indeed with our last bottle, the Gramona

Gran Reserva 2008, something bubbly to toast ourselves with. I haven't the remotest idea what this stuff was like. Cava, I suppose. Odd thing is, when we'd finished it we were thirsty for more and started eyeing up the bucket rather hungrily. You know you're in a bad way when that happens. We slept pretty much where we were, the Drive-By Truckers still blaring away until everything sort of went black and silent and lovely.

I checked the prices of some of those wines the next day, feeling guilty. It almost goes without saying that the wine we liked the best, the El Quintanal, was by some considerable margin the cheapest of those we had been sent, and you can pick one up for not much more than those Pinot Grigios to which, the following night, we returned, with a semblance of moderation.

STATUS ANXIETY

Toby Young

28 September

I should never have agreed to buy Sasha fish for her tenth birthday. But it seemed like such a modest request. It's not like you're going to come home one day to find they've escaped or starved to death – like certain rodents I can think of. I was also lulled into a false sense of security by Sasha's promise that she would look after them herself. I wouldn't have to lift a finger.

It wasn't until we were in the pet shop that I discovered she had something more exotic in mind than a couple of goldfish. She wanted tropical fish. That meant spending £100 on a 50-litre tank, complete with built-in filter and heating element. We were then told by the pet-shop owner that he wouldn't be able to sell us any fish until we could prove that the nitrate levels in our tank had fallen below a certain level. Luckily, all the products we'd need to 'prepare' the water just happened to be on sale in his shop. Handy, that.

Fast-forward two weeks, by which time I'd spent the best part of a

Saturday afternoon assembling the fish tank. Sasha's contribution was to watch me like a prison warder and scream if I deviated from the instructions by one jot. We went back to the shop with a water sample and – heaven be praised – were given permission to buy some fish. 'How about some zebrafish?' the man suggested. 'They fall into the category of "hard to kill".'

'Sounds good to me,' I said.

We returned to Acton with 12 zebrafish and began the process of introducing them to their new home. The most tedious part was standing beside my daughter as she painstakingly thought up names for all 12 of them.

By 6 p.m., I thought my labours were at an end, but no. Sasha came bursting into the kitchen in a state of hysteria, complaining that the filter wasn't working properly. I tramped back up the stairs and discovered she was right. The filter was positioned behind a couple of panes of plastic, creating a special chamber at the back of the tank, and for some reason it had managed to pump most of the water out of this chamber and was now making a continuous farting noise as it blew air into the rest of the tank. My solution was to push the filter deeper into the chamber until it was once again submerged.

'Are you sure that'll be all right, Dad?' asked Sasha. 'It's not going to hurt the fish?'

'It's fine,' I said. 'They're "hard to kill", remember?'

All was well until it was time for bed. At Sasha's insistence I went with her to her room to check on the fish, only to find that all hell had broken loose. My 'ingenious' solution hadn't worked. The filter had emptied its chamber of the remaining water and was sending a jet of air into the main tank with such force that it had created a kind of fish Jacuzzi. Two of the fish had been propelled out of the tank and now lay dead on the carpet.

'Dad!' said Sasha. 'You've killed Zip and Zap!'

I plunged my hand into the chamber to wrench out the filter, but it had somehow got wedged beneath the heating element. So I removed that and placed it on the carpet next to Zip and Zap, at which point Sasha, who was hopping from foot to foot with anxiety, trod on it. Cue meltdown. But before I could tend to her foot, I still had to deal with the rogue filter and in my haste I managed to break one of the panes of plastic. As the water levels equalised, the remaining ten zebrafish poured into the broken chamber and disappeared into the inner workings of the tank. It was fishmageddon.

After Sasha had been sedated and removed from the room by Caroline, I set about repairing the tank. That involved emptying 50 per cent of the water so I could stick the broken pane back together. By the time I'd completed the job and refilled the tank, only two fish survived.

Several weeks have passed, but I don't dare reinsert the filter in case it malfunctions again. The upshot is that the water has turned dark green and the nitrate level must be quite high because the two survivors are on their last legs. Less like Zip and Zap, more like Drift and Float. So much for low-maintenance pets. It's almost enough to make me want another hamster.

DIARY

Tristram Hunt

19 October

One of the minor sociological treats of being appointed shadow education secretary is a frontbench view of David Cameron's crimson tide – that half-hour journey, every Question Time, during which the Prime Minister's face turns from beatific calm to unedifying fury. It starts at 12.04 with the merest ripple of annoyance in his shiny, placid countenance. At 12.07, the ripple has become a swell of irritation, still far out to sea, at anyone daring to question the wisdom of government policy. By 12.10, it is a wave of indignation and wounded *amour propre* at the wilful duplicity of his opponents. And by 12.14, the crimson tide is crashing over the rocks of the dispatch box, back and forth for the next quarter of an hour. Close up, it is a marvel to behold.

FOOD

Tanya Gold

19 October

The Union Street Café is in a dismal, dingy part of London: dismal
dingy Southwark. Southwark, in fact, is almost charismatically dingy,
a land of despairing streets and brick arches and railway tracks heading suicidally for southern suburbs. Even the churches (small, brown,
bricked, almost bricked-up) look apologetic, as if they know they have
failed.

But it is here, on the junction of Union Street and Great Suffolk
Street, that Gordon Ramsay, the second most charismatic of the original
celebrity chefs – after Marco Pierre White, now selling stock cubes to
old ladies with his swiftly receding sexual charisma – has built his new
restaurant. It is his tenth in Britain. It was to be a co-venture with David
Beckham, the ex-footballer and human thong, but Beckham pulled
out; perhaps the restaurant was not thin enough for his terrifying wife
Victoria?

The cuisine is Italian, but food was never the point of Gordon
Ramsay; it was always about his anger, his face, and his chomping desire
for an empire; and also the fact that he was cynical enough to attempt
haute cuisine while punning, at Heathrow airport, with the appalling
Plane Food. Of course he isn't here in the kitchen of the Union Street
Café; who loves their tenth child? He is probably in some TV studio,
stuffing powder into the crevasses in his face, or perhaps shouting.
Instead there is a wall of smiling heads greeting us at the door. So
many happy heads smiling together. They are like the Tweenies, but
abducted.

DIARY

Sebastian Faulks

14/28 December

My favourite Christmas game is best played late at night on the 25th when you have had a lot to drink. Somebody goes out of the room. Then everyone else waits for a minute and tries to remember who it was.

2014

Rod Liddle; Tom Hollander; Melissa Kite;
Roger Alton; Dear Mary; Marcus Berkmann;
Bruce Anderson; Jeremy Clarke; Nicky Haslam;
Mark Amory; Barry Humphries; Jeremy Paxman;
Hugo Rifkind

I THINK IN MY ATTITUDE TOWARDS BREASTFEEDING, I'VE FOUND THE PERFECT MIDDLE GROUND

Rod Liddle

5 April

What attitude should we take towards women who wish to breastfeed their babies in public? Older, more conservative readers may feel a little squeamish about this sort of thing and would prefer mothers to do their breastfeeding in private; it is as much the hideous slurping noise as the sight of a female breast which offends, I think. At the other extreme, the modernist view is that they should be allowed to breastfeed when and where they want, without argument or hindrance, and that's an end to it.

As ever, I stalk what we might call the middle ground, the area where some sort of compromise can be found between these two diametrically opposed schools of thought. I think women should be allowed to get their breasts out when and where they want – but only if they are quite attractive breasts. In other words, if they are pert, firm and becoming. If, however, they are unpleasantly pendulous, or resemble in their shape, if not their colouring, a spaniel's ears, then I would argue it would be better for all concerned if they were to keep them hidden away under as many layers of clothing as possible. I think this suggestion strikes the right balance between conservatism and progressivism and I have written to a number of leading feminists suggesting that this would be an appropriate route out of the current impasse. I have not yet had a reply, which is an optimistic sign, I think – they are taking my attempt to forge a consensus very seriously and giving the matter a lot of thought. I will let you know how these important women respond.

THE SUMMER OF LOVE

Tom Hollander

12 April

Last time I was allowed to write a story for *The Spectator*, I managed to get away with a frankly smutty and boastful piece about sex. Well, it's been a while, so ... I do hope nobody minds if I do that again.

If I'm honest, when young, one of the reasons I decided to mortgage my life to showbiz was because I thought that if I did, I would get more than my fair share of bedroom action.

Hang on. Sorry, not more than my fair share. (I must stop putting myself down.) Firstly, as we all know there is no such thing as fair in these matters; very attractive women regularly confound the rest of us by sleeping with people everyone thinks are ghastly. And secondly, even if they didn't I am perfectly capable, on a good day, when not over-whelmed by various complexes there isn't space to describe, of actually being quite reasonably charming. But anyway, aged 21, I was entirely sure being in showbiz would definitely tip the scales in my favour. Think of the scenes of mass hysteria that greeted the Beatles. People actually threw their sodden underwear onto the stage. Not just the Beatles, David Essex, probably even Cliff Richard. OK, mostly pop stars rather than classical theatre actors, but come on, how many employment sectors can you think of that involve that sort of thing as even a remote possibility? The medical profession I grant you, out of necessity, and politics, for reasons which baffle everyone. But for spontaneous pants removal as an expression of sheer joie de vivre, it's got to be either sport, or for arts graduates, Lady Showbiz.

Twenty-five years ago. 1989. The beginning of the end of the 'second summer of love'. The sap was high. Beautiful young people were driving round the M25 on Ecstasy, dancing in fields till dawn. But I wasn't part of that. Born in the first summer of love, 1967, by the second, I was pulling on thick tights nightly at the Chichester Festival Theatre ready to skip about in the marriage masque at the end of *Love's Labour's Lost*. The idea that someone in the audience might be so overwhelmed by my performance as Costard the Clown that they would be impelled to hurl their knickers onto the stage had faded into the realms of distant fantasy. By the end of the season I'd got some good reviews, been to some lovely barbecues, and someone very encouraging had likened me to a young Ian Holm.

But as the colours began to turn autumnal I had to face the fact that my tally of conquests was nothing to write home about. Not that I ever would've done. Not, that is, until I got old enough to write about them in *The Spectator*.

The season was ending, I had no job to go to, an uncertain future beckoned. One evening, as I shuffled into the stage door for one of our final shows, the kindly but bored doorkeeper told me there was a package waiting for me. She produced a crumpled brown paper bag with 'for Tom Hollander' scrawled on it.

In the dressing room I poured its contents out. I was amazed. Could it be true? There before me lay a pair of lady's knickers. Black. More structured and supportive than I would have liked. But undeniably underwear of the female variety. And, oddly, two small carved wooden amphibians. These were slightly disconcerting, but I quickly realised that of course, they must be toads. Horny toads. A slightly ill judged but eloquent and humorous symbol of animal desire. And the right size for a postbox.

Ha! Nothing else. No note. No explanation. It seemed bizarre, but this was it. The fulfilment of my half-forgotten showbiz dream. Admittedly the toads were a bit weird, but an actual real woman had sent me her underwear. And what's more, I noticed, as I turned them over in my hand, she'd worn them first.

That night's performance passed in a euphoric daze. Was she out there? Eyes glinting in the darkness, a half-smile playing on her lips. In the marriage dance I skipped for her, and for all the other women out there who wanted me. Afterwards, forgoing drinks and compliment-fishing in the bar, I raced home on my moped, through the shining glory of the South Downs on a late summer night.

Leaving the toads to one side, I lay on my bed and considered my trophy. I tried to imagine the woman who had worn them so recently. What was she like? I held them to my nose and breathed in the traces of her scent. It wasn't only hers though. To me it was infinitely feminine. Whoever they belonged to, this flimsy material had been in enviably close contact with the most beautiful thing in all creation. Troy was besieged for this. I communed with it. I worshipped womankind through the talisman of this one anonymous gusset. We had a lovely night together, those pants and me. Next morning I awoke with them on my face.

About ten days later, when it was all nearly over, I was on the phone to my parents in Oxford.

'It was so good to see you in *Love's Labour's Lost* the other week.'

'Thanks, Mum.'

'Not your dancing at the end though – that was a bit silly.'

'Oh, OK, I'll tone it down.'

'But otherwise it was really good. Excellent. And very well directed. We really enjoyed it, darling ...'

She went on. 'Oh and just before we go. I've been meaning to tell you that when we came to see you last, I stupidly left some things at the bed and breakfast. Some knick-knacks I picked up for your cousins. But the nice lady who ran the place said she'd drop them off for me.'

'Oh right, I'll look out for them. What were they?'

'Two little wooden frogs. She said she'd leave a package at the stage door. Hello? Hello?'

'Sorry, I was just having a ... nothing. So ... er, just the frogs then. Anything else?'

'No, no, I don't think so ... Are you all right?'

'Yes, yes, fine ... I'll ... I'll look out for them.'

'Thanks, darling. Well done again. Bye.'

REAL LIFE

Melissa Kite

12 April

The Volvo has turned into a monster. It always did have a mind of its own. Fellow owners warned me when I got it that the sensors are incredibly sensitive. It is always faking injury.

I had only had it a few weeks when the warning light flashed and demanded a transmission service. In the interests of good relations – and also because I bought it from a dealer who was raided by police and trading standards a week later – I thought I would show willing.

But a few days after the mechanic changed the transmission oil, we were driving along and the light flashed: 'Transmission Service Required!' I took it back in, had it hooked up to the computer and the mechanics declared it fine.

A few days later the warning light flashed: 'Transmission Service Required!' I noticed that, as with the other times, it had flashed after I changed gears from drive to reverse a bit lumpily. Was it possible the car was complaining because I was being too rough? Could it be protesting at my driving skills? Emboldened by the Builder Boyfriend who insisted this was 'what Volvos do – ignore it', I decided to ignore it. And after a while it did stop.

But a few months after that, the light flashed again: 'Engine Service Required!' So I checked the service manual and, as it was due a full service soon anyway, I took it into the garage. It couldn't do any harm to give it the full once-over, I thought. When the mechanic had finished, he declared the Volvo in tip-top condition. He couldn't find a thing wrong. He had done all the usual stuff with oil and filters and made it as happy as he could.

And it didn't complain for a good few weeks. But then, halfway down a dirt track, as we went over a particularly big bump, it suddenly started: 'Transmission Service Required!' And then a few seconds later 'Engine Service Required!'

'Give it a break,' I said, 'you are having me on. Please, just try to be brave. We will be off this horrible track in a few minutes and back on to the nice smooth road, don't worry.'

But the Volvo was appalled. 'Engine Failure!' it flashed. But the engine did not fail at all. The engine was never going to fail. The warning lights are nothing to do with what is actually going to happen. The car's squeamishness is strange, on the face of it, because it is incredibly tough.

But I guess it's like a big bruiser of a man who looks butch, and who is capable of physical courage, but who whines constantly about having the flu when he has a touch of hay fever or a slight cold. 'Come on!' I say to the Volvo every time we hit a pothole. 'You can do this!' And it can. And it does. But it invariably flashes a warning light at me as it does it. Like a man demanding Beecham's Powders, its favourite has always been to whine about needing new transmission oil.

But the other day, it really did lose its nerve completely. We had a prang, you see. We were driving down a very narrow country lane and a boy racer in a souped-up yellow Celica was tailgating us. Very much against my better judgement I speeded up to get some distance between us, and an oncoming van swept past too fast and bashed my wing mirror.

I drove straight to my mechanic and he found that the motorised parts in the unit were still working and we only needed a new mirror and a backing panel. While it was on order, he taped a small, temporary mirror to the inside of the unit. The Volvo was appalled. We had only been driving for a few hours after the makeshift mirror had been put in, when it flashed at me: 'Transmission Service Required!' 'Yeah, all right, I know. It's not perfect. But we're getting a new one soon and it will all be fine. I promise.'

'Engine Service Required!'

'Come on, please. Don't panic. I'm sorting it.'

'Immobiliser!'

Oh dear. This was serious. It had never said that before. Was it threatening to turn itself off?

'Engine Failure!' I knew that was a ruse, so I told it I wasn't fooled.

'Anti-Skid Service Required!'

'Oh now you are just taking the p***,' I shouted.

'Anti-Skid Service Required!' it insisted.

'Are you threatening me? Are you threatening to slide off the road just because we've had to tape a too-small sticky-backed mirror into your wing mirror unit?'

'Engine Service Required! Transmission Service Required! Anti-Skid Service Required! Immobiliser! Immobiliser!'

'Pull yourself together, you're hysterical,' I told it. Sometimes, and I don't say this lightly, that car is worse than me.

SPECTATOR SPORT

Roger Alton

19 April

The brotherhood of cricket, as we know, transcends race, creed, class and nationality. It can also be a big help when it comes to dealing with the law, as this Easter parable demonstrates. My distinguished *Times* colleague Phil Webster, besides being a doyen of political writers, is also a ferocious cricketer and a man once described as the meanest captain who had ever pulled on a pair of whites. Phil at this time – about 20 years ago – led a press team loosely affiliated to a long–defunct magazine. As is the way with these things, the team had acquired an opening bowler, a large and imposing figure from Jamaica called, let's say, Courtney, who had little to do with journalism, more with the building trade.

Now Courtney's size belied his geniality, most of the time anyway. One day he was on his way home and inadvertently seems to have cut up a van full of white guys. They then forced him to stop and advanced on his car. Courtney took the view that their intentions were not entirely friendly (this was not long after the Stephen Lawrence murder) and got out of the car holding a crowbar that he happened to have with him. Vigorous views were exchanged, as were blows, and soon sirens sounded and police and ambulances rolled up. Courtney, who was unscathed, was charged with causing actual bodily harm and a court date was set.

This is where Phil comes in. He was called as a character witness, and dutifully made the journey to court.

'How do you know the defendant?' asked the magistrate. 'Well, your honour, I captain a cricket team and Courtney is my opening bowler.'

'Really?' said the magistrate, clearly interested. 'And is he an aggressive bowler?'

'Far from it, your honour. If anything I would like him to be more aggressive. If you follow cricket, your honour . . . ' 'I do, certainly,' said the bench. Webster continued, growing in confidence, 'Well, if anything I would compare him to Devon Malcolm, who is rated by many as the best in the country, but whose bowling often lacks the necessary bite and fizz.'

'You're here as a character witness for the defendant, Mr Webster. How did you feel when you heard the details of the case?'

'Well, your honour, I was astonished. I thought it would be quite a bonus if I ever saw any of that aggression on the cricket field, because I never have.' Which was all true, of course. Because although he loved a long run-up, Courtney's bowling rarely troubled any half-decent batsman.

'I see. Thank you.'

Courtney got off.

YOUR PROBLEMS SOLVED

Dear Mary . . .

17 May

Q. Although I have never experienced lesbian leanings, I really enjoy being frisked at airports, the more fully the better. To me, it is more relaxing than a full-body massage and it always gives me a little thrill to be found innocent. How can I ensure that I am always singled out for a searching? I find it so disappointing when I am just waved through.

– L.C., London W10

A. Just make sure that you always wear a bra with a large amount of underwiring, or a belt with metal fastening or studs, as all of these will set off the alerts. If you wear a belt the airport operative will also have to check that there is no weapon concealed underneath it, and this should extend the satisfaction of your customer experience as you transit security.

BOOKS

Marcus Berkmann

31 May

Simply English
by Simon Heffer
(RH Books, £14.99, pp. 384)

Did Simon Heffer's new book come out on St George's Day? If not, it probably should have done. If we ever needed someone to defend what's left of our national culture from the massed armies of lefties, foreigners, proles, riff-raff, illiterates, young people, thin people and David Cameron, he would be our man. For three decades he has fought the good fight, a squat colossus of unquenchable fury, his red hair forever threatening to burst into flames, just because it can. He is one of the marvels of the age and, I now discover to my shock, exactly four days younger than me. We Cancerians have to stick together – although my moon is in Aries and his is in Taurus, which I'm told makes all the difference.

Recently, then, young Simon has turned the white heat of his attention to the English language. *Strictly English* (2010) started life as a series of emails sent to *Telegraph* staffers who kept writing 'emend' when they meant 'amend' and foozling their subjunctives. Professional writers liked the book, whether or not they liked Heffer. Academics were less keen. The professor of general linguistics at Edinburgh university saw 'this perversely atavistic book' as a 'perversion of grammatical education'.

Still, it sold well, mainly to people who knew all the rules already, but liked reading them again for old times' sake. *Simply English* isn't so much a follow-up as a variation on the previous book. Expanded and rewritten, it has been rearranged into a handy A-to-Z format, enabling you to look up solecisms and barbarisms with the greatest of ease. It could be the pedant's loo book of 2014. (Heffer says that 'loo' is mere slang. I suspect he would prefer 'lavatory', or even the briskly utilitarian 'water closet'.)

Even in other rooms of the house, though, it's a bracing read. Heffer takes no linguistic prisoners. New and vogueish terms are swept aside with disdain. The use of the word 'source' as a verb (as in 'she sources her ingredients from organic farmers') dates only from 1972, and is therefore not to be countenanced. Nor does he like what one might call the 'dangling hopefully' (as in 'hopefully, it will stop raining soon'). 'It remains wrong, and only a barbarous writer with a low estimation of his readers would try to pass it off as respectable prose.' At times you can easily imagine the veins throbbing on the side of his forehead. 'Akimbo can only apply to arms, signifying hands on hips and elbows pointing outwards.' Which means that the only time anyone ever uses the word, in the phrase 'legs akimbo', it's wrong. Call me a softy, but when I read this, it felt as though a word had just died.

When he mirrors my own prejudices, though, Heffer can be quite brilliant. 'Brilliant in its figurative sense, meaning extremely clever or superlative talent, is a much over-worked adjective ... some newspapers apply it to so many columnists, series, special offers or free gifts that it is remarkable that their readers have not been blinded.' He is sound on 'refute', the misuse of which I have long felt should be punished by death.

There are omissions. There's nothing on 'national treasure' – maybe it'll appear in the paperback – and I was disappointed not to see his opinions on the popular half-witted confusion between 'parameter' and 'perimeter'. For there are quite a lot of opinions in here, elevated to the status of high judgement by Heffer's robust self-belief and, I would guess, extreme intellectual impatience. There's no room for shilly-shallying in Hefferland. 'Loo' is slang because he says it is, and that's all there is to it.

If you can forgive the eruptions of high-handedness, though, this is a useful, well-constructed and often absorbing book. The war goes on, and our man is up on the ramparts, armed to the teeth, and waiting to see the whites of their eyes.

YOUR PROBLEMS SOLVED

Dear Mary . . .

21 June

Q. In your column of 26 April, a correspondent wrote that, as a lawyer, he was irritated by people asking him for free advice at social gatherings. I have known of one way a lawyer dealt with this. A recently qualified doctor was at a party and said to a lawyer there, 'Now that I am a doctor, people – some of whom I hardly know – approach me and ask for advice about their various medical complaints. How do you, as a professional man, handle this situation?' The lawyer replied, 'I give them the advice that they want and the next day I send them an invoice for services rendered.' 'Excellent,' said the doctor, 'that's what I will do.'

The following day, at the doctor's rooms, an invoice arrived for him from the lawyer.

– L.S., by email

A. Thank you for supplying this material.

REAL LIFE

Melissa Kite

12 July

'I have a feeling,' said my father, 'that this evening is not going to go well.'

We were sitting in the bar of a local fish restaurant near my parents' home having pre-dinner drinks, and I was throwing a wobbly because my tomato juice wasn't right.

I had arrived at the table after putting my order in as I went off to park the car, only to find a drink in a bottle called Big Tom sitting on the table. You know the drill, it's the little things that get me.

I immediately went into one because I cannot understand why asking a bartender to make a tomato juice from scratch is considered beyond the call of duty these days. What is so arduous about opening two little bottles of Britvic, emptying them into a glass with some ice, adding a good splash of Lea and Perrins and Tabasco and stirring? Perhaps garnishing with a nice slice or two of crisp celery? Hmm?

But, no, that's way too much trouble. They have to buy in pre-made stuff that they promise has spice already in but you can't taste the spice. Of course you can't. And though you try, you can't taste the tomatoes either. All you can taste is generic red-flavoured mush.

'Why!' I gasped, as I slumped in front of the mush.

'Oh lord,' said Dad.

The Builder Boyfriend turned to my father and the two of them exchanged woeful glances.

My mother didn't flinch. 'It's ridiculous,' she agreed. 'Not being able to make a simple tomato juice properly. What is wrong with people?'

'Exactly.' I said. Clearly, I would need to post this trauma on Facebook. It was the only way to deal with it. I got out my iPhone but there was no reception.

'Excuse me,' I said to a passing waiter. 'Do you have wi-fi?'

'White wine?' he said, passing me a wine list.

'Wi-fi,' I said.

'White wine,' he said, pointing to the list.

'WI ... FI!' I shouted.

My father murmured 'Oh lord' again. He's an atheist but he often prays when I'm around.

'WHIIIITE WIIINE!' the waiter shouted back, and stabbed his finger at the list.

'WIIII-yuh! FIIII-yuh!'

'Oh,' he said. It turned out they hadn't.

So sans tomato juice, sans wi-fi, I brooded as we ordered our food and then trooped to our table.

It was one of those chain restaurants where there is a set spiel for everything, so a waitress appeared as we sat down and said chirpily: 'I will be your waitress for the evening!'

I felt like saying: 'Thank heavens you told us, because I thought you were going to strip and do us a lap dance while we ate our sea bream!' But I didn't. She worried me. She was too chirpy. Her chirpiness had a vicious edge, as if it was ready to burst at any moment and reveal something that was the opposite of chirpy underneath.

When our starters came, it was obvious what her game plan was. My mother had asked for no grapefruit in her crab salad and I had requested crevettes on ice. Four crevettes on a huge pile of ice came, and a crab salad that was almost entirely a mound of chopped-up red chilli peppers. My mother took a mouthful and promptly started choking.

I called the waitress over. She ignored me and walked the other way. Then Dad and the Builder realised they hadn't got their bottle of 'WHIIITE WIIINE!' So I walked over to her as she was talking happily to customers at another table and said, very politely: 'When you've got a minute, could we have a word?'

She ignored us for another five minutes then grudgingly appeared. 'What's the matter?' she said, obnoxiously.

I was direct: 'This starter is inedible and we haven't got our wine.'

She was more direct: 'What's wrong with it?'

My mother took over. 'I'm sorry, dear, but I really can't eat all this chilli. Would you mind taking it away?'

'What do you mean?' she barked. 'You asked for no grapefruit. It's what you wanted.'

Dad and the Builder groaned because they knew the game was up, so far as my behaving myself was concerned.

'Have you sampled this dish?' I said.

'There's no need to be rude!' she exclaimed.

'I'm simply saying, if you haven't tried it, with or without grapefruit, you can't argue.'

'That's it!' she squawked. 'I'm going to get the manager!' And she flounced off.

The four of us sat in silence like naughty schoolchildren. 'I've done it now, haven't I?' I said. 'We're going to be thrown out.'

'Don't be ridiculous,' said the Builder, drawing himself up. 'If the manager gets here and takes her side, I will throw this table in the air.'

'Oh lord,' said my dad.

DRINK

Bruce Anderson

19 July

A couple of decades ago, there was a Johnsonian journalist, George Gale. He often held court in the Cheshire Cheese, then a splendidly old-fashioned pub. The Cheese is only round the corner from Gough Square, and one day, a couple of American matrons came in to ask directions. 'Say, could you tell us the way to Dr Johnson's house?' George replied, 'I am Dr Johnson. This is my house. Now fuck off.'

LOW LIFE

Jeremy Clarke

26 July

'Oscar!' cried Miss Herd as I arrived. She was standing at the classroom door releasing her charges one by one as the parent, or in my case the grandparent, arrived to escort them safely back to their respective homes. Oscar came solemnly out in his navy Academy sweatshirt carrying his red Fireman Sam lunchbox and placed his four-year-old hand in his grandfather's 57-year-old one. We headed off to the car. 'Did Tom play with you today?' I said. Tom, by all reports, is omnipotent and capricious in his choice of playmates. 'No,' said Oscar tragically.

I was standing in on the school run for Daddy, who had to work an extra 12-hour shift at the care home unexpectedly. Oscar lives with Daddy and goes to stay with Mummy at the weekends. 'Are you having me?' said Oscar. 'Until eight o'clock,' I said. 'Is that long?' he said. 'Very,' I said. He looked up, pleased.

Before we did anything else, Grandad had to go to the doctor's for an anti-testosterone injection in the bum. While we were in the waiting area he sat on my lap and I read him a picture story called *Rupert and the Pirates*. Rupert was kidnapped by three vicious-looking, ill-mannered pirates, and one much older pirate with a kind face who eventually helped Rupert to escape. We wondered why such a decent old man should be keeping such disreputable company in the first place. When Rupert returned with a burly, laid-back policeman, the pirate with a kind face grassed up his mates, and the copper took his good behaviour into account and let him off with a caution.

And on that happy note we went into the treatment room, where Oscar sat on a chair clutching his red plastic lunchbox and watched as the practice nurse punctured Grandad in the buttock of his choice with a syringe. The nurse was extra cheerful, even festive, with a small witness present, and afterwards presented him with a Biro sponsored by a drug company as a souvenir. Then he put his small hand in mine again and we went out. 'I like your shirt,' he said when we were out in the street again.

After that we went to a literary festival. The main event was being held in a medieval banqueting hall. We sat on deckchairs on the lawned courtyard outside, eating peppermint ice cream from tubs with plastic scoops located in the lids, while observing the festival-goers coming and going. They were all fearfully old and not noticeably festive, though from time to time the current speaker in the Great Hall must have made a jest, because a gale of elderly, relieved, literary-minded laughter, amplified in the vast space between them and the hammer-beam roof, seeped out through the stained-glass windows.

We played a game of picking out individual festival-goers and guessing how old they were. 'How old do you think he is?' I said, pointing out a gentleman of about 90, gamely feeling his way along the path with two sticks. 'Twenty?' said Oscar. Then we went to the secondhand book-shop, where Oscar only partially succeeded in concealing his boredom. I bought for myself a biography of Frank Weston, Bishop of Zanzibar 1907–24; and for Oscar and myself equally, *The Tale of Pigling Bland*. 'I was patient, wasn't I?' said Oscar, inserting his hand in mine again as we went out. His use of a word describing such an abstract concept surprised me, and together we dissected its meaning in case he thought it meant merely that he had been bored out of his skull.

Then we went to the leisure centre learner pool, where Oscar made his Great Leap Forward. The week before he had bravely submerged his head beneath the surface for the first time. Today, while his submerged grandad sat smiling encouragement and giving him the thumbs up, Oscar found the courage not only to submerge his entire self, but also to take his feet off the tiles and propel himself forwards three yards under the water. We celebrated afterwards with onion rings and Slush Puppies all round, large blue ones, in the leisure centre café.

Then we went home and read *The Tale of Pigling Bland*, in which another burly policeman calmly arrests a pig whose papers aren't in order. Then we ate crisp-bottomed fried eggs on toast, and at ten past eight, Daddy, pale with exhaustion, appeared in the doorway wearing his sky-blue care assistant's shift. 'So what have you been up to, Oscar?' he said. Oscar cocked his head and thought about it. 'Can't remember,' he confessed. 'Well, you can have ten more minutes, then it's bedtime.' 'Is that long?' said Oscar. I thought about explaining how time is ultimately relative then thought better of it. 'No, not very,' I said.

YOUR PROBLEMS SOLVED

Dear Mary . . .

30 August

Q. When someone gives you anti-ageing cream as a present, is that an insult or a compliment?

– A.O., Provence

A. It is both, but such creams make pointless presents. Cosmetics are all to do with suggestibility: for them to work, the user must be the one who has studied the spiel on the packaging and decided it seems plausible. Well-wishers should also consider that products with names like 'emergency filler', 'intensive repair' and 'total elasticity loss rescue' on daily display on a bathroom shelf can eventually depress an onlooker.

DIARY

Nicky Haslam

13 September

Talking of baritones, after some recent in-depth radio news coverage on Israel/Gaza, the presenter announced: 'Now, a comment on the situation by Princess Anne.' We heard a sensible, cultivated, measured voice speaking surprisingly knowledgeably for several minutes. Then the presenter said: 'Thank you, Prince Hassan.'

DIARY

Mark Amory

20 September

Until recently I used to claim that I had been literary editor of *The Spectator* for over 25 years; now I say almost 30. The trouble is I am not quite sure and it is curiously difficult to find out. Dot Wordsworth arrived on the same day as me but she cannot remember either. Each of us assumed that the other was an established figure and so our superior. A similar imprecision may undermine other memories.

In the early Eighties then, when Alexander Chancellor had reinvented the magazine after a bad patch, and it seemed daring, anarchic and slightly amateurish, I wrote theatre reviews and one late afternoon went round to Doughty Street, where *The Spectator* then was. I could find no one sober in the building. How did it manage to come out so promptly each week? Charles Moore, the next editor, aged a mere 27, brought a certain coherence. Though Thursday lunches were still jolly and full of incident – Kingsley Amis never really got used to having his stories interrupted by Jennifer Paterson, the cook, and used to wave a fork in the air to convey that he still had the floor – sometimes cabinet ministers would attend and be asked serious questions. Margaret Thatcher came to the summer party. There was, however, a stretch when Moore had to be away and perhaps Dominic Lawson had not yet arrived, so there was no one to edit. For three weeks the editor's secretary and the literary editor were put in control. Luckily Julia Mount was the editor's secretary. The first week was fine – enough had been commissioned already to see us through. In the third week, help was going to return soon enough to stave off disaster. The second week presented problems. Unknown journalists, perhaps scenting weakness, rang up and proposed stories about which we knew nothing. One I remember was about a crucial European election, perhaps in Denmark? I stalled and asked Julia, 'What shall we say?' 'I'll ask Ferdy,' she said (her husband who knew a lot). 'No we can't,' I bravely replied. 'We have asked him two things already today.' I turned the story down. An hour later Julia reported, 'Ferdy said it was of no importance at all.' Thank heavens.

The years passed. *The Spectator* prospered. One day we were told that we had made a profit. 'Very bad news,' said the ancient librarian. 'They'll expect us to do it always now.' Auberon Waugh did not welcome success either. His view was that 'There are only nineteen thousand agreeable people in Britain and they all read *The Spectator* already.' I had found something similar, that too many people wanted to write or be written about, so the largest part of the job was repulsing unwanted reviewers and subjects. Enthusiasm was sometimes difficult to resist. I rang up the distinguished poet and scholar Peter Levi and asked him if he was interested in whales. 'Lived there for years,' he replied, 'couldn't know it better.' 'No, no,' I interrupted, 'I mean the large mammals that live in the sea.' 'Fascinating creatures,' he went on seamlessly. There was an excellent deaf poet who used to come into my room and simply make off with something he fancied. Perhaps genuinely unaware of my cries of protest, he would slip through the door without turning round and make his getaway. Almost everyone wrote best when off their familiar subjects. My favourite review was by Roy Jenkins, on croquet. I knew he was keen because I had watched him play, though not with success. He simply could not get through the first hoop. The onlookers jeered, he grew a little red. When I was putting the equipment away, I found that it was not his fault: his ball was larger than the others and could only be hammered through with great force.

IT'S HARD TO REFUTE STEREOTYPES ABOUT BRITISH PEOPLE BEING A BIT DISGUSTING

Rod Liddle

20 September

A few years back there was an opinion poll which asked the gentlemen of Italy, France, Germany and so on which country's women they would most like to sleep with. If I remember rightly, the Italian babes came top, while British women – perhaps on account of their slatternly behaviour, weight problems, screeched obscenities and propensity to vomit – were at the bottom. However, when the question was turned around a little and the men were asked which country's women they had already slept with, British girls topped the poll by a mile. A case of any port in a storm, I suppose. It occurred to me at the time that this perception of British women was probably a significant factor in our rapidly increasing tourist trade, with young foreign men flooding here on a sort of promise: they may yearn for the Ginas and the Lucianas, but at least with good old Kayleigh-Anne they can be guaranteed to fill their boots. Except of course not all British women are promiscuous. If the men arrived here and tried to pull the Queen, say, or one of those Liberal Democrat ministers you see on *Question Time*, for example, then I suspect that they would be given short shrift. Note – 'I suspect'. I don't know for sure.

DIARY

Barry Humphries

8 November

Do fish have loins? Last Tuesday, in a pretentious restaurant, I ordered a 'loin of sea trout'. It looked just like an ordinary piece of fish – a bit small, as is usual in pretentious restaurants – on a plate sprinkled and drizzled as though the chef had perhaps coughed over it rather violently or vigorously scratched his head before giving it to the waiter. In Australia, I was once offered a shoulder of some other fish, so I suppose one might even be able to enjoy a rump of whitebait or even a saddle of flounder. But generally speaking I don't mind loin when applied to the loinless, and somehow a loin of fruitcake sounds appetising, or even a loin of sourdough bread. After all, a loaf of bread has a 'heel', which I always pluck out of the proffered basket. It's crunchier.

DIARY

Jeremy Paxman

29 November

The most unfashionable show on television, *Songs of Praise*, has had a makeover. The BBC had apparently discovered that the average viewer of the show was in their mid-seventies. Quelle surprise: in the trade it is known as 'The Resurrection Show', because so many participants shuffle off their mortal coil before transmission. The new version was introduced by a bubbly presenter with hair dyed a fetching shade of cerise, slightly talking down to us. It ended with a cheery roomful of Salvationists and a brass band. I rather liked it, even if I had switched on wondering why publicly funded religious broadcasters were chasing the advertisers' target demographic. Actually, I think it's rather bold of the producers to tell us the average age of their viewers. The same ought to apply to all television programmes. Here's my hunch: *Match of the Day* – mid-forties men. *News at Ten* – both sexes, but skewed male and slightly older. *Gogglebox* – thirties and forties, not entirely sober. *The Only Way is Essex* – mid-twenties, both sexes, but with much of their brains removed.

REAL LIFE

Melissa Kite

29 November

The ambassador's receptions are noted in society for their host's exquisite taste that captivates guests. You know that, I know that. Anyone who enjoyed the cheesier television adverts of the early Nineties will know that.

Imagine my excitement, therefore, when I received an invitation to a buffet supper at the real Italian Embassy. The friend who invited me was notified immediately that I accepted, and was very much looking forward to it. 'See you at Ferrero Rocher House, 6 p.m. sharp!' I said. 'Let's hope he really spoils us!' And I hummed the old Ferrero Rocher theme tune.

'Yes, you might want to tone down the Ferrero Rocher allusions a bit,' said the friend, a businesswoman, who was thinking the occasion might provide her with an opportunity for some networking.

'I'm just saying, I hope a butler with a tray comes round with a carefully arranged pyramid of chocolates in gold wrappers. And then I can say, "Monsieur, with zis Rocher you are really spoiling us!" I mean, I'm going to be the Swiss lady in the black dress with the big blonde hairdo, right? You can be the one with the sleek black Miss Whiplash hair and the sparkly dress who sweeps past snootily, while swallowing a chocolate in one gulp.'

Such were my plans as the big evening approached. I don't think I have been so excited about a social outing in years. 'Really, you are becoming quite childish in your old age,' I told myself as I put on my best black dress.

When I arrived at the imposing stucco-fronted building in Grosvenor Square, I was ecstatic to find a scene exactly like the advert. We were ushered into a beautiful, ornate room with waiters in uniforms carrying around nibbles and drinks on silver trays.

In the next room, a vast table was laden with a delectable supper consisting of Italian delicacies of every conceivable kind: huge salvers of Parma ham, entire Parmesan cheeses, platters of vitello tonnato . . .

'The ambassador's receptions really are noted for their host's exquisite taste that captivates guests!' I said to my friend. 'Shh!' she said. We had to pass through a welcoming line before approaching the table to help ourselves to food. At the head of the line was a handsome, dark fellow who looked like he might be the ambassador. He had a twinkly smile on his face. But there was no one introducing him to us, or us to him.

'Is that the ambassador?' said a lady behind me in the queue. 'I don't know,' I said, 'but he looks just like the one in the advert so I'm going to give him a good shake anyway.'

With a little kick in the shins at the right moment from my friend, I managed not to tell him he was really spoiling us in a silly accent. 'Good evening,' I said instead. 'Very pleased to meet you. I'm Melissa.'

The handsome man we presumed to be the fount of chocolate pyramids nodded but didn't say a word as he looked us up and down. How very grand and sexy of him. Thus, we progressed to the table of delicacies. There were at least a dozen different dishes spread out on one side of the table, where the journey began, and a dozen more on the other.

I should explain that my friend and I both have eating issues, although mine are mainly confined to social situations when I'm nervous. We looked at each other and a moment of panic passed between us. The plates were not big enough. Not nearly big enough. They were what you would call medium plates.

As I began to fork pieces of Parma ham and salami on to mine it was obvious it would be full by the time we were a few dishes down unless we came up with a better plan. My friend, who is more experienced at panic eating than me, said, 'Right, I say we work our way to the halfway point then stop, eat, and start again at the other side of the table.'

'Brilliant!' I said. And that is what we did.

But after we had done the entire table and could barely move, and were sitting like beached whales at the side of the room on the ambassador's little gold-legged ornate chairs, the waiters cleared the table and started reloading it with tiramisus, panna cottas and cantuccini.

'Gah! We forgot to save room for desserts!'

We heaved ourselves up. My friend had long since forgotten her networking and began to reload her plate. We both made a beeline for a silver salver of chocolates, at which point I could contain myself no longer.

'Mmm, *délicieuse!*' I said loudly, popping one in my mouth.

My friend gave up: '*Excellente!*' she said, scoffing a confection.

THE GOOD OLD DAYS WHEN I HAD NO IDEA WHAT I WAS DOING

Hugo Rifkind

13/20/27 December

What I miss most about being very young is the cluelessness. It's enormously liberating, cluelessness. The boundaries of life are simply not comprehended. The boxes into which others will put you are not apparent. Thus, you float out with life, and you see all.

I moved to London at 22, with a vague plan to sleep on my dad's living-room floor until something better happened. He was very good about it, although I'm not sure he'd been consulted. Before long, I moved to Camberwell with an old schoolfriend. Lord knows why we chose Camberwell; very possibly because it's mentioned in *Withnail & I*. And anyway, this was more like Elephant & Castle, whatever the advert in *Loot* had said. Our back window looked out over Burgess Park, which was terraformed and *Blade Runner*-esque, and about which I still have strange and listless zombie nightmares.

I was an agency temp, and would be for the next few years. On good weeks, this meant proofreading; on bad ones something far more mundane, such as the month I spent in an engineering firm comparing printed lists of inconsequential bolts on the roof of the Northern Line with handwritten notebooks of the same. Altogether, this was a process

I'd describe as 'writing a novel'. At the weekends, friends in big, crumbly shared houses would throw parties, where we would all behave like the students we'd recently stopped being. After a year I moved to Brixton, into a mouldy flat with fleas. The previous inhabitants had all been Etonians and had left a syringe under the sofa. I liked it there enormously.

All of my strongest memories of this time are of stepping out onto frosty 3 a.m. streets, wobbly, and wondering how to get home. One night the Lambeth police were out in force, perhaps after some sort of riot. Few things make you crave sudden sobriety quite so strongly as the sight of two giant police horses clopping towards you down a deserted, glittery terraced street, steam whooshing from flaring nostrils. Have you ever seen *The Fisher King*? It was like that.

There was a precariousness to life that I remember very well: a sense that things were on the very edge of perhaps not quite working out after all. For every graduate generation there's that period of sudden disunity, where the lifestyles and identities of the newly salaried accelerate away from everybody else, and there begin bitter, lasting disputes over bills in pizzerias. It's about more than money, all this. There's an arrogance to graduate poverty, at least at first. It carries a weightlessness – a sense of being able to observe society as a collection of boxes, none of which you are in. Which is a delusion, probably, but a strong one. Remember, I was 'writing a novel'.

Obviously, you'll end up in a box, like everybody else. That's what it means to be middle-class: comfort is your destiny. Like a Terminator that never stops, stability will hunt you down. In the years to come I'd swap the urbs for the suburbs, night buses for taxis, and Saturday night parties for Sunday brunch. I'd even write the novel, and have it published, too, before the journalism caught. Today, strangers often remind me of the privileges I have enjoyed, as though this was how my life would always have been. By osmosis, I suppose I've come to believe them. Yet there's a sense of loss that comes with it, in the distance I now feel from the person I once was. Who would have been surprised indeed, and delighted too.

Or partly. Today, I like my little corner of London a lot, even for its absurdities. I like its cosiness and safety and savagely overpriced artisan cafés. I like the way that so many of the kids in my daughter's school have a second language, as do my own, even if they're usually safe, smug second languages such as Finnish and Swiss German, and not the ones parents are supposed to worry about, such as Kurdish and Somali. I like the benign hypocrisy a place like this indulges, whereby you can feel that the life you have built is at once fascinatingly unique, and exactly like everybody else's.

I don't miss the aimlessness of my early twenties, nor the cashlessness, but I do miss that weightlessness. That cluelessness. That sense that the whole world is yours, with all its edges and dangers and spikes. And not just this little bit of it I have found, into which I have poured myself like jelly into a mould.

WRITERS

Roger Alton
Mark Amory
Bruce Anderson
Wallace Arnold
Beryl Bainbridge
Jeffrey Bernard
Simon Barnes
Marcus Berkmann
Gyles Brandreth
Rory Bremner
Craig Brown
Bill Bryson
Julie Burchill
Alexander Chancellor
Kate Chisholm
Alan Clark
Jeremy Clarke
Joan Collins
Giles Coren
Simon Courtauld
Theodore Dalrymple
James Delingpole
Sally Emerson
Lloyd Evans
Nigel Farndale
Sebastian Faulks
Michael Frayn
Stephen Fry

A. A. Gill
Tanya Gold
Miriam Gross
Martyn Harris
Robert Harris
Nicky Haslam
Michael Heath
Simon Heffer
Ian Hislop
Simon Hoggart
Tom Hollander
Barry Humphries
Tristram Hunt
Boris Johnson
Frank Johnson
Paul Johnson
Mary Killen
Miles Kington
Melissa Kite
Dominic Lawson
Sam Leith
Roger Lewis
Rod Liddle
Leanda de Lisle
Richard Littlejohn
Camilla Long
Emily Maitlis
Hilary Mantel

Minette Marin
Mark Mason
Leah McLaren
Charles Moore
John Mortimer
Ferdinand Mount
Ozzy Osbourne
Matthew Parris
Jeremy Paxman
Frederic Raphael
Tim Rice
Hugo Rifkind
Byron Rogers
Deborah Ross
Alan Rusbridger
Brian Sewell
Mark Steyn
Taki
Michael Vestey
Mary Wakefield
Keith Waterhouse
Alan Watkins
Auberon Waugh
John Wells
A. N. Wilson
Dot Wordsworth
Toby Young

QUOTED WORKS

Amis, Kingsley, *Take A Girl Like You* (Gollancz, 1960)

Amis, Kingsley, *The Biographer's Moustache* (Flamingo, 1995)

Assorted writers, *Inspector Morse* (Zenith Productions for Central Independent Television, 1992)

Clark, Alan, *Diaries: In Power 1983–1992* (Weidenfeld & Nicolson, 1993)

Deedes, W.F., *At War With Waugh: The Real Story of Scoop* (Macmillan, 2003)

Guralnick, Peter, *Careless Love* (Little, Brown, 1999)

Heffer, Simon, *Simply English* (Random House Books, 2014)

Highfield, Roger, *Can Reindeer Fly?* (Metro, 1998)

King, Zalman and Knopp, Patricia Louisiana, *Wild Orchid* (Entertainment Film Distributors, MGM Home Entertainment, 1989)

Knight, Ronnie, *Memoirs and Confessions* (Blake, 1998)

Leader, Zachary, *The Life of Kingsley Amis* (Jonathan Cape, 2006)

Lowe, Rob, *Stories I Only Tell My Friends* (Bantam Press, 2011)

Morgan, Piers, *The Insider: The Private Diaries of a Scandalous Decade* (Ebury Press, 2005)

Rendell, Ruth, 'An Unwanted Woman', *The Copper Peacock And Other Stories* (Hutchinson, 1991)

Sellers, Robert, *What Fresh Lunacy Is This? The Authorised Biography of Oliver Reed* (Constable, 2013)

Straw, Jack, *Last Man Standing: Memoirs of a Political Survivor* (Macmillan, 2012)

Thatcher, Carol, *Below The Parapet: The Biography of Denis Thatcher* (HarperCollins, 1996)

Wallace, Randall, *Pearl Harbor* (Touchstone Pictures, Jerry Bruckheimer Films, 2001)

Who's Who 1995 (A&C Black, 1995)

ACKNOWLEDGEMENTS

My thanks are due, firstly, to Richard Beswick of Little, Brown, as the idea for this book was dreamt up over a delicious lunch, for which he paid; to Charles Moore, Dominic Lawson, Frank Johnson, Boris Johnson, Matthew d'Ancona and Fraser Nelson, for never quite getting round to sacking me; to Jenny Naipaul, Liz Anderson, Mark Amory, Igor Toronyi-Lalic, Sam Leith, Clare Asquith, Julia Mount, Ginda Utley and all the other wonderful, far-sighted people I have worked for at *The Spectator* over the years; to Kinga Rup, Laura Atkins, Maureen McGrory, Fiona Williams and the combined force of the Events and Marketing Departments on the third floor for making my Fridays in the office so easy and enjoyable; to Andrew Neil for the loan of his elegant sky-level eyrie; and to Freddy Gray and Shez Shafiq for oiling the wheels throughout. Thank you also to the contributors, to everyone at Little, Brown and Conville & Walsh, and to the following for their help, advice and encouragement: Stephen Arkell, James Berkmann, Martha Berkmann, Jean Berkmann-Barwis, Paula Bingham, Craig Brown, Chris Carter, William Cook, Amanda Craig, Susie Dowdall, Sally Ann Fitt, Sarah Hesketh, Ian Hislop, Sarah Jackson, Mark Jacobs, David Jaques, Bob Jones, Aalia Khan, Mary Killen, Nicholas Lezard, Leo McKinstry, Sophia Martelli, Mark Mason, Nick Newman, Simon O'Hagan, Julian Parker, Sandra Parsons, Alice Pitman, Chris Pollikett, Susy Pote, Padraig Reidy, Terence Russoff, Joanna Ryan, Kate Saunders, Mitchell Symons, D. J. Taylor, Russell Taylor, Jane Thynne, James Walton, Nathalie Webb, Francis Wheen, Alan White and Helen White.